Custodial Grandparenting

Individual, Cultural, and Ethnic Diversity

Bert Hayslip, Jr., Ph.D., received his doctorate in Experimental Developmental Psychology from the University of Akron in 1975. After teaching at Hood College in Frederick, MD for three years, he joined the faculty at the University of North Texas, where he is now Regents Professor of Psychology. Dr. Hayslip is a Fellow of the American Psychological Association, the Gerontological Society of America and the Association for Gerontology in Higher Education, and has held research grants from the National Institute on Aging, The Hilgenfeld Foundation, and the National Endowment for the Humanities. His published research deals with cognitive processes in aging, interventions to enhance cognitive functioning in later life, personality-ability interrelationships in aged persons, grandparents who raise their grandchildren, grief and bereavement, hospice care, death anxiety, and mental health and aging.

Julie Hicks Patrick, Ph.D., received her doctorate in Developmental Psychology/Applied Cognitive Aging from The University of Akron (Ohio). She has held appointments as Project Director for three federal grants related to family caregiving in Cleveland, Ohio, and Peoria, Illinois (Bradley University). In 1998, she joined the faculty at West Virginia University, where she is now an Associate Professor in Life Span Psychology. Dr. Patrick's research includes questions in social cognition, family caregiving, and successful aging. She teaches graduate and undergraduate courses in the areas of aging and cognition.

Custodial Grandparenting

Individual, Cultural, and Ethnic Diversity

Editors

Bert Hayslip, Jr., PhD

Julie Hicks Patrick, PhD

SPRINGER PUBLISHING COMPANY

Springer Publishing Company, Inc.
11 West 42nd Street
New York, NY 10036

Acquisitions Editor: Helvi Gold
Production Editor: J. Hurkin-Torres
Cover design by Mimi Flow
Typeset by International Graphic Services, Inc., Newtown, PA

05 06 07 08 09 / 5 4 3 2 1

Library of Congress Cataloging-in-Publication Data

Custodial grandparenting : individual, cultural, and ethnic diversity / [edited by] Bert Hayslip Jr., Julie Hicks Patrick. — 1st ed.
    p. cm.
    Includes bibliographical references and index.
    ISBN 0-8261-1998-0 (soft cover)
    1. Grandparents as parents. 2. Grandparents as parents—Cross-cultural studies.
    3. Kinship care. 4. Kinship care—Cross-cultural studies. I. Hayslip, Bert. II. Hicks
    Patrick, Julie
HQ759.9.C88 2006
306.874'5—dc22   2005018050

Printed in the United States of America by Sheridan Books, Inc.

To Stephen and Patrick Hayslip, who have made parenting so rewarding — BHJ

Velma and Darrel Hicks, Margaret Case, and Martha and Richard Hicks — JHP

Contents

Section 3   Cross-Cultural and Intra-Cultural Variation

Section 4   Variation Across Race and Ethnicity

Contributors

Annabel H. Baird, M.A.
Department of Applied
  Gerontology
University of North Texas
Denton, TX

Jennifer L. Cook, M.S.
Department of Child and Family
  Development
University of Georgia
Athens, GA

**Martha R. Crowther, Ph.D.,
M.P.H.**
School of Public Health
Department of Health Behavior
University of Alabama at
  Birmingham
Birmingham, AL

Kristie L. Earnheart, M.A.
Department of Psychology
University of North Texas
Denton, TX

Michelle A. Emick, Ph.D.
Department of Psychology
University of North Texas
Denton, TX

Margaret E. Ensminger, Ph.D.
Department of Health Policy and
  Management
Faculty of Social and Behavioral
  Sciences
Bloomberg School of Public
  Health
The Johns Hopkins University
Baltimore, MD

Esme Fuller-Thomson, Ph.D.
Faculty of Social Work
University of Toronto
Toronto, Canada

**Catherine Chase Goodman,
D.S.W.**
Department of Social Work
California State University
Long Beach, CA

Craig E. Henderson, Ph.D.
Department of Psychology
University of North Texas
Denton, TX

Tammy L. Henderson, Ph.D.
Department of Human
  Development
Virginia Polytechnic Institute and
  State University
Blacksburg, VA

Hyoun-Kyoung Higgerson, M.P.H.
School of Public Health
Department of Health Behavior
University of Alabama at
  Birmingham
Birmingham, AL

Patricia L. Kaminiski, Ph.D.
Department of Psychology
University of North Texas
Denton, TX

Jennifer King, M.A.
Department of Psychology
University of North Texas
Denton, TX

Steven J. Kohn, Ph.D.
Department of Counseling and
  Psychology
Valdosta State University
Valdosta, GA

Stacey R. Kolomer, Ph.D.
School of Social Work
University of Georgia
Athens, GA

Thomas A. LaVeist
Department of Health Policy and
  Management
Faculty of Health and Social
  Policy
Bloomberg School of Public
  Health
The Johns Hopkins University
Baltimore, MD

Rosalyn D. Lee, Ph.D.
Department of Substance Abuse,
  Mental Health, and Criminal
  Justice
NORC, University of Chicago
Chicago, IL

James L. Lyons, D.Min.
Adelphi Baptist Church
Adelphi, MD

Philip McCallion, Ph.D.
Center for Excellence in Aging
  Services
University of Albany
Albany, NY

Dorothy McKenney, M.A.
Initiatives on Aging
Boston College
Newton, MA

Carol M. Musil, Ph.D.
Bolton School of Nursing
Case Western Reserve University
Cleveland, OH

Paul Odhiambo Oburu, Ph.D.
Department of Psychology
Maseno University
Maseno, Kenya

Kerstin Palmérus, Ph.D.
Department of Psychology
Goteborg University
Goteborg, Sweden

Rachel Pruchno, Ph.D.
University of Medicine and
  Dentistry of New Jersey
Center on Aging
Stratford, NJ

Sara H. Qualls, Ph.D.
Department of Psychology
University of Colorado at
  Colorado Springs
Colorado Springs, CO

Suzanne M. Randolph, Ph.D.
Department of Family Studies
University of Maryland
College Park, MD

Karen A. Roberto, Ph.D.
Virginia Polytechnic Institute and
    State University
Center for Gerontology
Blacksburg, VA

Rachel L. Rodriguez, M.A.
Department of Psychology
University of Alabama
Tuscaloosa, AL

R. Jerald Shore, Ph.D.
Department of Psychology
University of North Texas
Denton, TX

Merril Silverstein, Ph.D.
Andrus Gerontology Center
University of Southern California
Los Angeles, CA

Gregory C. Smith, Ph.D.
School of Family and Consumer
    Studies
Kent State University
Kent, OH

Melissa Snarski, B.A.
Department of Psychology
University of Alabama
Tuscaloosa, AL

Theresa Standing, Ph.D.
Bolton School of Nursing
Case Western Reserve University
Cleveland, OH

Leslie M. Swanson, M.A.
Department of Psychology
University of Alabama
Tuscaloosa, AL

Jeff R. Temple, M.A.
Department of Psychology
University of North Texas
Denton, TX

Cecilia Toledo, B.A.
Department of Psychology
University of North Texas
Denton, TX

J. Rafael Toledo, M.D.
Department of Psychology
University of North Texas
Denton, TX

Jeffrey A. Watson, D.Min.
Director of Resident Life at
    Riderwood
Silver Spring, MD

Foreword

The role of grandparents in American society is significantly changing. In recent years, increasing numbers of grandparents have found themselves responsible for raising their grandchildren. Today, more than 4 million children are living in grandparent-headed families, often with no parent present or involved. Equally significant is the diversity found among these families with regard to race and ethnicity. These factors interact with and influence the grandparents' experience and, indeed, that of the children they are raising. Ten years ago a book on diversity among custodial grandparents would have seemed an esoteric subject and hardly one suitable for an edited book. Today there is an indisputable need for a book such as this one, which explores diversity from its many perspectives.

Discussions of custodial grandparents tend to begin with the reasons why the grandparents are assuming the parenting role. Parental abuse and neglect, substance abuse, HIV/AIDS, homicide, mental illness, incarceration, and child welfare policies that have a preference for relative caregivers are among the most commonly cited factors contributing to these restructured families. But, whatever the reason, most grandparents raising a grandchild had never anticipated they would be parenting again.

For most, this new role causes major interruptions in their lives. Many are forced to give up work, to reduce their working hours, to retire early, and to forgo leisure activities and their own plans in order to provide care. For many, the new responsibility also involves new financial strains and hardships as they find themselves struggling to support their grandchild while living on reduced incomes. Housing that had been comfortable and adequate may no longer suffice for the expanded family, while health and physical problems may be exacerbated by the demands of childrearing.

The problems encountered by the grandparents may be exacerbated by those of the grandchildren. Separation from the parent for whatever reason is a difficult experience, resulting in feelings of grief and loss, which if not resolved, can undermine efforts toward adjustment. Children who have been abused or neglected face particular difficulties in establishing trust and feeling secure in the new relationship. Behavioral problems and difficulties in school are common and can further tax the well-being of the grandparent and the family.

But given these challenges, grandparents also find new rewards and enjoyment in providing for their grandchildren and in the knowledge that they are maintaining the family and keeping their grandchildren out of the formal system. The pleasure of watching the child grow, the companionship they offer, and the knowledge that they are playing vital and irreplaceable roles in the lives of their grandchildren are among the rewards that grandparents frequently report.

Recognition of the needs of these families is occurring in several spheres. The 1995 White House Conference on Aging devoted several sessions to concerns of grandparent caregivers making recommendations for policy resolutions including establishment of comprehensive programs and supportive services, development of legal services, and removal of barriers to existing programs. Undoubtedly, the 2005 White House Conference on Aging will continue the work of the previous conference and focus again on the needs of custodial grandparents.

Further acknowledgment of the roles and issues faced by grandparents is found in the 2000 amendments to the Older Americans Act, National Family Caregivers Support Program, which enables states to provide funds for services and programs for grandparent caregivers. Although restricted to those over the age of 60, the program offers an important foundation for further policy interventions and programs.

Given the diversity of grandparent caregivers, it is critical that such interventions recognize the many influences that affect their roles and experiences. Without this understanding, such policies and programs are unlikely to meet the needs of the population and consequently, services that aim at assisting grandparents are at risk of not being utilized.

The 19 chapters in this book examine several dimensions of diversity among grandparent-headed families, age, gender, culture, race, and ethnicity. As this text brings together the many distinct facets of diversity, it provides a wealth of information that can be absorbed into policy and programs to support these families and to assure their well-being. As the number of children dependent upon their grandparents for care continue to grow, it is incumbent that we continue to learn as much as possible about the many factors affecting those children's lives and their futures.

Carole B. Cox, PhD
Fordham University
New York, New York

Preface

While four major previous coedited books focusing on grandparents raising their grandchildren dealt with (a) an overview of custodial grandparents (clinical, theoretical, empirical, applied perspectives) (Cox, 2000; Hayslip & Goldberg-Glen, 2000), (b) interventions with such grandparents (Hayslip & Patrick, 2003), and (c) grandparents raising grandchildren in the context of AIDS/HIV disease (Joslin, 2002), no book to date has spoken explicitly to the variability among custodial grandparent caregivers. This variability is brought into even sharper context when one considers custodial grandparenting as a nonnormative role, and thus, how individuals define and cope with that role is critical to its understanding. Indeed, one often thinks of grandparent caregivers as a homogenous group who face common problems (e.g., isolation from others, poverty, impairments of physical and emotional health, and the loss of their lives as they have come to know them). Yet, as most practitioners who work with grandparent caregivers and those who conduct research with such persons can attest, one cannot help but to be sensitized to their diversity, and being aware of their uniquenesses is essential to responding to them as human beings who have taken on an often thankless task.

As increased diversity is a hallmark of the aging process (see Nelson & Dannefer, 1992), it would indeed not be surprising to also observe such variability among middle-aged and older custodial grandparents. This text explicitly explores the many parameters of such diversity among custodial grandparents, with attention to individual variability utilizing multiple and diverse criteria. In this text, we specifically explore diversity across gender, age, and ruralness/urbaness, which to date, have largely been ignored as parameters differentiating caregiving grandparents. Importantly, driven by the seminal work of Meredith Minkler and her colleagues in the early 1990s who studied primarily African American custodial grandmothers raising the children of crack cocaine-addicted adult parents, we also attend to both cross cultural and ethnic diversity among custodial grandparents. It is important to recognize that in many respects, grandparent caregivers covary along more than one dimension simultaneously (i.e., gender and ethnicity), as well as along variables which cooccur with some frequency (i.e., grandchildren's difficulties, role demands and ethnicity, age, and health).

Attending to such diversity is essential if one wants to understand custodial grandparents' uniqueness in the context of their own as well as their grandchildren's development over time, and especially so if one is providing services to them. Thus, it is in both a basic research and an applied context that this text highlights the many variables differentiating grandparent caregivers and their grandchildren.

REFERENCES

Cox, C. (Ed.). (2000). *To grandmother's house we go and stay: Perspectives on custodial grandparents*. New York: Springer.

Hayslip, B., & Goldberg-Glen, R. (2000). *Grandparents raising grandchildren: Theoretical, empirical, and clinical perspectives*. New York: Springer.

Hayslip, B., & Hicks Patrick, J. (2003). *Working with custodial grandparents*. New York: Springer.

Joslin, D. (2002). *Invisible caregivers: Older adults raising children in the wake of HIV/AIDS*. New York: Columbia University Press.

Nelson, E., & Dannefer, D. (1992). Aged heterogeneity: Fact or fiction. The fate of diversity in gerontological research. *The Gerontologist, 32,* 17–23.

SECTION 1

Diversity Across Individuals

CHAPTER 1

Grandmothers Raising Grandchildren: The Effects of Work Disruptions on Current Work Hours and Income*

Rachel Pruchno and Dorothy McKenney

In 1997, 752,000 grandmothers were living in households that included at least one of their grandchildren and neither of the grandchild's parents. Close to half of these women (46.0%) were also part of the U.S. labor force (Bryson & Casper, 1999). Though the problems associated with balancing work and family responsibilities have long been acknowledged for employees who have young children (Emlen & Koren, 1984; Scharlach & Boyd, 1989; Voydanoff, 1988), and have recently been recognized for employees who have caregiving responsibilities for older persons with disabilities (Gorey, Rice, & Brice, 1992; Neal, Chapman, Ingersoll-Day-

*This research was supported by grant R01AG11041, "Psychological Well-Being of Co-Resident Grandparents," from the National Institute on Aging.

3

ton, & Emlen, 1993; Pavalko & Artis, 1997; Scharlach & Boyd, 1989; Wagner & Neal, 1994; Warshaw, Barr, Raymar, Schachter, & Lucas, 1986), these concerns have not been examined adequately for employees who are raising their grandchildren in the absence of the middle generation. It is particularly important to examine the intersection of work and family care responsibilities among grandmothers raising grandchildren because many grandmothers who become caregivers for their grandchildren face increased financial responsibilities at a time in their lives, close to or at retirement, when decreased income can have dramatic long-term effects (Kelley, Yorker, & Whitley, 1997). This chapter first identifies the work-related strains experienced by grandmothers who are both working and raising their grandchildren in the absence of the parent generation and then tests a model that predicts how work disruptions experienced because of grandchild caregiving responsibilities affect current annual income.

Parsons and Bales (1955), distinguishing between the instrumental orientation of the workplace and the affective orientation of the family, argued that the norms of the two are incompatible. For either to work effectively, they argue, the two must be separate. However, there is good evidence that, in reality, work and family roles are intricately entwined. Empirical research has connected employee concern for the care of their children or elderly relatives with productivity losses from increased absences, tardiness, and stress on the job. Sharlach and Boyd (1989), for example, comparing employees without children to those with children, found that the latter miss more days of work, have more conflict between work and family, and take more time off. Moreover, Cleary and Mechanic (1983) found that married female employees with children experience more depression than those without children. Similarly, Sharlach and Boyd (1989) found that employees caring for elders had more conflict between work and family, missed more days of work, and took more time off than their non-care giving peers. Research by Warshaw et al. (1986) found that employees who were caring for older relatives experienced numerous work productivity problems, with 75% taking unscheduled days off, 73% being tardy for work, 67% being absent from work because of their caregiving responsibilities, 64% requiring excessive use of the phone because of these responsibilities, and 58% requiring emergency hours off. Similar findings are reported by Enright and Friss (1987).

Further evidence of the impact that caregiving responsibilities have on the lives of employees comes from job or career opportunities that are lost because of care giving demands. Enright and Friss (1987), for example, report that 25% of caregivers would be working if they were not providing care. Gibeau and Anastas (1989) found that 31% of employed caregivers had considered quitting their jobs because of caregiving responsibilities; Stone, Cafferata, and Sangl (1987) found that between 5 and 14% of caregivers had quit work to become full-time caregivers; and Stephens and Christianson (1986) found that among recently unemployed caregivers, 35% had quit their jobs to provide care, 21% had turned down job offers to continue providing care, and 28% were prevented from looking for work because of their caregiving responsibilities.

Only a few studies of caregiving grandmothers have examined the effects of this caregiving role on work life. Minkler and Roe (1996) report that 30% of their respondents had left their jobs to become full-time caregivers, while Sands and Goldberg Glen (1998) report that 17.8% of the 123 custodial grandmothers they studied had quit their job because of the responsibility of raising a grandchild. Interestingly, 13.8% of the grandmothers participating in the latter study indicated that they had returned to work for the same reason.

Pavalko and Artis (1997), using data from the National Longitudinal Survey of Mature Women, found that employment status did not affect whether or not women start providing care, but that women who do start to provide care to a family member are more likely to reduce employment hours or stop working than women who do not provide this care. They conclude that the causal relationship between employment and caregiving in late midlife is largely unidirectional, with women reducing hours to meet caregiving demands. Consistent findings are reported by Pearson, Hunter, Cook, Ialongo, and Kellam (1997) who found that neither grandmother's age nor employment status was associated with grandmother's parenting involvement.

The effect of combining work and family roles weighs more heavily on the lives of women than men (Stone & Short, 1990). Yet, as demonstrated by Neal et al.'s (1993) study of employees caring for children, dependent adults, and elderly people, the factors predicting absenteeism from work because of these responsibilities are complex. In a sophisticated model that included personal characteristics of employees (e.g., gender, age, ethnicity, occupation), demand variables (e.g., hours worked, job shift, number of children under age 9, number of caregiving roles, extra time required for travel to child care, age of the youngest child, having a child with a disability, child care cost as a percentage of household income, and total hours of child care provided), and resources (e.g., income, work schedule flexibility, having an employed partner, number of children between the ages of 9 and 17, informal child care support from family, ease in finding child care, satisfaction with child care), these investigators were able to explain only 3% of the variance in number of days missed of work, 9% of the variance in arriving late for work or leaving early, and 8% of the variance in interruptions at work.

Although income is generally thought of as a resource, the relationships between household income and child care or work-family outcomes are often weak or negative (Neal et al., 1993). Vartuli and Stubbs (1986), for example, found that higher income was associated with higher job stress, higher absenteeism, and more use of out of home care services, but also with less difficulty in combining work and family responsibilities. As such, the negative effects of some occupations may outweigh the positive effects of increased income. Stone et al. (1987) found that professional, manager, clerical workers, and sales workers were more likely to reduce their work hours to rearrange their work schedules than were blue collar workers, while Brody, Kleban, Johnsen, Hoffman, and Schoonover (1987), in their study of caregivers to older mothers, found that those who had left the workplace to provide care were lower in educational status than those who had continued to work and managed their caregiving by making workplace accommodations. Gerstel and Gallagher (1994) conclude that among those who start caregiving, women with higher wages may have greater flexibility to reduce hours, while women who have difficulty making ends meet will be less likely to reduce hours or stop work after starting caregiving.

In addition to the effects that caregiving responsibilities have on concurrent employment, decisions made in order to accommodate these responsibilities can have dramatic long-term effects on the work lives and income of individuals. Resumption of full-time employment after an exit for family reasons is related to lower subsequent wages (Wenk & Rosenfeld, 1992), a greater likelihood of being located in a benefit-poor job (Harrington Meyer & Pavalko, 1996), and reduced retirement benefits (O'Rand & Henretta, 1982).

When caregiving is done in the years just prior to retirement eligibility, labor force exits or reductions in work hours can have a particularly powerful effect on long term income. Interruptions that occur when women are closer to retirement may lower their Social Security or private pension benefits (Kingston & O'Grady-LeShane, 1993). Furthermore, it is not clear whether work interruptions that occur later in the career essentially lead to early retirement because of difficulties in returning to the labor force after care giving responsibilities stop. Pavalko and Artis (1997) suggest that even though the length of time spent caregiving may be relatively short, it may be that women are unable to recover from the economic implications of this lost time.

THEORETICAL MODEL

The theoretical model that derives from this empirical research has current work hours and personal income as its primary outcomes. Penultimate outcomes include quitting work and missing work in order to care for a grandchild. Exogenous variables include current marital status (divorced vs. not divorced), education, and health. The hypotheses, deriving from the existing literature, include the following:

1. Grandmothers who are divorced are more likely to miss work for reasons associated with their role as caregiver than grandmothers who are not divorced.

2. The higher the education level of the grandmother, the more likely she is to miss work for reasons related to child care.

3. Grandmothers who miss work for reasons related to child care will be working fewer hours now than grandmothers who do not miss work for these reasons.

4. Grandmothers who have quit work for reasons related to child care will be working fewer hours now than grandmothers who have not quit work for these reasons.

5. Grandmothers who have quit work for reasons related to child care will have lower incomes than grandmothers who have not quit work for these reasons.

In order to control for known relationships, paths between health and work hours, health and income, work hours and income, and education and income are included in the model. In addition to these directional hypotheses, education and health are correlated with one another.

METHODS

Sample

Data for the following analyses come from telephone interviews with 506 grandmothers who were living with and providing care to a grandchild in households that did not include either the grandchild's mother or father. Inclusion in the analyses was limited to grandmothers who worked outside the home at some point during the years they lived with and had primary responsibility for their grandchild. Grandmothers were selected for study over grandfathers because women are more likely than men to assume the role of kin-keeper, either as parental replacement or parental supporter (Cohler & Grunebaum, 1980; Hagestad & Smyer, 1982). Women facilitate contact and exchanges between generations, and serve as "family monitors," observing the course of relationships and registering changes in them (Hagestad, 1985). Finally, these differences as well as differential life expectancies result in older women being more likely than older men to live with younger family members.

Individuals learned about the study primarily through media press releases (70.8%). Additional referral sources included 3.2% from paid advertisements, 5.3% from contact with social agencies, 3.2% from schools, 4.7% from word of mouth, 6.7% from support groups, and 5.1% were referred by others who had participated in the study. Identical outreach efforts were made throughout the United States. The sample for the analyses that follow included grandmothers living in 40 states throughout the United States. Respondents comprised 93.1% who lived in urban areas and 6.9% who lived in rural areas.

Though no attempt was made to randomly select participants for this study, an estimate of the extent to which participants are representative of, and hence yield data that are generalizable to, the population of grandmothers raising their grandchildren derives from comparing the demographics of this sample with that of national databases. More specifically, the demographic characteristics of people in our database were contrasted with the following datasets, all based on large representative samples: (a) the Current Population Survey analyzed by Chalfie (1994); (b) the National Survey of Families and Households analyzed by Fuller-Thomson et al. (1997), and (c) the 1997 Current Population Survey analyzed by Casper and Bryson (1998). These comparisons suggest that the grandmothers participating in our study are similar to women participating in the national datasets and to the population of grandmothers raising grandchildren in the United States with two exceptions: (a) they are less likely to be living in the Southern United States, and (b) they are less likely to be living under the poverty level.

Women were eligible to participate in the study if they had lived with at least one of their grandchildren in homes that did not include either the grandchild's mother or father for at least three months. Interviews were conducted between July 1996 and July 1998.

Grandmothers participating in the study ranged in age from 50 to 79 years. At the time they participated in the study, grandmothers had been living with their grandchild for a mean of 6.83 years. The grandmothers were between 33 and 70 years old (mean = 50.18, s.d. = 6.37) when they began living with and caring for their grandchild. Of the sample, 51.2% were Black; half were White. The majority of respondents (51.6%) were married; 28.3% were divorced; 14.0% were widowed; 2.5% not married, but living with a significant other; and 3.6% were never married. The women had an average of 13.6 years of education, with 9.2% having less than a high school education, 30.8% having a high school education, 36.5% having some college education, and 23.6% having four or more years of college.

The majority of the sample (73.3%) was currently working. Among those respondents who were currently working, the mean number of work hours per week was 34.6 (*s.d.* = 13.4). Respondents who were not currently working reported that they had last worked an average of 3.4 years ago (*s.d.* = 3.15 years). Respondents (whether currently working or not) reported that they worked in a variety of positions, with 34.6% holding professional positions requiring an advanced degree, 26.9% working in secretarial positions, 14.8% in service positions, and 21.6% in other blue collar positions. A minority of the sample (2.2%) indicated that they had been housewives for most of their lives. The majority of the sample (67.6%) was protestant, with 15.0% Catholic, 15.2% other (including Christian, nondenominational, Jehovah's Witnesses, Mormon), 1.0% Jewish, and 1.2% reporting no religion.

The grandchildren ranged in age from 9 months to 18 years. Half of the grandchildren were male; half were female. The majority of grandmothers (70.4%) were maternal grandmothers; 29.6% were paternal grandmothers.

The overwhelming majority of grandchildren moved into the grandmother's home (86.4%), whereas a minority had always lived with their grandmother (8.3%), and a few grandmothers moved into the grandchild's home (.8%) or grandmother and grandchild moved into a new home together (3.8%). While 54.2% of the grandmothers had only one grandchild living in her house, 27.3% had two grandchildren, 10.3% three grandchildren, and 8.3% had four or more grandchildren.

Measures

Each respondent participated in a confidential telephone interview that lasted for an average of 2.4 hours (range 61 minutes to 4.6 hours). The interviews were conducted by a staff of 17 part-time interviewers who received extensive training on the interview protocol, which was primarily structured and quantitative.

Respondents reported on three aspects of their physical health. First, subjective health of the grandmother was assessed by asking respondents the following four questions: (a) "How would you rate your overall health at the present time? Would you say: excellent, good, fair, or poor"; (b) "Is your health now better, about the same, or not as good as it was three years ago"; (c) "Does your own health stand in the way of your doing the things you want to do: not at all, a little, or a great deal?"; and (d) "Would you say that your health is better, about the same, or not as good as most people your age?" Scores on the scale ranged from 4 to 13, with higher scores reflecting better health. Coefficient alpha for the scale was .76. Second, grandmother's functional ability was assessed using the 10-item scale developed by Fitti and Kovar (1987). Grandmothers reported whether they had "no difficulty" (0), "some difficulty" (1), "much difficulty" (2), or were "unable" (3) to do activities that included walking a quarter of a mile, sitting for long periods, reaching up, and lifting or carrying something as heavy as ten pounds. Scores on the scale ranged from 0 to 23 (mean = 4.01, *s.d.* = 4.88). Coefficient alpha for the scale was .87. Finally, grandmothers reported on whether or not they had been diagnosed with any of 29 physical illnesses, including arthritis, cancer, heart trouble, and diabetes. The number of diagnosed health conditions ranged from 0 to 12 (mean = 2.58, *s.d.* = 2.35).

Work missed because of responsibilities to their grandchild was assessed by asking grandmothers whether, because of their grandchild, they had ever: (a) come late to work, (b) missed work, (c) left work in order to take their grandchild to a doctor's appointment, and (d) left work suddenly. Scores on the scale created from this information ranged from 0 (no work effects experienced as a function of responsibilities to grandchild) to 4 (mean = 2.21, *s.d.* = 1.50). Coefficient alpha for the scale was .76. Table 1.1 details the extent to which grandmothers raising their grandchildren missed work. Approximately half of the grandmothers participating in the study indicated that they had experienced each of the following: been late for work, missed work, had to leave work for a grandchild's medical appointment, and had to leave work suddenly because of their grandchild. Multiple work-related problems were common, as 16.8% of the sample reported two of these problems, 20.4% reported three of these problems, and 28.1% reported having experienced all of these problems.

Grandmothers stated whether or not they had ever quit a job because of responsibilities to their grandchild. A total of 89 women (17.6%)

TABLE 1.1   Effects of Providing Care to Grandchild on Missed Work

Because of responsibilities to your grandchild, have you ever had to:	Percent who answered "yes"
Come late to work?	49.8
Miss work?	59.9
Leave work to take your grandchild to a doctor's appointment?	64.4
Leave work suddenly?	46.6

participating in the study reported that they had quit a job in order to take care of their grandchild.

Current work hours were assessed by asking grandmothers to report on the number of hours per week that they were working. Work hours ranged from 0 (26.7%) to 90 (mean = 25.36, *s.d.* = 19.14).

Personal annual income was assessed by asking respondents to report their personal annual income, considering all sources such as jobs, Social Security, retirement income, unemployment compensation, profits, interest, and so forth. Personal annual income ranged from less than $3,000 to more than $70,000. The median annual personal income was $13,500.

Procedures

A series of three-phase model testing and development procedures were followed. These three phases of modeling, model evaluation, model readjustment, and model replication require two independent samples of data. The first two phases were carried out using a randomly selected sample of 406 of the 506 respondents (Sample 1). Data from the remaining 100 cases (Sample 2) were reserved and used for purposes of the third phase—model replication.

Once the sample was randomly split, t-tests examined whether there were significant differences between the two groups on model variables. These analyses revealed that there were no significant differences between the two groups on marital status (divorced vs. not) ($t = -.18$), education ($t = 1.22$), subjective health ($t = 1.23$), number of illnesses ($t = -.78$), having missed work to care for grandchild ($t = -1.25$), having quit work because of responsibilities to grandchild ($t = -.71$), and number of hours currently working ($t = .10$). The two groups were significantly different on functional ability ($t = -1.60$) with Sample 2 scoring higher, and personal annual income ($t = 1.51$) with Sample 1 having a higher income. These significant differences are most likely due to chance.

The AMOS (Analysis of Moment Structures) structural modeling equation program (Arbuckle, 1995) was used to test the fit of the data to the hypothesized model. AMOS is a computer program that estimates structural models through variance-covariance matrices. Multiple indices of fit were used to evaluate the fit of the data to the model. An overall chi-square index was used to assess the degree of fit between the estimated and observed covariance matrices. Lower values indicate better fitting models. Problems may arise with the chi-square index, so additional indices were used to assess model fit. Additional indices included a normed goodness of fit index in which .90 was the lowest acceptable value (Arbuckle, 1995; Hoyle & Panter, 1995), RMSEA or root mean square *error* of approximation (Browne & Cudeck, 1989), which compensates for the effects of model complexity and ideally has a value of .05 or less, and Hoelter's (1983) critical N (CN). Hoelter argues that a critical N of 200 indicates a satisfactory fit.

RESULTS

Bivariate correlations of model variables for Sample 1 are reported above the diagonal in Table 1.2 (those for Sample 2, below the diagonal), affording the first-level test of the hypothesized relationships as well as the opportunity to understand the relationships among the empirical variables. These data provide support for four of the five hypotheses: (a) divorced grandmothers were more likely to have missed work because of the demands of caring for a grandchild than were grandmothers who were not divorced, (b) grandmothers with higher levels of education were more likely to have missed work than grandmothers with lower levels of education, (c) grandmothers who had quit work in order to care for a grandchild were currently working fewer hours than grandmothers who had not quit, and (d) grandmothers who had quit work to care for a grandchild currently had lower incomes than grandmothers who had not quit work. However, contrary to the hypothesized relationship, grandmothers who missed work because of the demands of caring for a grandchild were actually working more hours now than grandmothers who had not missed work for this reason.

The five hypothesized paths as well as controls were tested simultaneously. The summary statistics (chi-square = 279.87; $d.f.$ = 27, p = .00; Bentler-Bonett index = .95; RMSEA = .15; Hoelter CN = 68) suggest a less than optimal fit of the data to the model. Two modifications made to the model, one at a time, significantly improved the fit. First, a path from education to quit work was added. Second, a regression path from education to hours working was added. Fit statistics for the final model included a chi square of 46.84 ($d.f.$ = 25, p = .00), Bentler-Bonett index of .99, RMSEA of .05, and a Hoelter CN of 384. These statistics indicate that the addition of these two paths resulted in an excellent fit of the model to the data. All hypothesized paths and controls were significant.

The final model developed using Sample 1 was then cross-validated using Sample 2. The resulting chi-square of 32.06 ($d.f.$ = 25, p = .16), Bentler-Bonett index of .98, RMSEA of .05, and Hoelter of 137 indicate that the model shows stability across samples, and that the paths added were, most likely, not due to chance.

To more carefully assess the stability of the paths across the two groups, we tested the final model simultaneously on Sample 1 and Sample

TABLE 1.2 Bivariate Correlations for Sample 1 (above diagonal) and Sample 2 (below diagonal)

	Divorced	Education	Subjective Health	Number Illnesses	Functional Ability	Miss Work	Quit Work	Hours work	Income
Divorced	1.0	.08	.06	.04	.03	.17**	.01	.04	.11*
Education	-.05	1.0	.10	-.01	-.015	.17**	-.04	.23**	.39**
Subjective health	-.04	.13	1.0	-.62**	-.66**	-.07	-.09	.16**	.19**
Number illnesses	.03	-.15	-.64**	1.0	.62**	.06	.08	-.15**	-.13**
Functional ability	.10	-.13	-.66**	.72**	1.0	.02	.04	-.24**	-.15**
Miss work	.14	.25*	-.14*	.03	.003	1.0	.03	.23**	.19**
Quit work	.01	-.09	-.01	-.03	-.03	-.04	1.0	-.32**	-.29**
Hours work	.17	.11	.27**	-.32**	-.42**	.31**	-.24*	1.0	.52**
Income	.14	.41**	.23*	-.31**	-.28**	.34**	-.31**	.58**	1.0

*Significant at .05 level. **Significant at .01 level.

2 using the nested procedures described by Joreskog and Sorbom (1986). Multisample AMOS analysis was first used to test a model in which the same parameter pattern was freely estimated within each group. This chi-square value was the starting point for the nested sequential analyses that follow. First the magnitudes of the regression paths were compared and then the magnitudes of the variances and covariances were compared. As seen in Table 1.3, these analyses reveal that there are parameter equivalencies in terms of both the regression paths and the variances and covariances across samples. Together, these analyses suggest stability of the structural equation paths in the model.

Finally, the fit of the model was tested using the complete sample of 506. Because of the parameter stability and equivalency across the two samples, it was possible to test the model on the complete sample. The increase in sample size acted to further stabilize the parameters. Results from that analysis yielded a chi-square of 58.72 ($d.f.$ = 25, p = .00), Bentler-Bonett index of .99, RMSEA of .05, and Hoelter of 382. The standardized estimates for the full sample on the final model can be obtained from the first author. The data provide support for the following direct relationships: (a) grandmothers who are divorced are more likely to miss work for reasons associated with their role as caregiver than grandmothers who are not; (b) the higher the education level of the grandmother, the more likely she is to miss work for reasons related to child care; (c) grandmothers who have quit work for reasons related to child care work fewer hours now than grandmothers who have not quit work for these reasons; (d) grandmothers who have quit work for reasons related to child care have lower incomes than grandmothers who have not quit work for these reasons; (e) grandmothers with more education are likely to be working more hours; and (f) grandmothers with more education are more likely to have quit their jobs in order to take care of

TABLE 1.3   Test of the Stability of the Model Across Two Samples

Step	Chi-Square	df	Change in Chi-Square	Change in df
1. No constraints	79.026	50	—	—
2. Equivalent regression weights between latent variables	96.809	63	17.78	13
3. Equivalent exogenous and residual covariances	106.197	74	9.388	11

their grandchild. Consistent with the trend identified at the bivariate level, grandmothers who had missed work for reasons related to child care at some point in the past were working more hours now than grandmothers who had not missed work for these reasons.

DISCUSSION

Minkler (1999) stated that "For grandparents who become the primary caregivers for their grandchildren, the personal decision to care often has profound economic consequences" (p. 210). These data provide support that assertion, as they find that the current annual personal income of grandmothers raising grandchildren who quit their jobs in order to assist their grandchild is less than that of grandmothers who did not quit their job for this reason. In addition to this decrease in income are the added expenses of caring for a grandchild—expenses not addressed in these analyses. Yet, as described by Simon-Rusinowitz, Krach, Marks, Piktialis, and Wilson (1996), many grandparents raising grandchildren watch their personal savings and retirement funds shrink as they save for their grand-child's current and future financial needs.

These analyses suggest that missing work and quitting work are very different phenomena for grandmothers raising their grandchildren. As such, they have different effects on grandmothers. While quitting work because of child care responsibilities leads to reduced current personal annual income and reduced current work hours, missing work is associ-ated with an increase in current work hours. These data lead one to wonder whether grandmothers who miss work because of child care responsibilities are currently working more hours in order to somehow make up for this lost time. Future research is needed to provide a greater understanding of this phenomenon.

Just as the effects of missing work and quitting work are different from one another, so too are the predictors. These data indicate that grandmothers who miss work because of their child care responsibilities are more likely to be divorced than are grandmothers who do not miss work. Grandmothers who are divorced may lack the support system within the household that enables them to both work and care for their grandchild. Grandmothers who miss work because of responsibilities to their grandchild are also more likely to be better educated than grand-mothers who do not miss work for this reason. Grandmothers with better education are most likely in occupations that provide the increased flexibility that they require in order to care for their grandchild and work. As such, it is possible that better-educated women miss more work in order to care for their grandchild than do less well-educated women because they can. Flexible hours and the opportunity to work at home may make it possible for grandmothers raising grandchildren to miss work without having serious repercussions for their current annual income. Unfortunately, these data do not adequately model the decision to quit work. The sole predictor of quitting work to care for a grandchild was education, and this path was one of the weakest in the model. Future studies must address this issue as they investigate the factors behind women leaving the work force in order to care for a grandchild.

Although these data are intriguing for their support of the relationship between missing work and quitting work for grandchild care and current income, they are limited because of the time constriction of these data. All of the grandmothers participating in the study were currently caring for a grandchild in households that did not include either of the grandchild's parents. Their reports of experiences of missing and quitting work are limited to retrospection, while the effects that these work experiences have on current income and work hours are short term, and limited to those grandmothers still providing care to a grandchild. In order to understand the long-term effects that caring for a grandchild can have on grandmother's income, a longitudinal study, tracking these women over time, is required. Such a study should follow grandmothers over a time period sufficient that their grandchildren would age out of their households and the long-term effects of this caregiving role on income could be examined, enabling an empirical test of Kingston and O'Grady-LeShane (1993) contention that interruptions that occur when women are closer to retirement may limit their Social Security or private pension benefits.

These data add to the growing empirical knowledge base that indicates that work and family roles are intricately entwined. The experiences of grandmothers raising grandchildren are similar to those of parents caring for young children and of persons caring for adults with a disability. What differentiates this population are both the time in their lives and the length of time during the course of their lives that they face the care giving role. Grandparents raising grandchildren face the caregiving role late in the history of their work lives, and often for extensive periods of time, while parents with young children, who may be involved in child care for similar lengths of time, meet these conflicting demands relatively early in the history of their work lives. Persons caring for an adult with a disability can experience their care giving role at a variety of times in their work life. When caregiving and spouse or parent care intersect, for example, while care may be provided toward the end of the work life, it is generally more short term than is the experience for grandmothers caring for grandchildren. When parents are involved in providing care to an adult child with disability, it is more likely to have been a constant throughout their working lives.

The number of grandmothers raising their grandchildren in the absence of the grandchild's parents continues to grow (Bryson & Casper, 1999). With their growth will come increased recognition from employers that, in order to remain competitive, and improve recruitment and retention, improve employee morale, and reduce stress, employers will need to create opportunities for their employees that enable them to both provide care for their young grandchildren and work. Galinsky and Stein (1990) contended that companies that have care giving responsibilities at the forefront and those that help to strengthen the relationship between family and work will be leaders in their industry. It is, as Martin, Polisar, and Bengtson (1988) says, "good business" (p. 11) for employers to help their employees balance their work and family lives. While many companies have developed programs that cater to parents of young children and to employees caring for a dependent adult, expanding these programs to reach employees caring for a grandchild does not seem unrealistic. Rather, the tendency for grandparent caregivers to be among the most experienced workers in a company make it essential that companies support grandparent caregivers in their family roles, thereby decreasing productivity loss, unplanned absences from work, or withdrawal from the work world.

Grandparents raising grandchildren have complex needs, which affect the work world. First, they often find themselves having to work long beyond the age when they believed they would retire. As indicated in focus groups with grandparent caregivers conducted by Simon-Rusinowitz et al. (1996), the fear that "I'm going to have to work into my 90s just to put food on the table" is central. Second, grandparents who are surrogate caregivers to their grandchildren need flexibility from their work that allows them to stay home with a sick child or attend a conference with the child's teacher. Third, they face difficulties finding quality and affordable child care and need advice with parenting issues (Simon-Rusinowitz et al., 1996). Finally, grandparent caregivers need health care coverage for their dependent grandchildren. Despite the fact that many grandparents have court-ordered custody of their grandchildren, they are often unable to provide health care insurance to these grandchildren under their employer-provided health insurance packages.

Finally, the policy implications of these findings are great. While there is a trend for political debate to move responsibility for dependent family care back to families, with the faulty assumption that families are shirking responsibility for care in favor of employment outside the home, solid research evidence suggests that this is not the case. Pavalko and Artis (1997), for example, documented that employed women are no less likely to start providing care for a family member than are unemployed women. As Glazer (1990) has noted, the pattern that emerges is not one of women forgoing caregiving because of employment, but rather, women squeezed as reductions in government programs and health insurance increase both their responsibility for providing care and their need for waged income. These data support Glazer's observations. In this study, close to three quarters of the women were both working and providing care to a dependent grandchild. On the other hand, these data provide support for only some of the economic cost borne by grandmothers who take on caregiving responsibilities for their grandchildren. That annual incomes for these women were reduced because of responsibilities to their grandchildren is only a small piece of a very complex picture. The reduced current income has important implications for long-term reductions in pension income and Social Security benefits that can only be surmised with these data.

REFERENCES

Arbuckle, J. (1995). *AMOS: Analysis of moment structures user's guide.* Chicago: Small Waters.

Brody, E. M., Kleban, M. H., Johnsen, P. T., Hoffman, C., & Schoonover, C. B. (1987). Work status and parent care: A comparison of four groups of women. *The Gerontologist, 27.* 201–208.

Browne, M. W., & Cudeck, R. (1989). Single sample cross-validation indices for covariance structures. *Multivariate Behavioral Research, 24,* 445–455.

Bryson, K. R., & Casper, L. M. (1999). *Coresident grandparents and grandchildren.* U.S. Bureau of the Census.

Chalfie, D. (1994). *Going it alone: A closer look at grandparents raising grandchildren.* Washington, DC: American Association of Retired Persons.

Cleary, P. D., & Mechanic, D. (1983). Sex differences in psychological distress among married people. *Journal of Health and Social Behavior, 24,* 111–121.

Cohler, B. J., & Grunebaum, H. U. (1980). *Mothers. grandmothers. and daughters: Personality and childcare in three-generation families.* New York: John Wiley & Sons.

Emlen, A. C., & Koren, P. E. (1984). *Hard to find and difficult to manage: The effects of child care on the workplace.* Portland, OR: Portland State University, Regional Research Institute for Human Services.

Enright, R. B., Jr., & Friss, L. (1987). *Employed caregivers of brain-impaired adults: An assessment of the dual role.* Final report submitted to the Gerontological Society of America. San Francisco: Family Survival Project.

Fitti, J. E., & Kovar, M. G. (1987). The supplement on aging to the 1984 National Health Interview survey. *Vital and Health Statistics: Series 1, 21,* 1–115.

Galinsky, E., & Stein, P. J. (1990). The impact of human resource policies on employees: Balancing work/family life. *Journal of Family Issues, 11*, 368–383.

Gerstel, N., & Gallagher, S. (1994). Caring for kith and kin: Gender, employment and the privatization of care. *Social Problems, 41*, 519–539.

Gibeau, J. L., & Anastas, J. W. (1989). Breadwinners and caregivers: Interviews with working women. *Journal of Gerontological Social Work, 14*, 19–40.

Glazer, N. Y. (1990). The home as workshop: Women as amateur nurses and medical care providers. *Gender and Society, 4*, 479–499.

Gorey, K. M., Rice, R. W., & Brice, G. C. (1992). The prevalence of elder care responsibilities among the work force population. *Research on Aging, 14*, 399–418.

Hagestad, G. O. (1985). Continuity and connectedness. In V. L. Bengtson & J. F. Robertson (Eds.), *Grandparenthood* (pp. 31–48). Beverly Hills, CA: Sage.

Hagestad, G. O., & Smyer, M. A. (1982). Dissolving long-term relationships: Patterns of divorcing in middle age. In S. Duck (Ed.), *Dissolving personal relationships* (pp. 155–188). London: Academic Press.

Harrington Meyer, M., & Pavalko, E. K. (1996). Family, work and access to health insurance among mature women. *Journal of Health and Human Behavior, 37*, 311–325.

Hoelter, J. W. (1983). The analysis of covariance structures: Goodness-of-fit indices. *Sociological Methods and Research, 11*, 325–343.

Hoyle, R. H., & Panter, A. T. (1995). Writing about structural equation models. In R. H. Hoyle (Ed.), *Structural equation modeling: Concepts, issues, and applications* (pp. 158–176). Thousand Oaks, CA: Sage.

Joreskog, K. G., & Sorbom, D. (1986). *LISREL VI: Analysis of linear structural relationships by maximum likelihood, instrumental variables, and least squares methods*. Chicago: National Educational Resources.

Kelley, S. J., Yorker, B. C., & Whitley, D. (1997). To grandmother's house we go . . . and stay: Children raised in intergenerational families. *Journal of Gerontological Nursing, 23*, 12–20.

Kingston, E. R., & O'Grady-LeShane, R. (1993). The effects of caregiving on women's Social Security benefits. *The Gerontologist, 33*, 230–239.

Martin, M. E., Polisar, D., & Bengtson, V. L. (1988). Silent issues: What older family members do not talk about. In San Francisco: 41st Annual Meeting of the Gerontological Society of America.

Minkler, M. (1999). Intergenerational households headed by grandparents: Contexts, realities, and implications for policy. *Journal of Aging Studies, 13*, 199–218.

Minkler, M., & Roe, K. M. (1996). Grandparents as surrogate parents. *Generations, Spring 1996*, 34–38.

Mullan, J. T. (1992). The bereaved caregiver: A prospective study of changes in well-being. *The Gerontologist, 32*, 673–683.

Neal, M. B., Chapman, N. J., Ingersoll-Dayton, B., & Emlen, A. C. (1993). *Balancing work and care giving for children, adults, and elders*. Newbury Park, CA: Sage.

O'Rand, A. M., & Henretta, J. C. (1982). Delayed career entry, industrial pension structure, and early retirement in a cohort of unmarried women. *American Sociological Review, 47*, 365–373.

Parsons, T., & Bales, R. (1955). *Family, socialization, and interaction process.* Glencoe, IL: Free Press.

Pavalko, E., & Artis, J. E. (1997). Women's caregiving and paid work: Casual relationships in late midlife. *Journal of Gerontology: Social Sciences, 52B,* S170–S179.

Pearson, J. L., Hunter, A. G., Cook, J. M., Ialongo, N. S., & Kellam, S. G. (1997). Grandmother involvement in child caregiving in an urban community. *The Gerontologist,* 650–657.

Sands, R. G., & Goldberg-Glen, R. S. (1998). The impact of employment and serious illness on grandmothers who are raising their grandchildren. *Journal of Women & Aging, 10,* 41–58.

Scharlach, A. E., & Boyd, S. L. (1989). Caregiving and employment: Results of an employee survey. *The Gerontologist, 29,* 381–387.

Simon-Rusinowitz, L., Krach, C. A., Marks, L. N., Piktialis, D., & Wilson, L. B. (1996). Grandparents in the workplace: The effects of economic and labor trends. *Generations, 20,* 41–44.

Stephens, S. A., & Christianson, J. B. (1986). *Informal care of the elderly.* Lexington, MA: Lexington Books.

Stone, R., Cafferata, G. L., & Sangl, J. (1987). Caregivers of the frail elderly: A national profile. *The Gerontologist, 27,* 616–626.

Stone, R. I., & Short, P. F. (1990). The competing demands of employment and informal caregiving to disabled elders. *Medical Care, 28,* 513–525.

Vartuli, S., & Stubbs, S. (1986). *Metropolitan child care project: Final report.* Kansas City: Missouri University, School of Education.

Voydanoff, P. (1988). Work role characteristics, family structure demands, and work/family conflict. *Journal of Marriage and the Family, 50,* 749–761.

Wagner, D. L., & Neal, M. B. (1994). Caregiving and work: Consequences, correlates, and workplace responses. *Educational Gerontology, 20,* 645–663.

Warshaw, L. J., Barr, J. K., Rayman, I., Schachter, M., & Lucas, T. G. (1986). *Employer support for employee caregivers.* New York: New York Business Group on Health.

Wenk, D., & Rosenfeld, R. A. (1992). Women's employment exit and reentry: Job leaving reasons and their consequences. *Research in Social Stratification and Mobility, 11,* 127–150.

CHAPTER 2

Determinants of Role Satisfaction Among Traditional and Custodial Grandparents

Bert Hayslip Jr., Jeff R. Temple, R. Jerald Shore,
and Craig E. Henderson

INTRODUCTION

Grandparents are increasingly adopting the role of custodial parents (i.e., primary caretakers of their grandchildren) (Simmons & Dye, 2003). For example, there was a 44% increase in the number of custodial grandparents from the 1980 to 1990 Census (Saluter, 1992). An analysis of data from the National Survey of Families and Households (NSFH) revealed that 10.9% of grandparents surveyed ($n = 3,477$) were considered custodial grandparents for at least six months of their life (Fuller-Thomson, Minkler, & Driver, 1997). This escalation in custodial grandparents is partially the result of the high rate of single parent families and families in which both partners work outside of their home (see Hayslip & Kaminski, 2005). Additionally, older adults are living healthier and longer lives (Kastenbaum, 1999), thus increasing the likelihood of custodial grandparenting. In this context, several variables are relevant to understanding grandparent role satisfaction, the focus of the present chapter.

Gender

Generally, grandmothers have inherited the role of custodial grandparents more often than men (Thomas, 1986; U.S. Bureau of the Census, 2000). In fact, in analyzing data from the NSFH, Fuller-Thomson et al. (1997) found that 77% of custodial grandparents were women. Moreover, in a logistic regression analysis, the researchers found women were twice as likely as men to be custodial grandparents. This is likely an extension of familial roles, where women are often the family caretakers.

In addition to gender differences in the role of custodial grandparents, there are also differences among men and women in the meaning and satisfaction associated with grandparenting. Whereas some studies suggest grandfathers are less involved and less expressive (Brubaker, 1990; Kivett, 1991), others find no significant differences between grandmothers and grandfathers (Bengtson & Harootyan, 1994). When such differences are occasionally found, they are usually consistent with traditional gender roles (e.g., grandmothers are thought of as warm and expressive, with a desire to preserve the family line, whereas grandfathers are thought to be more invested in practical or instrumental activities) (Baranowski, 1990). However, other studies have found no such gender differences (Shore & Hayslip, 1994). Although grandmothers are generally found to be more satisfied with their role as caregivers (Thomas, 1989, 1995), similar predictors of role satisfaction have been found for grandmothers and grandfathers (Thomas, 1986).

With respect to the gender of the grandchild and factors relating to custodial grandparents, Shore and Hayslip (1994) found that grandparents expressed more satisfaction and found more meaning in raising granddaughters as opposed to grandsons. Interestingly, granddaughters have been shown to feel closer to their grandparents than have grandsons (Kennedy, 1990). Kennedy (1992) reported that when asked about their "most close" grandparent, college-aged students chose their grandmother two thirds of the time.

Socioeconomic Status

In addition to the already stressful job of raising a child, custodial grandparents are often living in poverty. For example, the percentage of custodial grandparents living below the poverty threshold is 19%, whereas

14% of other types of families with children live below the poverty threshold (U.S. Bureau of the Census, 2000). As found with many impoverished groups, custodial grandparents often lack adequate benefits. For example, 33% of children under the care of their grandparents do not have health insurance; this figure is overwhelming when compared to the 20% of children in parent-headed homes (Bryson & Casper, 1999; Kirby & Kaneda, 2002). Moreover, 90% of all custodial grandparents do not receive Social Security benefits and 85% do not receive any type of public assistance (Dellmann-Jenkins, Blankemeyer, & Olesh, 2002). Compared with traditional grandparents, custodial grandparents are 60% more likely to be living below the poverty threshold (Fuller-Thomson et al., 1997). Not surprisingly, the mean educational level of custodial grandparents (10.7 years) was found to be one year less than traditional grandparents (11.7 years) (Solomon & Marx, 1995), impacting their ability to earn a living while raising a grandchild.

Health

Several stressors have been associated with the demands of child care and parenting (Hayslip, 2003). For several reasons, the impact of such stressors may be amplified in terms of their health impact being greater for custodial grandparents. Contributing to such distress is the stigma associated with the reasons the grandparent is now parenting (e.g., incarcerated parents, abusive parents) (Kelley & Whitley, 2003). Second, and as shown above, custodial grandparents often live in poverty (U.S. Bureau of the Census, 2000). Being responsible for another person likely increases (or may be the result of increases in) financial strain. In fact, the financial burden linked to raising a second generation of children is likely the most significant negative consequence of being a custodial grandparent (Burton & deVries, 1992; Kelley, Yorker, & Whitley, 1997; Simon-Rusinowitz, Krach, Marks, Piktialis, & Wilson, 1996). Third, normative declines in health related to age may be exacerbated by the daily activities associated with raising children. The number and age of grandchildren being cared for may affect all these stressors (Kelley, 1993; Musil, 1998).

A growing body of research illustrates the negative mental and physical health effects associated with grandparents' custodial caregiving (Fuller-Thomson & Minkler, 2000; Solomon & Marx, 1995). For example, using data from the National Survey of Families and Households, Fuller-Thomson and Minkler (2000) found that compared to traditional grandparents, custodial grandparents were significantly more likely to have depressive symptomatology and a decrease in daily activities. Additionally, data from the Health and Retirement Study (1995) revealed that custodial grandparents were 80% more likely to report physical health problems and a decline in physical health over the previous year than were traditional grandparents. Similar results have been found in the comparison of custodial grandparents and parents (Kelley, 1993; Musil, 1998) as well with reference to the general population (Kelley & Whitley, 2003).

Specific health complaints associated with custodial grandparenting include depression, insomnia, hypertension, back problems, and stomach problems (Miller, 1991). Because it is likely that the decreasing health of custodial grandparents would be related to lower levels of satisfaction in their role as grandparents, it is important to consider health as a predictor of role satisfaction.

Social Support

Because many custodial grandparents are satisfied with their role and because not every custodial grandparent has poor mental and physical health, there are likely to be numerous factors distinguishing resilient from nonresilient individuals. One such factor may be the availability of and satisfaction with social support. Assuming the stress associated with raising a child decreases satisfaction, and if social support buffers the negative effects of stress on health (Thoits, 1995; Turner & Marino, 1994), increases in social support should be associated with better health and increased role satisfaction. In contrast, lower levels of social support are expected to be associated with poorer health and decreased role satisfaction. Indeed, increased levels of emotional and instrumental support have been associated with less depression among custodial grandmothers (Musil & Ahn, 1997). Because of the cumulative effects of stress, the need for social support would likely increase as a function of several variables including the number, age, and gender of the grandchild as well as any behavioral and health problems the grandchild may have.

Age

The age of the grandparent and grandchild may also be an important predictor of the custodial grandparents' role satisfaction, especially considering the range of ages found with custodial grandparents (Simmons & Dye, 2003). The multiple roles (i.e., mothers, wives, children, and employees) associated with younger grandmothers (Brubaker, 1990) would likely have a negative impact on role satisfaction. However, older grandparents may have decreasing ability to participate in daily parenting tasks, which may contribute to negative affect (see Goodman, chapter 9) and exacerbate the age-related deterioration of their health. As a result, older grandparents may be more susceptible to dissatisfaction with their roles as caregivers than younger grandparents.

Child and Grandparent Variables

It is now well established that the quality of grandparents' relationship with their grandchildren in both custodial (see Hayslip, Shore, Henderson, & Lambert, 1998; Young & Dawson, 2003) and traditional dyads (see Reitzes & Mutran, 2004) may impact contact with one's grandchildren (for traditional grandparents) and role satisfaction via its negative impact on personal well-being and role-specific meaning for both traditional and custodial grandchildren. Consequently, such factors may emerge as most salient, relative to for example, social support, health, or age, in predicting role satisfaction in each group of grandparents, or in light of the demands of raising a grandchild, be more predictive of role satisfaction among caregiving grandparents.

Purpose of the Present Study

In the larger context of the often discussed rewards of traditional grandparenthood (see Szinovacz, 1998) and its potential disruption via raising a grandchild, little is known about the differential predictors of grandparent role satisfaction, especially in light of the fact that custodial grandparents, for a variety of reasons (see above) are likely to express less satisfaction with life in general, and with their roles as grandparents in particular. In this light, several questions about the satisfaction with being a grandparent are relevant: Why are some grandparents satisfied in their roles, while others are not? Do the determinants of role satisfaction differ between traditional and custodial grandparents? Consequently, in order to enhance role satisfaction in each grandparent group and intervene appropriately, it is necessary to attend to individual differences in such antecedent factors. It is in this context that this study will consider the roles of age, gender, socioeconomic status, social support, and health, in light of the contribution of child-specific factors and other more generic influences that might be expected to correlate with role satisfaction, such as role meaning and personal well-being, as predictors of role satisfaction in traditional and custodial grandparents.

METHOD

Sample

Participants (see Shore & Hayslip, 1994) in this study were 193 male and female grandparents from the Dallas–Fort Worth area of Texas.

Eighty percent of the traditional grandparents were female, whereas 79% of the custodial grandparents were female. Thirty-one percent of the traditional grandparents had a male grandchild, whereas 68% of the custodial grandparents had a male grandchild. Traditional grandparents generally had higher annual incomes than did their custodial grandparent counterparts. Marital status and race were similar across groups. Volunteers were recruited by a variety of methods to ensure a reasonably representative sample of both custodial and traditional grandparents. Both clinics and self-help groups were approached as potential sources of custodial grandparents due to the high incidence of family trauma that often leads them to become surrogate parents. Additionally, senior centers, older adult organizations, and newspaper announcements were used to identify both custodial and traditional grandparents. If a couple was parenting, only one member was permitted to volunteer to permit independence of responses; in such cases, the couple decided who would participate. Despite the diverse sources and methods by which the participants were recruited, the final sample must be considered somewhat biased due to the generally positive response bias associated with community samples of middle-aged and older adults (see Baltes, 1968). However, both groups of grandparents were equally likely to be recruited from each source (see Shore & Hayslip, 1994).

Several limitations should be noted regarding the sample of grandparents here, which was self-selected and thus may not represent the population of grandparents (custodial and otherwise) as a whole. The majority were middle-class Caucasian women, though approximately 20% of the participants were either African American or Hispanic. This sample of traditional and custodial grandparents does, however, resemble a national sample of custodial grandparents (Fuller-Thomson et al., 1997) in terms of age, gender, race, income, age of the grandchild when caregiving began, and duration of primary caregiving.

Measures

Independent Variables

The definition of traditional and custodial grandparents was of central concern in this study. Moreover, it was equally important to distinguish reliable subgroups of grandparents raising their grandchildren to disentangle role adjustments from the grandchildren's problems as sources of distress (personal, role-specific, and grandchild relationship) for custodial grandparents.

Traditional grandparents were defined as those whose grandchildren were in the care and custody of their parents. These participants provided little or no care for their grandchild who was age 18 or under and who lived in the grandparents' home. Custodial grandparents had legal custody of their grandchildren in just over half of the cases. When queried, custodial grandparents never described the extent of their caregiving responsibilities as "part-time" or "casual" in nature, whereas 100% of those in the traditional grandparent group did so.

Respondents reported on salient features of their relationship with only one grandchild age 18 or younger (Thomas, 1986, 1990). This procedure was used because different grandchildren affect grandparental feelings and perceptions in different ways (Cherlin & Furstenberg, 1986; Thomas, 1986, 1990); such perceptions are likely to be confounded by different feelings toward various grandchildren.

If respondents indicated that they did not parent a grandchild, they were asked to report on a grandchild age 18 or younger for whom the primary responsibility of care lay with the child's parents, whom they saw the most frequently of all their grandchildren, and for whom they provided only minimal or nominal care. Custodial grandparents were asked to report on the grandchild who had been in their care the longest (i.e., a grandchild age 18 or younger for whom they provided all of the grandchild's care, who might or might not be in their legal custody, and with whom they coresided).

The circumstances under which grandparents assumed responsibility for their grandchildren included divorce; incarceration; mental, emotional, or physical impairment of the parent; death of the parent; child abuse; or parents' drug abuse. Divorce, child abuse, and the parents' emotional disturbance and drug abuse were the most common. Sixty-four percent of custodial grandparents earned less than $30,000 per year, whereas 57% of traditional participants earned at least $50,000 annually.

Perceptions of social resources were evaluated in terms of visits and other contacts with the grandchild's parents, other relatives, or friends (Havighurst, 1973), as well as the extent to which this social network provided physical resources (e.g., transportation, money, food, clothing) and psychological help (e.g., "cheering me up") (Beyer & Woods, 1963). A measure of social support from the adult child, other family members, and friends was created by summing perceptions of the extent (1 = none to 5 = a great deal) to which such persons provided 11 different types of assistance, resulting in a 33-item scale assessing the extent of such support from others (alpha = .82). In this case, distinctions between instrumental (8 items in each case) and emotional support (3 items in each case) were made regarding social support.

Satisfaction with grandparenting was assessed using 15 questions (alpha = .79) used in the Thomas (1990) study. Each question was answered on a 5-point Likert-type scale (strongly disagree to strongly agree), and higher scores indicated greater satisfaction (alpha = .90 in this study).

The meaning of grandparenthood was evaluated via items from Thomas (1990) originally developed by Kivnick (1982, 1983), who derived five dimensions of meaning pertaining to grandparenthood: Centrality (having high personal salience), Valued Elder (being admired and sought out for advice and help by a grandchild), Immortality through Clan (being able to live on through a grandchild), Reinvolvement with Past (being able to relive earlier experiences), and Indulgence (being able to spoil and to be lenient with a grandchild). High scores reflected an important and increased meaning of grandparenthood. In previous research (Kivnick, 1982), coefficient alphas had ranged from .68 (Indulgence) to .90 (Centrality) (all alphas exceeded .73 in the present study). For purposes of this study, total meaning scores were utilized in light of the factor structure of role meaning (see Hayslip, Shore, & Henderson, 2003).

Grandparents' perceptions of their relationships with grandchildren were measured by the Positive Affect Index (10 items) and Negative Affect Index (10 items) (Thomas, 1986, 1990). The former index asked the grandparents to describe the extent (Likert format, none to a great amount) of their mutual understanding with, trust in, respect for, and affection for their grandchildren, whereas the latter measured the extent of the grandparents' negative feelings toward irritating behaviors of the grandchild (alpha = .79; Thomas, 1989). The Positive and Negative Affect Indices predict well-being in samples of grandparents (Thomas, 1986, 1990). Alphas for these scales in this study were .92 and .93, respectively. An additional question asked the participants to rate the quality of the grandchild relationship (Likert 5-point scale, very negative to very positive).

Psychological well-being was assessed via Liang's (1985) 15-item self-report scale, which includes items that span a long-term time frame to reduce the possible distortion of results due to the effects of temporary situations. Positive and negative affect (transitory affective components), happiness (a long-term affective component), and congruence (a long-term cognitive component) were assessed by an integration of items from the Bradburn Affect Balance Scale (Bradburn, 1969) and the Life Satisfaction Index A (Neugarten, Havighurst, & Tobin, 1961). Total scores for well-being were used in this study; alpha for this sample was .67.

Grandparents responded to questions regarding the extent to which their grandchildren manifested nine specific problem behaviors and to one additional general category that asked grandparents to write in problems and behaviors not listed in the questionnaire. Respondents rated the problem behaviors (nine specific problems in addition to an "other" category) on a continuum of severity (1 = no problem to 5 = severe problem), with a score of 13 being the median. Total scores indexing the perception of grandchild problems were used here.

In completing the single item Likert rating of the quality of their relationship with the grandchild and in completing the above measures as they related to the grandchild, traditional grandparents referenced the grandchild with whom they had the most contact, while custodial grandparents referenced the grandchild whom they had been raising for the longest period of time.

RESULTS AND DISCUSSION

Hierarchical regression analyses were used to examine predictors of role satisfaction in representative samples of custodial and traditional grandparents. Variables were entered as blocks in the following order: (a) grandchild age, grandchild gender (dummy coded), number of grandchildren, duration in months of part-time/full-time caregiving; (b) instrumental support provided by the adult child, friends, and other family; (c) emotional support provided by the adult child, friends, and other family; (d) extent of caregiving responsibility along 11 dimensions (see Shore & Hayslip, 1994), positive and negative affect, perceptions of child difficulties; (e) level of education, health, age, and gender of the grandparent; and (f) well-being and role meaning.

These analyses (conducted separately for traditional and custodial grandparents) found that in the context of the above blocks of variables to predict role satisfaction, for traditional grandparents ($p < .05$), greater role duration ($\beta = -.22$), fewer grandchild problems ($\beta = -.29$), higher grandchild relationship quality ($\beta = .36$ and $\beta = -.27$ for positive and negative affect, respectively), fewer caregiving responsibilities ($\beta = -.11$), and younger age ($\beta = -.19$) positively predicted role satisfaction, $F(6, 93) = 36.29$, $p < .01$, $R^2 = .70$, $R^2_{adj} = .69$. In contrast, for custodial grandparents ($p < .05$), having fewer grandchildren ($\beta = -.13$, $p < .05$), perceiving fewer custodial grandchild problems ($\beta = -.13$), greater role meaning ($\beta = .34$), higher well-being ($\beta = .17$), more emotional support from family ($\beta = .10$), higher grandchild relationship quality ($\beta = .20$ and $-.30$ for positive and negative affect, respectively), and to a certain extent ($p < .09$), more instrumental support from friends ($\beta = .08$), positively predicted role satisfaction, $F(8, 93) = 63.67$, $p < .01$, $R^2 = .85$, $R^2_{adj} = .83$. Thus, 70% of the variance in grandparent role satisfaction was accounted for among custodial parents and 85% of such variance among the traditional grand-parents was accounted for via the above respective sets of predictors. Surprisingly, in no case did grandparent age, gender, level of education, or health as a block uniquely contribute to the prediction of role satisfac-tion in either subgroup of grandparents.

In general, these results are consistent with previous research (see Reitzes & Mutran, 2004; Szinovacz, 1998) targeting satisfaction with the grandparental role. For traditional grandparents, greater role duration (i.e., the longer one has been in the grandparental role) was a predictor of role satisfaction. Interestingly, this was not found for custodial grand-parents, suggesting that increased experience with being the primary caregiver does not necessarily increase satisfaction with the role, in con-trast to a deepening of the relationship with the grandchild over time or increased involvement for traditional grandparents. Fewer caregiving responsibilities (e.g., babysitting, cooking, dressing) was also predictive of greater role satisfaction among traditional grandparents. In relating this finding to custodial grandparents, increased instrumental support may decrease the extent of caregiving responsibilities, and, as was the case for traditional grandparents, may increase their role satisfaction. Age was inversely predictive of role satisfaction with traditional grandparents. This is consistent with previous research (see Goodman, chapter 9), as older grandparents may have increased health problems and may not be able to physically "keep up" with their grandchildren. In light of the importance of social support in affecting role satisfaction among custodial grandparents (see below), such support may buffer the otherwise negative impact of either older age or more tenuous health on role satisfaction (see Hayslip, Shore, & Emick, chapter 5). As being the primary caregiver to a grandchild, in addition to being an employee and a spouse, may be overwhelming for custodial grandparents, social support is especially critical in helping persons deal with role strain, role conflict, or role overload.

Because the stress of raising a grandchild is likely multiplied by the demands on one's time associated with having more grandchildren, it is not surprising that custodial grandparents who report greater satisfaction have fewer grandchildren. Moreover, the anecdotal reports of guilt associ-ated with giving one grandchild extra attention (i.e., grandchild being cared for) at the expense of another may decrease satisfaction with the role of grandparent (Shore & Hayslip, 1994) are borne out in these objective data.

The fact that instrumental or emotional support from family and friends predicted role satisfaction in custodial grandparents is consistent with the notion that social support acts as a buffer against the negative impact of stressors. Greater family contact (most likely correlated with more opportunities for greater social support) may then be associated with more extensive interpersonal resources to manage role demands and a subsequent increase in role satisfaction. Unfortunately, many custodial grandparents are isolated from sources of social support (Wohl, Lahner, & Jooste, 2003). Thus, one goal of counselors or community psychologists working with custodial grandparents should be to increase the amount of social support and family contact available to grandparents raising their grandchildren.

The finding that higher role meaning was a predictor of role satisfaction suggests that custodial grandparents feel they are central to the family, feel valued, and will be remembered for the job they have done in raising their grandchildren. Indeed, custodial grandparents who believe their role serves a purpose and is meaningful are more likely to be satisfied with their role and accept the daily hassles, stressors, and negative health consequences associated with raising a grandchild. This is especially the case among Mexican-born grandparent caregivers (see Toledo, Hayslip, Emick, Toledo, & Henderson, 2000), underscoring its importance as a determinant of role satisfaction among American-born samples, for whom caregiving is seen as an imposition or as a disruptive influence on one's life plans (Jendrek, 1994). Psychological well-being was also a predictor of role satisfaction among custodial grandparents, indicating that custodial grandparents who generally feel positive, happy, and congruent are increasingly likely to feel satisfied with their role. This is not surprising given the research linking positive feelings with a positive assessment of one's life (see Neugarten et al., 1961).

It is notable that the only variables predicting role satisfaction in both grandparent groups were higher grandchild relationship quality and perceiving the grandchild to have fewer emotional and behavioral problems. This suggests that irrespective of the degree of caregiving in which one is engaged (i.e., custodial vs. traditional grandparents), having a positive relationship with a grandchild and having a grandchild with fewer behavioral problems is related to greater satisfaction with the grandparent role. Indeed, it is often the case that grandparents who are raising their grandchildren report that their dedication to the grandchild's welfare, and satisfaction in seeing the grandchild enjoy the security and stability of an intact home outweigh the demands on their time, the toll on their health, and the disruption in their lives that raising a grandchild may bring about (see Hirshorn, 1998; Ruiz, 2003).

In sum, these results generally suggest diverse sets of antecedents of role satisfaction for each grandparent group, and have implications for interventions to enhance the role adjustment of such persons, especially that of custodial grandparents. By understanding individual differences in relationships between a variety of factors and role satisfaction, we can more effectively intervene to enhance the quality (and perhaps the quantity) of life for grandparents who raise their grandchildren. These data therefore reinforce the wisdom of utilizing support groups, increasing support from family and friends, and the development of programs that provide instrumental assistance (e.g., financial support, health care) to custodial grandparents, increasing their personal well-being and satisfaction with their role as primary caregivers to their grandchildren.

REFERENCES

Baltes, P. B. (1968). Longitudinal and cross-sectional sequences in the study of age and generation effects. *Human Development, 11*, 145–171.

Baranowski, M. D. (1990). The grandfather-grandchild relationships: Meaning and exchange. *Family Perspective, 24*, 201–215.

Bengtson, V. L., & Harootyan, R. A. (Eds.). (1994). *Hidden connections: A study of intergenerational linkages in American society*. New York: Springer.

Beyer, G. H., & Woods, M. E. (1963). Living and activity patterns of the aged. *Research Report No. 6*. Ithaca, NY: Center for Housing and Environmental Studies, Cornell University.

Bradburn, N. (1969). *The structure of psychological well-being*. Chicago: Aldine.

Brubaker, T. H. (1990). *Family relationships in later life* (2nd ed.). California: Sage.

Bryson, K., & Casper, L. M. (1999). *Coresident grandparents and grandchildren: U.S. Bureau of the Census current population reports* (Series P. 23 No. 198). Washington, DC: U.S. Government Printing Office.

Burton, L. M., & deVries, C. (1992). Challenges and rewards: African American grandparents as surrogate parents. *Generations, 16*, 51–54.

Cherlin, A. J., & Furstenberg, F. F. (1986). *The new American grandparent: A place in the family, a life apart*. New York: Basic Books.

Dellman-Jenkins, M., Blankemeyer, M., & Olesh, M. (2002). Adults in expanded grandparent roles: Considerations for practice, policy, and research. *Educational Gerontology, 28*, 219–235.

Fuller-Thomson, E., & Minkler, M. (2000). The mental and physical health of grandmothers who are raising their grandchildren. *Journal of Mental Health and Aging, 6*, 311–323.

Fuller-Thomson, E., Minkler, M., & Driver, D. (1997). A profile of grandparents raising grandchildren in the United States. *The Gerontologist, 37*(3), 406–411.

Goodman, C. C. (in press). Grandmothers raising grandchildren: The vulnerability of advancing aging. In B. Hayslip & J. Hicks Patrick (Eds.), *Diversity among custodial grandparents*. New York: Springer.

Havighurst, R. J. (1973). Social roles, work, leisure, and education. In C. Eisdorfer & M. P. Lawton (Eds.), *The psychology of adult development and aging* (pp. 598–618). Washington, DC: American Psychological Association.

Hayslip, B. (2003). The impact of a psychosocial intervention on parental efficacy, grandchild relationship quality and well being among grandparents raising grandchildren. In B. Hayslip & J. Hicks Patrick (Eds.), *Working with custodial grandparents* (pp. 163–178). New York: Springer.

Hayslip, B., & Kaminski, P. (2005). Grandparents raising their grandchildren: A review of the literature and suggestions for practice. *The Gerontologist, 45*, 262–269.

Hayslip, B., Shore, R. J., & Emick, M. (in press). Age, health, and custodial grandparenting. In B. Hayslip & J. Hicks Patrick (Eds.), *Diversity among custodial grandparents*. New York: Springer.

Hayslip, B., Shore, R. J., & Henderson, C. (2003). The structure of grandparental role meaning. *Journal of Adult Development, 10*, 31–39.

Hayslip, B., Shore, R. J., Henderson, C., & Lambert, P. (1998). Custodial grandparenting and grandchildren with problems: Impact on role satisfaction and role meaning. *Journal of Gerontology: Social Sciences, 53B*, S164–S174.

Hirshorn, B. (1998). Grandparents as caregivers. In M. E. Szinovacz (Ed.), *Handbook on grandparenthood* (pp. 200–216). Westport, CT: Greenwood.

Jendrek, M. (1994). Grandparents who parent their grandchildren: Circumstances and decisions. *The Gerontologist, 34*, 206–216.

Kastenbaum, R. (1999). Dying and bereavement. In J. Cavanaugh & S. Whitbourne (Eds.), *Gerontology: An interdisciplinary perspective* (pp. 155–185). New York: Oxford.

Kelley, S. J. (1993). Caregiver stress in grandparents raising grandchildren. *Image: Journal of Nursing Scholarship, 25*, 331–337.

Kelley, S. J., & Whitley, D. M. (2003). Psychological distress and physical health problems in grandparents raising grandchildren: Development of an empirically based intervention model. In B. Hayslip, Jr. & J. H. Patrick (Eds.), *Working with custodial grandparents* (pp. 127–144). New York: Springer.

Kelley, S., Yorker, B. C., & Whitley, D. (1997). To grandmother's house we go . . . and stay: Children raised in intergenerational families. *Journal of Gerontological Nursing, 23*, 12–20.

Kennedy, G. E. (1990). College students' expectations of grandparent and grandchild behaviors. *The Gerontologist, 30*, 43–48.

Kennedy, G. E. (1992). Quality in grandparent/grandchild relationships. *International Journal of Aging and Human Development, 35*, 83–98.

Kirby, J .B., & Kaneda, T. (2002). Health insurance and family structure: The case of adolescents in skipped-generation families. *Medical Care Research and Review, 59*, 146–165.

Kivett, V. R. (1991). The grandparent-grandchild connection. *Marriage and Family Review, 16*, 267–290.

Kivnick, H. Q. (1982). Grandparenthood: An overview of meaning and mental health. *The Gerontologist, 22*, 59–66.

Kivnick, H. Q. (1983). Dimensions of grandparenthood meaning: Deductive conceptualization and empirical derivation. *Journal of Personality and Social Psychology, 44*, 1056–1068.

Liang, J. (1985). A structural integration of the Affect Balance Scale and the Life Satisfaction Index A. *Journal of Gerontology, 40*, 552–561.

Miller, D. (1991). *The "Grandparents Who Care" support project of San Francisco*. Paper presented at the annual meeting of the Gerontological Society of America, San Francisco.

Musil, C. M. (1998). Health, stress, coping, and social support in grandmother caregivers. *Health Care for Women International, 19*, 441–455.

Musil, C. M., & Ahn, S. (1997, November). *Grandmothers raising grandchildren: Is support linked to depression?* Paper presented at the meeting of the Gerontological Society of America, Cincinnati, OH.

Neugarten, B. L., Havighurst, R. J., & Tobin, S. S. (1961). The measurement of life satisfaction. *Journal of Gerontology, 16*, 134–143.

Reitzes, D. C., & Mutran, E. (2004). Grandparenthood: Factors influencing frequency of grandparent-grandchild contact on grandparent role satisfaction. *Journal of Gerontology: Social Sciences, 59B*, S9–S16.

Ruiz, D. (2003). *Amazing grace: African American grandmothers as caregivers and conveyors of traditional values*. Westport, CT: Praeger.

Saluter, A. F. (1992). *Marital status and living arrangements: March 1991. U.S. Bureau of the Census current population reports* (Series P-20 No. 461). Washington, DC: U.S. Government Printing Office.

Shore, R. J., & Hayslip, B. (1994). Custodial grandparenting: Implications for children's development. In A. E. Gottfried & A. W. Gottfried (Eds.), *Redefining families: Implications for children's development* (pp. 171–218). New York: Plenum.

Simmons, T., & Dye, J. (2003). *Grandparents living with grandchildren: 2000, Census 2000 Brief* (pp. 1–10). Washington, DC: U.S. Department of Commerce.

Simon-Rusinowitz, L., Krach, C. A., Marks, L. N., Piktialis, D., & Wilson, L. B. (1996). Grandparents in the workplace: The effects of economic and labor trends. *Generations, 20*, 41–44.

Solomon, J. C., & Marx, J. (1995). "To grandmother's house we go": Health and school adjustment of children raised solely by grandparents. *The Gerontologist, 35*, 386–394.

Szinovacz, M. E. (1998). *Handbook on grandparenthood*. Westport, CT: Greenwood.

Thoits, P. A. (1995). Stress, coping, and social support processes: Where are we? What next? *Journal of Health and Social Behavior, 35*, 51–79.

Thomas, J. L. (1986). Gender differences in satisfaction with grandparenting. *Psychology and Aging, 1*, 215–219.

Thomas, J. L. (1989). Gender and perceptions of grandparenthood. *International Journal of Aging and Human Development, 29*, 269–282.

Thomas, J. L. (1990). The grandparent role: A double bind. *International Journal of Aging and Human Development, 31*, 169–177.

Thomas, J. L. (1995). Gender and perceptions of grandparenthood. In J. Hendricks (Ed.), *The ties of later life* (pp. 181–193). Amityville, NY: Baywood.

Toledo, R., Hayslip, B., Emick, M., Toledo, C., & Henderson, C. (2000). Cross cultural differences in custodial grandparenting. In B. Hayslip & R. Goldberg-Glen (Eds.), *Grandparents raising grandchildren: Theoretical, empirical, and clinical perspectives* (pp. 107–124). New York: Springer.

Turner, R. J., & Marino, F. (1994). Social support and social structure: A descriptive epidemiology. *Journal of Health of Social Behavior, 35*, 193–212.

U.S. Bureau of the Census. (2000). *Current populations survey.* Washington, DC: U.S. Government Printing Office.

Wohl, E., Lahner, J., & Jooste, J. (2003). Group processes among grandparents raising grandchildren. In B. Hayslip & J. Hicks Patrick (Eds.), *Working with custodial grandparents* (pp. 195–212). New York: Springer.

Young, M. H., & Dawson, T. J. (2003). Perception of child difficulty and levels of depression in caregiving grandmothers. *Journal of Mental Health and Aging, 9*, 111–122.

CHAPTER 3

Diversity and Caregiving Support Intervention: Lessons from Elder Care Research

Sara H. Qualls and Karen A. Roberto

Few grandparents—regardless of race, ethnicity, or social class—plan, anticipate, or are prepared for a second parenthood. As they assume responsibility for rearing their grandchildren, grandparents may confront several personal and social challenges in making adjustments in their daily lives to accommodate their acquired parental roles. The research on how cultural minority populations care for elderly family members distinctively offers guidance for the study of cultural variations in grandparent caregiving. This chapter describes different intervention strategies used by minority family caregivers of older adults and reveals how educators, practitioners, and clinicians can transfer and transform elements of these programs as they develop and implement interventions for minority grandparents who are now in a parenting role. In addition, this chapter introduces the topic of diversity in family care with a brief overview of the merging demographic revolutions changing the face of our nation and focuses on factors that influence beliefs about elder care and families' responsiveness to formal assistance. As we identify specific types of intervention programs designed to support minority families providing care of their older members, we note their effectiveness in meeting caregivers' needs and challenges of delivering intervention programs. The chapter ends with a discussion of strategies for transferring and building upon what we have learned about from the late-life minority caregiving intervention literature to develop and implement successful programs and interventions for minority grandparents raising grandchildren.

DIVERSIFICATION OF AN AGING AMERICA

Since 1900, the percentage of Americans age 65 and older has tripled. About 35.6 million persons, representing 12.3% of the population, were 65 years of age or older in 2002 (Administration on Aging [AoA], 2003). The ethnic minority populations of older Americans are growing at even faster rates than that of the older adult population as a whole. In 2002, 17.2% of persons age 65 and older represented minority groups—8.1% were African Americans, 2.7% were Asian or Pacific Islander, and less than 1% were American Indian or Native Alaskan. Persons of Hispanic origin represented 5.5% of the older population (AoA, 2003). Almost 7% of minority race and Hispanic populations were age 65 and older (8.2% of African Americans, 8.18% of Asians and Pacific Islanders, 6.6% of American Indians and Native Alaskans, 5.1% of Hispanics), compared with 15.0% of White Hispanic elders.

Approximately 20.8 million older Americans are women, 7.9 million of whom live alone. Although an economically diverse population, approximately 3.6 million elderly persons (10.4%) report annual incomes below the poverty level and another 2.2 million (6.4%) of the older persons have income between the poverty level and 125% of poverty. Older women have a higher poverty rate (12.4%) than older men (7.7%) and older persons living alone are much more likely to be poor (19.2%) than were older persons living with families (6.0%) (AoA, 2003). One of every 12 (8.3%) elderly Whites was poor in 2002, compared to 23.8% of elderly African Americans and 21.4% of elderly Hispanics. The highest poverty rates (47.1%) were experienced by older Hispanic women who lived alone.

Changes in health and functioning often require older adults to seek assistance from informal and formal sources. When the need arises, older adults turn to family members, typically their spouse or adult children, for instrumental support (e.g., helping with transportation, running errands) and more intense care activities (e.g., personal care). According to a national survey conducted by AARP (2001), nearly 78% of baby boomers age 45 to 55 provide intermittent caregiving services to their parents or other older adults, but do not consider themselves to be caregivers. Of the 22% who identify themselves as caregivers for their parents, 17% provide personal assistance, whereas approximately 5% provide mainly financial support. Midlife White Americans are the least likely of any racial or ethnic group to provide care for their parents or other older adults (19% vs. 28% of African Americans, 33% of Hispanic Americans, and 42% of Asian Americans). Compared to White, Hispanic American, and Asian American midlife caregivers, African Americans are more likely to rely on their individual faith and include other family members and formal care to meet parent care needs. With family being a central part of most Hispanic American lives, it is no surprise that they provide more care for aging parents than any other group. Asian Americans report more often than do other ethnic groups that family care responsibilities influence how they live their own lives and, thus, this group reports the most stress in their lives.

A late life family care situation receiving greater attention in the past decade is that of grandparents assuming full-time parenting responsibilities for their grandchildren. Approximately 2.4 million grandparents have primary responsibility for their grandchildren, of whom 840,000 have been caring for their grandchildren for 5 or more years (U.S. Bureau of the Census, 2003). The majority of grandparents rearing grandchildren are between the ages of 30 and 59 (60%), married (73%), and female (62%). More than one half of them are in the labor force and about one fifth have incomes below the poverty threshold. However, there is marked variation in income by household type with grandmother-only households averaging $19,750 per year and households with two grandparents plus at least one parent averaging $61,632 (Bryson & Casper, 1999). Contradictions appear in the literature with regard to the health of these caregivers; some grandparents viewed their health as not affected or improved as a result of a more active lifestyle, whereas others reported increased physical and mental health problems (Grinstead, Leder, Jensen, & Bond, 2003). Although older adults representing all race and ethnic groups are raising grandchildren, minority grandparents are 2 to 3 times as likely as their White counterparts to assume the parenting role (Fuller-Thomson, Minkler, & Driver, 1997).

CAREGIVING FOR ELDERLY FAMILY MEMBERS IN CULTURALLY DIVERSE HOUSEHOLDS

Culture refers to a way of life as manifested by those elements of a particular group's history, traditions, values, practices, and social organizations that are meaningful to individual members (Hinrichsen & Ramirez, 1992). Specific to the issue of caregiving, values and customs influence families' willingness to provide care and how they structure that care. Thus, family culture plays a central role in defining roles and responsibilities as well as help-seeking and help-accepting behaviors.

Norms of Family Care

Cultural norms strongly influence the extent and type of care provided by family members. In contrast with the majority White American culture, which emphasizes democracy and individuality, the needs and well-being of the family unit is of utmost importance and a driving influence in the lives of many members of minority groups. Extended family models are common among African American families, whose system of kin and quasi-kinship network is defined not only by blood ties, but also by a complex system based on proximity, shared values, and functional affiliations (Scannapieco & Jackson, 1996). Hispanic culture, with its strong basis in familism, promotes strong reliance on family ties and preference for assistance from within the family (Sotomayor & Randolph, 1988). Although the extent of acculturation varies across immigrant groups, Asian and Pacific Islander cultures continue to uphold traditional family values, including filial piety. For Japanese Americans, traditional family values, including interdependency, hierarchical relationships, and cohesiveness predominate (Tempo & Saito, 1996). Family, not the individual, is the most important unit of social organization in Chinese culture (Elliott, Di Minno, Lam, & Tu, 1996); thus, family goals and interests take precedence over the goals and interests of any individual family member. Putting family welfare before the self also is deeply embedded in the Filipino culture. The family is the major source of emotional, moral, and economic support and caring for elders is a strongly held family value (McBride & Parreno, 1996).

Cultural assumptions about familial beliefs and supports have been subject to limited empirical tests. The family caregiving literature consistently, however, reports differences in burden between White and ethnic minority caregivers. White caregivers typically report greater burden than other family groups (e.g., Adams, Aranda, Kemp, & Takagi, 2002). Potential explanations have been offered for these differences in the level of perceived burden, including stronger feelings of family obligation and greater acceptance of the family of the caregiving situation (Aranda & Knight, 1997; Connell & Gibson, 1997). Yet, a set of individual studies comparing responses of Latino, Korean and Korean American, Japanese American, and African American caregivers found the relationship of familism to caregiver burden was not consistent across ethnic groups and was either independent of caregiver outcomes or was positively associated with distress (Knight, Robinson, Flynn Longmire, Chun, Nakao, et al., 2002). Calderon and Tennstedt (1998) argue that members of ethnic groups may be experiencing similar levels of burden as that of their White counterparts, but cultural factors impede the expression or admission of burden. Their qualitative study of White, African American, and Puerto Rican caregivers revealed that White caregivers openly expressed strong feelings of burden, whereas the minority caregivers expressed burden more indirectly through expressions of frustration, anger, isolation, and somatic complaints. Similarly, although Pueblo Indian caregivers expressed a variety of frustrations with their caregiving situations, including family members not contributing to the caregiving effort or criticizing the primary caregiver's efforts, most negative constructs constituting caregiver burden were not endorsed (Hennessy & John, 1995). Rather, the caregivers actively engaged in activities aimed at achieving an acceptable caregiving arrangement that promoted family harmony and interdependence. Collectively, these findings suggest the importance of taking into consideration cultural differences and idiosyncrasies in the design, planning, implementation, and evaluation of interventions for ethnic minority caregivers.

Immigration patterns and acculturation processes create diversity within as well as across cultural groups that influence family caregiving patterns for elderly as well as young. The contexts of migration to the United States shape life contexts in such significant ways that they cannot be ignored in discussions of family caregiving patterns. Immigration due to famine or war produces a very different life context than migration to seek improved business opportunity or to join financially successful family members. In addition to economic resources, access to cultural organizations that bridge the old and new cultures also influences style of adaptation and family structuring. Time since immigration within the lineage is a powerful predictor of acculturation in some groups, yielding distinctive generational support structure challenges.

Contexts of Family Care

Structural characteristics of families shape who provides care and how. Elder care research documents patterns of care provider preference that yield predictable patterns for who will take over care. A "hierarchical compensatory" model suggests that the closest, most available person provides the care (Cantor, 1975). Thus, with elder care, spouses are most preferred, but if unavailable due to disability or death, adult children are the next likely providers, with daughters more likely to take on the duties than sons. Certainly, other structural variables also influence the likelihood of particular members taking on family caregiving roles. Geographic propinquity (Finley, Roberts, & Banham, 1988) and competing role demands (Brody & Schoonover, 1986) influence decision to care.

The internal dynamics of families also shape the elder caregiving experience. In particular, alliances and bonds between members often influence the likelihood that a particular person will provide care for another, but cut-off relationships preclude availability for caregiving. Just as missing or broken relationships between aging parents and middle aged children disrupt available caretakers for elders, the same disruption complicates care for grandchildren.

Decision-making structures have received considerable attention in the elder care literature because they have been documented to influence well-being of both caregiver and care recipient, and use of formal systems such as nursing homes (Fisher & Lieberman, 1999). Families with a more focused decision making style and positive conflict resolution strategies provided more support than families with ambiguous or democratic structures (Lieberman & Fisher, 1999).

Variations in family caregiving structures, decision patterns, and adjustment to caregiving have been documented across several ethnic groups (see summaries of research in Gallagher-Thompson et al., 2000; Yeo & Gallagher-Thompson, 1996). Several authors have noted that some cultural groups value more extreme sacrifice to provide care within the family than other populations, across stages of the life span (Gallagher-Thompson et al., 2003). For example, within the elder care literature, cultural variations have been documented regarding the values underlying end of life decisions. African American and Caucasian respondents differed in preferences regarding use of CPR, tube feeding, and ventilation in persons with dementia, with Caucasians recommending less intervention than African Americans (Allen-Burge & Haley, 1997). This finding illustrates variations among cultural groups in the level of self-sacrifice individuals make for other family members or the preservation of the family structure itself.

Formal advanced planning for elder care decisions in the form of advance directives is more likely in Euro-Americans than in other cultural groups (Hopp & Duffy, 2000; Vaughn, Kiyasu, & McCormick, 2000). The emphasis in Euro-American culture on autonomy and determining one's own destiny through legal advance directives may be less relevant in cultural groups that view family as more interdependent (High, 1991). Applying that finding to grandparent caregivers might suggest variations in the cultural rules about the extent of self-sacrifice expected in care of family as well as the appropriateness of planfulness for potential difficulties ahead. Reliance upon family may lead some groups to engage in less formal planning for future care needs because they presume that family will handle what comes (Hopp & Duffy, 2000), although other factors such as concern for being disrespectful of elderly family members or fear of generating conflict may be more powerful inhibitors (Knopman, Donahue, & Gutterman, 2000).

Recent longitudinal analyses of the trajectory of dementia caregiving suggests that the abruptness of onset of the caregiving experience affects outcomes (e.g., institutional placement) (Gaugler, Zarit, & Pearlin, 2003). Easing into the elder caregiving role appears to have less deleterious impact on caregiving, as well as less dramatic outcomes for the care recipient. Role onset and role induction have been useful ways of examining the emergence of coping strategies in elder caregiving contexts that may be useful to apply to grandparent caregivers (Aneshensel, Pearlin, Mullan, Zarit, & Whitlatch, 1995). Furthermore, cultural differences in timing of initiation of medical care for illnesses influence the timing and initiation of roles across cultural groups (e.g., Watari & Gatz, 2004). In essence, cultural rules structure role transitions (or leave them ambiguous), prescribe roles in clearer or more ambiguous ways, and vary in the extent to which the person learning new roles is supported.

SUPPORTING MINORITY GRANDPARENT CAREGIVERS: LESSONS FROM ELDER CARE INTERVENTION RESEARCH

Researchers and practitioners have come to understand that ignoring the plurality of American culture leads to incorrect assumptions about sociocultural influences and the need for and use of programs by different ethnic families. Successful program development for minority populations must focus on service accessibility, availability, and acceptability (Wallace, 1990). The American Psychological Association's (APA, 2002) guidelines for providing service to culturally diverse populations provide a foundation from which to design effective interventions for families providing care. Specific principles include awareness and acknowledgment that culture is a primary aspect of human existence, and that culture and ethnicity inevitably shape behavior. Sensitivity, knowledge, and understanding of cultural backgrounds of both the intervener and client are required in persons and programs seeking to assist individuals. Of particular importance is sensitivity to the client's cultural background and preferences, including language, family values, community, and religious systems. Sensitivity requires trust building within the community so interventions are integrated within community structures and sanctioned by community leaders. Thus, the process of designing and building the intervention requires thoughtful planning at the level of community and culture. Specific suggestions include the importance of understanding the demographic characteristics of the community targeted for intervention, identifying key members within the community who can work as liaisons for the programs, actively recruiting families through personal contacts with programs already serving minority families, and having bilingual and culturally competent individuals interact with families in recruiting for and conducting the intervention (Gallagher-Thompson, Leary, Ossinalde, Romero, Ward, et al., 1997; Gallagher-Thompson et al., 2000; Valle, 1998).

Many of the APA guidelines are apparent in the published reports of formal interventions designed specifically to address the needs of culturally diverse groups of family caregivers of older adults. An examination of the development, implementation, and outcomes of successful educational programs, support groups, respite programs, and skills training provides valuable insights for designing interventions to support and empower minority elders caring for their grandchildren.

Psychoeducational Interventions

Community psychoeducational interventions, which often provide printed educational materials and guides, are a common, low-cost means of providing information to individuals faced with the challenges of providing care for aging relatives. Successful educational efforts to reach minority caregivers require culturally competent leaders who recognize and reinforce the basic family infrastructure, acknowledge the family's desire to remain self-reliant, and address language preference and translation issues. The "train-the-trainer" workshop model is an effective approach to providing caregiver education programs that can be replicated and sustained within minority communities (Coogle, 2002). One advantage of implementing this model is that the trainer typically is a community member who can serve as a resource for families upon completion of the program.

Psychoeducational programs typically do not carry the stigma often associated with counseling or other intervention programs; thus, giving them greater appeal to ethnic caregivers whose beliefs about illness and family responsibility may place them at a disadvantage for accessing social and professional programs from which they may benefit (Sotomayor & Randolph, 1988). For example, Hispanic and Latino caregivers who participated in an 8-week class designed to teach specific cognitive and behavioral skills for coping with the frustrations of caregiving reported a decrease in depressive symptoms and greater control over angry feelings at the post-intervention interview, compared to those on the program's waiting list (Gallagher-Thompson, Arean, Rivera, & Thompson, 2001). Program participants consistently assessed the program favorably and reported increased knowledge, hope, and self-confidence along with decreased guilt and despair.

Support Groups

Support groups, a popular form of caregiver intervention, are generally not well attended by minority individuals caring for older relatives. In African American and Hispanic families, lack of participation may be due in part to the caregivers' reliance on others in their informal network for caregiving assistance and the internalization of the caregiving role, which makes seeking formal services a contradiction from the strong cultural norms of family responsibility (Cox & Monk, 1993). Because cultural experiences and expectations may make it difficult for caregivers to turn to formal networks for support, group leaders must be sensitive to the differing personal values and beliefs held by caregivers of diverse backgrounds. Success in attracting support group participants may be increased with personal contact with caregivers and knowledge of local ethnocultural factors and social norms. Henderson and colleagues (Henderson, Gutierrez-Mayka, Garcia, & Boyd, 1993) reported increasing attendance of African American and Hispanic families in Alzheimer's disease support group sessions by holding sessions in culturally neutral sites within communities that do not violate the intraethnic variability of social organization, and gaining the support of individuals respected within the local communities.

Respite Programs

Respite programs provide temporary, short-term supervisory, personal, and nursing care for older adults with physical and cognitive impairments. Family caregivers benefit from these programs as they provide relief from the constant responsibilities of caring for dependent older adults. Although the availability of these community-based programs has increased, there continues to be low participation by minority families. Employing Anderson's behavioral model to predict service use, Kosloski, Montgomery, and Karner (1999) report that predisposing factors (i.e., elder's age, caregiver's sex, relationship of the caregiver to the elder, ethnicity, and caregiver's employment status) explained three times as much of the variance in adult day care and in-home respite use among African American and Hispanic caregivers relative to White caregivers. The impact of need variables was similar across caregiving groups for adult day care, but differed dramatically for in-home respite use. Need variables (i.e., elders' activity of daily living abilities, ADLs, IADLs, diagnosis of Alzheimer's disease) were the most important among Hispanic caregivers than among African American and White caregivers. The findings reinforce the need to understand sociocultural influences, such as under which condition they should be used and by whom, so that services can be tailored to meet the specific needs of the caregivers.

REACH Project

A large multi-site research project was funded by the National Institute on Aging and the National Institute for Nursing Research in the late 1990s to investigate the efficacy of several interventions that had shown promise for reducing the burden on family caregivers to older adults while improving the quality of care (Schulz et al., 2003). Each site in the Resources for Enhancing Alzheimer's Caregiver Health (REACH) tested distinctive interventions targeted at particular caregiving populations while sharing common evaluation tools and coordinated research methods. This massive clinical trial represents a remarkable investment in learning how best to help diverse cultural groups handle the demands of caregiving.

The REACH study provides the grandparent caregiving literature with interesting models of well-designed interventions targeting particular populations with specific interventions in particular geographic regions. For the purpose of this chapter, the conceptual frameworks and the strategies for promoting services accessed by particular cultural groups are what have the most potential applicability to the design of interventions for grandparent caregivers. Each site targeted particular caregiving populations with individually designed interventions ranging from psychoeducational support classes to telephone-linked computer tools to foster communication among professionals and a caregiving network. Thus, interventions varied across site, but evaluation tools were shared across sites to allow for meta-analyses of the impact of active treatment [further description of the study sites, conditions, and multi-site outcomes are published in a special section of *Psychology and Aging* (2003), and site-specific methodologies and findings are published in a special section of *The Gerontologist* (2003)]. The following descriptions are offered to illustrate the strategies used by the various sites to meet needs of particular cultural groups and do not attempt to summarize all of the interventions at any site, or the process and outcome data on how the interventions worked.

The Birmingham, Alabama, site focused on economically disadvantaged African American elder caregivers (Burgio, Stevens, Guy, Roth, & Haley, 2003). The intervention was designed to be meaningful and useful to individuals with limited education, competing time demands, and inflexible work hours. The design team was also concerned about "cost, convenience, suitability of available written material, and limited trust and rapport with non-minority health professionals and university-based researchers" (Gallagher-Thompson et al., 2003, p. 427). With the goal of modifying an existing skill training program designed to teach behavior management skills (to address care recipient problem behavior) and general problem-solving skills, the program required modification to meet the contextual constraints. The intervention was delivered in a combination of home visits and videotaped instruction after the initial orientation workshop. Caregivers' schedules could be fully accommodated within this flexible delivery strategy.

The training materials and setting were shaped to build trust and maximize educational effectiveness. Pilot work had demonstrated that the target group did not prefer group settings because they were hesitant to speak in a group; thus, individualized contact bypassed this common requirement of caregiver interventions. Furthermore, the individualized contact allowed for greater trust between the intervener and the particular family, a trust that was enhanced by the sending of birthday, sympathy, and holiday cards in honor of particular family events and values. In addition, in-home observation of caregiver and care recipient interaction was very informative about which particular skills were most needed. Multiple modes of presentation materials (oral, written, video, and interactive sessions) maximized learning opportunities. Materials were presented in written format in language appropriate to the education level and cultural context of the participants in order to avoid demands for intensive note taking during sessions. A challenging component of elder care is the advocacy role that demands assertiveness from the caregiver within various medical and services systems. Initial data from this REACH site had shown that the African American caregivers were unwilling to challenge or even directly question health care providers. This aspect of the caregiving role required training in assertiveness with medical personnel, including training to address racism and other barriers in accessing care.

Hispanic/Latino caregivers were the focus of interventions designed to address the barriers to help-seeking behavior that leave elder caregivers isolated in the stress and burden of their daily responsibilities. A core barrier is the social stigma of allowing outsiders to observe a loved one while that loved one is engaging in unusual or difficult behaviors, which brings shame to the elder and the family (Valle, 1998). Hispanic/Latino cultural values that emphasize family well-being over individual well-being can inhibit caregivers from attempting to reduce their distress, burden, or depression because their duty is to endure without complaint while providing support (Henderson & Gutierrez-Mayka, 1992; Henderson et al., 1993). As a cautionary note, however, the familistic cultural structure has not always explained additional burden, so it must be examined more closely for its impact on caregiver well-being (Aranda & Knight, 1997). The very high rates of depression that have been observed in Hispanic/Latino caregivers as compared to other cultural groups are well documented and serve as an inhibiting factor to engaging them in interventions (Adams et al., 2002).

Diversity within Hispanic/Latino populations is based on a multiplicity of variables, including their country of origin, the number of generations their families have resided in the United States (or number of first-generation immigrants), their socioeconomic status, their political strength, and their history of settlement patterns. The distinctive nature of particular subcultures and particular communities require differentiated approaches to intervention. The Miami, Florida, intervention was designed for Cuban American caregivers. In recognition of the particularly strong *familisimo* values of Cuban American culture (Szapocznik, Scopetta, Aranalde, & Kurtines, 1978), a family systems intervention was employed to empower families to communicate differently about caregiving demands (Szapocznik, Scopetta, Ceballos, & Santisteban, 1994). For example, the intervention addressed common family interaction patterns that added to the burden experienced by caregivers. One observed pattern was the tendency of caregivers to lash out in anger about the previous absence of family help once family members actually offered help. Obviously, the anger inhibited the much-needed flow of assistance to the caregiver. Another example of interactions that were the focus of intervention was family conflicts about handling the disease that arose because of different levels of acculturation experienced by different family members (for a summary of the intervention strategy and efficacy, see Eisdorfer et al., 2003). Given the importance of family communication, the Miami site also included a strategy to increase the frequency of communication among family members. A telephone-based communication system that facilitated conference calls among family members was located in the caregiver's home. The combined benefits of family therapy and this relatively simple technological intervention had the strongest impact on caregiver depression of the REACH interventions (Gitlin et al., 2003).

The Palo Alto site tested delivery of a previously developed small group psychoeducational intervention to Mexican and Mexican American caregivers (Gallagher-Thompson et al., 2001) because it was nonstigmatizing, interactive, short term, and active directive (Gallagher-Thompson et al., 2003). A set of cognitive-behavioral strategies were engaged to teach female caregivers specific cognitive and behavioral skills needed for effective mood management. Many skills were consistent with the cognitive-behavioral approach for treating depression, as appropriate for addressing depression and excessive burden in caregivers. The focus of the intervention was explicitly on caregiver well-being.

The format for the sessions was a small group/workshop offered over 10 weeks in community locations in both English and Spanish (Gallagher-Thompson et al., 1996). Consistent with the cultural expectations, each session began with social conversation (or *platica*). Following a review of the previous week's homework, brief minilectures and small group practice sessions were intermixed to engage participants in applying and practicing the principles in their own lives. A graduation ceremony that completed the series was valued by Hispanic/Latino caregivers more than the Euro-American participants.

Findings from the elder care intervention literature, and the REACH project in particular, offer substantial guidance for professionals designing interventions for grandparent caregivers of grandchildren. Descriptions of the methodologies used in the REACH interventions are rich with highly thoughtful efforts to address variations in cultural, geographic, gender, socioeconomic, and educational backgrounds. Furthermore, the interventions illustrate the alternatives for targeting multiple entities (e.g., caregiver, care recipient, caregiver's support system), across multiple domains of functioning (e.g., behavior, cognition, or affect), using multiple strategies for intervention (e.g., information, problem solving, mood management, or environmental design), and delivered through a variety of mechanisms (e.g., one-on-one counseling, group psychoeducational classes, family meetings, videotaped materials) (Schulz, Gallagher-Thompson, Haley, & Czaja, 2000).

CONCLUSION

Borrowing ideas from the elder caregiving literature is one strategy for rapid identification of interventions to assist the rapidly increasing population of older adults who are taking on child rearing responsibilities at the same time that they deal with their own aging, the aging of their parents, and management of what is often a troubled family context with cut-off relationships or dysfunctional relationships with the middle generation (Roberto & Qualls, 2003). Although the results of intervention studies on depression, burden, and well-being have been only moderate, the impact on variables such as maintaining and enhancing family care arrangements (e.g., Mittelman et al., 1993) and appreciation/satisfaction with the intervention have been impressive (e.g., Gitlin et al., 2003). Specific strategies as well as general principles are now available as foundational work for designing innovative interventions for grandparent caregivers from multiple cultural groups.

REFERENCES

AARP. (2001). *In the middle: A report on multicultural boomers coping with family and aging issues.* Washington, DC: Author.

Adams, B., Aranda, M. P., Kemp, B., & Takagi, K. (2002). Ethnic and gender differences in distress among Anglo American, African American, Japanese American, and Mexican American spousal caregivers of persons with dementia. *Journal of Clinical Gerontology, 8,* 279–301.

Administration on Aging. (2003). A profile of older Americans: 2003. Retrieved April 7, 2004, from http://www.aoa.gov/prof/Statistics/profile/2003/profiles 2003.asp

Allen-Burge, R., & Haley, W. E. (1997). Individual differences and surrogate medical decisions: Differing preferences for life-sustaining treatments. *Aging and Mental Health, 1,* 121–131.

American Psychological Association. (2002). *Guidelines on multi-cultural education, training, research, practice, and organizational change for psychologists.* Washington, DC: APA.

Aneshensel, C. S., Pearlin, L. I., Mullan, J. T., Zarit, S. H., & Whitlatch, C. J. (1995). *Profiles in caregiving: The unexpected career.* San Diego: Academic Press.

Aranda, M. P., & Knight, B. G. (1997). The influence of ethnicity and culture on the caregiver stress and coping process: A sociocultural review and analysis. *The Gerontologist, 37,* 342–354.

Brody, E. M., & Schoonover, C. B. (1986). Patterns of parent-care when daughters work and when they do not. *The Gerontologist, 26,* 372–381.

Brown, D. R., & Mars, J. (2000). Profile of contemporary grandparenting in African-American families. In C. Cox (Ed.), *To grandmother's house we go and stay: Perspectives on custodial grandparents* (pp. 203–217). New York: Springer.

Bryson, K., & Casper, L. M. (1999). Coresident grandparents and grandchildren. (Publication No. P23-198). Retrieved March 23, 2004, from Current Population Reports at http://www.census.gov/prod/99pubs/p23-198.pdf

Burgio, L., Stevens, A. B., Guy, D., Roth, D. L., & Haley, W. E. (2003). Impact of two interventions on White and African-American family caregivers of patients with dementia. *The Gerontologist, 43*, 568–579.

Calderon, V., & Tennstedt, S. (1998). Ethnic differences in the expression of caregiver burden: Results of a qualitative study. *Journal of Gerontological Social Work, 30*, 159–178.

Cantor, M. H. (1975). Life space and the social support system of inner city elderly of New York. *The Gerontologist, 15*, 23–27.

Chumbler, N. R., Dobbs-Kepper, D., Beverly, C., & Beck, C. (2000). Eligibility for in-home respite care: Ethnic status and rural residence. *Journal of Applied Gerontology, 19*, 151–169.

Connell, C. M., & Gibson, G. D. (1997). Racial, ethnic, and cultural differences in dementia caregiving: Review and analysis. *The Gerontologist, 37*, 355–364.

Coogle, C. (2002). The families who care project: Meeting the educational needs of African American and rural family caregivers dealing with dementia. *Educational Gerontology, 28*, 59–71.

Coon, D. W., Gallagher-Thompson, D., & Thompson, L. W. (Eds.). (2003). *Innovative interventions to reduce dementia caregiver distress.* New York: Springer.

Coon, D. W., & Zeiss, L. M. (2003). The families we choose: Intervention issues with LGBT caregivers. In D. W. Coon, D. Gallagher-Thompson, & L. W. Thompson (Eds.), *Innovative interventions to reduce dementia caregiver distress: A clinical guide* (pp. 267–295). New York: Springer.

Cox, C. (1998). The experience of respite: Meeting the needs of African American and White caregivers in a statewide program. *Journal of Gerontological Social Work, 30* (3/4), 59–72.

Cox, C., & Monk, A. (1993). Black and Hispanic caregivers of dementia victims: Their needs and implications for services. In C. M. Barresi & D. E. Stull (Eds.), *Ethnic elderly and long-term care* (pp. 57–67). New York: Springer.

Cox, C., Brooks, L. R., & Valcarcel, C. (2000). Culture and caregiving: A study of Latino grandparents. In C. Cox (Ed.), *To grandmother's house we go and stay: Perspectives on custodial grandparents* (pp. 218–232). New York: Springer.

Degenholtz, H., Kane, R., & Kivnick, H. Q. (1997). Care-related preferences and values of elderly community-based LTC consumers. Can case managers learn what's important to clients? *The Gerontologist, 37*, 767–776.

Edgerly, E., Montes, L., Yau, E., Stokes, S. C., & Redd, D. (2003). Ethnic minority caregivers. In D. W. Coon, D. Gallagher-Thompson, & L. W. Thompson (Eds.), *Innovative interventions to reduce dementia caregiver distress: A clinical guide* (pp. 223–242). New York: Springer.

Eisdorfer, C., Czaja, S. J., Loewenstein, D. A., Rubert, M. P., Argüelles, S., Mitrani, V., et al. (2003). The effect of a family therapy and technology-based intervention on caregiver depression. *The Gerontologist, 32*, 521–531.

Elliott, K. S., Di Minno, M., Lam, D., & Tu, A. M. (1996). Working with Chinese families in the context of dementia. In G. Yeo & D. Gallagher-Thompson (Eds.), *Ethnicity and the dementias* (pp. 89–108). New York: Taylor & Francis.

Finley, N. J., Roberts, M. D., & Banham, B. F. (1988). Motivators and inhibitors of attitudes of filial obligation toward parents. *The Gerontologist, 28,* 73–78.

Fisher, L., & Lieberman, M. A. (1999). A longitudinal study of predictors of nursing home placement for patients with dementia: The contribution of family characteristics. *The Gerontologist, 39,* 677–686.

Fuller-Thompson, E., Minkler, M., & Driver, D. (1997). A profile of grandparents raising grandchildren in the United States. *The Gerontologist, 37,* 406–411.

Gallagher-Thompson, D., Arean, P., Coon, D., Menéndez, A., Tagaki, K., Haley, W. E., et al. (2000). Development and implementation of intervention strategies for culturally diverse caregiving populations. In R. Schulz (Ed.), *Handbook on dementia caregiving* (pp. 151–186). New York: Springer.

Gallagher-Thompson, D., Arean, P., Rivera, P., & Thompson, L. W. (2001). Reducing distress in Hispanic caregivers using a psychoeducational intervention. *Clinical Gerontologist, 23,* 17–32.

Gallagher-Thompson, D., Haley, W., DeLois, G., Rupert, M., Argüelles, T., Zeiss, L. M., et al. (2003). Tailoring psychological interventions for ethnically diverse dementia caregivers. *Clinical Psychology: Science and Practice, 10,* 423–438.

Gallagher-Thompson, D., Leary, M., Ossinalde, C., Romero, J., Ward, M., & Fernadez-Gamarra, E. (1997). Hispanic caregivers of older adults with dementia: Cultural issues in outreach and intervention. *Group, 21,* 211–232.

Gallagher-Thompson, D., Ossinalde, C., Menéndez, A., Fernandez, E., Romero, J., Valverde, I., et al. (1996). *Como mantenar su bienestar: Una clase para cuidadores* (How to maintain your well-being: A class for caregivers; class leader and participant manuals). Palo Alto, CA: Department of Veterans Affairs Medical Center.

Gaugler, J. E., Zarit, S. H., & Pearlin, L. I. (2003). The onset of dementia caregiving and its longitudinal implications. *Psychology and Aging, 18,* 171–180.

Gitlin, L. N., Belle, S. H., Burgio, L., Czaja, S., Mahoney, D., Gallagher-Thompson, D., et al. (2003). Effect of multi-site interventions on caregiver burden and depression: The REACH multi-site initiative at 6 months follow-up. *Psychology and Aging, 18,* 361–374.

Grinstead, L., Leder, S., Jensen, S., & Bond, L. (2003). Review of the research on the health of caregiving grandparents. *Journal of Advanced Nursing, 44,* 318–326.

Haley, W. E., Han, B., & Henderson, J. (1998). Aging and ethnicity: Issues for clinical practice. *Journal of Clinical Psychology in Medical Settings, 5,* 393–409.

Henderson, J. N., & Gutierrez-Mayka, M. (1992). Ethnocultural themes in caregiving to Alzheimer's patients in Hispanic families. *Clinical Gerontologist, 11,* 59–74.

Henderson, J. N., Gutierrez-Mayka, M., Garcia, J., & Boyd, S. (1993). A model for Alzheimer's disease support group development in African-American and Hispanic populations. *The Gerontologist, 33,* 409–414.

Hennessy, C. H., & John, R. (1995). The interpretation of burden among Pueblo Indian caregivers. *Journal of Aging Studies, 9,* 215–229.

High, D. M. (1991). A new myth about families of older people? *Gerontologist*, *31*, 611–618.

Hinrichsen, G., & Ramirez, M. (1992). Black and White dementia caregivers: A comparison of their adaptation, adjustment, and service utilization. *The Gerontologist, 32*, 375–381.

Hopp, F. P., & Duffy, S. A. (2000). Racial variations in end-of-life care. *Journal of American Geriatrics Society, 48*, 658–663.

Kennet, J., Burgio, L., & Schulz, R. (2000). Interventions for in-home caregivers: A review of research 1990 to present. In R. Schulz (Ed.), *Handbook of dementia caregiving* (pp. 61–125). New York: Springer.

Knight, B., Robinson, G. S., Flynn Longmire, C. V., Chun, M., Nakao, K., & Kim, J. H. (2002). Cross cultural issues in caregiving for persons with dementia: Do familism values reduce burden and distress? *Ageing International, 27*(3), 70–94.

Knopman, D., Donahue, J. A., & Gutterman, E. M. (2000). Patterns of care in the early stages of Alzheimer's disease: Impediments to timely diagnosis. *Journal of the American Geriatrics Society, 48*, 300–304.

Kosloski, K., Montgomery, R. J., & Karner, T. X. (1999). Differences in perceived need for assistive services by culturally diverse caregivers of persons with dementia. *Journal of Applied Gerontology, 18*, 239–256.

Lauderdale, S. A., D'Andrea, J. A., & Coon, D. W. (2003). Male caregivers: Challenges and opportunities. In D. W. Coon, D. Gallagher-Thompson, & L. W. Thompson (Eds.), *Innovative interventions to reduce dementia caregiver distress: A clinical guide* (pp. 243–266). New York: Springer.

Lieberman, M. A., & Fisher, L. (1999). The effects of family conflict resolution and decision making on the provision of help for an elder with Alzheimer's Disease. *The Gerontologist, 39*, 159–166.

McBride, M. R., & Parreno, H. (1996). Filipino American families and caregiving. In G. Yeo & D. Gallagher-Thompson (Eds.), *Ethnicity and the dementias* (pp. 123–136). New York: Taylor & Francis.

Mittelman, M. S., Ferris, S. H., Steinberg, G., Shulman, E., Mackell, J. A., Ambinder, A., et al. (1993). An intervention that delays institutionalization of Alzheimer's disease patients: Treatment of spouse-caregivers. *The Gerontologist, 33*, 730–740.

Roberto, K., & Qualls, S. (2003). Intervention strategies for grandparents raising grandchildren: Lessons learned from the late life caregiving literature. In B. Hayslip & J. Hicks Patrick (Eds.), *Working with custodial grandparents* (pp. 13–26). New York: Springer.

Scannapieco, M., & Jackson, S. (1996). Kinship care: The African-American response to family preservation. *Social Work, 41*, 190–196.

Schulz, R., Belle, S. H., Czaja, S. J., Gitlin, L. N., Wisniewski, S. T., & Ory, M. G. (2003). Introduction to the special section on Resources for Enhancing Alzheimer's Caregiver Health (REACH). *Psychology and Aging, 18*, 357–360.

Schulz, R., Gallagher-Thompson, D., Haley, W., & Czaja, S. (2000). Understanding the interventions process: A theoretical conceptual framework for intervention approaches to caregiving. In R. Schulz (Ed.), *Handbook on dementia caregiving: Evidence-based interventions for family caregivers* (pp. 33–60). New York: Springer.

Sotomayor, M., & Randolph, S. A. (1988). Preliminary review of caregiving issues among Hispanic elderly. In M. Sotomayor & H. Curriel (Eds.), *Hispanic elderly: A cultural signature* (pp. 137–160). Edinburg, TX: Pan American University Press, National Hispanic Council on Aging.

Szapocznik, J., Scopetta, M. A., Aranalde, M. A., & Kurtines, W. M. (1978). Cuban value structure: Treatment implications. *Journal of Consulting and Clinical Psychology, 46,* 961–970.

Szapocznik, J., Scopetta, M. A., Ceballos, A., & Santisteban, D. A. (1994). Understanding, supporting, and empowering families: From microanalysis to macrointervention. *Family Psychologist, 10,* 23–27.

Tempo, P. M., & Saito, A. (1996). Techniques for working with Japanese American families. In G. Yeo & D. Gallagher-Thompson (Eds.), *Ethnicity and the dementias* (pp. 109–122). New York: Taylor & Francis.

U.S. Bureau of the Census. (2003, October). *Grandparents living with grandchildren: 2000* (Publication No. C2KBR-31). Retrieved November 15, 2003, from Census 2000 Briefs and Special Reports at http://www.census.gov/prod/2003pubs/c2kbr-31.pdf.

Valle, R. (1998). *Caregiving across cultures: Working with dementing illness and ethnically diverse populations.* Washington, DC: Taylor & Francis.

Vaughn, G., Kiyasu, E., & McCormick, W. C. (2000). Advanced directive preferences among subpopulations of Asian nursing home residents in the Pacific Northwest. *Journal of the American Geriatrics Society, 48,* 554–557.

Wallace, S. (1990). The no-care zone: Availability, accessibility, acceptability in community-based long term care. *The Gerontologist, 30,* 254–261.

Watari, K., & Gatz, M. (2004). Pathways to care for Alzheimer's disease among Korean Americans. *Cultural Diversity and Ethnic Minority Psychology, 10,* 23–38.

Yeo, G., & Gallagher-Thompson, D. (1996). *Ethnicity and the dementias.* Washington, DC: Taylor & Francis.

CHAPTER 4

Variability in the Need for Formal and Informal Social Support Among Grandparent Caregivers: A Pilot Study

Jennifer King, Bert Hayslip Jr., and Patricia L. Kaminiski

As the number of grandparents raising grandchildren continues to rise (Simmons & Dye, 2003), their needs for a variety of formal social services, social support from formal service providers, and informal support from family members, neighbors, and friends have been highlighted (see Hayslip & Kaminski, 2005). Directly or indirectly, becoming a custodial grandparent can result in numerous challenges to a person's health and well-being, ability to parent, economic stability, and relationships with others (see Cox, 2000; Hayslip & Goldberg-Glen, 2000; Hayslip & Hicks Patrick, 2003 for reviews). Other stressors are borne of isolation from others, feeling different and personally vulnerable (see Wohl, Lahner, & Jooste, 2003), and the demands of child care (Hayslip, 2003), especially if the grandchild is experiencing physical or emotional health difficulties (Hayslip, Shore, Henderson, & Lambert, 1998; Young & Dawson, 2003).

However, adequate social support—both emotional and instrumental—can mitigate the effects of the numerous stressors grandparent caregivers face (see Hayslip & Shore, 2000; Kolomer, McCallion, & Overeynder, 2003; Landry-Meyer, 1999; Smith, 2003).

Musil, Schrader, and Mutikani (2000) further differentiate social support as either "formal" or "informal." Formal support is described as professionally delivered, specific social services available to grandparent caregivers to meet their instrumental (e.g., income maintenance, health care, legal assistance) or emotional (e.g., professional counseling) needs. Informal support may come from friends, family, neighbors, or the church. It includes instrumental support such as transportation and child care as well as emotional support such as friendship. While purposefully constructed grandparent support groups and social service agency support most likely fall within the arena of formal social support, important informal, emotional support can also occur in these contexts. For example, developing an ongoing relationship with a staff member, a support group leader, or fellow grandparents can be an important outgrowth of requesting formal support from a social service agency or joining a grandparent caregiver support group. Thus, in some cases, while the two types of social support can and are often distinguished from one another, this distinction may be difficult to draw, especially if one emphasizes the *perception* of social support, wherein grandparents' estimates of the support they receive from others or from formal social service agencies may differ from the actual degree of support offered (see Burton, 1992; Kolomer et al., 2003; Landry-Meyer, 1999).

Smith (2003), in his discussion of how grandparent caregivers view support groups, highlights the diversity in needs for social support among grandparent caregivers, as well as diversity in the content of what might be provided in the context of support groups. Needs range from emotional support from peers to information to professional assistance (i.e., psychotherapeutic). Some custodial grandparents are most in need of programmatic formal support (e.g., accessing services regarding health care, insurance, transportation, employment, or housing), but needs for support also vary by persons consistent with their own or a grandchild's health, whether a grandchild is male or female or is younger or older, whether the child is transitioning in school, whether the grandparent has left or returned to the workforce, and whether the grandparent has divorced or experienced a loss of emotional support from family (i.e., the adult child whose child he or she is raising) or friends (Kolomer et al., 2003). Such recognition of the diversity in needs for social support is crucial to the design and implementation of both formal and informal support for grandparent caregivers. Understanding specific social support

needs is particularly important for the development of public policy advocating for grandparent caregivers and their grandchildren. In this context,
and in light of a lack of attention to the topic, the present pilot study
explored the extent of variability in needs for social support in a sample
of grandparents who are raising grandchildren.

METHOD

Participants

Thirty-nine custodial grandparents (36 females, 3 males) ranging in age
from 44 to 76 years ($M = 58.74$) participated in the survey. Their level
of education ranged from 9 to 20+ years ($M = 13.72$). Of the participants,
79.49% were Caucasian, while 15.38% of the remaining grandparent
caregivers were African American and 5.13% were Hispanic. Hours per
week of employment were recorded with 35.90% ($n = 14$) indicating
that they were retired, 33.33% ($n = 13$) reporting 30+ hours of weekly
employment, 7.69% ($n = 3$) reporting 21 to 25 hours per week, and
23.08% ($n = 9$) stating that they were unemployed (e.g., due to chronic
illness, being disabled, or being a full time homemaker). The gender of
grandchildren they cared for was evenly split between males and females.
Twenty-nine participants responded to our inquiry about the length of
time they had been in the custodial role for a grandchild. Durations
ranged from 6 months to 22 years ($M = 7.84$ years). Persons reported
caring for between one and two grandchildren, ranging in age from 2
and 20 years ($M = 9.02$).

Materials

A predominantly open-ended survey was developed collaboratively by
the first and second authors to ascertain demographic information (e.g.,
age, gender, race, employment) and to principally address grandparent
caregivers' needs for formal and informal support in the context of their
perceptions of the agency's adequacy in meeting their needs. Participants
were also assured that everything discussed would be confidential and
that they would not be identified by name.

Procedure

An address and phone contact list of 120 grandparents raising their
grandchildren was provided by a social service agency, which had devel-

oped an information and referral program specifically for grandparents raising their grandchildren in north Texas. This program, providing information and referrals for legal assistance, child care, and family counseling, had been in existence for approximately 2 years.

First, surveys were mailed to 37 grandparents whose contact information did not include a phone number. Reminder letters were sent one month after the original mailing. Eight (21.62%) people responded with completed surveys, 3 surveys were returned with wrong addresses, and 26 surveys were not returned.

The authors attempted to contact the remaining 83 persons by phone. Of these, 24 phone numbers were no longer valid (i.e., disconnected, out of service, or wrong numbers). Nine other grandparents could not be reached by phone or did not respond to our messages. Language barriers inhibited the participation of five grandparents. Two other custodial grandparents were not interested in completing the phone survey. Finally, 12 of the completed surveys were not included in the following analyses, as these grandparents were not raising grandchildren at the time they completed the survey. Thus, our analyses included data from 39 people, 33% of the grandparents on our original contact list. When only English-speaking custodial grandparents with valid contact information are considered, our response rate was 51% (39 of 76).

RESULTS

Variability in Grandparent Caregivers' Needs for Informal Social Support

Twenty-five participants (64.10%) related that they received help from someone else in caring for their grandchild including one or more of the following: spouse (64%; $n = 16$), adult child (40%; $n = 10$), other relative (24%; $n = 6$), friend (12%; $n = 3$), other (12%; $n = 3$; i.e., day care, church), and neighbor (8%; $n = 2$). Their total number of grandchildren ranged from 1 to 25 ($M = 5.77$). When asked about the number of grandchildren each was caring for, an average of 1.59 was found with ages ranging between 2 and 20 years ($M = 9.02$).

Formal Support: Barriers to Service Use

In discussing the difficulties they experienced in getting services for their grandchildren, 56.41% ($n = 22$) reported no difficulties in obtaining services, while others related difficulties with counseling (17.95%; $n =$

7), legal help (12.82%; $n = 5$), medical services (12.82%; $n = 5$), medical insurance (10.26%; $n = 4$), dental care (10.26%; $n = 4$), food stamps (5.13%; $n = 2$), Medicaid (2.56%; $n = 1$), and/or "other" (7.69%; $n = 3$; i.e., getting child support, needing child care, paying an electric bill). No difficulties were reported with school registration, special education services, or Social Security benefits.

To assess factors serving as impediments to accessing services, participants were asked why they might not have attended workshops and other organized efforts that were offered to them (by the agency that provided the contact list). Each of the 36 grandparents responding to this item gave one or more reasons for not attending programs. These reasons fell into five broad categories. Our category titles and grandparents' verbatim responses are listed below:

Lack of Time (in general or because of child care demands, work demands, or other caregiving responsibilities) or Programs Scheduled at an Inconvenient Time

- I was caring for my mother who lives with me
- My husband was out of town during the week, so I must watch the child during week, and weekends are family time
- Home schooling my child—I have no time
- Scheduling (work or other grandchild activities)
- I must work during the week
- Grandchild's schedule
- Busy schedule (all I can do to keep up with grandchild)
- Schedule difficulties (we both work)
- Caring for 88-year-old mother in Ohio. Schedule is busy (e.g., grandchild dances, models)
- Scheduling problems with work
- Work full-time (sometimes even on weekends)
- Inconvenient times. Behavior problems with youngest grandchild, and I must be available at all times to go to the school
- Busy—school, personal business
- Scheduling (something comes up)
- So busy and embroiled in legal issues with grandchild

- I didn't attend because I didn't have time or a sitter
- Wonderful organization that I want to get involved in as my schedule changes
- I would like to attend more workshops but my work schedule prevents me from attending in the middle of the day.

Disability or Illness (of self or child)

- Illness—I can't get around very well
- Sick
- Health
- Sick—myself, son, and grandchild have had health problems over last 2 years, so hard to get to events
- Disability

Lack of Transportation

- Transportation
- Transportation difficulty due to illness
- Too far away but I would like to gain knowledge of some of the topics offered
- Transportation—I have no money for a car; I don't know how to drive
- Location. I am disabled, so my transportation is limited

Programs Not Personally Relevant

- Did not feel connected because different issues for me than for other grandparents (grandchild is disabled) but I thought the service was important
- No information about raising teens
- Grandchild too old to really need services by time it was established
- Not available when I started caring for my grandchild
- Agency tried to provide services (for my grandchildren), but the grandchildren weren't interested in the activities

- What I needed was relief from the stress and workshops didn't help me there—my church did

Did Not Know About the Programs

- I am unaware of many services

- Unaware of workshops

Perceived Helpfulness of Services for Grandparent Caregivers

Participants were asked to rate the level of helpfulness of the services, information, or referrals they had been provided on a scale of 1 (not helpful at all) to 5 (very helpful). Twenty-eight participants responded. The average helpfulness rating was 4.09 with three ratings of 1, one rating of 2.5, two ratings of 3, seven ratings of 4, and fifteen ratings of 5. The 11 participants who did not respond to this item had received no services upon which to base their ratings.

When asked about what services they received were helpful to them, participants responded in the following verbatim manner:

- Information is good. Nice to know it is there if I need it

- I asked for information not readily available—as a volunteer at school, others ask for information and I inquire for them

- Not available when I started caring for my grandchildren, but I try to help others now

- Newsletter and/or resources/information in mail ($n = 17$)

- Referral for legal services ($n = 2$)

- None ($n = 6$)

- Information about Medicaid

- Information at gatherings—none applicable to our situation, but good information

- I have not asked for anything

- I don't know what was offered, so none

- List of services, flyers, housing, clothes/food for kids (Stockings for Santa)

- Call and ask what I need and what my grandchildren may do for activities over the summer

- Bulletins, but no information related to teens

- Information for assistance financially, but I have not qualified for the programs

- Resources, but I have not needed them

- Helped with planning (e.g., food stamps, day care)

- Information in the mail but I have not read any of it

- Information in the mail, but I didn't need anything

- Support that someone is there

- Resource list

- We are relatively new. Thought the seminar very informative

- Counseling

- Activities to do with grandchildren; workshops; social gatherings with grandparents

Perceived Helpfulness of Services for Grandchildren

Participants were also asked to rate the level of helpfulness of the services, information, or referrals they were provided for their grandchildren on a scale of 1 (not helpful at all) to 5 (very helpful). Three of the 39 participants responded resulting in an average helpfulness rating of information relating to their grandchildren of 4.33 with two ratings of 4 and one rating of 5. The 35 of the 36 grandparents who did not provide a rating to this item had not received services upon which to base a rating, and one participant left the page blank.

When asked about what specific services had been provided for their grandchildren, participants mentioned one or more of the services listed below:

- Counseling. Referred to local clinic but difficult to make times to go and (long) waiting lists

- Took kids to camp

- Stockings for Santa programs

- Social gatherings with others
- Provided child care so that I could attend workshops

Perceived Needed Improvements for Information and Referral Services

In light of the above benefits and barriers to formal social support provided by the agency, grandparents were asked how the agency could improve its workshops. We grouped participants' responses into categories, including a category for those responses that were essentially a restatement of barriers faced (without suggestions for how the agency could help eliminate the barrier). Each of the 32 participants who answered this question gave one or more of the following verbatim responses:

Restatement of Barriers Faced

- Problems with location
- Too far to come
- Some grandparents still working. They need Saturdays need to rest and prepare for next week
- If my grandchild goes back in public school, I would try to attend but there just isn't time now
- Just too busy with work and trying to spend time with my grandchild
- Schedule. I just started a new job and I have no set schedule, so I don't know when may be able to attend but want to
- I don't participate due to scheduling issues
- Grandparents are busy
- Some are sick and can't go
- Health is a major problem
- Language barriers
- None—our lifestyle just won't work with any time

Improve Attendance, Grandparents Need to Change

- Main problem—no one attends
- Grandparents have yet to understand the value of networking

- If you don't want to raise them find someone else; I know the staff, but not really through the programs, as I have little interest in being around negative attitudes of many grandparents

- Problem—older generation not interested or don't see value in the services. They don't see anything they should change

Change the Day or Time of Programs

- Work prevents me from attending in the middle of the day

- Schedule on evenings or weekends—weekends are best because I am busy at work during week

- More afternoon times

- Weekends are better

- Weekends would help some but very busy

- Weekends are better

- Weekends or evenings are better because of work

- Weekends are better but it still is a trip from where I live

- Time of day (evening or weekend better)

- Evenings or weekends are best

- Schedule during Friday mornings or during school hours

- Different times—both an evening and a daytime meeting

Change Location of Programs, Offer Transportation (especially for disabled clients)

- Location closer to me

- Provide transportation but health varies whereby I may not attend due to that

- Transportation—you need to get an old van to transport grandparents like myself

- Location. Transportation has no lift on van

- Great program and if there was one closer

Offer Information and Support Through Other Means

- Set up a website so I can get answers to questions anytime (maybe even a question/answer page so those who cannot attend can ask questions of others and get responses)
- Mentor volunteers (more one-on-one; sit down and have coffee at a time that's good for those two people)

Provide Child Care and Refreshments

- Important to provide refreshments and child care
- Child care or activities for kids, as it is hard to get a sitter

Offer Programs or Information on Topics Relevant to Me/My Family

- Need topics on teens
- Also parenting classes for parents
- Help in obtaining medical insurance and medication expenses

Other Comments and Suggestions

- Rehashing the past is sometimes difficult but would not mind mentoring those with younger grandchildren
- Grandparents are not included in planning
- I do not want to share personal problems such as grandchild's past

I Am Not Interested in Attending Programs

- Not interested
- None—those grandparents I met felt sorry for themselves
- I am glad they are there if I need them, but I have family support now and am busy with grandchild's activities

No Change Needed

- Keep doing what you are doing—even if not many attend, it is new so give it time

Desired Services Not Currently Being Provided for Grandparents

Fifty-four percent ($n = 21$) of our sample indicated that there were no services needed that were not being provided at this time. Sixteen participants responded in the following manner when asked what kind of services or information for themselves that the agency could provide that they were not providing:

More Opportunities to Build Supportive Relationships

- Calling partner with someone with an older grandchild
- Mentors or support group because of much stress
- E-mail buddies
- Support group for grandparents with teens (new issues arise with this age group)
- Open forum (like AA) to say what the concern is without the pressure
- Support group
- More relationships with others like in a support group
- I think a "grandparents night out" once a month would be great
- (Agency is) always there to call if need information for resources but I need support from others in similar situation

Counseling

- Information on counseling
- More information about counseling for grandchildren

Written Resources

- Reading list for information (especially for those who cannot attend)

Parenting Advice

- Information on raising a teen
- Parenting a child with trouble making friends (how to help him/her)

- Want information about answering questions that grandchild will have later but may attend meetings once grandchild starts school
- Information on ADD (attention deficit disorder) and discipline
- Information on child care after I get custody

Legal Advice

- Help on how to get child support from unwilling parents
- More on legal concerns in newsletter

Accessing Other Services

- Information about starting Medicaid or getting other services
- Baby sitting referrals that are reasonable priced

Other Responses

- None—I am solving my own problems
- Build another day into the week!
- Transportation to workshops

Desired Services Not Currently Being Provided for Grandchildren

Seven (18%) of the grandparents provided the following recommendations for services or information needed for their grandchildren that were not currently being provided:

More Opportunities for Grandchildren to Build Supportive Relationships

- More counseling
- Support group for teens (feels he is the only one being raised by grandparents)
- I would like to see groups for grandchildren that meet 2 to 3 times a year

Attention to Age Diversity Among Custodial Grandchildren

- Activities for all ages of grandchildren
- My grandson was much older that the children at the picnic

Information and Services for Children With Special Needs

- Information on tutoring (trouble with attention but just getting tested so don't know what he needs yet)
- Information on children with ADHD (attention deficit/hyperactivity disorder) and bipolar disorder
- Medical insurance information and help with obtaining medication or lower cost for psychotropic medication

Written Resources

- More information in newsletter or pamphlets that could be mailed to you on particular topics if called for them (especially for those who physically cannot attend)
- I wish I could participate more but my job responsibility limits my participation. I look forward to receiving the newsletter

Improved Communication with Agency and Other Grandparents

- E-mail would help
- Advertise more because I have told other grandparents who did not know the service existed; this would get more people of color; get the word out
- Telephone mentoring or e-mail so people can connect without having to make many schedules match

Other Responses

- Extreme class differentiation in the county, so there are different needs for low versus middle incomes; may need to offer different groups: one on meeting basic needs and one for emotional support

DISCUSSION

Implications for Service Delivery and the Provision of Social Support

Agencies such as those studied here face the challenge of meeting the needs of a diverse set of grandparent caregivers. Indeed, despite the pilot study nature of the sample, it is clear that grandparents' needs for both formal and informal support are quite diverse. Such needs seem to covary with the following factors: being married versus being single; being older versus younger; being employed versus being retired; and having infants or children versus teenage grandchildren. In addition, variability in grandparents' health (covarying with age), driving distance from services (covarying with their need for transportation), socioeconomic status, as well as the extent to which either the grandparent or the grandchild were experiencing loneliness, personal distress, or school difficulties influenced perceived needs for formal and informal support as well as perceived barriers to accessing such support.

These qualitative data mirror those collected from larger and more representative samples of grandparent caregivers, utilizing objective measures of social support (see Hayslip & Kaminski, 2005), documenting both the variability in needs for social support across not only grandparent physical and mental health, but also as a function of grandchild behavioral and emotional difficulties (see Hayslip et al., 1998; Musil et al., 2000; Young & Dawson, 2003). Both sets of findings suggest that poorer such health or less adaptive functioning necessitates greater needs for support from others.

As grandparents and grandchildren age and face new developmental issues, agencies will encounter new challenges in targeting their emotional and physical needs. Indeed, in this study, there was some evidence to suggest that the needs of grandparents raising children who were younger (e.g., infants, preschoolers) were distinct from those raising older children. Consequently, most social service agencies providing some form of social support to grandparent caregivers would be wise to attend to their diverse and changing needs for formal and informal social support. Importantly, new needs for information, referral, and direct service will emerge as the health and developmental needs of custodial grandparents and grandchildren change over time.

Considering employment status alone, it is clear that many grandparents continue to work either out of necessity or because they are not of retirement age, creating schedules that are as hectic and demanding as those of traditional parents. Schedule overload was the most commonly stated impediment to grandparents' access to services, creating challenges for social service agencies seeking to provide them some form of help. However, several grandparents suggested alternate modes of information dissemination (e.g., newsletters, e-mail, reading lists) and emotional support (e.g., e-mail buddies, one-on-one meetings) to minimize scheduling as a barrier to social support.

Our data also suggest that sensitivity to individuals' job and school-related schedules would require that activities and workshops be offered in the evening or on the weekends, with advance notice, so that busy grandparents can make appropriate plans. Moreover, provision of transportation, child care, and refreshments would allow more grandparents to participate.

Our data also suggest that custodial grandparents can be grouped into two distinct subpopulations: (a) those needing instrumental support—information and services to meet basic everyday living necessities (e.g., financial assistance, medical care), and (b) those wanting emotional support (e.g., support groups, mentoring, counseling for themselves or their grandchildren). Meeting the needs of grandparents in each of these groups may necessitate keeping the subpopulations fairly separate. That is, busy grandparents with adequate emotional support who are seeking information, referrals, and other types of instrumental support may experience agency-sponsored opportunities for emotional support as unnecessary or even a violation of their privacy. Grandparents who are feeling overwhelmed and isolated, on the other hand, may need to make use of agency-sponsored opportunities for emotional support (coupled with the necessary instrumental support to make participation possible) before they can really benefit from informational programs.

Based on these data, it was evident that many custodial grandparents feel disconnected from the agency that was created to assist them. Our data suggest that this disconnection is due, in part, to the very diversity of their needs for formal and informal social support. At the minimum, this would suggest the development of multiple strategies for disseminating information (e.g., e-mail, phone calls, home visits, mailed flyers). For grandparents who are homebound due to health difficulties or child care responsibilities, we advocate the use of websites with helpful resources and Internet links. This would also allow for the exchange of questions and answers, where grandparents can interact online. Moreover, some grandparents' needs for informal social support may be met by creating a "buddy system," where grandparents are matched with one another and can jointly decide how best to interact with one another (e.g., e-mail, phone, meet for coffee). This strategy may be especially valuable for grandparents who are reticent to disclose personal information in a group setting. The importance of attending to such diversity regarding scheduling and flexible means of reaching grandparent caregivers has also been noted by Kolomer et al. (2003) in the context of providing informal support to grandparent caregivers.

Importantly, these diversity data suggest that agencies develop two different types of activities: (a) information meetings for those needing knowledge of services and (b) support groups for those seeking to relate to others in a similar situation. Both should be open to all, but the purpose of each should be clearly communicated. Such diversity should also be reflected in workshops encompassing not only topics on gaining basic services, but also child difficulties, parenting, stress relief, and self care (see Kolomer et al., 2003; Wohl et al., 2003). Such workshops and support groups would therefore better reflect the diversity among grandparent caregivers found here, and avoid the concerns voiced by many (see Smith, 2003; Strom & Strom, 2000) that such efforts are actually counterproductive for persons whose needs are not being addressed.

Many grandparents in this admittedly small sample did not feel that they needed any information and referral services. Rather than accept this at face value, it may be prudent to encourage grandparents in planning and decision making, and promote their involvement through actively seeking ongoing feedback and implementing recommended changes. This would likely also "bind" them more completely to available opportunities for formal and informal support, wherein they would feel that their voices are heard and respected.

Finally, it may be necessary for agencies to engage in "multimodal" service provision, wherein they may be required to go beyond simply making referrals or providing information. Indeed, at least on a part-time basis, more direct service provision (e.g., on Saturdays, more one-on-one contact) where ongoing communication, assessment, and feedback can occur might complement these basic functions, especially for smaller, younger agencies with fewer resources. In this manner, agencies can develop an ongoing relationship with each grandparent caregiver. Support groups, a service fair, and having persons on site (i.e., social service agency representatives, counselors) are all avenues by which to achieve these goals.

Ultimately, taking such diversity of needs seriously suggests that personalized contact with grandparent caregivers who feel "invisible" (Wohl et al., 2003) is necessary to create an environment that meets their needs. Such a perspective on the provision of social support will more adequately reflect grandparents' individual life situations, and therefore promote not only their success, but also their continued happiness and growth, enabling them to cope with the stressors and transcend the isolation that many grandparent caregivers experience on a daily basis.

REFERENCES

Burton, L. (1992). Black grandparents rearing children of drug-addicted parents: Stresses, outcomes, and social service needs. *The Gerontologist, 32*, 744–751.

Cox, C. (Ed.). (2000). *To grandmother's house we go and stay: Perspectives on custodial grandparents.* New York: Springer.

Hayslip, B. (2003). The impact of a psychosocial intervention on parental efficacy, grandchild relationship quality, and well-being among grandparents raising grandchildren. In B. Hayslip & J. Hicks Patrick (Eds.), *Working with custodial grandparents* (pp. 163–178). New York: Springer.

Hayslip, B., & Goldberg-Glen, R. (2000). *Grandparents raising grandchildren: Theoretical, empirical, and clinical perspectives.* New York: Springer.

Hayslip, B., & Hicks Patrick, J. (2003). *Working with custodial grandparents.* New York: Springer.

Hayslip, B., & Kaminski, P. (2005). Grandparents raising their grandchildren: A review of the literature and suggestions for practice. *The Gerontologist, 45,* 262–269.

Hayslip, B., & Shore, R. J. (2000). Custodial grandparenting and mental health. *Journal of Mental Health and Aging, 6,* 367–384.

Hayslip, B., Shore, R. J., Henderson, C., & Lambert, P. (1998). Custodial grandparenting and grandchildren with problems: Impact on role satisfaction and role meaning. *Journal of Gerontology: Social Sciences, 53B,* S164–S174.

Kolomer, S., McCallion, P., & Overeynder, J. (2003). Why support groups help: Successful interventions for grandparent caregivers of children with developmental disabilities. In B. Hayslip & J. Hicks Patrick (Eds.), *Working with custodial grandparents* (pp. 111–126). New York: Springer.

Landry-Meyer, L. (1999). Research into action: Recommended intervention strategies for grandparent caregivers. *Family Relations, 48,* 381–389.

Musil, C., Schrader, S., & Mutikani, J. (2000). Social support, stress, and special coping tasks of grandmother caregivers. In C. Cox (Ed.), *To grandmother's house we go and stay: Perspectives on custodial grandparents* (pp. 56–70). New York: Springer.

Simmons, T., & Dye, J. (2003). *Grandparents living with grandchildren: 2000, Census 2000 Brief,* 1–10. Washington, DC: U.S. Department of Commerce.

Smith, G. (2003). How caregiving grandparents view support groups: An exploratory study. In B. Hayslip & J. Hicks Patrick (Eds.), *Working with custodial grandparents* (pp. 69–92). New York: Springer.

Strom, R., & Strom, S. (2000). Goals for grandparents and support groups. In B. Hayslip & R. Goldberg-Glen (Eds.), *Grandparents raising grandchildren: Theoretical, empirical, and clinical perspectives* (pp. 289–304). New York: Springer.

Wohl, E., Lahner, J., & Jooste, J. (2003). Group processes among grandparents raising grandchildren. In B. Hayslip & J. Hicks Patrick (Eds.), *Working with custodial grandparents* (pp. 195–212). New York: Springer.

Young, M. H, & Dawson, T. J. (2003). Perception of child difficulty and levels of depression in caregiving grandmothers. *Journal of Mental Health and Aging, 9,* 111–122.

SECTION 2

Diversity Across Age and Gender

CHAPTER 5

Age, Health, and Custodial Grandparenting

Bert Hayslip Jr., R. Jerald Shore, and Michelle A. Emick

Grandparents who raise their grandchildren on a full-time basis often do so under adverse circumstances that either exacerbate existing health difficulties or lead to health-related problems. Indeed, there is ample evidence to support the fact that the demands of caregiving are associated with deleterious physical and mental health-related consequences for such persons. For example, Minkler and Fuller-Thomson (1999) found grandparent caregivers to have more difficulty in performing activities of daily living than their noncaregiving peers, and Minkler, Fuller-Thomson, Miller, and Driver (2000) found that the incidence of such illnesses as depression, diabetes, hypertension, and insomnia was greater among grandparent caregivers. Strawbridge, Wallhagen, Shema, and Kaplan (1997) found that over a 20-year period, custodial grandparents to be more likely to experience declines in their physical and mental health than noncaregiving grandparents. Indeed, Goodman (chapter 9) has found that with increased age, such effects are negative (being more depleted by a grandchild's behavior problems) and positive (greater life satisfaction, less negative affect, more benefited by religious activity involvement). Consequently, it is not surprising to learn that grandparent caregivers often express concerns over the worsening of their health, potential impairment, and death as factors threatening the security and happiness of the grandchildren they are raising (Kelly, 1993; Shore & Hayslip, 1994). Among women who were caring for their grandchildren, even moderate involvement in child care (i.e., 9 hours per week) increases such persons' risk for coronary heart disease over time (Lee, Colditz, Berkman, & Kawachi, 2003). Alternatively, older age may independently (via more distance from active parenting) or in concert with poorer health (undermining one's existing resources) influence the experience of raising a grandchild, by depleting energy available to invest in the daily tasks of parenting, creating more negative affect (Goodman, chapter 9) and perhaps for some persons, leading to diagnosable depression, further interfering with the ability to care for oneself and attend to the needs of one's spouse and grandchildren. Recently, Park (2003) has found among younger grandmother caregivers, more severe grandchild behavioral problems to be linked to higher levels of depressive symptoms. Whether such findings are unique to younger grandmothers has yet to be determined. Conjointly or independently then, age and age-related losses in physical health, stamina, and energy (see Whitbourne, 1999) may serve to undermine middle aged and older persons' ability to parent as well as impact their relationships with age peers and friends. Ultimately, their influence may detract from the quality of grandparent caregivers' own lives, as well as those of their spouses and grandchildren. On a very practical, everyday level, the demands of raising a grandchild are likely to be very different then for older persons versus younger/middle-aged persons, and for grandparents who report their health to be poorer versus those whose health is more adequate. As an individual difference parameter contributing to the diversity among grandparent caregivers, both health status and age have received little empirical attention in the custodial grandparenting literature. With this in mind, the present project seeks to explore the relationships among age, self-rated health, and custodial grandparent stress and adjustment in three independent samples of grandparent caregivers.

SAMPLES AND PROCEDURE

The three samples in question were gathered over a 10-year period, and consisted primarily (70%) of community-residing grandmothers whose average age was approximately 55 years, 60% of whom were raising boys under the age of 8 (see Emick & Hayslip, 1999; Hayslip, 2003; Shore & Hayslip, 1994; Hayslip, Shore, Henderson, & Lambert, 1998). The samples varied in size ($N = 102$, $N = 53$, $N = 40$), but were each drawn from the Dallas–Ft. Worth Metroplex.

MEASURES

Each custodial grandparent completed measures of self-rated Likert-type single item estimates of health and energy, and in Sample 1 ($N = 102$), for purposes of the present study, these indicators were combined to define an overall self-perceived health variable. In Sample 1, the correlation between health and energy was .73. Relationships between health, energy, and age were .46 and −.52 (each $p < .01$). The relationship between age and the combined index of health was −.53, indicating that as expected, older age was associated with poorer self-perceived health. In Sample 2 ($N = 53$), the correlation between health and energy was .66, but those between age, health, and energy were considerably smaller (−.14, .02). This was equally true in Sample 3 ($N = 40$) ($r = .69$, $r = .10$, $r = −.11$, respectively) and thus, health and energy were treated as separate indicators of self perceived health in Samples 2 and 3.

Additionally, in each case, participants completed common measures of satisfaction with grandparenting (Bence & Thomas, 1988), grandparental role meaning (Kivnick, 1982), and positive and negative affect regarding the grandchild's behavior (Bence & Thomas, 1988). Although the samples differed with regard to the specific measure of well-being/psychological distress utilized [i.e., the CES-D (Radloff, 1977), the Liang (1985) well-being measure, and the Parental Stress Index (Abidin, 1990)], each of these measures reflects an underlying dimension of personal well-being.

Stress associated with the parental role was assessed with the Parenting Stress Index/Short Form (PSI/SF) (Abidin, 1990), a 36-item self-report measure consisting of three subscales: the Parental Distress Factor, the Parent-Child Dysfunctional Interaction Factor, and the Difficult Child Factor. The Parental Distress Factor measures parental distress, the Parent-Child Dysfunctional Interaction Factor evaluates whether the parent derives satisfaction from interactions with the child and whether the child meets parental expectations, and the Difficult Child Factor measures the child's ability to self-regulate. The PSI/SF demonstrates high internal consistency (alpha = .91), high test-retest stability ($r = .84$), adequate construct, discriminant and predictive validity, acceptable concurrent validity with clinical and self-report criteria, and acceptable cross cultural validity (Abidin, 1990). PSI Total Stress scores were used here. All PSI/SF items were reframed to apply to "my grandchild." As the PSI/SF primarily applies to custodial grandparents, persons in those groups completed the PSI/SF as it related to their newly acquired roles as the grandchild's functional parent. This measure was unique to Samples 2 and 3.

Satisfaction with grandparenting (Thomas, 1988) was assessed with 15 Likert-type questions, for example, "life has more meaning for me because of my grandchild," "sometimes it is hard to say I love my grandchild." Its alpha coefficient is .79.

To assess the grandparent's perception of the behavioral and emotional difficulties experienced by the grandchild, persons rated the extent to which they believed 10 such problems (e.g., sexual difficulties, depression, learning disabilities, alcohol and drug abuse) to be severe, where 1 = no problem, to 5 = severe problem (see Emick & Hayslip, 1999; Hayslip et al., 1998). Total problem scores were used here and unique to Samples 1 and 2. Also unique to such samples were single Likert-type ratings of the quality of the relationship with the grandchild as well as the degree of satisfaction with this relationship.

Psychological distress/depression (Center for Epidemiologic Studies Depression Scale-CES-D) (Radloff, 1977) was assessed via a 20-item self-report scale designed to measure current level of depressive symptomatology with emphasis on depressed mood. Participants were asked to endorse the response that best described how often they had felt a particular way in the past week. Questions were answered on a four-point Likert-type scale [rarely or none of the time (less than once a day) to most or all of the time (5 to 7 days)]. The scale exhibits high internal consistency (alpha = .85), adequate test-retest stability (correlations range from .45 to .70), exceptional concurrent validity with clinical and self-report criteria, and substantial evidence of construct validity (see Radloff, 1977).

The Positive and Negative Affect Index assessed aspects of one's perceptions of the relationship with the grandchild (i.e., extent of mutual trust, respect and understanding, affection for the grandchild versus negative feelings about irritating behaviors of the grandchild) (Bence & Thomas, 1988). The Positive Affect Index asks grandparents to describe the extent of mutual understanding, trust, fairness, respect, and affection for the grandchild. In contrast, the Negative Affect Index measures the extent to which the grandparents feel negatively toward irritating behaviors of the grandchild. Two single questions each asked the respondent to rate the quality of the relationship with the grandchild (very negative to very positive) and the satisfaction with this relationship (very unsatisfied to very satisfied).

Parental role strain was derived from the Structure of Coping Scale (Pearlin & Schooler, 1978), and used to identify potential strains in participants' roles as parents, as well as to identify emotional stress experienced by participants connected to this role. It was unique to Sample 2.

Psychological well-being (Liang, 1985) was assessed via a 15-item self-report scale which is designed to measure respondents' feelings about their lives. The scale integrates items from the Bradburn Affect Balance Scale (Bradburn, 1969) and the Life Satisfaction Index A (Neugarten,

Havighurst, & Tobin, 1961). The Liang scale allows for the assessment of positive and negative affect (transitory affective components), happiness (long-term affective component), and congruence (long-term cognitive component). Inclusion of items of a long-term nature is intended to diminish potential distortion of results due to the consequences of transient circumstances.

The meaning of grandparenthood was evaluated with Likert-type items from the Thomas (1988) questionnaire, for example, "I value the fact that my grandchild confides in me," "I value being able to teach things to my grandchild." These items were originally developed by Kivnick (1982), who derived five dimensions of meaning pertaining to grandparenthood (i.e., Centrality, Valued Elder, Immortality through Clan, Reinvolvement with Past, and Indulgence), where scores for each meaning dimension were used here. Coefficient alphas range from .68 (indulgence) to .90 (centrality) (Kivnick, 1982). For our purposes, total scores were used here, reflecting the single factor identified by Hayslip, Henderson, and Shore (2003) for this measure of grandparental role meaning.

To assess life disruption as a function of assuming the parental role, grandparents were also asked to indicate the extent to which, in the context of the extent of care they provided their grandchild, they were satisfied with a variety of aspects of their lives, (i.e., "doing things for fun and recreation," "having my own privacy," "the need to alter routines and plans," "enjoyment of daily activities," "feeling physically tired," "worrying about things") (see Jendrek, 1994). These items tap the extent to which a variety of aspects of one's life have been disputed by child care responsibilities (Jendrek, 1994). Life disruption total scores were used here.

A measure of overall social support (see Emick & Hayslip, 1999; Hayslip et al., 1998) was also utilized here, to reflect both instrumental and emotional support provided by the adult child, other family, and friends. A 33-item scale assessing the extent of such support possessed an alpha of .82.

All of the above self-report scales and/or ratings have been successfully utilized in previous custodial grandparenting research by the first author (Emick & Hayslip, 1999; Hayslip & Shore, 2000; Hayslip et al., 1998; Shore & Hayslip, 1994) to differentiate custodial grandparents by the extent of problems in their grandchildren, to explore the determinants of well-being and role satisfaction in grandparent caregivers, and to examine relationships to mental health service attitudes in such persons. As noted above, nearly all of the above measures possess more than adequate reliability (see Emick & Hayslip, 1999; Hayslip et al., 1998). In each case, higher scores indexed more positive feelings about the parental role, greater well-being, greater role satisfaction, more depression, more role strain, more social support, greater role meaning, and greater life disruption. Each questionnaire required approximately an hour to complete.

To measure parental efficacy, a 9-item scale (see Bachicha, 1997) of generalized parental efficacy was employed to assess the grandparent's perceptions of their ability as a parent to solve problems and understand the grandchild. This scale is unique to Sample 3, and has been successfully used to assess the impact of a psychosocial intervention targeting grandparent caregivers by Hayslip (2003).

RESULTS

While age and health, energy, and a combined measure of health and energy covaried ($r = -.47, -.52, -.53$, respectively, all $ps < .01$) (with older persons reporting poorer health and vitality) in the largest sample, such constructs were not interrelated in two smaller samples (rs ranged from .02 to $-.14$). For this reason, and because health and energy covaried highly ($r = .93$) in the largest sample, versus doing so to a lesser degree in the two smaller samples ($r = .66$ and $r = .68$), independent analyses regarding the relationship between age, energy, and health and the above variables were carried out in the latter two samples, while a combined measure of energy and health was utilized in this respect for the largest sample of custodial grandparents (see above).

For the largest sample ($N = 102$) of grandparent caregivers (see Table 5.1), better self-rated health/more personal energy was associated with more positive overall grandparental role meaning ($r = .41, p < .01$), greater personal well-being ($r = .43, p < .01$), greater affection, trust, and respect for the grandchild (positive affect) ($r = .26, p < .01$), and greater tolerance for a grandchild's disruptive and irritating behaviors (negative affect) ($r = .35, p < .01$). Additionally, in the largest sample, better health/energy were associated with greater quality of and more satisfaction with one's relationship to the grandchild, as well as the perception that the grandchild was experiencing fewer emotional and behavioral problems. Importantly, age was weakly related to only less negative affect ($r = -.20, p < .05$), and when relationships between health/energy and a variety of grandparental well-being indicators were statistically adjusted for the effects of age, little change was noted. Additionally, it is clear in Table 5.1 that the strength of such relationships with health/energy is notably stronger than those for age.

For the second sample ($N = 53$) (see Table 5.2), better self-rated health and vitality was associated with less parental stress ($r = -.29, p <$

TABLE 5.1 Study 1 ($N = 102$) Bivariate and Partial rs

	Age	Health[a]
N affect[b]	−.200*	.352**
N affect	−.026[c]	.293**[d]
P affect[e]	−.057	.265**
P affect	.102[b]	.277**[c]
Meaning[f]	−.191	.408**
Meaning	.033[b]	.368**[c]
WB[g]	−.192	.427**
WB	.044[b]	.391**[c]
GP Sat[h]	.050	.155
GP Sat	.157[b]	.214*[c]
Support[i]	−.121	−.063
Support	−.182[b]	−.150[c]
Child Prob[j]	.192	−.329**
Child Prob	.022[b]	−.273**[c]
Quality[k]	−.080	.302**
Quality	.099[b]	.307**[c]
Satis[l]	−.161	.357**
Satis	.035[b]	.324**[c]

[a]Composite measure of health. [b]Negative affect. [c]Controlling for health. [d]Controlling for age. [e]Positive affect. [f]Grandparental role meaning. [g]Well-being. [h]Grandparental role satisfaction. [i]Social support. [j]Perceptions of grandchild's problems. [k]Quality of relationship with grandchild. [l]Satisfaction of relationship with grandchild.
*$p < .05$; **$p < .01$

.05), and to a lesser extent, greater tolerance for grandchild disruptive behaviors ($r = .26$, $p < .06$) and greater well-being ($r = .26$, $p < .06$). In contrast to Sample 1, in this second, smaller sample, relationships between grandparent variables and age were more pervasive, wherein older age related to more positive grandparent role meaning ($r = .60$, $p < .01$), greater well-being ($r = .31$, $p < .02$), and less depression ($r = −.38$, $p < .01$). Neither set of relationships was altered when controlling for either the effects of age or health and energy, in light of the latter's independence from one another.

In the third sample ($N = 40$) (see Table 5.3), better health/vitality was associated with greater role satisfaction ($rs = .40$ and $.38$, $ps < .05$), less life disruption ($r = −.42$, $r = −.39$, $p < .01$), less depression ($r = −.34$,

TABLE 5.2   Study 2 ($N = 53$) Bivariate and Partial rs

	Age	Health	Energy
WB[a]	.310*	.147	.260
WB	.314*[b]	.212[c]	.289[c]
CESD[d]	−.379**	−.104	−.099
CESD	−.450**[b]	−.164[c]	−.191[c]
Disrupt[e]	−.244	−.166	−.070
Disrupt	−.336*[b]	−.215[c]	−.147[c]
N affect[f]	.092	.167	.257
N affect	.190[b]	.215[c]	.232[c]
P affect[g]	.209	−.144	.093
P affect	.050[b]	.048[c]	.186[c]
GP Sat[h]	.158	.116	.198
Gp Sat	.145[b]	.152[c]	.206[c]
PSI[i]	−.205	−.284*	−.271*
PSI	−.261	−.294*[c]	−.298*[c]
Meaning[j]	.595**	.038	.070
Meaning	.582**[b]	.021[c]	.064[c]
Par strain[k]	−.053	−.240	−.152
Par strain	−.145[b]	−.195[c]	−.180[c]
Child prob[l]	−.145	−.328	−.153
Child prob	−.225	−.337*	−.157

[a]Well-being. [b]Controlling for health and energy. [c]Controlling for age. [d]Depression. [e]Life disruption. [f]Negative affect. [g]Positive affect. [h]Grandparent role satisfaction. [i]Parental stress index. [j]Grandparental role meaning. [k]Parental strain. [l]Perceptions of grandchild's problems.
*$p < .05$; **$p < .01$.

$r = −.40$, $p < .05$), as well as (energy only) greater positive affect toward the grandchild ($r = .34$, $p < .05$). In contrast, in this third sample, older age was associated with both less positive affect toward the grandchild ($r = −.40$, $p < .01$), and less negative affect (less tolerance) regarding the grandchild's behavior ($r = −.54$, $p < .01$). As was true for the second sample, in the third sample, these relationships were not altered substantively when the effects of age or health/energy were statistically controlled.

DISCUSSION

These data clearly suggest that as an individual difference parameter, more favorable self-ratings of one's health and vitality, as well as older

TABLE 5.3 Study 3 ($N = 40$) Bivariate and Partial rs

	Age	Health	Energy
GP Sat[a]	−.106	.404*	.385*
GP Sat	−.068[b]	.504***[c]	.453***[c]
P Affect[d]	−.398*	.194	.338*
P Affect	−.378*[b]	.302[c]	.373*[c]
N Affect[e]	−.543**	−.013	.211
N Affect	−.500***[b]	.057[c]	.186[c]
Disrupt[f]	−.205	−.422**	−.388*
Disrupt	−.230[b]	−.411*[c]	−.436***[c]
CESD[g]	−.122	−.343*	−.398*
CESD	−.164[b]	−.312[c]	−.406*[c]
Par Eff[h]	−.261	.038	.062
Par Eff	−.278[b]	.196[c]	.149[c]
Support[i]	−.187	.060	.072
Support	−.169[b]	.102[c]	.071[c]

[a]Grandparental role satisfaction. [b]Controlling for health and energy. [c]Controlling for age. [d]Positive affect. [e]Negative affect. [f]Life disruption. [g]Depression. [h]Parental efficacy. [i]Social support.
*$p < .05$; **$p < .01$.

age (which are sometimes, but not always interrelated) are each in varying degrees linked to more positive role meaning, greater personal well-being, less parental stress, a more adaptive stance toward the grandchild's disruptive behavior, and more positive feelings toward the grandchild. However, they also indicate that age and health can also operate independently as correlates of custodial grandparents' parental skills in raising their grandchildren. This, to a certain extent, reflects the status of age as a proxy for poorer health, and in this respect, mirrors the concerns of Wohlwill (1970), who argued (see also Baltes, 1987) that age is best treated as nonpsychological in nature, and indeed, age-related declines in health and energy, borne of both primary (physiological) and secondary (lifestyle, disease) age-related influences, rather than increased age per se, can lessen role satisfaction, personal well-being, and undermine one's tolerance for the demands of parenting and a grandchild's misbehavior. In this respect, they parallel to an extent the findings of Goodman (chapter 9) and Park (2003) who have explored variability and vulnerability among younger and older caregiving grandparents. Clearly, this suggests that practitioners pay special attention to not only the short-term, but also the long-term impact of grandparental caregiving on older grandparents, who are more likely to report greater limitations associated with their health, mobility, and energy.

In light of facts that (a) self-rated health, versus objective assessments of health, were utilized here, (b) older persons often overestimate the quality of their health, and (c) persons were not asked to estimate their health and vitality relative to that of their age peers (see George, 1996; Jette, 1996; Marx & Solomon, 2000; Solomon & Marx, 2000), one might easily reach different conclusions regarding the relationships between age, health, and psychosocial functioning, versus those discussed here. Perceptions of one's health are impacted by a variety of factors, (e.g., race/ethnicity, gender, education, income, degree of social support and social integration, coexistent stress) (see George, 1996), as well as the extent to which one has access to health care. In this respect, caregiving grandparents are less likely to seek help for themselves than they are for their grandchildren (Hayslip & Shore, 2000), and thus, their estimates of their health may reflect efforts to cope with the demands of caregiving, and thus mirror the resiliency that we find among custodial grandparents in the face of the personal, interpersonal, and role demands on them. Thus, self-estimates of health might reflect more adequate coping and greater self-efficacy (see George, 1996), rather than impact psychosocial functioning, among grandparent caregivers here. It is certainly possible that one's estimates of health may or may not reflect an awareness of a real physical basis for one's ratings, and therefore, higher or lower such ratings may reflect an awareness of the consequences for oneself as well as for one's grandchild should one's health actually deteriorate in the future, or they may be influenced by greater levels of activity and involvement with a grandchild (see Marx & Solomon, 2000; Solomon & Marx, 2000). For all of these reasons, it would not be surprising to observe that indeed, grandparent caregivers may use a different subjective standard in evaluating their health (i.e., other older persons, other caregiving grandparents, or other grandparents more generally speaking) (see George, 2001 for a review). Indeed, had we asked persons to estimate their health and vitality relative to their noncaregiving age peers, their ratings in this respect may have been unduly and negatively biased. It is worth noting that as most of the grandparents in these samples were women, and in light of gender differences often found in self rated health (George, 2001), our findings may not generalize to men who raise their grandchildren.

A last caveat regarding these findings is to simply suggest that not all grandparent caregivers' health is negatively impacted by the demands of caregiving. Not only do the correlations presented here between age, health, and psychosocial functioning substantiate this fact, but the literature on custodial grandparenting clearly documents this as well (see e.g.,

Hirshorn, 1998). Dependent upon perhaps socioeconomic status, the quality of social support, or the degree to which one's grandchild is experiencing emotional or behavioral difficulties, the health and vitality of some custodial grandparents may suffer and affect their personal well-being and undermine their ability to meet the demands of parenting, while for others, this may not be the case. Notably, in Sample 3, and to a certain extent in Sample 1, older grandparents were less tolerant of disruptive behaviors in their grandchildren, and as a consequence, the quality of their relationships with these children declined. On the other hand, better health (see Samples 1 and 2) apparently is advantageous in these respects.

It is interesting to find here that neither age nor health and vitality were associated with lessened social support, perhaps suggesting that vulnerable grandparent caregivers can nevertheless cope with the stresses of raising a grandchild with at least no less social support than their younger, healthier counterparts. Also, it is perhaps fortunate as well to not find relationships between parental strain and parental efficacy and neither age nor health/energy, suggesting that one's parental skills and related strains of this role are not compromised by older age/lessened health. This suggests that independently of age-related changes in health, that grandparent caregivers can retain their skills as parents, perhaps through utilizing their life experience, accessing parental skills training programs, or relying on earlier developed child-rearing expertise to over-come any health-related limitations that they may be experiencing, and thus maintain their role of caregivers to their grandchildren and remain emotionally connected to their spouses by finding time to seek respite from their parental responsibilities.

Despite the above considerations, these findings for the most part do mirror the reports (see above) of caregiving grandparents who are fearful of their continued ability to parent in light of anticipated age-related declines in their health and vitality. Thus, monitoring one's health becomes a key element in being able to raise a grandchild, so that one can enjoy the fruits of one's labor in seeing this grandchild grow and prosper.

REFERENCES

Abidin, R. R. (1990). *Parenting Stress Index/Short Form*. Charlottesville, VA: Pediatric Psychology Press.

Bachicha, D. (1997). *A validation study of the parental self-efficacy scale*. Unpublished doctoral dissertation, University of New Mexico.

Baltes, P. (1987). Theoretical propositions of life span developmental psychology: On the dynamics between growth and decline. *Developmental Psychology, 23*, 611–626.

Bence, S. L., & Thomas, J. L. (1988, November). *Grandparent-parent relationships as predictors of grandparent-grandchild relationships*. Paper presented at the Annual Scientific Meeting of the Gerontological Society of America. San Francisco.

Bradburn, N. M. (1969). *The structure of psychological well-being*. Chicago: Aldine.

Emick, M., & Hayslip, B. (1999). Custodial grandparenting: Stresses, coping skills, and relationships with grandchildren. *International Journal of Aging and Human Development, 48*, 35–62.

George, L. K. (1996). Social factors and illness. In R. H. Binstock & L. K. George (Eds.), *Handbook of aging and the social sciences* (4th ed., pp. 229–253). San Diego, CA: Academic Press.

George, L. K. (2001). The social psychology of health. In R. H. Binstock & L. K. George (Eds.), *Handbook of aging and the social sciences* (5th ed., pp. 217–237). San Diego, CA: Academic Press.

Hayslip, B. (2003). The impact of a psychosocial intervention on parental efficacy, grandchild relationship quality, and well-being among grandparents raising grandchildren. In B. Hayslip & J. Patrick (Eds.), *Working with custodial grandparents* (pp. 163–178). New York: Springer.

Hayslip, B., Henderson, C., & Shore, R. J. (2003). The structure of grandparental role meaning. *Journal of Adult Development, 10*, 1–11.

Hayslip, B., & Shore, R. J. (2000). Custodial grandparenting and mental health services. *Journal of Mental Health and Aging, 6*, 367–384.

Hayslip, B., Shore, R. J., Henderson, C., & Lambert, P. (1998). Custodial grandparenting and grandchildren with problems: Impact on role satisfaction and role meaning. *Journal of Gerontology: Social Sciences, 53B*, S164–S174.

Hirshorn, B. (1998). Grandparents as caregivers. In M. E. Szinovacz (Ed.), *Handbook on grandparenthood* (pp. 200–216). Westport, CN: Greenwood.

Jendrek, M. (1994). Grandparents who parent their grandchildren: Circumstances and decisions. *The Gerontologist, 34*, 206–216.

Jette, A. (1996). Disability trends and transitions. In R. H. Binstock & L. K. George (Eds.), *Handbook of aging and the social sciences* (4th ed., pp. 94–117). San Diego, CA: Academic Press.

Kelly, S. J. (1993). Caregiver stress in grandparents raising grandchildren. *Image, 25*, 331–337.

Kivnick, H. G. (1982). Grandparenthood: An overview of meaning and mental health. *The Gerontologist, 22*, 59–66.

Lee, S., Colditz, G., Berkman, L., & Kawachi, I. (2003). Caregiving to children and grandchildren and risk of coronary heart disease in women. *American Journal of Public Health, 93*, 1939–1944.

Liang, J. (1985). A structural integration of the Affect Balance Scale and the Life Satisfaction Index A. *Journal of Gerontology, 40*, 552–561.

Marx, J., & Solomon, J. C. (2000). Physical health of custodial grandparents. In C. Cox (Ed.), *To grandmother's house we go and stay: Perspectives on custodial grandparents* (pp. 37–55). New York: Springer.

Minkler, M., & Fuller-Thomson, E. (1999). The health of grandparents raising grandchildren: Results of a national study. *American Journal of Public Health, 93*, 1384–1389.

Minkler, M., Fuller-Thomson, E., Miller, D., & Driver, D. (2000). Grandparent caregiving and depression. In B. Hayslip & R. Goldberg-Glen (Eds.), *Grandparents raising grandchildren: Theoretical, empirical, and clinical perspectives* (pp. 207–220). New York: Springer.

Neugarten, B. L., Havighurst, R. J., & Tobin, S. (1961). The measurement of life satisfaction. *Journal of Gerontology, 16,* 134–143.

Park, H. (2003, November). *Younger grandmothers caring for grandchildren: The effects of poverty and caregiving demands on psychological distress.* Paper presented at the Annual Scientific Meeting of the Gerontological Society of America. San Diego, CA.

Pearlin, L. I., & Schooler, C. (1978). The structure of coping. *Journal of Health and Social Behavior, 19,* 2–21.

Radloff, L. S. (1977). The CES-D Scale: A self-report depression scale for research in the general population. *Applied Psychological Measurement, 1,* 385–401.

Shore, R. J., & Hayslip, B. (1994). Custodial grandparenting: Implications for children's development. In A. Gottfried & A. Gottfried (Eds.), *Redefining families: Implications for children's development* (pp. 171–218). New York: Plenum.

Solomon, J. C., & Marx, J. (2000). The physical, mental, and social health of custodial grandparents. In B. Hayslip & R. Goldberg-Glen (Eds.), *Grandparents raising grandchildren: Theoretical, empirical, and clinical perspectives* (pp. 183–206). New York: Springer.

Strawbridge, W. J., Wallhagen, M. I., Shema, S. J., & Kaplan, G. A. (1997). New burdens or more of the same? Comparing grandparent, spouse, and adult–child caregivers. *The Gerontologist, 37,* 505–510.

Thomas, J. L. (1988, November). *Relationships with grandchildren as predictors of grandparents' psychological well-being.* Paper presented at the Annual Scientific Meeting of the Gerontological Society of America. San Francisco.

Whitbourne, S. (1999). Physical changes. In J. C. Cavanaugh & S. K. Whitbourne (Eds.), *Gerontology: An interdisciplinary perspective* (pp. 91–122). New York: Oxford.

Wohlwill, J. (1970). The age variable in psychological research. *Psychological Review, 77,* 49–64.

CHAPTER 6

Grandmothers' Diaries: A Glimpse at Daily Lives*

Carol M. Musil and Theresa Standing

There is a resurgence of interest in the role of women in the lives of their children and grandchildren. This interest is spurred, in part, by growing recognition of the contribution of grandmothers with primary responsibility for raising grandchildren, and comparisons to grandmothers in diverse caregiving roles to grandchildren (Fuller-Thomson & Minkler, 2001; Goodman & Silverstein, 2002; Jendrek, 1994; Musil & Ahmad, 2002; Strawbridge, Wallhagen, Shema, & Kaplan, 1997). Although various family circumstances contribute to grandmothers' participation in daily care of grandchildren, how the specific daily stresses of primary caregivers to grandchildren and grandmothers in multigeneration homes differ from those of grandmothers who are non-caregivers to grandchildren has not been previously examined.

Clarifying these issues is important because the stresses and demands faced by grandmothers reflect not only issues in their own lives, but also issues in their families' lives. For example, grandmothers with custodial

*The authors gratefully acknowledge the assistance of Trang Chou, Muayyad Ahmad, Katherine Barzilai, and Jacqueline Russek in various phases of this project. This research was supported by grants NIA R15AG15438 and NINR 5R01NR005067.

responsibility for raising their grandchildren, regardless of whether they have legal custody of grandchildren, undertake this role out of necessity, usually related to psychological, drug, or alcohol problems in the parents (Jendrek, 1994). They often describe financial concerns and attention to special needs of children with health problems, behavioral problems, or learning disabilities (Ghuman, Weist, & Shafer, 1999; Ohio Department of Aging, 1999). Less frequently identified are issues with adult children and the relationship between generations when grandparents are raising grandchildren (Goodman & Silverstein, 2002). Since primary caregiver grandmothers take on both parenting and grandparenting responsibilities, they are accountable for all aspects of daily care to children, and may experience a range of problems that are distinct from those of other grandparents (Kelley, Whitley, Sipe, & Yorker, 2000; Musil, Youngblut, Ahn, & Curry, 2002).

Grandmothers who live in the same home as a grandchild and the grandchild's parent(s) frequently help in the care of grandchildren and experience a different constellation of issues. Their stresses have received less attention, although some work has focused on caregiving situations with a teenage parent (Caldwell, Antonucci, & Jackson, 1998; Chase-Lansdale, Brooks-Gunn, & Zamsky, 1994). Because the role of a grandmother living in a home with a grandchild and the grandchild's parent(s) may be less clearly defined, grandmothers in these homes may experience stress (Jendrek, 1994) as well as ambivalence related to their caretaking responsibilities to grandchildren. Primary caregiver grandmothers and those with child care responsibilities in multigeneration homes were found not to differ from each other in the level of appraised stress (Musil & Ahmad, 2002), but have reported more stress than non-caregiver grandmothers, especially stress related to parenting aspects of their role (Musil, 1998). Studying the daily lives of grandmothers permits a detailed look at how caregiving to grandchildren affects the stresses, personal concerns, normal routines, and salient family interactions of grandmothers.

METHOD

This is a content analysis of three-week diaries that detail the stresses reported by a random subsample of grandmothers with different degrees of caregiving to grandchildren.

Sample

The 64 grandmothers who completed the three-week health diary were a randomly selected subsample of a convenience sample of 283 community-dwelling grandmothers living in northeast Ohio who had participated in a cross-sectional study using mailed questionnaires. Details of the study and a description of the complete sample are reported elsewhere (Musil & Ahmad, 2002). To obtain the diary sample, grandmother participants in the larger study were asked in the questionnaire if they were interested in completing a 3-week health diary and 244 of the 283 women indicated an interest in doing so. Those interested in keeping the diary were more likely to be White (89.4%) than non-White (79%), $\chi^2 = 5.92$, $p < .05$, but differed on no other demographic characteristics. From the list of interested participants, 23 grandmothers from each of three caregiver groups (grandmothers raising grandchildren, grandmothers in intergenerational homes, and grandmothers who were not caregivers to their grandchildren) were systematically (every third) selected and invited, by telephone, to participate in the diary study.

Grandmother caregiver status was based on self-report during a screening phone call at initial recruitment into the study and validated by their written responses in the demographic portion of the questionnaire. Criteria for each group was as follows: The *primary caregiver group* included grandmothers who (1) lived in the same home as one or more grandchildren under the age of 18; (2) had primary responsibility for raising their grandchildren because (a) they or the state had custody of the grandchild(ren) due to parental abuse, neglect, incompetence, death, or incarceration; or (b) the grandmother was raising the children without a formal custody arrangement due to parental disinterest, child abandonment, or family instability; and (3) did not reside in the same home as the parents of the grandchildren. The *intergenerational group* included grandmothers who were living (1) with one or more grandchildren under the age of 18 and at least one of the child(ren)'s parents in the same home, and (2) who helped the grandchild's parents with the children's daily care. Grandmothers living in a home with a teenage (minor) parent and grandchild were regarded as intergenerational or multigenerational home caregivers. The *non-caregiver group* included grandmothers who (1) lived in a separate residence from their grandchildren under the age of 18 and the grandchildren's parents; (2) had no responsibility for raising their grandchildren; (3) lived within a one-hour drive; and (4) had regular contact with their grandchildren, including occasional babysitting or child care. Grandmothers who were a child's principal day care provider/babysitter were excluded.

A total of 68 women were contacted by telephone and told about the diary study, 67 agreed to maintain the diary, and 65 women returned complete diaries; one grandmother became the primary day care provider and was not eligible for sample inclusion, and thus, 64 diaries were analyzed. Due to transitions in caregiver status from the time of question-naire completion to time of diary participation, there were not equal numbers of grandmothers in each of the three groups. There were 21 primary caregivers, 18 grandmothers in multigenerational homes, and 25 grandmothers with no responsibility for caregiving to grandchildren who completed the diary.

The diary subsample was 73% ($n = 47$) White and 27% ($n = 17$) Black, and ranged in age from 39 to 85 years old, with a mean age of 57.3 years; 35 women (57%) were 57 years of age or younger. At least one third of the participants had some college education, with only three women (5%) having a college degree or postgraduate studies. Ten women (16.4%) never finished high school. Thirty women worked full- or part-time (47%) and 34 women (53%) were married. Two women (3%) reported monthly incomes of under $500, 25 (39%) reported $500 to $1,500, 20 women (31%) reported $1,501 to $2,500, and 17 (27%) reported over $2,501 monthly.

Measures

Data were recorded in two health diaries, one diary for Week 1 and a second diary for Weeks 2 and 3. Each page of the diary represented one day of the week and had separate sections for recording daily stresses, symptoms, health activities, and other comments. This free-format diary, similar to that used in a previous study (Musil et al., 1998), allows the diary keeper to report any information related to the topic of interest, rather than responding to a predetermined list of problems or concerns. Although information about daily stresses, health symptoms, and health activities were recorded in the diaries, only stresses are examined in this analysis.

Procedure

After agreeing to participate in the diary study, all participants were mailed the two diaries; a cover letter that included the informed consent and an explanation of the diary procedure; and two stamped return-addressed envelopes. All participants were asked to begin recording in the diary on Sunday April 19, 1999. Participants received a reminder postcard in the middle of the first week, and were instructed to return the Week 1 diary at the end of that week. Project staff reviewed the Week 1 diaries for completeness and quality, and most diaries were thorough and detailed. Participants received a check for $50.00 after returning the second diary.

Coding and Analysis

The handwritten diaries were transcribed verbatim and imported into NUD*IST 4 software. Initial coding categories for the content analysis were established using the categories of stress, symptoms, and health activities as a priori codes. Developing the categories was a collaborative, iterative process involving the investigators and graduate assistants. Categories and subcategories were agreed upon, category definitions were developed, and the data were coded by graduate assistants. Inter-coder reliability was calculated on four diaries coded by three different graduate assistants, with agreements ranging from 79 to 89%. Inconsistent codes were examined within the context of the participant's other diary entries and the analysis team made a coding decision. After all stress data were coded, printouts of each category were reviewed, assessed for accuracy and internal consistency, and final coding adjustments were made. Table 6.1 displays frequencies of grandmothers in each caregiver group who

TABLE 6.1   Stresses as Reported by Grandmothers N = 64

Stresses	Primary $n = 21$	Intergenerational $n = 18$	Non-caregiver $n = 25$	χ^2
Child-rearing issues	15	11	12	.25
School routine issues	15	12	0	30.03**
School progress	4	0	0	8.74*
Grandchildren's activities	9	3	2	8.51*
Grandchildren's health	9	4	2	7.75*
Effects on personal life	6	3	0	7.85*
Stressful interactions (grandchildren)	13	6	2	15.05**
Family tasks	17	16	16	3.95
Situational worries	13	10	16	.32
Stressful interactions with others	6	6	5	1.02
Financial worries	13	9	11	1.49
Health issues	12	14	16	1.87
Time issues	12	8	6	5.35#
Life events	3	3	8	2.49
Work issues	4	9	16	9.53*

* $p < .05$
** $p < .001$

made journal entries in each coding category, and χ^2 values of group differences. Illustrative comments are reported in the text below.

Results

All grandmothers reported some stresses related to child-centered stresses. These included child-rearing issues, school routine and progress, grandchildren's activities, effects on grandmothers' personal lives, grandchildren's health, and stressful interactions with grandchildren.

Child-Rearing Issues

Fifteen primary caregivers, 11 grandmothers in multigeneration homes, and 12 non-caregivers reported child-rearing concerns. The nature of the child care issues was strikingly different for primary caregiver grandmothers who were raising their grandchildren compared with grandmothers in the other categories, reflecting their unique status as grandparents and parents. For example, one primary caregiver expressed her hope that she lives long enough to raise her grandchildren to adulthood. Two grandmothers raising grandchildren reported interactions with Children's Services during the diary period. One grandmother reported that her grandchildren missed school for two weeks, and as a foster grandparent she needed to report this to the county, adhering to guidelines of her custody arrangement. Another grandmother reported a visit by Children's Services requesting that she assume temporary custody of an additional grandchild, a teenager. Grandmothers in all groups were stressed by the mundane issues of child care; however, primary grandmothers often mentioned watching additional grandchildren from multiple families. Caregivers often reported stresses that were centered on feeding, bathing, and transporting children as well as supervising play and homework. One wrote about her stresses, "Another grandchild showed up [ill] . . . I will have to keep him for a few days." The child care *activities* of the non-caregiving grandmothers often reflected child care in their homes as grandchildren were dropped off while parents worked overtime or went to social functions or appointments. This was stressful for them as evidenced by entries such as "Watching babies is getting more difficult," and another, "I am feeling OK today except for the added stress when the baby is here."

School Routines

Unlike non-caregivers to grandchildren, 15 of 21 primary caregivers and 12 of 18 grandmothers living in intergenerational homes reported rushing to get children ready for school as a stress ($\chi^2 = 30.03$, $p \leq .001$); many grandmothers reported awakening children at 6:00 a.m. to complete morning routines. According to one grandmother: "Getting sleepy irritable grandson up for daycare was stressful . . . most days he is easy to handle but he needed a little extra loving today and I did not have time to give it to him." Grandmothers in multigenerational homes also described morning activities with grandchildren, such as, "hurried to help kids get off to school." One intergenerational grandmother said, "I spend my mornings with my 5-year-old granddaughter, [eating] breakfast and she loves to read." Another chaperoned her granddaughter's field trip. Grandmothers in both primary and intergenerational caregiving roles reported helping grandchildren study for tests or complete homework in the morning.

School Progress

Four primary caregivers expressed concerns about their grandchildren's progress in school, including grandchildren not turning work in on time, failing classes, skipping school, or receiving detentions and school suspensions ($\chi^2 = 8.74$, $p \leq .05$). No intergenerational home grandmothers expressed such concerns, although one non-caregiver grandmother reported similar problems with her own teenage son, but not with her grandchildren.

Activities

Nine primary caregiver grandmothers, compared with three intergenerational and two non-caregivers reported activities of grandchildren as stressful ($\chi^2 = 8.51$, $p \leq .05$). Primary caregiver grandmothers were responsible for transporting children to and attending programs, plays, soccer practices, track meets, and other activities: "had a lot of driving to do for the kids, was gone from 1:20 to 6 p.m." Being responsible for their grandchildren's daily care, they reported responsibility for looking after clothing and uniforms, such as Girl Scouts Brownie vests; fixing hair for school pictures, and arranging play dates for the children. Whereas other grandparents attend "grandparents' days" only, primary caregivers also attend Parents' Day too, "because we are both." One primary caregiver reported being unable to take her own mother to a medical appointment because of a grandchild's activity. Intergenerational home grandmothers infrequently reported driving grandchildren, but frequently reported accompanying the grandchildren's parent(s) to activities such as ball games, music programs, or school plays. Only two non-caregiver grandmothers reported attending a grandchild's school play or concert.

Grandchildren's Health

The grandmother's role in the care of sick and healthy children varied by her responsibility ($\chi^2 = 7.75$, $p < .05$); nine primary, four intergenerational, and two non-caregiver grandmothers reported such activities. Six primary caregivers documented making decisions about sick children, such as illness-related absences, child care arrangements, and physician/nurse practitioner visits for sick children. One grandmother wrote on Day 16, "both kids have head colds . . . wanted to stay home . . . but I sent them out the door." Day 17, "Kept [grandson] home from school today . . . he has an ear infection . . . picked up [granddaughter] from school, she has a fever." Day 18 "Kept both kids home today . . . need I say more about my stress." Two grandmothers in intergenerational homes reported helping with sick children, including physician visits for sick grandchildren and also supportive care, "spend a lot of time . . . to make her feel better." Five of eight grandmothers with acutely ill grandchildren reported that more than one grandchild in the household was sick at the same time, and one primary caregiver reported caring for up to six ill grandchildren on 10 of the 21 diary days. Primary caregivers also reported taking grandchildren for visits to neurologists, dentists, orthodontists, psychiatrists, therapists, pediatricians, dermatologists, and eye doctors. Grandmothers in the other two categories also took children in to optometrists, dentists, and for x-rays.

Effects on Personal Life

Six primary caregivers and three intergenerational home grandmothers, unlike non-caregivers to grandchildren, revealed that their responsibilities affected their personal life ($\chi^2 = 7.85$, $p < .05$). Two primary caregiver grandmothers wrote that they did not expect to be in the position of raising a child again. Occasionally, grandmothers reported that responsibilities to their families interfered with their own activities, and although they accepted this, it was sometimes disappointing that they could not participate as fully in their own activities as they might like. One grandmother said, "The kids wanted to go to the playground but I wanted to sit and meditate." Another had to leave a much anticipated luncheon to "meet the school bus." Another grandmother noted that it is often difficult because she works two jobs, night shift in the emergency room and home health care, and that she takes her granddaughter with her when she does home health care. An intergenerational home grandmother reported being unable to attend a paid sporting event because she was babysitting, but also "felt guilty at being angry."

Stressful Interactions With Grandchildren

Thirteen of the primary grandmothers, six of the intergenerational home grandmothers, but only two of the non-caregiver grandmothers described difficult interactions with grandchildren ($\chi^2 = 15.05, p \le .001$). Problems ranged from children acting up in church, or not cleaning their rooms and talking back, to more serious concerns such as worries about a granddaughter becoming pregnant or a grandson stealing. One custodial grandmother wrote, "There's not much I can do to escape the stress they cause . . . I wish I could have a break from them once in a while." Another primary caregiver grandmother expressed concerns about similarities between her grandchildren and the children's parent; she stated, "trying to teach a child whose daddy is an abusive alcoholic to not hit . . . is stressful." Grandmothers reported using time-outs and activity restrictions to discipline grandchildren.

Other Stresses

All grandmothers reported other stresses not focused exclusively on grandchildren. The other stresses included family tasks, situational stresses, stressful interactions with adult children, financial and health problems, time pressures, life events, and work.

Family Tasks

In general, over three fourths of all diary-keepers reported some stress from family tasks during the diary period, but the nature of these tasks differed across groups. Seventeen of 21 primary caregivers reported family tasks, which included trying to do housework with children underfoot, cleaning, making beds, preparing meals, washing clothes, grocery shopping, and going to work. Others also reported redecorating and/or refinishing furniture (3) and car maintenance/repairs (3). All but two grandmothers in intergenerational homes also reported family tasks, many related to general family life. Grandmothers in multigeneration homes reported shopping, especially for groceries, cleaning, washing, paying bills, and doing yardwork. One wrote: "Woke up with my mind racing with things I have to do—made a list, . . . got busy." Another wrote: "Burned my fingers making cinnamon toast for them, . . . lost my keys . . . had quiet time after they left for school . . . Afternoon, grandson and I went to doctor, evening, dad didn't get home until 9 p.m." In contrast, 16 of 25 non-caregivers to grandchildren reported shopping, cleaning, running errands, and involvement with others outside the home, such as siblings, cousins, and parents. This involvement included visiting others, meeting others for lunch, caring for others' pets, and cooking for others. One primary, three intergenerational and three non-caregivers reported providing tangible help with elderly parents, in-laws, or other relatives, and two additional non-caregivers reported telephone conversations with their fathers.

Situational Worries

Grandmothers made numerous diary entries related to situational stresses. Grandmothers worried over the instability of children and grandchildren as they changed jobs, boyfriends, and living arrangements. They worried about children divorcing and grandchildren being caught in the shuffle. One intergenerational home grandmother wrote, "My child leads such a chaotic and sad life that I get chest pains and anxiety symptoms." Another said, "I just prepare myself to end up raising my granddaughter." Non-caregiver grandmothers also expressed concerns: "I have a granddaughter who is estranged from her mother. I worry about her constantly." Grandmothers in all groups had concerns about children or grandchildren in trouble with the law for stealing, drug use, or other violations. One primary caregiver reported that her granddaughter had been suspended from school and taken for drug testing, and an intergenerational grandmother wrote that her grandson was being evaluated for alcohol and drug use. Eight grandmothers indicated concerns about alcohol and drug use by their adult children and children-in-law.

During the period of data collection, the shootings of students and teachers occurred at Columbine High School in Littleton, Colorado. Eleven grandmothers across all three groups recorded reflections on this tragedy. "Couldn't sleep—worried about the schools my grandchildren are in." One intergenerational caregiver wrote, "the Columbine School [shooting] incident happened. I thought about comparisons of my kids to [the] killers/victims. So many similarities with the profile of killers . . . I worry about the similarities."

Stressful Interactions With Adult Children and Others

Some grandmothers in all groups expressed stress from difficult interactions with sons, daughters, and in-laws. Some custodial grandmothers were stressed because the grandchildren's fathers let them down by not visiting or calling. Grandmothers in intergenerational homes expressed stress from living with their adult children such as a son who is "bossy" or a daughter who "picks on me so I go to my room." Other issues in intergenerational homes centered on differences in child rearing approaches. As one grandmother said about her daughter, "she's too nervous and short with her child . . . so I stepped in and reminded her that the child is only two and not twenty." More grandmothers in the non-caregiver group indicated stress from husbands, even though equal numbers of grandmothers in each of the primary and non-caregiver groups were married.

Worries Related to Finances

Financial matters were a source of stress for over 50% of all the grandmothers, with 13 custodial, 9 intergenerational, and 11 non-caregiver grandmothers citing concerns such as extra bills or no incomes. One primary caregiver grandmother wrote, "My grandchildren are still here and I don't have money to buy milk and cereal." Another described giving her grandson money for a school activity that she had planned to use to pay a bill. She later wrote, "Raising him just doesn't leave any money for lunch or dinner away from home." Grandmothers did not only worry about money for themselves and their grandchildren, they sometimes helped out their adult children. A grandmother in an intergenerational home commented, "Trying to live on Social Security is not easy . . . gave our daughter money to pay for her glasses since she didn't have money." Non caregiver grandmothers reported concerns over bills, rising living costs, and taxes, but not financial worries related to children or grandchildren.

Worries Related to Health

Two thirds of the grandmothers reported stress about medical issues. These worries included the health of elderly parents, spouses, siblings, friends, and the grandmothers' own health. Twelve of the primary, 14 of the intergenerational home, and 16 of the non-caregiver grandmothers identified problems ranging from anticipating medical tests and learning the results, to dealing with surgery, and coping with arthritis, heart disease, or cancer. In describing these stresses, two of the non-caregiver grandmothers related that they "keep my health problems to myself" or they "tried not to show my stress" to their family.

Stress Related to Time Pressure

Many grandmothers (41%) listed stress from a lack of time in their busy lives. The custodial grandmothers, who were trying to juggle child care, jobs, and household chores, described these stresses more often than the intergenerational home or non-caregiver grandmothers. One grand-mother raising a grandchild wrote, "I don't have time to rest or think about myself. I have to take care of the children." Another wrote, "I feel like everyone wants a piece of me." Grandmothers in multigenerational homes also reported time pressures, "I would really like to have Sunday just for my husband and myself. Is this selfish? Our kids make us feel like it is but we really need it!" Non-caregiving grandmothers did not reflect such time stresses related to children and grandchildren.

Life Events

This category included stress from events such as deaths, births, and major moves. Three primary, two intergenerational, and six non-caregiver grandmothers reported dealing with the death of family or friends during the diary period. For two, this prompted memories of sons who had died. One non-caregiver also wrote that her children wanted her to move in with them, but that she did not want to do that.

Work

Grandmothers in all categories reported stress from their employment, however 16 non-caregivers reported this source of stress compared to four primary and nine intergenerational caregivers ($\chi^2 = 9.53$, $p \leq .05$). The nature of the stress was similar across the groups and centered on issues such as office politics, physical demands, busy workdays, and job security.

DISCUSSION

This content analysis examined the stresses of grandmothers as entered into daily health diaries. Grandmothers in all groups reported a variety of stresses, and these stresses differed by caregiving to grandchildren. Primary grandmothers reported more stress related to grandchildren's activities and health issues as well as from difficult personal interactions with grandchildren. Primary and intergenerational grandmothers re-ported more stress from their grandchildren's school routines and effects on their personal lives, whereas non-caregivers to grandchildren reported more work-related problems. All grandmothers reported stresses associ-ated with family tasks, health issues, family situations, and financial issues, but more primary caregivers reported the latter concern. Grandchildren being raised by one grandparent are most likely to be poor (Casper & Bryson, 1998), which adds to family stress in many ways. Even if married, grandparents are at a time in their lives when their incomes may become more limited, yet the expenses from raising grandchildren are increasing at the same time (Kelley et al., 2000).

For primary and intergenerational home grandmothers, many stresses were child and school related. Getting children off to school or day care, along with general child care, were among the most frequently reported stresses for these grandmothers, whereas the non-caregiver grandmothers rarely have this responsibility. School mornings are stressful for most parents, and for grandmothers who are generally older and have more health issues, especially musculoskeletal problems, mornings are apt to be uncomfortable and difficult. In addition, four primary caregiver grandmothers but no grandmothers in the other groups recorded their grandchild's school progress as a concern. Solomon and Marx (1995) reported that children being raised solely by grandparents were not as successful in school as children in two parent families, but were as successful as children being raised by only one parent. Solomon and Marx (1999) also noted that 27% of the primary grandparent caregivers felt their children misbehaved at school. In this current study, behavior and discipline problems were listed as stresses by two thirds of primary caregiver grandmothers and a third of those in intergenerational homes. Many of these children have had a troublesome childhood, and their grandmothers are dealing with the daily consequences of these difficulties. However, there remains limited available data about the needs of children living with grandmothers. Programs sponsored by schools or local offices on aging designed to help caregiving grandmothers support their grandchildren's academic progress and to manage behavior-related problems are critical.

Grandmothers across all three groups reported stress from difficult interactions or confrontations with their adult children or in-law children, but the nature of the difficulties differed. Grandmothers in multigeneration homes reported stresses from disagreements over child rearing and other criticisms from their adult children, whereas primary grandmothers were stressed from adult children not visiting their grandchildren or relational problems between their adult children and their significant others. Although the role of social support as an important factor in decreasing stress and improving health has been well documented, the grandmothers who reported relationship stress face a diminished circle of support that may place them at risk for health problems. This risk may be compounded if such grandmothers also have limited opportunities for employing active coping strategies that reduce depression (Musil &

Ahmad, 2002), such as if they have many time constraints or share living space with other adults.

More primary grandmothers reported stress from general child care activities than the intergenerational or non-caregiver grandmothers. Pruchno and McKenney (2002), in describing caregiver burden of grandmothers, emphasize that the demands of caregiving compete with other roles and responsibilities of the grandmothers. In addition to school issues, getting grandchildren to activities and medical appointments as well as the general tasks of maintaining a family with children added to their daily activity level. Although the nature of the family tasks differed by the caregiver groups, grandmothers across groups reported spending time attending to family needs. Minkler, Fuller-Thomson, Miller, and Driver (1997) found that depression in grandmother caregivers is higher in those who had more recently begun caring for their grandchildren, suggesting that grandmother caregivers might benefit from support early in their caregiving experience. Attention to the needs of grandmothers in multigeneration homes is also warranted, especially given their interpersonal concerns.

Many diary entries focused on the grandmothers' connections with others, regardless of caregiving group. This is consistent with the work of those who consider women in relationship to others, especially in their roles as caregivers (Gilligan, 1982; Moen, Robison, & Demster-McClain, 1995). Thomas (1997) refers to "vicarious stresses," or the stresses of loved ones, which are evident in the grandmothers' reports of situational stresses, such as children's marriages, grandchildren's school problems, and reflections on the Columbine incident. In contrast, some were reluctant to share their own concerns with their families, which may reflect a view of self as "caregiver" rather than as one who is equally in need of care from others.

This analysis provides some beginning insights about grandmothers and their roles in three types of family structures, but has several limitations. The smaller proportion of non-White grandmothers who expressed an initial interest in keeping a diary is noteworthy, although whether such lack of interest reflects lack of time, less comfort with diary writing, or other concerns about participation is not known; the completion rate was 97%, however. Further, the participation of the non-caregiver grandmothers in the care of the grandchildren may be unique to this sample which required grandmothers to have ongoing relationships with the grandchild's family. Additional work examining ethnic as well as structural differences in grandmothers' participation in extended families continues to be important.

In summary, this study, designed to identify the stresses of grandmothers according to their caregiving status to grandchildren, highlights the diverse roles of women with their grandchildren. There were some distinct differences between the grandmothers according to caregiver groups that reflected not only their caregiving responsibilities but also hinted at interpersonal issues that have not been well articulated to date. Despite these differences, there were similarities as well, with grandmothers' concerns for family safety and drug use crossing all groups. Thus, while grandmothers may carry a specific label as a certain type of caregiver to grandchildren, such labels are but one indication of women's stresses, activities, and interactions with their immediate and extended families.

REFERENCES

Caldwell, C., Antonucci, T., & Jackson, J. (1998). Supportive/conflictual family relations and depressive symptomatology: Teenage mother and grandmother perspectives. *Family Relations, 47*, 4, 395–402.

Casper, L. M., & Bryson, K. R. (1998). *Co-resident grandparents and their grandchildren: Grandparent maintained families.* Washington, DC: Population Division. U.S. Bureau of the Census.

Chase-Lansdale, P., Brooks-Gunn, J., & Zamsky, E. (1994). Young African American multi-generational families in poverty: Quality of mothering and grandmothering. *Child Development, 65*, 373–393.

Fuller-Thomson, E., & Minkler, M. (2001). American grandparents providing extensive child care to their grandchildren: Prevalence and profile. *Gerontologist, 41*, 2, 201–209.

Ghuman, H., Weist, M., & Shafer, M. (1999). Demographic and clinical characteristics of emotionally disturbed children being raised by grandparents. *Psychiatric Services, 50*, 11, 1496–1498.

Gilligan, C. (1982). *In a different voice: Psychological theory and women's development.* Cambridge, MA: Harvard University Press.

Goodman, C., & Silverstein, M. (2002). Grandmothers raising grandchildren: Family structure and well-being in culturally diverse families. *Gerontologist, 42*, 5, 676–689.

Jendrek, M. (1994). Grandparents who parent their grandchildren: Circumstances and decisions. *Gerontologist, 34*, 2, 206–216.

Kelley, S. J. (1993). Caregiver stress in grandparents raising grandchildren. *Image: Journal of Nursing Scholarship, 25*, 331–337.

Kelley, S., Whitley, D., Sipe, T., & Yorker, B. (2000). Psychological distress in grandmother kinship care providers: The role of resources, social support, and physical health. *Child Abuse & Neglect, 24*, 3, 311–321.

Minkler, M., Fuller-Thomson, E., Miller, D., & Driver, D. (1997). Depression in grandparents raising grandchildren. *Archives of Family Medicine, 6*, 445–452.

Moen, P., Robison, J., & Dempster-Mclain, D. (1995). Caregiving and women's well-being: A life course approach. *Journal of Health and Social Behavior, 36*, 3, 259–273.

Musil, C. (1998). Health, stress, coping, and social support of grandmother caregivers. *Health Care for Women International, 19*, 5, 441–453.

Musil, C., Ahn, S., Haug, M., Warner, C., Morris, D., & Duffy, E. (1998). Health and illness among community dwelling older adults: Results of a health diary study. *Applied Nursing Research, 11*, 3, 138–147.

Musil, C., & Ahmad, M. (2002). Health of grandmothers: A comparison by caregiver status. *Journal of Aging and Health, 14*(1), 96–121.

Musil, C., Youngblut, J., Ahn, S., & Curry, V. (2002). Parenting stress: A comparison of grandmother caretakers and mothers. *Journal of Mental Health and Aging, 8*, 3, 197–210.

Ohio Department of Aging. (1999, September). *A report to the Ohio general assembly on the problems and concerns of Ohioans raising their children's children.* Columbus, OH: Grandparents Raising Grandchildren Task Force.

Pearson, J. L., Hunter, A. G., Cook, J. M., Ialongo, N. S., & Kellam, S. G. (1997). Grandmother involvement in child caregiving in an urban community. *Gerontologist, 37*, 5, 650–657.

Pruchno, R., & McKenney, D. (2002). Psychological well-being and Black and White grandmothers raising grandchildren: Examination of a two-factor model. *Journal of Gerontology, 57*, 5, 444–452.

Solomon, J., & Marx, J. (1995). To grandmother's house we go: Health and school adjustment of children raised solely by grandparents. *Gerontologist, 35*, 5, 386–394.

Solomon, J., & Marx, J. (1999). Who cares? Grandparent/grandchild households. *Journal of Women and Aging, 11*, 1, 3–25.

Thomas, S. P. (1997). Distressing aspects of women's roles, vicarious stress, and health consequences. *Issues in Mental Health Nursing, 18*, 539–557.

U.S. Bureau of the Census. (1998). *Co-resident grandparents and their grandchildren: Grandparent maintained families.* (Population Division Working Paper No. 26.). Washington, DC.

CHAPTER 7

Depression and Caregiver Mastery in Grandfathers Caring for Their Grandchildren*

Philip McCallion and Stacey R. Kolomer

For the past two decades grandparent caregiving has been recognized as a new trend in families. Historically grandparent-headed households have always occurred often during times of crisis (Burton, 1992; Mullen, 1996). Between 1980 and 1994 there was almost a 40% increase in these households (Burnette, 1997; Fuller-Thomson, Minkler, & Driver, 1997; Hanson & Opsahl, 1996; Kelley, Yorker, & Whiteley, 1997; Mullen, 1996). However, today 1 in 10 grandparents will take on the role of primary caretaker to a grandchild for at least six months before the child is age 18 (Burnette, 1999; Silverstein & Vehvilainen, 1998).

Several factors have contributed to the recent increases in the prevalence of grandparent headed households. One frequently identified source

*Project funded by grants from the Joseph P. Kennedy Jr. Foundation and the Center for Excellence in Aging Services.

has been the dramatic increase in substance abuse. Another reason has been the increase in reported child abuse and neglect. There was a 24% increase in reports of child abuse and neglect between 1985 and 1994, which totaled more than 3 million reports each year (Kelley et al., 1997), and thirty-one percent of all reports in 1996 were substantiated or indicated abuse and/or neglect, and resulted in children being removed from their parents' care (The Greenbook, 1998). Additional reasons for the growth in grandparent-headed households include divorce, death, mental illness, homelessness, HIV/AIDS, teenage motherhood, incarceration, abandonment, and unemployment/employment out of area/military service (Burnette, 1997; Burton, 1992; Emick & Hayslip, 1999; Fuller-Thomson et al., 1997; Hayslip, Shore, Henderson, & Lambert, 1998; Jendrek, 1994; Kelley et al., 1997; Minkler, 1994; Pinson-Millburn, Schlossberg, & Pyle, 1996; Silverstein & Vehvilainen, 1998).

GRANDPARENTS AS PRIMARY CAREGIVERS

Grandparents becoming primary caregivers to their grandchildren is a phenomenon that cuts across all ethnic groups and socioeconomic backgrounds. In looking at grandparent-headed households by ethnicity/race it is reported that 43.6% of the grandparents are Caucasian, 35.9% are Black, and 18% are Hispanic/Latino (Generations United, 1999).

Most non-parental kin or related caregivers to children are grandmothers, followed by aunts (Burnette, 1997; Dressel & Barnhill, 1994). This is consistent with traditional views that caregiving is part of a woman's role in the family. In a profile of 173 grandparents, Fuller-Thomson et al. (1997) found that 77% of the participants were grandmothers. In Hayslip and colleagues' study (1998) of 193 grandparents, 80% of the custodial grandparents were women. A telephone survey of 134 grandparent caregivers conducted by the University of Massachusetts–Boston found 86% of the carers to be women (Silverstein & Vehvilainen, 1997). However, the greater likelihood of women being in the role does not preclude grandfathers being primary caregivers.

Rewards and Stressors of Providing Primary Care to Grandchildren

Becoming caregivers to another generation of children can have unexpected rewards as well as unwelcome stressors. Previous studies of grandparents have indicated that becoming a caregiver to one's grandchildren provides a purpose for living, increases love and companionship, feelings of being appreciated, hope for the future, and the satisfaction of helping others (Burton, 1992; Burton & deVries, 1992; Chase-Lansdale, Brooks Gunn, & Zamasky, 1994; Dressel & Barnhill, 1994; Emick & Hayslip, 1996, 1999; Hayslip et al., 1998; Janicki, McCallion, Grant-Griffin, & Kolomer, 2000; Jendrek, 1994; Minkler & Roe, 1993; Minkler, Roe, & Price, 1992). In addition, parenting another generation of children has been reported to help the aging grandparent feel youthful.

Despite the rewards of caregiving, it has been well documented that the role of caregiver also has disadvantages for grandparents. One strain that can be particularly problematic is risk of illness and disability for the caregiver. Common physical health problems reported by grandparent caregivers include arthritis, hypertension, insomnia, pain, stiffness, head-aches, and hearing problems (Emick & Hayslip, 1999; Kelley et al., 1997; Silverstein & Vehvilainen, 1998). Grandparents also often deny their own health problems for fear of having the grandchildren removed from their care. Limited housing space and financial strain are other challenges for grandparent caregivers. Often grandparents are unable to move and are powerless to increase their income to meet their new responsibilities. This can lead to additional stress for the caregiver. Other identified strains for grandparent caregivers include difficulty with grandchildren's school system, social isolation, exhaustion, embarrassment, regret, and bereavement.

A negative effect of these stressors can be the development of anxiety and/or depression for the grandparent caregiver (Burnette, 2000; Flint & Perez-Porter, 1997; Generations United, 1999; Janicki et al., 2000; Kelley et al., 1997; Kolomer, 2000; Phillips & Bloom, 1998; Roe, Minkler, Saunders, & Thomson, 1996). In a previous study increased symptoms of anxiety were found (Sands & Goldberg-Glen, 1998), but the most common concern is heightened symptoms of depression (Burnette, 2000; Fuller-Thomson et al., 1997; Janicki et al., 2000). Silverstein and Vehvi-lainen's (1998) study of 134 grandparents raising grandchildren in Massa-chusetts found 9% reported feeling depressed often, while 54% reported sometimes feeling depressed. In a study of grandparents caring for children with developmental disabilities more than half of the 97 grandparent caregivers experienced symptoms of depression at levels of clinical con-cern as measured by the CES-D depression scale (Janicki et al., 2000). The reality that samples in the studies cited comprised exclusively or overwhelming of grandmothers does raise unanswered questions as to whether grandfathers experience the same concerns and consequences as grandmothers. In the most comprehensive review of symptoms of depression among grandparent caregivers for example, Fuller-Thomson and colleagues' analysis of the National Survey of Families and Households found 25% of grandparent caregivers exhibiting symptoms of depression (1997). However, there are no separate analyses for men and women in the role.

Differences Between Men and Women as Caregivers

Although there have been no published studies specifically focused on grandfather caregivers, there have been some studies regarding men as primary caregivers. Heller, Hsieh, and Rowitz (1997) reported that mothers caring for adult children with developmental disabilities are more likely than fathers to report experiencing subjective burden, dysphoria, and strain. In contrast, Pruchno and Hicks Patrick (1999) found no significant differences between mothers and fathers who provide care to an adult child with a chronic disability on either the CES-D (Center for Epidemiology Studies Depression Scale) or the LSIA (Life Satisfaction Index). Additionally, Essex, Seltzer, and Krauss (1999) measured psychological distress among married couples caring for adults with intellectual disabilities and found no significant difference between spouses in depressive symptoms or in subjective burden. However, fathers of sons were found to experience increasing symptoms of depression over an 18-month period in comparison to fathers of daughters.

Grandfathers as Caregivers

Often unnoticed and underserved are the grandfathers who take on the responsibility of becoming primary caregiver to their grandchildren. Small in number in comparison to women, several questions arise. Who are the grandfathers and what are their thoughts about caring for their grandchildren? Do they experience their caregiving role differently from grandmothers? As several studies have indicated, many grandmother caregivers experience elevated levels of symptoms of depression more frequently than other women in their same age cohort. Do grandfather caregivers experience similar levels of symptoms of depression? Grandfather caregivers are a unique population that warrants further study.

METHOD

Sample

For the purposes of this study grandparent caregiver was defined as an individual who has assumed primary care for a child, is at least one generation removed from the child's own parent, and perceives himself in a grandparenting relationship with the child (Janicki et al., 2000). Some grandfathers who self-selected into the study were single carers (19), others were the primary caregiver in situations where their spouse was not the maternal grandmother and the decisions and management of care were primarily theirs (6) and still others were identified by their spouse as an equal partner in caregiving (8). Nonprobability techniques were used to obtain this snowball sample of 33 grandfather caregivers. The grandfathers were primarily recruited from two Relatives as Parents Programs in counties outside New York City and from two support groups for grandparents caring for grandchildren with developmental disabilities in Queens, New York. Approximately 10 of the grandfathers also participated in focus group interviews.

Questionnaire Data

As shown in Table 7.1 the mean age of the grandmothers was 58.3 years and the mean age for the grandfathers was 57.8 years and for both more than half of the participants were less than 60 years old. Seventy-four percent of the grandmothers were African American whereas 49% of the grandfathers were African American. Only 13% of the grandmothers were Caucasian in comparison to 36% of the grandfathers. Seven percent of the grandmothers and 3% of the grandfathers were Latino. Only 28% of the total sample of grandmothers reported themselves as being married, whereas 73% of the grandfathers were married. Twenty-eight percent of the grandmothers were separated or divorced as compared to 9% of the grandfathers. Thirty percent of the grandmothers were widowed and only 9% of the grandfathers were widowers. As Table 7.1 indicates, in addition to providing care for their grandchildren, 29% of the grandmothers and 45% of the grandfathers worked outside of their homes. Thirty-one percent of the grandmothers and 54% of the grandfathers reported owning their own home as compared to 68% of grandmothers and 46% of the grandfathers renting.

Fifty-six percent of grandmothers and 55% of grandfathers planned to care for their grandchildren until the grandchildren could care for themselves. Few grandparents, 3% of grandmothers and 9% of the grandfathers, expected to always have to provide care for their grandchildren. Eight percent of the grandmothers and 24% of the grandfathers did not know how long they should expect to provide care. In terms of planning for future care should the grandparent no longer be able to, 20% of the grandmothers and 51% of the grandfathers thought that the child's biological parent would become the primary caregiver. Twenty percent

TABLE 7.1 Comparisons of Grandmother and Grandfather Caregivers

	Grandmothers ($n = 540$)	Grandfathers ($n = 53$)
Age		
< 60	57%	58%
60–69	31%	30%
> 70	12%	12%
	Mean = 58.3 years, sd = 9.2 years	Mean = 57.8 years, sd = 10.1 years
Race		
African American	74%	49%
Caucasian	13%	36%
Latino	7%	3%
Other	6%	12%
Marital Status		
Married	28%	73%
Separated/divorced	28%	9%
Widowed	30%	9%
Single	7%	7%
Work outside of home		
Yes	29%	45%
No	71%	55%
Own or rent home		
Own	31%	54%
Rent	68%	46%
Live with friend/relative	1%	0%

of the grandmothers and 6% of the grandfathers did not know who would provide care.

Focus Group Interviews

A structured series of questions was developed to guide discussions with the grandfathers. With the participants' permission notes were taken and the sessions tape recorded. One focus group session was held with three groups of 3 to 4 grandfathers. The sessions were organized to cumulatively address the discussion questions. At the end of the first session, the two researchers made a preliminary identification of emergent themes and then used the second and third groups to confirm or clarify these themes.

TABLE 7.2   Expectations by the Grandmother and Grandfather Caregivers for the Children Under Their Care

	Grandmothers ($n = 540$)	Grandfathers ($n = 33$)
Expectation for length of care		
Until grandchild can care for self	56%	55%
Will always provide care	3%	9%
Until son/daughter can	10%	6%
Until my son/daughter are released from prison	2%	0%
Don't know	8%	24%
Other	2%	6%
Plan for child if grandparent can no longer provide care		
Grandchild's parent	20%	51%
Other relative	51%	30%
Foster care	1%	0%
Don't know	20%	6%
Other	7%	13%

Questionnaire Interviews

Thirty-three grandfathers were interviewed via telephone or through in-person interviews lasting 40 minutes to 1 hour. A 17-page questionnaire included a total of 121 closed ended questions with 6 follow-up open-ended questions. The questionnaire was originally developed and used to gather data to measure differences among families who were or were not caring for a child with a developmental disability (see Janicki et al., 2000; McCallion, Janicki, Grant-Griffin, & Kolomer, 2000). Use of this previously developed questionnaire made it possible to draw for comparison purposes a matched sample of 33 grandmothers from a previously collected database of 540 grandparents.

Measures

The instrument used included demographic questions about the grandparent caregiver and the grandchild, and about need, use, and satisfaction with formal services. Specific information collected included age, sex, education, ethnicity, religion, marital status, employment, and number of children under the grandparent's care. Two different Likert-type scales, the Center for Epidemiological Studies Depression (CES-D) (Radloff, 1977), and the Caregiving Mastery Scale (CMS) (Pearlin & Schooler, 1978) were included in the questionnaire. The CES-D scale measures symptoms of depression by summing the scores of 20 questions on a scale from 0 to 3. Statements in this scale include "You were bothered by things that do not usually bother you" and "You felt as if you could not shake the blues even with the help of family or friends." Scores over 16 are considered likely to indicate symptoms of depression at a clinical level. Internal consistency of the CES-D with this population was similar to Radloff's original reports (.80 compared to .85, McCallion & Kolomer, 2000; Radloff, 1977). Caregiving Mastery was measured using the 7-item CMS scale drawn from work by Pearlin and Schooler (1978). The scale measures generalized expectations about one's ability to influence events in life using a four-point agree/disagree format (Huyck, 1991). Statements in the scale include: "This month you've been feeling that you could make your financial situation better if you wanted to." Some wording changes were made so the scale would be more applicable to grandparent caregivers. Higher scores are indicative of higher locus of control. Both of the scales have been used in previous studies and have been found to have good validity and reliability. Internal consistency in this study at .85 was higher than previously reported with caregiver populations (.67–.70, Pruchno, Patrick, & Bryant, 1997).

Data Analysis

Demographic characteristic of the 33 grandfathers were compared to those of 540 grandmothers in an existing dataset. A cross comparative approach using grounded theory was used to derive and confirm themes from the focus group discussions. The process began with the development of ideas and discussion points. These beginning points were then systematically tested, expanded, modified, and codified in a cumulative manner, using a constant comparative approach to the analysis of both tape recorded and written notes on successive focus groups. Depression and caregiving mastery scores of the grandfathers and 33 matched grandmothers were compared using student's t-tests.

RESULTS

Focus Group Themes

Several common themes emerged in the focus group discussions: the feeling of missing freedom, experiencing child rearing differently than they had with their own children, and fear of what would happen to the grandchildren should the grandfather's health fail.

Missing Freedom

Some of the grandfathers expressed that they were envious of friends who could go out to dinner or go on vacations on a whim. In taking responsibility for their grandchildren, some of the grandfathers had to change their vision for retirement. Plans for travel changed, and hobbies that were going to be the focus of attention were put aside: "Prior to the children coming to live with me I was footloose and fancy free. Can't do that anymore. I still miss doing things on the spur of the moment."

Some animosity was also expressed toward agencies that placed their grandchildren with them. Many of the grandfathers related stories that they felt pushed into a corner and not given the chance to consider taking on the role of caregiver. However, they all agreed they would have taken the responsibility of caring for their grandchildren; they just wanted the opportunity to think about it.

A Different Experience

Despite the feeling of loss the grandfathers also talked about how different it was raising children a second time. Many admitted to having played a relatively minor caregiving role with their own children when they were small but now enjoying being with their grandchildren. One grandfather shared the story of how strange and uncomfortable it was to accompany his granddaughters dressed in their tutus to ballet class. However, the grandfathers also expressed regret that they were losing the opportunity to "spoil" their grandchildren like other grandparents.

Health Concerns

Several grandfathers reported experiencing cardiac and other chronic health problem and their recognition that further deterioration may be in their future. One grandfather stated "I worry about what will happen to them in the future. Emotion gave way to reason (when we took them in)." All the grandfathers expressed concern about what would happen if their own health situation got worse and who would provide care for their grandchildren in their absence.

An independent samples t-test was used to analyze the differences between the grandmothers and grandfathers' mean CES-D and caregiving mastery scores. There was a statistically significant difference in the mean CES-D scores of the grandparent caregivers ($p > .05$) but there was no statistically significant difference in the mean caregiving mastery scores. As reflected in Table 7.3 the mean score on the CES-D for the matched (matching was on the basis of age, race, and marital status) grandmother caregivers was 20.3 (sd 4.55). The mean score on the CES-D for the grandfathers was 12.71(sd 7.4). This also reflects therefore that a greater number of grandmothers scored above the usual clinical cutoff of a score of 16 than the grandfathers.

DISCUSSION

The samples of both grandfathers and grandmothers reported on here may not necessarily be typical. However, the range of ethnicity, level of incomes, and location in large urban, suburban, and rural communities found here at least yielded findings worthy of further investigation and the data point out directions for such investigation. The grandfather caregivers in this sample looked different from the grandmothers. The grandfathers in this study were more likely to be Caucasian, to be married, to be working outside of their homes, and to own their own homes in comparison to the grandmother caregivers. Such differences have the potential to influence stressors. For example, 45% of the grandfathers worked outside of the home. Grandparents having more disposal income available may help alleviate financial and other burdens. Alternatively, grandfathers who work outside of the home may have less time to provide hands-on care with their grandchildren and therefore may be missing some of the caregiving experiences that have been identified as rewarding.

TABLE 7.3 Differences in Symptoms of Depression and Caregiving Mastery for Grandmother and Grandfather Caregivers

	Grandmothers ($n = 33$)			Grandfathers ($n = 33$)			
	Mean	SD	Range	Mean	SD	Range	F
CES-D	20.3	12.1	3–54	12.7	7.4	0–32	4.1*
Caregiving mastery	20.5	4.6	12–32	17.03	4.8	6–27	3.8

*$p > .05$.

Another important difference was that 73% of the men had spouses in comparison to only 25% of the women. Caregivers who have a spouse may have more social support and feel less isolation than caregivers who are not married. However, there were also spouse situations where the spouse was not the biological grandmother and she was not active in caregiving suggesting that such support should not be assumed.

A further interesting difference between the grandparents in this study was who identified themselves as legally responsible for their grandchild. Eighty-three percent of the grandmothers reported themselves to be responsible for their grandchildren in comparison to 34% of the grandfathers. Yet the objective reality of actual legal establishment of custody in these families was similar. This may suggest that grandfathers and grandmothers have different understandings of these issues or may reflect different emphases on these issues as they respond to the challenges of caregiving.

The issue of primary interest in this study was the experience of grandfather caregivers. The focus group participants appeared committed to caregiving, spoke of the rewards they experienced, and acknowledged the difficulties. Two issues that appeared different from grandmothers were their discussions of "loss of freedom" and of their own health concerns. Loss of freedom appeared related to their view of what retirement should be like and the comparisons they made with their age peers. For all grandparent caregivers, caring for a grandchild is an activity out of life sequence and unexpected. However, the literature has not described this concern to the same extent for grandmothers. Further investigation should consider the extent to which retirement expectations are attributed to gender role and paid work history. Also the influence in turn of such "loss of freedom" concerns on subsequent feelings of stress and depression should be considered. The presence of and anticipation of physical health problems among grandfathers and their relationship to psychosocial concerns such as depression should also be considered. Such investigation should also seek to better capture these issues among grandmothers.

There were statistically significant differences between the grandfathers' and grandmothers' mean scores on the CES-D. Symptoms of depression as measured by the CES-D for the grandfathers were below the traditional cutoff of 16 indicating that as a group grandfathers in this sample were not depressed. The mean score for the matched sample of grandmothers was above 16, suggesting high levels of depressive symptoms. More work is clearly warranted in understanding what factors may protect male caregivers from symptoms of depression. As previously stated, as compared to the grandmothers more grandfathers had a spouse, owned their own home, worked outside of the home, and were connected to formal resources. Perhaps these differences protect grandfather caregivers from experiencing symptoms of depression at the same level as grandmothers. Further investigation may also help establish circumstances that place grandparents, male or female, potentially at risk for symptoms of depression.

Men as Primary Caregivers

Despite grandfathers in this sample experiencing low symptoms for depression, grandfathers were experiencing some difficulty with their caregiving role. Grandfathers were somewhat (if not significantly) less likely than grandmothers to feel in control over their caregiving situation as indicated by the lower mean for this group found on the caregiving mastery scale. In the focus groups grandfathers also reported hesitancy about their caregiving role and uncertainty for the future. Further investigation collecting data from a national more demographically representative sample would greatly contribute to our understanding of this group. The design of interventions that assist grandfathers who are primary caregivers to their grandchildren that address both their concrete service needs and their psychological needs would also be beneficial.

REFERENCES

Burnette, D. (1997). Grandparents raising grandchildren in the inner city. *Families in Society, 78*(5), 489–501.
Burnette, D. (1999). Custodial grandparents in Latino families: Patterns of service use and predictors of unmet needs. *Social Work, 44*(1), 22–34.
Burnette, D. (2000). Latino grandparents rearing grandchildren with special needs: Effects of depressive symptomatology. In P. McCallion & M. Janicki (Eds.), *Grandparents as carers of children with disabilities: Facing the challenges* (pp. 1–16). Binghamton, NY: Haworth Press.
Burton, L. (1992). Black grandparents rearing children of drug addicted parents: Stressors, outcomes, & social services needs. *The Gerontologist, 32*(6), 744–751.
Burton, L., & DeVries, C. (1992). Challenges and rewards: African American grandparents as surrogate parents. *Generations, 16*(3), 51–54.
Chase-Lansdale, P., Brooks-Gunn, J., & Zamsky, E. S. (1994). African American multigenerational families in poverty: Quality of mothering and grandmothering. *Child Development, 65*, 373–393.
Dressel, P. L., & Barnhill, S. (1994). Reframing gerontological thought and practice: The case of grandmothers with daughters in prison. *The Gerontologist, 34*(5), 685–691.

Dubowitz, H., Feigelman, S., Harrington, D., Starr, R., Jr., & Zuravin, S. (1994). Children in kinship care: How do they fare. *Children and Youth Services Review, 16*(1–2), 85–106.

Emick, M. A., & Hayslip, B., Jr. (1996). Custodial grandparenting: New roles for middle aged and older adults. *International Journal of Aging and Human Development, 43*(2), 135–154.

Emick, M. A., & Hayslip, B. (1999). Custodial grandparenting: Stresses, coping skills, and relationships with grandchildren. *International Journal of Aging and Human Development, 48*(1), 35–61.

Essex, E. L., Seltzer, M. M., & Krauss, M. W. (1999). Differences in coping effectiveness and well-being among aging mothers and fathers of adults with mental retardation. *American Journal on Mental Retardation, 104*(6), 545–563.

Flint, M., & Perez-Porter, M. (1997). Grandparent caregivers: Legal and economic issues. *Journal of Gerontological Social Work, 28*(1/2), 63–76.

Fuller-Thomson, E., Minkler, M., & Driver, D. (1997). A profile of grandparents raising grandchildren in the U.S. *The Gerontologist, 37*(3), 406–411.

Generations United. (1999). *Fact sheet: Grandparents and other relatives raising children: Challenges of caring for the second family.* (202) 662-4283.

Hanson, L., & Opsahl, I. (1996). Kinship caregiving: Law and policy. *Clearinghouse Review, 30*(5), 481–501.

Hayslip, B., Jr., Shore, J., Henderson, C. E., & Lambert, P. R. (1998). Custodial grandparenting and the impact of grandchildren with problems on role satisfaction and role meaning. *Journals of Gerontology: Series B: Psychological Sciences and Social Sciences, 53B*(3), s164–s173.

Heller, T., Hsieh, K., & Rowitz, L. (1997). Maternal and paternal caregiving of persons with mental retardation across the lifespan. *Family Relations, 46,* 407–415.

Huyck, M. H. (1991). Predicates of personal control among middle aged—and young—old men and women in Middle America. *International Journal of Aging and Human Development, 32,* 261–275.

Janicki, M. P., McCallion, P., Grant-Griffin, L., & Kolomer, S. R., (2000). Grandparent caregivers I: Characteristics of the grandparents and the children with disabilities they care for. *Journal of Gerontological Social Work, 33*(3), 35–55.

Jendrek, M. P. (1994). Grandparents who parent their grandchildren: Circumstances and decisions. *The Gerontologist, 34*(2), 206–216

Kelley, S. J., Yorker, B. C., & Whiteley, D. (1997). To Grandma's house we go . . . and stay. *Journal of Gerontological Nursing,* 13–20.

Kolomer, S. R. (2000). Kinship foster care and its impact on grandmother caregivers. *Journal of Gerontological Social Work, 33*(3), 85–102.

McCallion, P., Janicki, M. P., Grant-Griffin, L., & Kolomer, S. R. (2000). Grandparent Caregivers II: Service needs and service provision issues. *Journal of Gerontological Social Work, 33*(3), 57–84.

McCallion, P., & Kolomer, S.R. (2000). Depressive symptoms among African American caregiving grandmothers: The factor structure of the CES-D. *Journal of Mental Health and Aging, 6*(4), 525–538.

Minkler, M. (1994). Grandparents as parents: The American experience. *Aging International, 21*(1), 24–28.

Minkler, M. (1999). Paper Presentation at the 52nd Annual Scientific Meeting of The Gerontological Society of America, San Francisco.

Minkler, M., & Roe, K. M. (1993). *Grandmothers as caregivers: Raising children of the crack cocaine epidemic.* Newbury Park, CA: Sage Publications.

Minkler, M., Roe, K. M., & Price, M. (1992). The physical and emotional health of grandmothers raising grandchildren in the crack cocaine epidemic. *The Gerontologist, 32*(6), 752–761.

Mullen, F. (1996). Public benefits: Grandparents, grandchildren, and welfare reform. *Generations, 20*(1), 61–64.

Pearlin, L. I., & Schooler, C. (1978). The structure of coping. *Journal of Health and Social Behavior, 19*, 2–21.

Phillips, S., & Bloom, B. (1998). In whose best interest? The impact of changing public policy on relatives caring for children with incarcerated parents. *Child Welfare, 77*(5).

Pinson-Millburn, N. M., Schlossberg, N. K., & Pyle, M. (1996). Grandparents raising grandchildren. *Journal of Counseling and Development, 74*(6), 548–555.

Pruchno, R., & Hicks Patrick, J. (1999). Mothers and fathers of adults with chronic disabilities. *Research on Aging, 21*(5), 682–713.

Pruchno, R., Patrick, J., & Bryant, C. J. (1997). African American and White mothers of adults with chronic disabilities. *Family Relations, 46*(4), 335–346.

Radloff, L. S. (1977). The CES-D scale: A self-report depression scale for research in the general population. *Applied Psychological Measurement, 1*(3), 385–401.

Roe, K. M., Minkler, M., Saunders, F., & Thomson, G. E. (1996). Health and grandmothers raising children of the crack cocaine epidemic. *Medical Care, 34*(11), 38–51.

Sands, R. G., & Goldberg-Glen, R. S. (1998). Impact of employment and serious illness on grandmothers who are raising their grandchildren. *Journal of Women and Aging, 10*(3), 41–58.

Silverstein, N. M., & Vehvilainen, L. (1998). *Raising awareness about grandparents raising grandchildren in Massachusetts.* University of Massachusetts–Boston: Gerontology Institute.

www.gpo.ucop.edu/. 1998 Green Book. Section 11: Child Protection, Foster Care, and Adoption Assistance. Ways and Means Committee.

U.S. House of Representatives Committee on Ways and Means. (1998). Section 11: Child Protection, Foster Care, and Adoption Assistance. The Greenbook. Retrieved January 16, 2004, from http://instruct1.cit.cornell.edu/courses/econ321/public_html/favors/greenbook/1998/11CPS.TXT

CHAPTER 8

African American Grandmothers: The Responsibility Continuum*

Rosalyn D. Lee, Margaret E. Ensminger,
and Thomas A. LaVeist

The tendency in research on Black grandparents has been to focus on crisis contexts or comparisons to White counterparts, with less examination of within group variation, context, and general behavior (Hunter & Taylor, 1998). Studies have tended to be unidirectional, focusing on the benefits of certain roles to younger generation family members without accounting for the costs to elders (Burton & Dilworth-Anderson, 1991). Szinovacz (1998a) suggests deeper understanding of grandparenthood will come from work on heterogeneity and the dynamics and contingencies of inter-generational and extended family relationships. King, Russell, and Elder (1998) advocate work examining how extra-familial conditions and envi-

*This research was based on a dissertation conducted at Johns Hopkins School of Public Health using data from the Woodlawn Longitudinal Study. The study was supported by minority supplemental grant (5R01MH52336) from the National Institute on Mental Health. Postdoctoral support came from National Institute on Aging postdoctoral fellowship 5T32AG0024308.

ronments influence intra-familial processes. This chapter responds to these needs by expanding on previous research to broaden our knowledge about experiences of African American grandmothers.

African American families have historically been more likely than other groups in the United States to transition into and to maintain extended family households over time (Hunter & Ensminger, 1992). Cherlin and Furstenberg (1986) found that nearly twice as many Black (27%) as White grandparents (15%), exhibit an involved grandparenting style (parent-like behavior and exchange of services). Also, Black women are more likely than White women to be parents at all ages, with the most pronounced differences occurring during both the early and late years of adulthood (King, 1999). Black household extension, involved grandparenting, and extended parenting can be understood as forms of organization or behaviors utilized by the elderly to stabilize families. The involved style of the stabilizer or extended parent is rooted in the age-graded family systems of West African culture and enacted as a means of survival amid the social, political, and economic adversities experienced by Black families (Burton & Dilworth-Anderson, 1991; Cherlin & Furstenberg, 1986).

BACKGROUND

In 1950 when coresidence of minor children in grandparental homes was highest (5.8%), married adults lived in parents' homes or brought parents into their homes. By the mid-1980s when the coresidence rate began ascending again (Szinovacz, 1998b), coresident homes formed frequently in response to the middle generation's difficulty establishing or sustaining families and households (Goldscheider & DaVanzo, 1989; Whittington & Peters, 1996). Szinovacz (1998b) found a majority of coresident households were downward extended, serving the needs of adult children and grandchildren. Using homeownership to demarcate direction of transfer, Bryson and Casper (1999) found that grandparent-maintained homes, where grandchildren and/or adult children resided in the homes of grandparents, greatly outnumbered parent-maintained homes, where grandparents resided in homes headed by their adult children. Their analysis of data from the March 1997 Current Population Survey (CPS), indicated 75% of families with coresident grandparents and grandchildren were grandparent maintained.

In-depth caregiver studies have focused more on grandparents with custody or primary responsibility, regardless of legal status, than grandparents living with grandchildren (Pebley & Rudkin, 1999). Population-based studies have revealed that caregiver and coresident grandmother status occurs regardless of class and race lines; that recently bereaved, Black and young grandmothers, as well as, those from poor households are over represented; and that the most frequently observed coresident household type contains three or more generations (Bryson & Casper, 1999; Caputo, 1999; Fuller-Thomson, Minkler, & Driver, 1997; Pebley & Rudkin, 1999). Analysis of CPS data spanning 1983 through 1994 showed that foster care households headed by relatives compared to parent-child households were more likely to have no earned income, to rely on public assistance; and, to be headed by widows, those with less education and those out of the labor force (Harden, Clark, & Maguire, 1997). The grandmother role has frequently been defined in studies by household composition (e.g., skip generation, where child's parent is absent) or self-identification of primary role. Also, it usually has been represented dichotomously (e.g., primarily responsible vs. all others). Few studies have focused on grandparents who take on significant responsibility without "crossing the line" to become primary or custodial parents (Caputo, 1999; Fuller-Thomson & Minkler, 2001). Likewise, level of parenting or grandparenting that non-coresident grandparents engage in has not garnered much consideration. Some of these limitations result from the design of national surveys that do not include items on coresidence, caregiving, or grandparenting.

Grandparents take on many degrees of caregiving. Within coresidence settings, depending on the extent of formalization of the living or caregiving arrangement, grandparents become some variant of surrogate parent with full responsibility, coparents or helpers with shared responsibility, or members of the household without child care responsibilities. Even so, many studies focus on the skipped generation or primary caregiver, and the non-caregiver reference group by default becomes all other grandparents. Such an approach can result in classification bias as those who do not see themselves as primary—because of level of care, residential setting, or informality of arrangement—may place themselves or be placed into the non-caregiver category. Using a broader definition of caregiver that considers functional, temporal, and residential criteria may increase our understanding of the variations in family composition and functioning, as well as, the implications for a range of older, involved grandmothers.

Pearson, Hunter, Cook, Ialongo, and Kellam (1997) examined differing levels of caregiving by type of coresidential household in a community sample in Baltimore, Maryland. Grandmothers acting as sole parent or coparent with a grandfather were the most engaged in four parenting behaviors and had the least help. Those living with single mothers were the next most engaged. The results replicated an earlier analysis of a community sample in Chicago, Illinois (Pearson, Hunter, Ensminger, & Kellam, 1990). Additionally, Fuller-Thomson and Minkler (2001) used the National Survey of Families and Households to conduct five-way comparisons of grandmother types. Custodial grandmothers were operationalized by self-report of ever having had primary responsibility of at least one grandchild for six or more months. Four non-custodial grandmother types ranged from having provided 30+ hours per week of child care or 90 overnight stays per year to having provided no hours per week of child care and no overnight stays during the year. The present research expands on these studies in four ways. First, the grandmother role construct incorporates (a) behavioral components of role enactment (i.e., quantity and types of activities executed in the role), (b) household composition, and (c) self-identification of primary caregiver status during lifetime. This approach expands the pool of caregivers by including grandmothers who engage in parenting but who may not self-identify as the primarily responsible person. Second, the design allows for the comparison of grandmothers who currently, formerly, or never engaged in caregiving. The classification scheme acknowledges variation in the timing of caregiving role and responsibilities of non-custodial caregivers. Third, the sample is derived from a large, community-based, longitudinal study of women and children from a predominantly African American neighborhood so the data includes prospectively collected information on the grandmother's and grandchildren's characteristics and family history. Fourth, the findings contribute to knowledge on heterogeneity within Black grandparenthood, the prevalence of lifetime exposure to caregiving, and the persistence of relationships between social risk factors, household structure, and grandmother role.

METHOD

This study includes 542 African American grandmothers from the Wood-lawn Longitudinal Study (WLS), a longitudinal epidemiological study of children and their families who in the mid-1960s resided in Woodlawn, an urban community on the south side of Chicago. This secondary analysis utilized data from interviews conducted in 1966 and 1967 (Time 1) and 1997 and 1998 (Time 3). The initial cohort consisted of 1,224 mothers, the follow-up targeted 1,136 biological or adoptive mothers of the original target children. About 66% ($n = 752$) were located and alive, 90% of which ($n = 680$) were interviewed. Disposition analysis indicated that compared to those interviewed at Time 3 those who refused were more likely to have received welfare and to live below the poverty line in the 1960s. Women deceased at Time 3 were less likely to have graduated from high school. The grandmothers did not, however, differ in family type in 1966 and 1967 or teenage motherhood. At Time 3, 96% of the women interviewed were grandmothers, the majority of which (86%) headed their own homes. Most women, whether householders or not, did not live with grandchildren (70%). Furthermore, 82% of coresident grandmothers headed households. This secondary analysis includes respondents who were grandmothers and householders in 1997 and 1998. Thirty-nine percent were between 50 and 59 years old, 52% were between 60 and 69 years old, and 9% were between 70 and 79 years old. Though only 26% of the respondents were 65 years of age or older, 44% were retired. Fifty percent of the women had their first child at age 19 or younger. Slightly more than a third were married. About one quarter lived alone. Forty-one percent lived below the government-defined poverty level and nearly 50% had at some point in time received welfare benefits. The vast majority of the women (89%) continued to live in the Chicago metropolitan area, particularly within the city limits. Only 13% continued to live in the Woodlawn community; while 5% had migrated into the Chicago suburbs.

Three major categories of grandmothers were constructed, those who: (a) lived with and assumed responsibility for grandchildren, (b) did not live with grandchildren but who had assumed primary responsibility for one year or more at some prior point in time, and (c) did not live with and had never assumed primary responsibility for a grandchild. The grandmothers were further stratified by the magnitude and frequency of engaging in parenting tasks and the presence of middle generation family members in the household at Time 3. This systematic sorting provided a method of identifying the degree to which women assumed caregiving responsibilities for grandchildren. See Table 8.1 for a description of the seven profiles and acronyms used for each grandmother type defining the Grandmother Role Construct.

The grandmother types were compared on demographic characteristics, financial resources, grandchild characteristics, and social stress. Chi-square tests were used for categorical variables and one-way analysis of variance (ANOVA) tests were used for continuous measures. The measures included: age, education, marital status, employment status, poverty status, foster care income, personal or household public assistance (i.e., welfare, SSI, or food stamps), total number of grandchildren, number of coresident grandchildren, age of coresident grandchildren, age of youngest and oldest coresident grandchild, duration of grandchild coresidence, and whether any resident grandchild had lived in the respondent's home their

TABLE 8.1 Grandmother Role Construct

Category Label	Acronym	Definition of Category
Skip generation	SG	Grandchild(ren) in home, adult children not in home
Three-generation, high responsibility	3GH	Second and third generations in home, high parenting score
Three-generation, moderate responsibility	3GM	Second and third generations in home, moderate parenting score
Past primary, moderate responsibility	PPM	No grandchildren in the home, moderate (or high) parenting, assumed primary responsibility in the past
Past primary, low	PPL	No grandchildren in the home, low parenting score, assumed primary responsibility in the past
Never primary, moderate responsibility	NPM	No grandchildren in the home, moderate (or high) parenting score, never had primary responsibility
Never primary, low responsibility	NPL	No grandchildren in the home, low parenting score, never had primary responsibility

entire childhood. With respect to social stress, a large body of literature has established a clear connection between health status and scores on event check lists (Aneshensel, 1992; Turner & Lloyd, 1995). These reports of life events have been used as measures of social stress. Because these stressful life events may precipitate coresidence and may also increase the burden of grandparenting, we compare the grandparent profiles by events that happened to the respondent or household members from 1975 to 1997. The events include serious illness, work difficulties, trouble with the law or police, incarceration, drug problems, alcohol problems, parental caregiving (direct or financial), death of parents, and domestic violence. We construct a global score and a caregiver specific score (using four events identified as determinants of coresidence and caregiving).

FINDINGS

Table 8.2 presents the profile of grandmothers in the Woodlawn population, 67.7% of which were engaged in moderate or high levels of parent-

TABLE 8.2 Cross-Tabulations/ANOVA: Grandmother Types by Primary Status, Marital Status, Economic Measures, Employment Status, Household Size, and Family Life Event Scores

Grandmothers (N = 542)	% of Total (N)	% Ever Primary Caregiver, One or More Years	% Below Poverty	% SSI, Food Stamps, or Welfare	% Employed	% Ever Welfare	Mean Household Size [SD]	Mean Family Life Events [SD]	Mean Alcohol/ Drug Law/ Jail Events [SD]
Skip generation	8.7 (47)	87	41	30	32	38	3.34 [1.24]	3.53 [2.07]	1.32 [1.37]
Three-generation, high	8.1 (44)	71	70	59	32	48	5.55 [2.46]	3.89 [2.04]	1.39 [1.48]
Three-generation, moderate	10.1 (55)	42	71	55	42	62	5.10 [1.69]	3.04 [2.26]	1.15 [1.50]
Past primary, moderate	14.9 (81)	100	30	31	32	49	2.19 [1.25]	3.43 [1.94]	1.18 [1.30]
Past primary, low	12.9 (70)	100	41	47	47	60	2.15 [1.25]	3.70 [2.06]	1.29 [1.35]
Never primary, moderate	25.8 (140)	0	30	28	51	40	2.17 [1.07]	2.91 [1.93]	.84 [1.30]
Never primary, low	19.4 (105)	0	36	28	48	37	1.96 [1.17]	3.20 [2.02]	.73 [1.21]
Chi-square	N/A	N/A	46.8	31.04	14.02	17.83	N/A	N/A	N/A
F statistic	N/A	N/A	N/A	N/A	N/A	72.30	2.27	2.90	N/A
p value	N/A	N/A	.01	.01	.029	.01	.01	.035	.009

ing. Of those who coresided, 87% in SG and 70% in 3GH households had assumed a primary caregiving role for at least one year compared to less than 50% of women in 3GM households. Grandmother types significantly differed by age ($p < 0.05$) with a majority of 3GM grandmothers 50 to 59 years old and a majority of SG and 3GH women 60 to 69 years old. About one third of PPM and 3GH types were over 65 and received Social Security benefits; but retirement rates for them and women in the SG group exceeded the average (49 to 52%). Thus, considerable proportions of women retired prior to retirement age and were not receiving Social Security benefits. There were vast differences in financial resources by grandmother type. Though a small percentage of women received foster care income, SG women reported it nearly twice as often as women in three-generation households. Also, women in three-generation households were much more likely than other women to be living below poverty (70% vs. 30 to 41%, $p < .00$). Personal receipt of welfare and food stamps was relatively low. Rates of household receipt were higher and significant differences ($p < .00$) were found on public assistance as a source of household income. The three-generation (55 to 59%) and PPL (47%) households were much more likely to have SSI, food stamps, or welfare as a source of household income; compared to about 33% of other household types. When examining specific types of assistance, significant differences were found on each. Highest welfare (25 to 26%) and food stamps (26 to 37%) receipt was found in three-generation households. With respect to disability-related assistance, household SSI, PPL (31.8%) and both three generation households (21.5%) had the highest rates of receipt. The NPL profile reported the lowest frequencies of household welfare and food stamps; while SG reported lowest household SSI. Thus, highest rates of receipt of public assistance were found in three-generation households while lowest rates were in the SG and NPL profiles. Those receiving assistance due to disability were found most frequently in PPL and three-generation homes. This paralleled significant differences in welfare history. Women in three-generation and past primary households (50 to 60%) had the highest rates of welfare history compared to about 40% in the other types. With respect to employment, nearly half of the PPL and never primary grandmothers were employed compared to about one third of the women in the remaining profiles. The differences were significant and indicated that coresident grandmothers with high responsibility and moderately involved women with a history of primary caregiving were the least likely employed.

Table 8.2 also shows significant differences among the grandmother types on life events ($p < .05$). The highest average family life event score was in the 3GH household (3.89); while the lowest score was in the NPM household (2.91). Differences on specific events were significant at ($p <$ .01) with scores similarly being highest in the 3GH household (1.39) and lowest in the NPL household (0.73). Nearly half (47%) of the grandmothers reported at least one caregiver specific event, while almost one third (30.5%) reported at least two. Current and past caregivers more frequently reported multiple events. About 40% of SG, 3GH, and both past primary groups experienced at least two events. Three of the specific events had strong associations with grandmother types—drug problem, incarceration, and trouble with the law. About one third of SG and 3G grandmothers reported family drug problems; while SG, 3GH, and PPL households more frequently indicated family jail events (36 to 40%). As for trouble with the law, a measure highly correlated with incarceration, over one third of grandmothers in SG, 3GH, and both past primary groups reported such events. The never primary grandmother type consistently had low rates of specific events (14 to 22%). Differences among profiles on recent family alcohol problems were significant ($p < .05$). The 3GM (25.4%) type most frequently reported the problem within the last five years; while the NPL group had the lowest occurrence (6.6%). A trend for recent jail events was noted with highest rates amongst PPL and both three-generation profiles (20 to 26%) compared to the low of 11% amongst NPL.

Household size differed significantly by grandmother type ($p < .01$). The 3GH group had the highest mean number of household members (5.55); while the NPL group had the lowest number of household members (1.96). Among coresident grandmothers, 55% lived with more than one grandchild (27% with two or more and 28% with three or more) while 45% lived with one coresident grandchild. Consistent with mean household size, the three-generation, high households tended to be most represented among those with two or more grandchildren. Ages of coresident grandchildren significantly differed by grandmother type. Women in three-generation households cared for children about three years younger than children in SG households, 9.4 versus 12.5 years standard deviation (SD) 4. Also the gap in age of youngest child in three-generation and SG homes was about 4 years, 6.8 versus 10.8 years, SD 5. These differences suggest women in SG households were raising teenagers while those in three-generation homes were coresiding with and/or raising preteens. The mean years of grandchild coresidence ranged from 7.9 to 9.3, SD 6; the age of oldest coresident grandchild ranged from 12.3 to 14.1, SD 5. Grandchildren who resided in the home their entire life were reported by each coresident type at rates ranging from 61 to 68%. Significant differences were found in the number of total grandchildren ($p < .01$). Women in PPL and 3GH households had the highest mean number of grandchildren—about 12.5. Women in NPM households had the lowest mean number of grandchildren—6.8. Women with the highest numbers of grandchildren also had the highest number of children. Two thirds of women in PPL and 3GH had five or more children compared to a low of 39% among women in NPM households.

To summarize, descriptive statistics indicate that within a community population of mothers followed from the time they parented first grade children to the time they averaged 60 years of age, 27% had grandchildren living in their homes, 28% had assumed a primary caregiving role at some earlier time and 45% were not coresiding and had never been primary caregivers. Coresidence and caregiving were found to be significantly associated with demographic, economic, and social characteristics. As expected there is heterogeneity within coresidence/caregiving categories. Contrary to earlier findings, women in SG households did not have worse personal or household characteristics as compared to non-caregivers or other types of caregivers. In this population of grandmothers, prior primary responsibility, current level of caregiving, younger coresident grandchildren, and three or more generations in the home were associated with negative economic and socioenvironmental characteristics.

DISCUSSION

Using data from the Woodlawn Longitudinal Study, we found that in an inner city population of mature African American women the coresidence rate in a specific year, 27%, was about two to three times the rate for Black women found by Beck and Beck (1989) using a nationally representative sample of mature women (10 to 15%). The lifetime coresidence estimate, however, was comparable to that found by Beck and Beck (40 to 50%). The discrepancy in the specific year rate may be explained, in part, by the fact that the Woodlawn population contains many of the subgroups overrepresented in the recent caregiver population. In addition to overall rates of coresidence, we importantly found that many non-coresiding grandmothers take on similar levels of responsibility as coresident caregivers. Fifty-six percent of non-coresidental grandmothers were moderately to highly involved in parenting grandchildren. Thus many who are classified as non-caregivers in other studies could be non-residential caregivers. Furthermore, we learned that more than one third of those non-residential grandmothers had been primary caregivers at some earlier point in time. Thus, assuming that grandchildren were coresident at the time grandparents were primarily responsible, at least 55% of the Woodlawn grandmothers have ever coresided with one or more of their grandchildren. Additionally, we were able to specify that at least 46% of the Woodlawn sample identified themselves as having ever been primarily responsible for a grandchild for 1 year or more.

We also learned about variation within coresident households. The findings suggest that different characteristics or outcomes are likely associated with different pathways to household extension and caregiving. For example, two main grandmother types differentiated by current parenting level were found in three generation homes. Only 40% of women with moderate responsibility had ever assumed primary responsibility for grandchildren compared to 71% of women with high responsibility. It is likely that grandmothers in three-generation, high households were currently parenting the children without much help from the child's parent (if present) or the child's aunts or uncles. Thus, they were similar to the skip generation grandmother but had the added burden of assisting adult children in the home. This is posited as grandmothers in this household type seemed to be helping adult children who had economic and other social problems. On the other hand, grandmothers in three-generation, moderate households could more easily be characterized as helpers to single parents who were in the home perhaps to pool economic resources. The data bear out these assumptions, as both household types were the most impoverished, but the high responsibility group had the highest event scores, while the moderate group had lower event scores.

Another factor which may explain the differences in these two grandmother types is age. Three-generation, moderate grandmothers tended to be younger while three-generation, high grandmothers tended to be older. So, in addition to differences in life events, younger and older grandmothers may make decisions based on different notions of responsibility and cultural norms. Older grandmothers socialized at a different time may select into the stabilizer role, perhaps even caring for great-grandchildren, while younger grandmothers may decide to be less involved. In Woodlawn, the three-generation, high caregiving profile had the highest proportion of older grandmothers. Also compared to other profiles, they had lower marriage rates, less education, more welfare history, more children and grandchildren, the largest households, younger coresident grandchildren, and the highest proportion of two or more coresident grandchildren. Additionally, they were most likely to be living in poverty, more reliant on public assistance, and more affected by family life events.

Our findings also suggest the value of examining characteristics of past caregivers separately from current caregivers. Over 50% of grandmothers not living in coresident situations were moderately to highly involved in rearing grandchildren. Those who assumed primary roles at an earlier time and currently had low parenting involvement were worse off. They faced many of the same challenges faced by grandmothers in multigenerational households. These women may have selected out of the caregiving role upon reaching a certain economic or social threshold; or, upon completion of caregiving duties, they found themselves in poor economic and social situations. Additionally, continued responsibility among those who report past primary status may indicate that earlier primary role assumption places them at risk for future responsibility. Such vulnerability may extend from their present non-residential situation into a future residential situation; suggesting potential fluidity between the statuses of coresident and non-resident caregivers. Key questions for future research therefore are: Why do past primary caregivers, particularly those involved in low parenting, have poor outcomes? Which current caregiver group, if any, do they most closely resemble in terms of determinants and context of role assumption? Have they permanently or temporarily selected out of their primary caregiver roles? What are the implications for programs and policies which aim to prevent or mitigate poor outcomes in caregivers?

To summarize, using a broader definition of caregiver that considers functional, temporal, and residential aspects of the grandmother role allowed us to examine heterogeneity among African American grandmothers in the Woodlawn sample. We found that grandmothers were in coresident and non-coresident living situations and their level of participation in child rearing was not automatically determined by their residential context. Two grandmother types fared poorly on economic and social measures—(a) those in households of three or more generations who take on high levels of parenting and (b) those with a history of caregiving, who are not coresiding, but who take on low levels of parenting responsibility. Grandmothers who fared the best were those with fewer children and grandchildren, no history of primary caregiving, and fewer reports of life events affecting themselves or household members. These findings contribute to knowledge on heterogeneity within Black grandparenthood, the prevalence of lifetime exposure to caregiving, and the persistence of relationships between social risk factors, household structure, and grandmother role and functioning. The findings should be of interest to practitioners, policy makers, and family scholars concerned with diverse family structures and the social and economic factors that shape and/or impinge upon family members.

REFERENCES

Aneshensel, C. S. (1992). Social stress: Theory and research. *Annual Review of Sociology, 18*, 15–38.

Beck, R. W., & Beck, S. H. (1989). The incidence of extended households among middle-aged Black and White women: Estimates from a 15-year panel study. *Journal of Family Issues, 10,* 147–168.

Bryson, K. B., & Casper, L. M. (1999). Coresident grandparents and grandchildren. Census Bureau. (1999, May). P23–198, 1 p. Current Population Reports, Special Studies.

Burton, L. M., & Dilworth-Anderson, P. (1991). The intergenerational roles of aged Black Americans. *Marriage and Family Review, 16,* 311–330.

Caputo, R. K. (1999). Grandmothers and coresident grandchildren. *Families in Society: The Journal of Contemporary Human Services, 80*(2), 120–126.

Cherlin, A., & Furstenberg, F. (1986). *The new American grandparent: A place in the family, a life apart.* New York: Basic Books, Inc.

Fuller-Thomson, E., & Minkler, M. (2001). American grandparents providing extensive child care to their grandchildren: Prevalence and profile. *The Gerontologist, 41*(2), 201–209.

Fuller-Thomson, E., Minkler, M., & Driver, D. (1997). A profile of grandparents raising grandchildren in the United States. *The Gerontologist, 37*(3), 406–411.

Goldscheider, E., & DaVanzo, J. (1989). Pathways to independent living in early adulthood: Marriage, semi-autonomy and premarital residential independence. *Demography, 26*(4), 597–614.

Harden, R. L., Clark, R. L., & Maguire, K. (1997). Formal and informal kinship care (Executive summary). U.S. Department of Health and Human Services.

Hunter, A., & Ensminger, E. (1992). Diversity and fluidity in children's living arrangements: Family transitions in an urban Afro-American community. *Journal of Marriage and the Family, 54,* 418–426.

Hunter, A., & Taylor, R. J. (1998). Grandparenthood in African-American families. In M. E. Szinovacz (Ed.), *Handbook on grandparenthood* (pp. 70–86). Westport, CT: Greenwood Press.

King, R. B. (1999). Time spent in parenthood status among adults in the United States. *Demography, 36*(3), 377–385.

King, V., Russell, S. T., & Elder, G. H., Jr. (1998). Grandparenting in family systems: An ecological perspective. In M. E. Szinovacz (Ed.), *Handbook on grandparenthood* (pp. 53–69). Westport, CT: Greenwood Press.

Pearson, J., Hunter, A., Cook, J., Ialongo, N., & Kellam, S. (1997). Grandmother involvement in child caregiving in an urban community. *The Gerontologist, 17,* 650–657.

Pearson, J., Hunter, A., Ensminger, M., & Kellam, S. (1990). Black grandmothers in multigenerational households: Diversity in family structure and parenting involvement in the Woodlawn community. *Child Development, 61,* 434–442.

Pebley, A. R., & Rudkin, L. L. (1999). Grandparent's caring for grandchildren. *Journal of Family Issues, 20*(2), 218–242.

Szinovacz, M. E. (1998a). Grandparent research: Past, present, and future. In M. E. Szinovacz (Ed.), *Handbook on grandparenthood* (pp. 1–20). Westport, CT: Greenwood Press.

Szinovacz, M. E. (1998b). Grandparents today: Demographic profile. *The Gerontologist, 38*(1), 37–52.

Turner, R. J., & Lloyd, D. A. (1995). Lifetime traumas and mental health: The significance of cumulative adversity. *Journal of Health and Social Behavior, 36*(4), 360–376.

Whittington, L. A., & Peters, H. E. (1996). Economic incentives and residential independence. *Demography, 33*(1), 82–97.

CHAPTER 9

Grandmothers Raising Grandchildren: The Vulnerability of Advancing Age[*]

Catherine Chase Goodman

INTRODUCTION

The nature of family has shifted over the past 30 years. In 1970, families with two parents and children represented about two of five households (40.3%). By 2000, only 24.1% of all households were two-parent families with children (Fields & Casper, 2001). This change, driven primarily by increases in single-parent families, has been accompanied by aging of the population and increases in the numbers of grandparents raising grandchildren (custodial) or helping their single adult children raise their grandchildren (coparenting). Grandchildren living in grandparent-headed families have increased from 3.2% of all the children in 1970 to over

*This study was supported by grant RO1AG14977 from the National Institute on Aging and in part by a Scholarly and Creative Activity Award, California State University, Long Beach.

5% of all children in 2002 (Casper & Bryson, 1998; Fields, 2003). Although grandparents in these households are primarily middle aged, they show considerable age diversity: Of those assuming responsibility for their grandchildren, 28% were age 60 and over (Simmons & Dye, 2003). Thus, aging and some of the declines associated with advancing age have an important impact on the capacity of grandparents to provide for their grandchildren and on their psychological well-being as they confront this challenging task.

Grandparents raising grandchildren constitute an older adult population experiencing parenting demands "off-time," when expectations would be for empty nest, retirement, and greater leisure time. Comparisons of grandparents raising grandchildren to non-caregiving grandparents show grandparent caregivers to be more depressed (Fuller-Thomson & Minkler, 2000; Minkler, Fuller-Thomson, Miller, & Driver, 1997) and to have worse physical health (Solomon & Marx, 1998) than their non-caregiving peers. These findings suggest that the demands of caregiving and the circumstances surrounding assuming the role—crisis, ambiguity, and indeterminacy—have an overall negative impact. Thus while family relationships appear to increase in importance as people age (Lang, 2000; Pinquart & Sorensen, 2000) and religious involvement appears to provide a resource (Diener & Suh, 1998), the disruption of relationship that is characteristic of many grandparent-headed families may provide a particularly disadvantageous environment for aging.

This study addresses age diversity among grandmothers raising grandchildren when the grandparent is head of the household. Specifically, the study addresses the following questions among grandmother caregivers: (a) In what ways do different aspects of subjective well-being vary with age; (b) To what extent are well-being and age influenced by social loss characteristic of aging, such as widowhood and declines in health and income; (c) To what extent are the difficult circumstances of grandparent caregiving an increased threat as age increases and does religion provide a greater resource with increasing age?

Aging and Well-Being

Argyle (1999) reviewed studies in which age was related to well-being and found small increases in subjective well-being with older age groups (with a correlation of about .10). One large sample of 60,000 people across 43 nations found different results for different aspects of well-being: Specifically decreases with age were found for positive affect, while stability for women and decreases for men with age were found for negative affect (Diener & Suh, 1998). This study showed life satisfaction to have a significant upward trend for men and a slight decline for women through the '80s. Other studies of adulthood have found increased age to be related to decreased positive affect, whereas other aspects of well-being increased with age: Negative affect declined with age (Steverink, Westerhof, Bode, & Dittmann-Kohli, 2001) and life satisfaction increased with age (Chen, 2001; Steverink et al., 2001) when age losses, such as marital status, income, and health were controlled. A study focusing on persons of advanced age, (age 70 to 103) similarly found positive affect decreased and negative affect was constant. However, controlling for functional health, age was positively related to well-being—higher positive affect and lower negative affect (Kunzmann, Little, & Smith, 2000). Functional health, such as capacity to bath and dress, climb stairs, and carry groceries, was most directly related, rather than general health appraisals or comparison to other people. Thus it appears that health disabilities may suppress a positive association between well-being and age.

Positive aspects of aging have been identified which may contribute to well-being, such as wisdom (Ardelt, 1997), altruism (Lapierre, Bouffard, & Bastin, 1997), enhanced ability for management of relationships, and greater importance given to emotionally meaningful tasks (Cantor & Sanderson, 1999; Lang, 2001) and high quality relationships (Pinquart & Sorensen, 2000). Diener and Suh (1998) found religiosity increased with age, but the relationship between life satisfaction and religiosity did not change over the life course. Krause (2003), examining religious meaning in older adults, found that church attendance and private prayer were related to life satisfaction until the more influential factor, religious meaning, was considered. However, all of these indicators of religious involvement were related to optimism. Even when older people experience functional limitations, religious involvement is maintained over time (Kelley-Moore & Ferraro, 2001) suggesting consistent involvement for those who find religion to be a resource.

Vulnerability of Grandparent Caregivers

Grandparent caregivers may consider the tasks of providing for their grandchildren to be altruistic or meaningful; or they may see caregiving as a disruption of their personal proactive goals (Holahan & Chapman, 2002). Furthermore, disrupted relationships with adult children are tenuous and often unsupportive, leading to the term bonding ambiguity (Hirshorn, Van Meter, & Brown, 2000). Grandparents are particularly distressed when caring for children with behavioral problems (Hayslip, Shore, Henderson, & Lambert, 1998) and these problems may be result of parental child abuse or neglect. Family stresses, such as relationship strains often experienced by grandparent caregivers, have been shown to be related to lower well-being and health for women across the life span (Walen & Lachman, 2000). Therefore, older grandparent caregivers may find that health declines make parenting even more difficult. Furthermore, they express anxiety that they will not live long enough to provide for their grandchildren (Kelley, 1993). While grandparent caregivers often express satisfaction with their grandchildren, they also express burden and loss (Pruchno, 1999; Pruchno & McKenney, 2002).

METHOD

Sample and Data Collection

Subjects were 1,054 grandmothers raising grandchildren without a parent in the household (custodial, $n = 576$), or assisting their adult son or daughter and grandchildren by providing a home (coparenting, $n = 478$). The sample was recruited through grandchildren attending school in the Los Angeles Unified School District and through media announcements during 1998 through 2001. An attempt was made to recruit near equal numbers of African American, Latina, and White grandmothers. Children in 223 schools received notices in English and Spanish announcing the study. Interested grandmothers mailed in a tear-off or telephoned and were subsequently interviewed in their homes by ethnically and linguistically matched interviewers from the Survey Research Center at University of California, Los Angeles.

Measures

Grandmothers were the sole respondents and they described one grandchild, either the one from the targeted school or one selected randomly. Measures not already available in Spanish were translated by a bilingual mental health professional and reviewed by three bilingual persons of different nationalities (Mexican, Spanish, and Salvadoran).

Age Loss and Control Factors

Yearly per capita income, marital status, and health were factors that represented possible age losses. The Physical Functioning Subscale of the SF-36 was used as the most direct indicator of age disability (Kunzmann et al., 2000; Ware, 1993). This subscale addressed physical capacities, such as lifting, carrying, bending, climbing stairs, walking, and bathing. Coefficient alpha for this sample was .93. Grandmother's ethnicity (African American, Latina, and White) and recruitment method (school or media) were control variables to adjust for the quota sampling and different strategies of recruitment. The current presence of the parent in the household was also a control factor reflecting the grandmother's role as primary caregiver versus coparenting with an adult son or daughter.

Family Functioning Factors

The grandchild's behavior and the reasons grandmothers assumed care represent the unique challenges faced by grandparent caregivers. The grandchild's *behavior problems* were measured using by a 10-item Behavior Rating Index for Children (BRIC), with problems rated on a 5-point scale from 1 (rarely or never) to 5 (most or all of the time) (Stiffman, Orme, Evans, Feldman, & Keeney, 1984). Coefficient alpha in this sample was .78. Reasons the grandmother assumed care for the grandchild were described for her adult son or daughter: Reasons suggesting dysfunction were summed for a *parental dysfunction index* (drug use, alcohol use, child neglect, emotional/mental problem, and legal trouble; coefficient alpha = .76).

Religious Involvement

Religious involvement was assessed by a single item based on frequency of attendance at religious services or events, rated from 1 (never) to 7 (daily).

Grandmother Well-Being

The 20-item Positive and Negative Affect Scale (PANAS) was used to measure mood (Watson, Clark, & Tellegen, 1988) based on descriptive positive adjectives, such as "interested" or "strong," and negative adjectives, such as "distressed" or "hostile." Feelings over the past few weeks were described on a 5-point scale from 1 (very slightly or not at all) to 5 (extremely) and a Spanish version, the SPANAS, was developed through forward and back translations (Joiner, Sandín, Chorot, Lostao, & Marquina, 1997). Coefficient alpha for this sample was .87 for positive affect and .88 for negative affect. Life Satisfaction, a cognitive judgement of well-being, was measured using the Satisfaction With Life Scale (Diener, Emmons, Larson, & Griffin, 1985). Five items were rated on a 7-point scale, from 1 (strongly agree) to 7 (strongly disagree) and coefficient alpha was .84.

RESULTS

Age Phases

Table 9.1 shows bivariate relationships between age phases and factors used in subsequent analyses. Age is grouped here into three categories to provide a view of the ways in which age phases relate to age loss and control factors, indices of family functioning, religious involvement, and well-being. Age distribution was from 37 to 86 (mean = 56.8, sd = 8.51). Therefore, cut-off points for age phases approximate 1 standard deviation (younger 37 to 49; middle age 50 to 64; older 65 to 86). Marital status and functional health decreased with the grandmother's age, whereas income was highest in the middle-aged group. The proportion of African American and Latina grandmothers decreased with age, whereas the proportion of White grandmothers increased with age. There were no differences in school recruitment or whether the parent was living in the household by grandmother's age phase. There was a higher level of parental dysfunction among families with middle-aged grandmothers compared to families of younger grandmothers, although no differences were evident for the grandchild's behavior by grandmother's age. Similarly, religious involvement did not differ by grandmother's age phase groupings. Only negative affect showed any age phase difference in the well-being indicators, with the middle-aged grandmothers having higher negative affect than older grandmothers.

Predictors of Well-Being

Hierarchical multiple regression was used to examine age and well-being for each of the three dependent variables: positive affect, negative affect, and life satisfaction (see Table 9.2). A log linear transformation was used to improve the skew in the distribution of negative affect. Models were arranged to examine age as the main predictor (Model 1: age). Then age was examined with the additional impact of age loss and control factors (Model 2: physical functioning, per capita income, marital status, school recruitment, ethnicity, and parental presence in the household). Finally, family function factors and involvement in religious activities were added and tested for direct effects and interaction with age. To examine whether family functioning factors and religious involvement had a different impact on older versus younger grandparents, interaction terms were added to the regressions. These interaction terms were the cross product of age and each variable centered on its mean and they were subsequently graphed to show the direction of the interaction (Tabachnick & Fidell,

TABLE 9.1 Grandmother's Age by Demographic, Family, and Well-Being Factors

Variable		Younger ($n = 199$)	Middle Age ($n = 667$)	Older ($n = 188$)	Total ($n = 1,054$)	F or χ^2	df
Age Loss and Control Factors							
Marital status	%	52.3	42.4	34.6	42.9	12.50**	2, 1,054
Per capita income ($)[a]	M	7,510.4$_b$	9,099.5$_a$	8,277.5	8,652.9	5.41**	2, 1,051
	SD	6,106.2	6,299.1	6,081.1	6,250.8		
Poverty	%	30.2	22.2	25.0	24.2	5.38	2, 1,054
Physical	M	86.1$_a$	76.1$_{bc}$	68.9$_{bd}$	76.7	20.15***	2, 1,051
functioning	SD	22.0	27.5	29.6	27.4		
Ethnicity							
African American	%	37.2	33.6	31.4	33.9	21.61***	4, 1,054
Hispanic	%	42.7	33.1	27.7	34.0		
White	%	20.1	33.3	41.0	32.2		
School recruitment	%	65.3	60.6	69.1	63.0	5.20	2, 1,054
Parent presently at home	%	42.7	46.0	45.7	45.4	69	2, 1,054

(continued)

TABLE 9.1 (continued)

Variable		Younger (n = 199)	Middle Age (n = 667)	Older (n = 188)	Total (n = 1,054)	F or χ^2	df
Family Function and Religious Involvement							
Child's	M	23.5	24.6	22.1	23.9	1.95	2, 1,051
behavior BRIC	SD	14.7	15.5	15.9	15.5		
Parental	M	$.9_b$	1.3_a	1.1	1.2	3.96*	2, 1,051
dysfunction	SD	1.4	1.5	1.5	1.5		
Religious	M	4.4	4.4	4.6	4.4	1.32	2, 1,051
involvement	SD	1.7	1.7	1.8	1.7		
Grandmother's Well-Being							
Negative	M	17.2	17.7_a	16.3_b	17.3	3.23*	2, 1,051
affect	SD	6.4	7.3	6.2	6.9		
Positive	M	37.3	37.9	36.6	37.6	2.10	2, 1,051
affect	SD	8.1	8.0	8.2	8.1		
Life satisf-	M	24.0	24.6	25.6	24.7	2.33	2, 1,051
action	SD	7.3	7.5	7.2	7.4		

Note: Younger age = 37–49; middle age = 50–64; older = 65–86.
[a]Data on yearly income were collected in categories with intervals of $5,000, and midpoint used for dollar amount. Mean substitution based on results from more general income question.
*$p \leq .05$. **$p \leq .01$. ***$p \leq .001$. Subscripts denote significant ($p < .05$) differences using Bonferroni post hoc tests a > b; c > d

TABLE 9.2 Hierarchical Multiple Regressions for Grandmother Well-Being Indicators: Standardized Betas (N = 1054)

Characteristics	Positive Affect			Negative Affect[a]			Life Satisfaction		
	1	2	3	1	2	3	1	2	3
Age	-.02	-.00	-.02	-.06	-.12***	-.11***	.09**	.14***	.12***
Age Loss and Control Factors									
Per capita income		.08**	.08*		-.07*	-.05		.17***	.16***
Married		.02	.00		-.06*	-.05		.17***	.15***
Functional health		.21***	.19***		-.15***	-.12***		.12***	.09**
School recruitment		-.00	-.01		-.13***	-.10***		.14***	.12***
African American versus others		.17***	.13***		-.26***	-.22***		.10**	.03
Hispanic versus others		-.18***	-.22***		-.18***	-.13***		.20***	.14***
Parent present currently		-.04	-.05		-.10**	-.00		.07*	.00

(continued)

141

TABLE 9.2 (continued)

Characteristics	Positive Affect			Negative Affect[a]			Life Satisfaction		
	1	2	3	1	2	3	1	2	3
Family Function and Religious Involvement									
Parental dysfunction			-.00			.16***			-.11***
Behavior rating index for children			-.11***			.23***			-.17***
Religious involvement			.09**			-.01			.08**
Age X parental dysfunction			-.07*			-.06*			.04
Age X behavior rating index for children			.01			.00			-.03
Age X religious involvement			.01			.00			.06*
Model R²	.00	.15	.17	.00	.11	.20	.01	.13	.18
F	.50	22.69***	15.24***	3.62	16.49***	17.98***	7.62**	21.12***	17.38***
df	1, 1,052	8, 1,045	14, 1,039	1, 1,052	8, 1,045	14, 1,039	1, 1,052	8, 1,045	14, 1,039

Note: Dichotomous variables coded 1 = yes.
[a] A log linear transformation used to correct for positive skew.

142

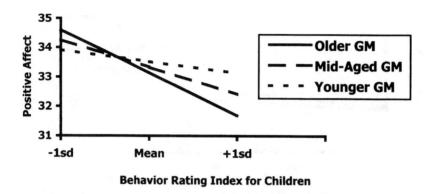

FIGURE 9.1 Interaction age by behavior rating index for children.

2001; Model 3: BRIC; parental dysfunction; religious involvement; and interaction age and BRIC, age and parental dysfunction, and age and religious involvement).

Positive Affect

Age was not related to positive affect in any of the three models. In Model 2, age loss factors were significantly positively related (income and functional health), although marital status was not related. Ethnicity was related, with African American grandmothers showing higher positive affect and Hispanic grandmothers showing lower positive affect. In Model 3, the index of child's behavior problems (BRIC) was negatively related to positive affect and religious involvement was positively related. The child's behavior problems interacted with age such that greater levels of behavior problems were related to decline in positive affect, with greater declines for older grandmothers than younger or middle-aged grandmothers (see Figure 9.1). It should be noted that the interaction was marginal: Although the Beta was significant for the interaction explanatory power was small. R^2 increase and the F change statistic were not significant when only interaction terms were added as a separate step (not shown: $R^2_{change} = .00$, $F (3, 1039) = 1.69$ $p = .17$).

Negative Affect

Age was not related to negative affect in Model 1. In Model 2, age became a negative predictor, showing negative affect to decrease with advancing age when age loss factors are controlled. Age loss factors (marital status,

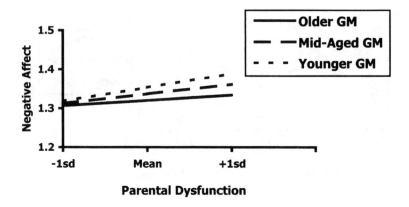

FIGURE 9.2   Instruction age by parental dysfunction.

income, and functional health) were all significant negative predictors, demonstrating that negative affect was higher when grandmothers were unmarried, low income, and disabled. Additionally control variables, ethnicity, school recruitment, and parental presence in the household were all negative predictors. Thus the parent's presence in the household was related to lower negative affect; African American and Latina grandmothers had lower negative affect than White grandmothers; and school recruitment was related to lower levels of negative affect. In Model 3, parental dysfunction and the child's behavior problems were both related to negative affect. One interaction showed significance: age by parental dysfunction (see Figure 9.2). Older grandmothers were less affected by the parent's dysfunction than other age groups. Once again, the interaction was marginal. Introducing only the interaction terms as a separate step (not shown) resulted in very small nonsignificant change in predictive power (R^2_{change} = .00, F (3, 1039) = 1.64, p = .18).

Life Satisfaction

Age was significantly related to life satisfaction, a relationship, which became stronger in Model 2 when age loss and control factors were added. All age loss and control factors were significantly and positively related to life satisfaction. Thus grandmothers who were married, higher income, and had better functional health were more satisfied with their lives. Similarly, African American and Latina grandmothers had higher life satisfaction than White grandmothers. Grandmothers recruited through schools and those living with the parent in the household had

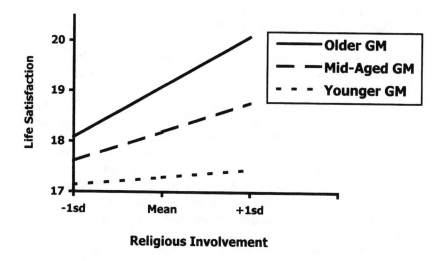

FIGURE 9.3   Interaction age by religious involvement.

higher life satisfaction. In Model 3, child's behavior problems and parental dysfunction were negatively related to life satisfaction and religious involvement was positively related. The interaction, age by religious involvement, was significant, showing a slightly stronger relationship between life satisfaction and religious involvement for older grandmothers (see Figure 9.3). Once again, the interaction was suggestive and marginal, with increase in explanatory power minimal if only interactions were added to all other factors (not shown: R^2_{change} = .01, F (3, 1039) = 1.97, p = .12).

DISCUSSION

In summary, consistent with studies of other older populations, this study has shown an increase in life satisfaction with age for grandmothers raising grandchildren. Well-being as seen in lower negative affect was also related to age when losses associated with age were controlled, such as being alone without a spouse, having lower income, and being disabled. These gains in well-being were not augmented when family functioning factors were controlled. Across most indicators, the circumstances often surrounding grandmother caregiving (parental dysfunction and children's behavior problems) were negatively related to well-being and religious participation was positively related to well-being. Although offering little explanatory power, interactions between age and family functioning factors suggests that older grandmother caregivers are more vulnerable to the grandchild's difficult behaviors but not parental dysfunction. Furthermore, interactions between age and religious involvement suggest that older grandmothers benefit more from their religious involvement than younger grandmothers.

It should be noted that it is impossible to disentangle age effects from cohort differences and selective mortality with this cross sectional design. Amongst older caregiving grandmothers, many may have given up caregiving because of declining health and advanced age. Additionally older grandmothers may have shared positive attitudes about caregiving resulting from characteristics of their generation. Another limitation is the age range of this sample, which does not include those of very advanced age and has a limited proportion over 75 (only 2.6%). Because of the limited number of old-old grandmothers little can be concluded about changes among old-old persons. Furthermore, interaction effects were not strongly explanatory, although they did offer suggestive results characteristic of older caregiving grandmothers.

Despite these limitations, results provide a positive view of aging for caregiving grandmothers. Like older persons who are not caregiving, those who are married, in good health, and who have a satisfactory income level have greater life satisfaction and lower negative affect as they age (Chen, 2001; Diener & Suh, 1998; Kunzmann et al., 2000; Steverink et al., 2001). Positive affect, similar to results of other studies (Diener & Suh, 1998; Steverink et al., 2001) did not show this age advantage. It may be that the vitality implied by self-description as "strong," "energetic," and "active" is not likely to increase with age.

In contrast, aging brings little or no gain for those who make up a large proportion of caregiving grandmothers—those that are single, low income, or have some health disability. Most (57%) of the grandmothers in the study were not married and therefore lacked the support that a husband might have provided. Among those in the study who were older (65 and over), more than 65% were unmarried compared with 47% unmarried women age 65 to 74 in the United States (Smith, 2003). The poverty rate among the 65 and over group for this sample was 25%. Nationally, the poverty rate among those 65 and over is 10.4% (Proctor & Dalaker, 2003), a rate that has been fairly stable since the mid-1990s. Thus, the disadvantages of low income and being unmarried were pervasive. In terms of health and disability, older grandmothers in the sample enjoyed a higher level of physical functioning compared to women aged 65 or over in the general U.S. population (68.9 mean compared to 61.9 mean for the U.S. general population on the SF-36; Ware, 1993). However, according to comparisons developed through the National Survey of Functional Health Status, of those scoring in the 60 to 69 range, 21% could not walk one block or more (Ware). Thus a subgroup of grandmothers are struggling to raise young children with a substantial level of functional disability.

There is also some indication that the daily stresses of children with behavioral problems are particularly difficult for older grandmothers. These day-to-day challenges deplete the grandmother's positive mood—her strength, enthusiasm, and activity level is felt more than by younger grandmothers. The results echo the statements of older grandmothers who describe the difficulties they have experienced with their grandchildren, "The patience I need . . . my age," or "When I can't take him to the park or out because of the heat or how I am feeling." On the other hand, older grandmothers also display strengths in dealing with the parent's difficult problems: Declines in negative mood related to the parent's dysfunction appeared to be less severe for older grandmothers than for younger or middle-aged grandmothers. The emphasis of older people on emotional regulation and generativity (Lang, 2001) may represent a refocusing on the needs of grandchildren over adult children. Additional strength appears to come from religious involvement amongst grandmothers: The interaction identified in this study suggested that older grandmothers are more benefited by their religious involvement than younger grandmothers. Furthermore, religious involvement was related to higher life satisfaction and positive affect amongst all caregiving grandmothers, supporting other studies that have found benefits from religious involvement (Diener & Suh, 1998; Krause, 2003).

Other results are suggestive regarding the parent's role in the household. The parent's presence in the household is related to higher well-being (lower negative affect and higher life satisfaction) until family functioning factors extract variance from parental dysfunction. These parental problems are more prevalent among custodial families (Goodman & Silverstein, 2002). However, physical presence or absence is not important per se—rather the parent's serious problems are important.

Implications for Practice

The current trend toward increases in grandparent caregivers would be likely to continue due to the greater availability of middle aged and older caregivers, particularly women (Meyer, 2001). However, this population of aging adults continues to show women living without a spouse, in poverty, and without labor force participation in higher proportions compared to men (Smith, 2003). These risk factors for poverty are particularly prominent for grandmothers raising their grandchildren, who face additional challenges when their adult children and grandchildren have serious problems. A beginning step was accomplished toward providing a service network for older caregivers when the Administration on Aging earmarked 10% of funds from the National Caregiver Support Act of 1999 (P. L. 106-501) to Area Agencies on Aging to develop programs for older (60 or over) relatives providing care to children. The formation of multigenerational households provides for grandchildren and assists the parent or compensates when parents are unable to parent their children: Expansion of service networks is essential to assist these at-risk caregivers.

REFERENCES

Ardelt, M. (1997). Wisdom and life satisfaction in old age. *Journal of Gerontology: Psychological Sciences, 52B*, P15–P27.

Argyle, M. (1999). Causes and correlates of happiness. In D. Kahneman, E. Diener, & N. Schwarz (Eds.), *Well-being: The foundations of hedonic psychology* (pp. 353–373). New York: Russell Sage.

Cantor, N., & Sanderson, C. A. (1999). Life task participation and well-being: The importance of taking part in daily life. In D. Kahneman, E. Diener, & N. Schwarz (Eds.), *Well-being: The foundations of hedonic psychology* (pp. 230–243). New York: Russell Sage.

Casper, L. M., & Bryson, K. R. (1998). *Co-resident grandparents and their grandchildren: Grandparent maintained families* (Population Division Working Paper No. 26). Washington, DC: U.S. Census Bureau.

Chen, C. (2001). Aging and life satisfaction. *Social Indicators Research, 54*, 57–79.

Diener, C., Emmons, R. A., Larson, R. J., & Griffin, S. (1985). The Satisfaction With Life Scale. *Journal of Personality Assessment, 49*, 71–75.

Diener, E., & Suh, M. E. (1998). Subjective well-being and age: An international analysis. In K. W. Schaie (Ed.), *Focus on emotion and adult development* (pp. 304–324). New York: Springer.

Fields, J. (2003). *Children's living arrangements and characteristics: March 2002* (Current Population Reports P20–547). Washington, DC: Bureau of the Census. Retrieved July 18, 2003, from http://www.census.gov/prod/2003pubs/p20-547.pdf

Fields, J., & Casper, L. M. (2001). *America's families and living arrangements: 2000 Current Population Reports* (P20–537). Washington, DC: U.S. Census Bureau, Retrieved March 24, 2003, from http://www.census.gov/prod/2001pubs/p20-537.pdf

Fuller-Thomson, E., & Minkler, M. (2000). The mental and physical health of grandmothers who are raising their grandchildren. *Journal of Mental Health and Aging, 6*(4), 311–323.

Goodman, C., & Silverstein, M. (2002). Grandmothers raising grandchildren: Family structure and well-being in culturally diverse families. *The Gerontologist, 42,* 676–689.

Hayslip, B., Jr., Shore, R. J., Henderson, C. E., & Lambert, P. L. (1998). Custodial grandparenting and the impact of grandchildren with problems on role satisfaction and role meaning. *Journal of Gerontology: Social Sciences, 53B,* S164–S173.

Hirshorn, B. A., Van Meter, M. J., & Brown, D. R. (2000). When grandparents raise grandchildren due to substance abuse: Responding to a uniquely destabilizing factor. In B. Hayslip Jr. & R. Goldberg-Glen (Eds.), *Grandparents raising grandchildren: Theoretical, empirical, and clinical perspectives* (pp. 269–288). New York: Springer.

Holahan, C. K., & Chapman, J. R. (2002). Longitudinal predictors of proactive goals and activity participation at age 80. *Journal of Gerontology: Psychological Sciences, 57B,* P418–P425.

Joiner, T. E., Sandín, B., Chorot, P., Lostao, L., & Marquina, G. (1997). Development and factor analytic validation of the SPANAS among women in Spain: (More) cross-cultural convergence in the structure of mood. *Journal of Personality Assessment, 68,* 600–615.

Kelley, S. J. (1993). Caregiver stress in grandparents raising grandchildren. *Journal of Nursing Scholarship, 25*(4), 331–337.

Kelley-Moore, J. A., & Ferraro, K. F. (2001). Functional limitations and religious service attendance in later life: Barrier and/or benefit mechanism? *Journal of Gerontology: Social Sciences, 56B,* S365–S373.

Krause, N. (2003). Religious meaning and subjective well-being in late life. *Journal of Gerontology: Social Sciences, 58B,* S160–S170.

Kunzmann, U., Little, T. D., & Smith, J. (2000). Is age-related stability of subjective well-being a paradox? Cross-sectional and longitudinal evidence from the Berlin Aging Study. *Psychology and Aging, 15,* 511–526.

Lang, F. R. (2000). Endings and continuity of social relationships: Maximizing intrinsic benefits within personal networks when feeling near to death? *Journal of Social and Personal Relationships, 17,* 157–184.

Lang, F. R. (2001). Regulation of social relationships in later adulthood. *Journal of Gerontology: Psychological Sciences, 56B,* P321–P326.

Lapierre, S., Bouffard, L., & Bastin, E. (1997). Personal goals and subjective well-being in later life. *International Journal of Aging and Human Development, 45,* 287–303.

Meyer, J. (2001). *Age: 2000* (Census 2000 Brief C2KBR/01-12). Washington, DC: U.S. Census Bureau. Retrieved December 31, 2003, from http://www.census.gov/prod/2001pubs/c2kbr01-12.pdf

Minkler, M., Fuller-Thomson, E., Miller, D., & Driver, D. (1997). Depression in grandparents raising grandchildren: Results of a national longitudinal study. *Archives of Family Medicine, 6,* 445–452.

Pearlin, L. I. (1993). The social contexts of stress. In L. Goldberger & S. Breznitz (Eds.), *Handbook of stress: Theoretical and clinical aspects* (2nd ed., pp. 303–315). New York: Free Press.

Pinquart, M., & Sorensen, S. (2000). Influences of socioeconomic status, social network, and competence on subjective well-being in later-life: A meta-analysis. *Psychology and Aging, 15,* 187–224.

Proctor, B. D., & Dalaker, J. (2003). *Poverty in the United States: 2002.* Washington, DC: U.S. Bureau of the Census. Retrieved February 28, 2004, from http://www.census.gov/prod/2003pubs/p60-222.pdf

Pruchno, R. (1999). Raising grandchildren: The experiences of Black and White grandmothers. *The Gerontologist, 39,* 209–221.

Pruchno, R. A., & McKenney, D. (2002). Psychological well-being of Black and White grandmothers raising grandchildren: Examination of a two-factor model. *Journal of Gerontology: Psychological Sciences, 57B,* P444–P452.

Simmons, T., & Dye, J. L. (2003). *Grandparents living with grandchildren: 2000.* Washington, DC: U.S. Census Bureau. Retrieved February 4, 2004, from www.census.gov/prod/2003pubs/c2kbr-31.pdf

Smith, D. (2003). *The older population in the United States: March 2002* (Current Population Reports P20-546). Washington, DC.: U.S. Census Bureau. Retrieved December 31, 2003, from http://www.census.gov/prod/2003pubs/p20-546.pdf

Solomon, J. C., & Marx, J. (1998). The grandparent grandchild caregiving gradient: Hours of caring for grandchildren and its relationship to grandparent health. *The Southwest Journal of Aging, 14*(2), 31–39.

Steverink, N., Westerhof, G. J., Bode, C., & Dittmann-Kohli, F. (2001). Personal experience of aging, individual resources, and subjective well-being. *Journal of Gerontology: Psychological Sciences, 56B,* P364–P373.

Stiffman, A. R., Orme, J. G., Evans, D. A., Feldman, R. A., & Keeney, P. A. (1984). A brief measure of children's behavior problems: The Behavior Rating Index for Children. *Measurement and Evaluation in Counseling and Development, 17,* 83–90.

Tabachnick, B. G., & Fidell, L. S. (2001). *Using multivariate statistics* (4th ed.). Boston: Allyn & Bacon.

U.S. Census Bureau. (2001). *Census 2000 PHC-T-17. Multigenerational households for the United States, states, and for Puerto Rico: 2000.* Washington, DC: U.S. Census Bureau. Retrieved December 31, 2003, from http://www.census.gov/population/cen2000/phc-t17.pdf

Walen, H. R., & Lachman, M. E. (2000). Social support and strain from partner, family, and friends: Costs and benefits for men and women in adulthood. *Journal of Social and Personal Relationships, 17,* 5–30.

Ware, J. E., Jr. (1993). *SF-36 health survey: Manual and interpretation guide.* Boston: The Health Institute, New England Medical Center.

Watson, D., Clark, L. A., & Tellegen, A. (1988). Development and validation of brief measures of positive and negative affect: The PANAS Scales. *Journal of Personality and Social Psychology, 54,* 1063–1070.

CHAPTER 10

Gender Differences Among Custodial Grandparents

Bert Hayslip Jr., Patricia L. Kaminiski,
and Kristie L. Earnheart

Marriage and parenthood are described as "turning points," shaping the life course for men and women; in this context, Riley, Kahn, and Foner (1994) discuss "counterpoints"—life transitions persons experience whose occurrence depends upon the behavior of others rather than that of oneself, often associated with negative life events such as the illness or death of a spouse. Custodial grandparenting clearly qualifies as a counterpoint in this respect, as the assumption of the parenting role by middle-aged and older persons depends upon the actions of a son or daughter (in-law). That is, an adult child's divorce, unemployment, child abuse, drug abuse, incarceration, or death is what typically leads grandparents to assume parental responsibility for their grandchild (Fuller-Thomson & Minkler, 2000; Hirshorn, Van Meter, & Brown, 2000).

The number of grandparents raising grandchildren has increased over the last decade (Simmons & Dye, 2003). In 2000, 5.7 million grandparents lived with their grandchildren. Moreover, 2.4 million of such persons reported raising their grandchildren on a full-time basis, often without an adult parent's presence (Simmons & Dye). Such figures also indicate that the majority (64%) of custodial grandparents are women.

This is especially the case for African American custodial grandparents (see Simmons & Dye). In light of these facts, it is not surprising that nearly all of the published research on grandparents raising grandchildren is based on grandmothers.

As most custodial grandparenting research is based on women, little is known regarding the impact of grandparent caregiving on men. There is reason to believe that gender differences in the experience of custodial grandparenting would exist. First, older men are less likely than older women to have had as many and varied caregiving experiences across their lifetimes. For example, women are more likely than men to have cared for an ill spouse (Moen, 2001), performed the majority of child care tasks while raising children together (Pleck, 1997; Silverstein, 1996), and been in the caregiving role for other family members and friends (Moen, 2001; Moen, Robison, & Fields, 1994). Second, research with traditional families has shown gender to be a key variable when studying parents' behaviors and experiences (see Cowan, Cowan, & Kerig, 1993). For example, the gender differences reported in two recent studies (i.e., Lahner & Hayslip, 2003; Perez-Albeniz & de Paul, 2004) highlight the particular importance of considering parent gender when attempting to understand parenting stress.

Thus, the purpose of this chapter is to explore gender differences in custodial grandparenting, on the assumption that what is known about custodial grandmothers may not be accurate for grandfathers who have assumed custodial responsibility for their grandchildren. In particular, we will explore gender as it relates to grandparents' (a) perceptions of the custodial role and its impact, (b) experiences of parenting stress, (c) levels of social support, (d) parental efficacy, and (e) parenting attitudes.

METHOD

Samples

Data from five separate studies of custodial grandparenting collected over a 10-year period were analyzed with respect to gender differences in the experience of raising a grandchild in middle age and later life. Study 1 involved 102 custodial grandparents, 21 of whom were males (see Hayslip, Shore, Henderson, & Lambert, 1998); Study 2 involved 52 such grandparents, 12 of whom were males (see Emick & Hayslip, 1999); Study 3 consisted of 38 grandparent caregivers, 8 of whom were males (see Hayslip, 2003); and Study 4 consisted of 36 grandparent caregivers, 6 of whom were males (see Kaminski & Hayslip, 2004). Study 5 data was taken from the 1992 Wave of the HRS (Health and Retirement Study, 2002). Participants, age 51 to 61, consisted of 45 married women, 45 single women, 45 married men and 45 single men. In Study 5, it is important to note that there were no married men who reported caring for their grandchildren on a full-time basis.

Measures

Across Studies 1 to 4, each grandparent caregiver completed several self-report measures assessing numerous dimensions of the experience of caregiving. In most cases, such measures were identical, while in a few cases (e.g., parenting attitudes) such measures were study-specific (see below).

Perceptions of the Custodial Role and Its Impact

A number of self-report instruments were combined to form one question-naire to assess various aspects of grandparents' perceptions of their custo-dial role and its impact. Each of these self-report scales and ratings have been successfully utilized in previous custodial grandparenting research by the first author (Emick & Hayslip, 1999; Hayslip & Shore, 2000; Hayslip et al., 1998; Shore & Hayslip, 1994) to differentiate custodial grandparents by the extent of problems in their grandchildren, explore the determinants of well-being and role satisfaction in grandparent caregivers, and examine relationships to mental health service attitudes in such per-sons. Nearly all of the measures possess more than adequate reliability (see Emick & Hayslip, 1999; Hayslip et al., 1998). Additional information about each scale, whose use varied across samples (see Tables 10.1 to 10.4), is provided below.

Feelings Regarding Role Assumption (10 items) assessed the grand-parent's positive/negative attitude toward the resumption of the parental role (Emick & Hayslip, 1999). Examples of items are feelings of guilt over not having been a good parent, anger at having to parent again, and being able to make up for past mistakes. Higher scores indexed more positive overall attitudes (see Hayslip, 2003).

Satisfaction with Grandparenting (Thomas, 1988) was assessed with 15 Likert-type questions such as "life has more meaning for me because of my grandchild," "sometimes it is hard to say I love my grandchild." Its alpha coefficient is .79 (Thomas, 1988).

Psychological Distress/Depression (Center for Epidemiologic Studies Depression Scale-CES-D) (Radloff, 1977) was assessed via a 20-item self-

TABLE 10.1 Study 1 ($N = 102$, $F = 81$, $M = 21$)

	GM[a]		GF[b]	
	Adj M[c]	SD	Adj M	SD
GP Meaning[d]	88.63	26.53	96.92	20.91
P affect[e]	46.50	9.03	39.18	10.99
N affect[f]	25.42	8.65	29.14	10.94
WB[g]	42.99	8.12	40.50	7.66
GP sat[h]	50.92	7.10	50.61	9.59

[a]Grandmothers. [b]Grandfathers. [c]Age, health, and education as covariates. [d]Grandparental role meaning. [e]Positive affect. [f]Negative affect. [g]Well-being. [h]Grandparent role satisfaction.

TABLE 10.2 Study 2 ($N = 52$, $F = 40$, $M = 12$)

	GM[a]		GF[b]	
	Adj M[c]	SD	Adj M	SD
GP Meaning	95.71	15.24	92.97	20.52
P affect	43.94	5.94	43.07	6.88
N affect	34.25	5.86	34.52	6.30
CESD[d]	29.04	8.50	36.07	16.38
WB[e]	50.56	12.24	42.82	13.64
GP sat	57.18	7.10	54.18	50.43
Life disrupt[f]	54.14	15.12	54.67	15.86
Support[g]	19.09	13.11	9.86	9.57
PSI[h]	76.22	22.50	77.63	38.20

[a]Grandmothers. [b]Grandfathers. [c]Age, health, and education as covariates. [d]Depression. [e]Well-being. [f]Life disruption. [g]Social support. [h]Parental Stress Index.

report scale designed to measure current level of depressive symptomatology with emphasis on depressed mood. Participants were asked to endorse the response that best described how often they had felt a particular way in the past week. Questions were answered on a four-point Likert-type scale [rarely or none of the time (less than once a day) to most or all of the time (five to seven days)]. The scale has exhibited high internal consistency (alpha = .85), adequate test-retest stability (correlations range from .45 to .70), exceptional concurrent validity with clinical and self-

TABLE 10.3   Study 3 ($N = 38$, $F = 30$, $M = 8$)

	GM[a]		GF[b]	
	Adj M[c]	SD	Adj M	SD
Feeling[d]	31.02	5.73	36.77	5.03
PSI	76.33	26.28	72.87	15.41
GP sat	60.61	7.82	57.10	7.30
P affect	40.25	5.56	37.77	2.94
N affect	32.77	4.77	33.31	5.75
Par strain	27.26	6.93	30.24	7.94
Life disrupt	54.22	17.91	55.20	12.18
CESD	38.64	6.97	34.43	3.83
Par Eff[e]	320.13	63.25	271.44	61.49

[a]Grandmothers. [b]Grandfathers. [c]Age, health, and education as covariates. [d]Feelings about role assumption. [e]Situational parental efficacy.

TABLE 10.4   Study 4 ($N = 36$, $F = 30$, $M = 6$)

	GM[a]		GF[b]	
	Adj M[c]	SD	Adj M	SD
PSI	79.80	23.02	78.83	20.61
AAPI inapp expectations	21.13	4.32	20.00	1.78
AAPI role reversal	26.16	4.16	21.83	1.94
AAPI power independence	20.81	1.91	19.33	1.36
AAPI empathy	40.46	4.23	35.83	2.48
AAPI corporal punishment	37.10	5.02	36.00	3.58
Parental efficacy[d]	37.56	7.23	36.16	3.06
Financial strain	7.40	3.09	5.16	1.16
Life Disruption	55.36	18.53	44.00	15.65
PSI	79.80	23.02	78.83	20.61

[a]Grandmothers. [b]Grandfathers. [c]Age and education as covariates. [d]Generalized parental efficacy.

report criteria, and substantial evidence of construct validity (see Radloff, 1977).

Participants also completed the Positive and Negative Affect Index, assessing aspects of one's perceptions of the relationship with the grandchild (i.e., extent of mutual trust, respect and understanding, affection for the grandchild versus negative feelings about irritating behaviors of the grandchild) (Bence & Thomas, 1988). The Positive Affect Index asks grandparents to describe the extent of mutual understanding, trust, fairness, respect, and affection for the grandchild. In contrast, the Negative Affect Index measures the extent to which the grandparents feel negatively toward irritating behaviors of the grandchild. Two single questions each asked the respondent to rate the quality of the relationship with the grandchild (very negative to very positive) and the satisfaction with this relationship (very unsatisfied to very satisfied).

Parental and Financial Role Strain were derived from the Structure of Coping Scale (Pearlin & Schooler, 1978), and used to identify potential strains in participants' roles as parents and as financial managers, as well as to identify emotional stress experienced by participants connected to these roles.

Psychological Well-Being (Liang, 1985) was assessed via a 15-item self-report scale that was designed to measure respondents' feelings about their lives. The scale integrates items from the Bradburn Affect Balance Scale (Bradburn, 1969) and the Life Satisfaction Index A (Neugarten, Havighurst, & Tobin, 1961). The Liang scale allows for the assessment of positive and negative affect (transitory affective components), happiness (long-term affective component), and congruence (long-term cognitive component). Inclusion of items of a long-term nature is intended to diminish potential distortion of results due to the consequences of transient circumstances.

The meaning of grandparenthood was evaluated with Likert-type items from the Thomas (1988) questionnaire such as "I value the fact that my grandchild confides in me" and "I value being able to teach things to my grandchild." Subscales can be derived according to Kivnick's (1982) five dimensions of meaning pertaining to grandparenthood (i.e., Centrality, Valued Elder, Immortality through Clan, Reinvolvement with Past, and Indulgence). Reported coefficient alphas range from .68 (Indulgence) to .90 (Centrality) (Kivnick, 1982). For our purposes, total scores were used, reflecting the single factor identified by Hayslip, Henderson, and Shore (2003).

To assess Life Disruption as a function of assuming the parental role, grandparents were also asked to indicate the extent to which, in the context of the extent of care they provided their grandchild, they were satisfied with a variety of aspects of their lives (e.g., "doing things for fun and recreation," "having my own privacy," "the need to alter routines and plans," "feeling physically tired") (see Jendrek, 1994). These items tap the extent to which a variety of aspects of one's life have been disrupted by child care responsibilities (Jendrek, 1994). Life Disruption total scores were used here. Grandparents also made single ratings of the quality of and satisfaction with their relationship with their grandchild (Emick & Hayslip, 1999).

Parenting Stress

Stress associated with the parental role was assessed with the Parenting Stress Index/Short Form (PSI/SF) (Abidin, 1990), a 36-item self-report measure consisting of three subscales: the Parental Distress Factor, the Parent-Child Dysfunctional Interaction Factor, and the Difficult Child Factor. The Parental Distress Factor measures parents' expressions of burden and distress both related to parenting and more generally; the Parent-Child Dysfunctional Interaction Factor evaluates whether the parent derives satisfaction from interactions with the child and whether the child meets parental expectations; and the Difficult Child Factor measures the child's ability to self-regulate. However, the PSI Total Stress scores were used here. The PSI/SF demonstrates high internal consistency (alpha = .91), high test-retest stability ($r = .84$), adequate construct, discriminant and predictive validity, acceptable concurrent validity with clinical and self-report criteria, and acceptable cross-cultural validity (Abidin, 1990). All PSI/SF items were reframed to apply to "my grandchild." That is, custodial grandparents completed the PSI/SF as it related to their newly acquired roles as the grandchild's functional parent.

Social Support

A measure of overall social support (see Emick & Hayslip, 1999; Hayslip et al., 1998) was used to reflect both instrumental and emotional support provided by the adult child, other family, and friends. This 33-item scale assessing the extent of such support possessed an alpha of .82.

Parental Efficacy

To measure Parental Efficacy, grandparents rated the extent of confidence they had in their ability to manage the child's behavior in a variety of situations (e.g., at home, in a store, in the presence of company) reflecting several underlying dimensions (suitability, communication, discipline) (Bachicha, 1985, 1997). This scale reflected grandparents' self-confidence regarding situation-specific time management skills, sensitivity to child's feelings, handle situations when a mistake has been made, ability to solve problems with the child, ability to perform one's duties as a parent and spouse, and ability to take credit to one's own and the child's good and bad behavior (Bachicha, 1997). An additional 9-item scale (see Bachicha, 1997) of generalized parental efficacy was employed to assess the grand-parent's perceptions of their ability as a parent to solve problems and understand the grandchild. These scales were unique to Studies 3 and 4.

Parenting Attitudes

The Adult-Adolescent Parenting Inventory-2 (AAPI-2; Bavolek & Keene, 1999) was unique to Study 4. The AAPI-2 is so named because it can be used to assess the parenting attitudes of both adolescent and adult parents. In our case it was adapted to measure the parenting attitudes of custodial grandparents. Attitudes assessed reflect five dimensions of risk of poor parenting: (a) Belief in the Value and Use of Corporal Punishment as Discipline, (b) Lack of Empathy toward the Child's Needs, (c) Suppression of Children's Power and Independence, (d) Reversal of Parent-child Role Responsibilities, and (e) Inappropriate Expectations of Children. Scale names are "backward" in that higher scores indicate *less* risk for poor parenting. Alpha coefficients for each scale range from .71 to .82 (Bavolek & Keene, 1999).

Variables Unique to Study 5 (the HRS Data Set)

For the HRS data set, measures included items from Section 0: Demographics; Section B: Health Status; Section E: Family Structure and Transfers; and Section N: Income, of the HRS Wave 1 Interview. They include questions about activities of daily living, depressive symptoms, time spent caring for grandchildren, contact with adult child, perceived social support, education, and income. Items that asked about the ability to perform daily tasks were used to create a measure of Activities of Daily Living. The items were further separated to form two distinct scales: (a) Independent Activities of Daily Living (IADLs) (8 items) and (b) Activities of Daily Living (ADLs) (8 items). IADLs refer to everyday activities such as walking around the block, grocery shopping, and so forth, and ADLs refer to more basic activities such as grooming and toileting. Higher scores indicated higher levels of functioning; alpha reliability for the ADL measure was .80 and for the IADL measure was .86.

Fourteen items used to measure depressive symptoms were taken from the shortened form of the CES-D (Center for Epidemiological Studies Depression Scale), where higher scores indicated higher levels of depressive symptoms. Alpha reliability for this measure was .72.

Total perceived social support included seven items from the interview that described general social support. The participant was asked about satisfaction with different areas of their social support system related to family, friends, and neighbors. Alpha internal reliability for this created measure was .60.

Education was measured using an item that asked the highest grade level of the individual. Income was measured by asking the amount of income earned in the past year from salary, wages, tips, Social Security, pension, annuities, and so forth, and a total income variable was calculated by summing the income received for each area. One item was used to measure the number of hours spent caring for grandchildren over the last year. Self-rated health was measured along a 4-point continuum, ranging from excellent to poor, with higher scores indexing better health.

RESULTS

Study 1 yielded no gender differences in role satisfaction, role meaning, and positive affect when controlling for age, education, and health, but males expressed somewhat less well-being (F 1,97 = 2.89, $p < .09$) and somewhat more negative affect (F 1,97 = 2.87, $p < .09$). For the most part however, gender differences in Study 1 were minimal. Similar analyses of Study 2 data suggested that males were more depressed (F 1,39 = 4.68, $p < .05$) and reported less social support (F 1,39 = 4.41, $p < .05$). There was also a nonsignificant but notable gender difference on well being (F 1,39 = 3.17, $p < .08$), with men having lower scores. Analyses of Study 3 data indicated that while males felt more positive about assuming the custodial role (F 1,28 = 4.12, $p < .05$), they still reported somewhat less parental efficacy (F 1,28 = 3.00, $p < .09$). Study 4 analyses indicted that males' AAPI-2 Role Reversal (F 1,31 = 8.78, $p < .05$) and Empathy (F 1,31= 4.55, $p < .05$) scores were lower (i.e., more problematic) than those of females. In addition, in the absence of controls for age and education, males reported less financial strain (F 1,31 = 9.00, $p < .01$). Tables 1 to 4 summarize the comparisons across gender for each of the four samples.

In Study 5, a series of ANCOVAs were conducted to determine if there was a significant difference in hours spent caring for grandchildren over the last year, IADLs, ADLs, depressive symptoms, and social support between each of above four sets of custodial grandparent pairs. Income, health, and education were included as covariates. For married women and married men, results suggested differences between males and females in ADLs, $F 1,91 = 5.10$, $p < .03$ (where men had higher scores), and in hours spent caring for the grandchild, $F 1,91 = 12.66$, $p < .01$ (favoring women). For married men versus single women, similar differences ($p < .01$) were found for hours spent in caregiving, but no other differences were obtained. For single men versus married women, no differences existed regarding hours spent caring for the grandchild, but women tended to report greater IADLs ($p < .09$). For single men versus single women, the latter spent more hours in caring for a grandchild, $F 1,85 = 4.50$, $p < .04$, had higher IADLs, $F 1,85 = 12.80$, $p < .01$, while men experienced somewhat more depression, $F 1,85 = 3.53$, $p < .06$ (see Table 10.5). Except when single men were compared to married women, where such men reported less social support, $F 1,85 = 4.90$, $p < .03$, there were no differences in social support among any of the four groups broken down by gender and marital status.

DISCUSSION

Based on these five studies, our findings suggest that there are likely some gender differences among custodial grandparents. A phenomenon that is clearly deserving of additional study is our finding in Study 2 that custodial grandfathers endorsed more symptoms of depression and lower levels of social support than did custodial grandmothers. While the sample of men in Study 2 was small, the merit of these findings is strengthened by similar results among the men in Study 1 and the single male caregivers in Study 5. Specifically, the men in Study 1 tended to report lower well-being and higher rates of negative affect as compared to their wives. Single custodial grandfathers in Study 5 experienced somewhat more depression and reported less social support than their female counterparts. Compared to their female counterparts, grandfathers in Study 5 also reported more difficulties with self-care.

In addition, the men caring for grandchildren in Study 3 felt less efficacious as parents, a self-assessment that may have validity given the poorer parenting attitudes expressed by grandfathers in Study 4. Specifically, as compared to custodial grandmothers, custodial grandfathers were less able to empathize with their grandchildren's needs and more apt to turn to them to get their own needs met (e.g., children should comfort a parent figure after a hard day's work).

These findings should be considered exploratory, as to date, grandfather caregivers have yet to be studied systematically, if at all, in the

TABLE 10.5 Study 5

| | Married | | | | | | Single | | | | | |
| | GF[a] ($n = 45$) | | GM[b] ($n = 45$) | | GF[c] ($n = 45$) | | GM[d] ($n = 45$) | |
	Adj. M	SD	Adj. M	SD	Adj. M	SD	Adj. M	SD
Hours[c]	50.22	156.24	705.71	981.17	477.93	590.74	922.96	1,093.96
IADL[d]	1.82	.80	1.65	.60	1.53	.50	2.10	.80
ADL[d]	1.20	.45	1.03	.40	1.05	.14	1.18	.29
CESD[d]	3.30	.51	3.43	.29	3.37	.42	3.13	.56
Support[d]	1.85	.82	1.67	.78	1.68	.49	1.68	.77

[a]Grandmothers. [b]Grandfathers. [c]Hours spent caregiving over the past year. [d]Figures represent averages, divided by the number of items in each scale.

custodial grandparenting literature. Moreover, what factors might explain the gender differences reported here remain unclear. It is also possible that our results reflect the selective (i.e., negatively biased) nature of grandfathers who volunteered for the respective research projects, or who were still alive long enough to experience the resumption of the caregiving role for their grandchildren later in life.

Alternatively, our results might be indicative of the manner in which the current cohort of older men was socialized. That is, physical and emotional caregiving roles have not been central in the lives of men in this cohort. As fathers their responsibilities were primarily in the realms of provider and disciplinarian. In addition to the lack of practice and knowledge related to caregiving that results from traditional gender roles, exchange theory would predict that grandchildren would be more oriented toward their grandmothers than their grandfathers due to feelings of indebtedness to them as a function of earlier caregiving experiences (Spitze & Ward, 1998). It may be that, for all these reasons, when asked to assume either full-time or secondary responsibility for their grandchildren, men are likely to be at a disadvantage compared to women. Not only may building a healthy relationship with a grandchild be more difficult for men, but custodial grandfathers may also be or feel ill prepared to do so. It is not surprising then, that older men hold attitudes that reveal some difficulty understanding the physical and emotional needs of their grandchildren. Moreover, when compared to custodial grandmothers, custodial grandfathers express less confidence in themselves as parents. It is reasonable that these real or perceived deficits, especially when coupled with inadequate social support, would put custodial grandfathers at risk for psychosocial consequences such as depression and poor self-care.

Another reason why the transition from grandparent to custodial grandparent may differentially affect men and women has to do with the meaning that each gender assigns to the traditional grandparent role. There is some evidence to suggest that men perceive the grandfather role as an outlet for their need to express themselves emotionally later in life (Neugarten & Weinstein, 1964; Thomas, 1989, 1995). For example, grandfathers take particular pleasure in indulging grandchildren (Thomas, 1989, 1995). Thus, being "counterpointed" back to the disciplinarian role may represent a significant loss for custodial grandfathers.

In interpreting the generally negative impact of custodial grandparenting on men in our samples, it is unclear regarding how involved men in Studies 1 through 4 were in the rearing of their grandchildren, though Study 5 results clearly suggest that women do assume the bulk of such responsibilities, especially with regard to their husbands. As secondary caregivers also experience role-related stress in raising their grandchildren (Goldberg-Glen & Sands, 2000), however, it would not be surprising to observe that men, even if they are not assuming the bulk of the child care responsibilities, would experience some distress in doing so. Consistent with this hypothesis, the single men in Study 5 were both more involved in caregiving and significantly more depressed than single women. Furthermore, and analogous to gender differences among parents, both married and single grandfathers performed significantly fewer hours of child care compared to married and single grandmothers.

It is also important to note that, despite devoting fewer hours to child care overall, custodial grandfathers scored similarly to custodial grandmothers on measures of role strain, life disruption, and parenting stress. Clearly, these data reveal the extent to which grandfathers, who have been referred to as "the forgotten men" of the family (see Baranowski, 1990) do indeed experience many of the negative consequences to their emotional and physical health that have been associated with custodial grandmothers. Once again, what we know about the demands of caregiving on grandmothers may be an underestimate of such demands on grandfathers. Moreover, men may be especially vulnerable to social isolation, depression, and both skill-related and attitudinal deficits regarding child rearing. Practitioners, therefore, may need to pay special attention to identifying such men (especially if they are single) and facilitate the provision of both formal (programmatic) and informal (interpersonal) social support, education about self-care, respite from child care, and parent education.

While our data represent the first attempt to describe custodial grandfathers and seem to have implications for their emotional, physical, and parental functioning, it should be made clear that in some cases, small numbers of males were studied, undermining the utility of multivariate analysis as well as statistical power. Moreover, dependent variables were not identical across data sets. Nevertheless, these findings serve as a baseline against which to understand the relative demands on custodial grandmothers and grandfathers, and have important implications for both grandparent caregivers and the grandchildren they are raising.

REFERENCES

Abidin, R. R. (1990). *Parenting stress index* (3rd ed.). Charlottesville, VA: Pediatric Psychology Press.

Bachicha, D. (1985). *The parental self-efficacy scale and its relationship to maternal variables in a triadic model for parent training.* New Mexico: Unpublished master's thesis, New Mexico Highland University.

Bachicha, D. (1997). *A validation study of the parental self-efficacy scale*. New Mexico: Unpublished doctoral dissertation, University of New Mexico.

Baranowski, M. D. (1990). The grandfather-grandchild relationships: Meaning and exchange. *Family Perspective, 24,* 201–215.

Bavolek, S. J., & Keene, R. G. (1999). *Adult-adolescent parenting inventory: Administration and development handbook*. Park City, UT: Family Development Resources, Inc.

Bence, S. L., & Thomas, J. L. (1988, November). *Grandparent-parent relationships as predictors of grandparent-grandchild relationships*. Paper presented at the Annual Scientific Meeting of the Gerontological Society of America, San Francisco.

Bradburn, N. M. (1969). *The structure of psychological well-being*. Chicago: Aldine.

Cowan, P. A., Cowan, C. P., & Kerig, P. K. (1993). Mothers, fathers, sons, and daughters: Gender differences in family formation and parenting style. In P. A. Cowan & D. Field et al. (Eds.), *Family, self, and society: Toward a new agenda for family research* (pp. 165–195). Hillsdale, NJ: Erlbaum.

Emick, M., & Hayslip, B. (1996). Custodial grandparenting: New roles for middle aged and older adults. *International Journal of Aging and Human Development, 43,* 135–154.

Emick, M., & Hayslip, B. (1999). Custodial grandparenting: Stresses, coping skills and relationships with grandchildren. *International Journal of Aging and Human Development, 48,* 35–62.

Fuller-Thomson, E., & Minkler, M. (2000). The mental and physical health of grandmothers who are raising their grandchildren. *Journal of Mental Health and Aging, 6,* 311–323.

Goldberg-Glen, R., & Sands, R. (2000). Primary and secondary caregiving grandparents: How different are they? In B. Hayslip & R. S. Goldberg-Glen (Eds.), *Grandparents raising grandchildren: Theoretical, empirical, and clinical perspectives* (pp. 161–180). New York: Springer.

Hayslip, B. (2003). The impact of a psychosocial intervention on parental efficacy, grandchild relationship quality, and well-being among grandparents raising grandchildren. In B. Hayslip & J. Hicks Patrick (Eds.), *Working with custodial grandparents* (pp. 163–178). New York: Springer.

Hayslip, B., Henderson, C., & Shore, R. J. (2003). The structure of grandparental role meaning. *Journal of Adult Development, 10,* 1–11.

Hayslip, B., & Shore, R. J. (2000). Custodial grandparenting and mental health. *Journal of Mental Health and Aging, 6,* 367–384.

Hayslip, B., Shore, R. J., Henderson, C., & Lambert, P. (1998). Custodial grandparenting and grandchildren with problems: Their impact on role satisfaction and role meaning. *Journal of Gerontology: Social Sciences, 53B,* S164–S174.

Health and Retirement Study (HRS) (2002). *Documentation Report 2002*. Ann Arbor: University of Michigan.

Hirshorn, B., Van Meter, J. V., & Brown, D. R. (2000). When grandparents raise grandchildren due to substance abuse: Responding to a uniquely destabilizing factor. In B. Hayslip & R. Goldberg-Glen (Eds.), *Grandparents raising grand-*

children: Theoretical, empirical, and clinical perspectives (pp. 269–288). New York: Springer.

Jendrek, M. (1994). Grandparents who parent their grandchildren: Circumstances and decisions. *The Gerontologist, 34,* 202–216.

Kaminski, P., & Hayslip, B. (2004, August). *Parenting attitudes of custodial grandparents.* Paper presented at the Annual Convention of the American Psychological Association. Honolulu, Hawaii.

Kivnick, H. G. (1982). Grandparenthood: An overview of meaning and mental health. *The Gerontologist, 22,* 59–66.

Lahner, J. M., & Hayslip, B. (2003). Gender differences in parental reactions to the birth of a premature low birth weight infant. *Journal of Prenatal & Perinatal Psychology & Health, 18,* 71–88.

Liang, J. (1985). A structural integration of the Affect Balance Scale and the Life Satisfaction Index A. *Journal of Gerontology, 40,* 552–561.

Moen, P. (2001). The gendered life course. In R. Binstock & L. George (Eds.), *Handbook of aging and the social sciences* (pp. 179–196). San Diego, CA: Academic Press.

Moen, P., Robison, J., & Fields, V. (1994). Women's work and caregiving roles: A life course approach. *Journal of Gerontology: Social Sciences, 49,* S176–S186.

Neugarten, B. L., Havighurst, R. J., & Tobin, S. (1961). The measurement of life satisfaction. *Journal of Gerontology, 16,* 134–143.

Neugarten, B. L., & Weinstein, K. K. (1964). The changing American grandparent. *Journal of Marriage and the Family, 26,* 199–204.

Pearlin, L. I., & Schooler, C. (1978). The structure of coping. *Journal of Health and Social Behavior, 19,* 2–21.

Perez-Albeniz, A., & de Paul, J. (2004). Gender differences in empathy in parents at high- and low-risk of child physical abuse. *Child Abuse & Neglect, 28,* 289–300.

Pleck, J. H. (1997). Paternal involvement: Levels, sources, and consequences. In M. E. Lamb (Ed.), *The role of the father in child development* (pp. 66–103). New York: Wiley.

Radloff, L. S. (1977). The CES-D Scale: A self-report depression scale for research in the general population. *Applied Psychological Measurement, 1,* 385–401.

Riley, M., Kahn, R., & Foner, A. (1994). *Age and structural lag: The mismatch between people's lives and opportunities in work, family, and leisure.* New York: Wiley.

Shore, R. J., & Hayslip, B. (1994). Custodial grandparenting: Implications for children's development. In A. Gottfried & A. Gottfried (Eds.), *Redefining families: Implications for children's development* (pp. 171–218). New York: Plenum.

Silverstein, L. B. (1996). Fathering is a feminist issue. *Psychology of Women Quarterly, 20,* 3–37.

Simmons, T., & Dye, J. L. (2003). *Grandparents living with grandchildren: 2000. Census 2000 Brief,* 1–10. Washington, DC: U.S. Department of Commerce.

Spitze, G., & Ward, R. A. (1998). Gender variations. In M. E. Szinovacz (Ed.), *Handbook on grandparenting* (pp. 113–130). Westport, CT: Greenwood Press.

Thomas, J. L. (1988, November). *Relationships with grandchildren as predictors of grandparents' psychological well-being.* Paper presented at the Annual Scientific Meeting of the Gerontological Society of America, San Francisco.

Thomas, J. L. (1989). Gender and perceptions of grandparenthood. *International Journal of Aging and Human Development, 29,* 269–282.

Thomas, J. L. (1995). Gender and perceptions of grandparenthood. In J. Hendricks (Ed.), *The ties of later life* (pp. 181–193). Amityville, NY: Baywood.

SECTION 3

Cross-Cultural and Intra-Cultural Variation

Cross-Cultural Differences in Traditional and Custodial Grandparenting: A Qualitative Approach

Bert Hayslip Jr., Annabel H. Baird, J. Rafael Toledo,
Cecilia Toledo, and Michelle A. Emick

Studies have documented that the numbers of grandparents drawn into the role of parents to their grandchildren has risen alarmingly in the past decade (Simmons & Dye, 2003), and that this phenomenon has been seen across all ethnic and socioeconomic boundaries (e.g., Burnette, 1997; Chalfie, 1994; Fuller-Thomson, Minkler, & Driver, 1997; Goodman & Silverstein, 2002; Hayslip & Kaminiski, 2005; Jendrek, 1994; Kornhaber, 1996; Minkler, 1994; Minkler, 1994; Morrow- Kondos, Weber, Cooper, & Hesser, 1997; Pinson-Milburn, Fabian, Schlossberg, & Pyle, 1996).

While substantial research has been conducted dealing with the incidence of custodial grandparents, as well as to causal factors giving rise to this new form of caregiving in middle and later life, few studies address the attitudes and needs of the various ethnic and cultural communities that are embedded within the cultural grandparent population. Most efforts to this end have been oriented to the African American community (Burton, 1992; Burton & Bengston, 1985; Wilson, 1984, 1986), especially that segment directly affected by the drug epidemic of the 1980s and 1990s (Burton, 1992; Joslin, 2002; Minkler & Roe, 1993; Minkler, Roe, & Price, 1992). Less attention has been paid to the Hispanic community (see however, Burnette, 1997; Burnette, 1997; Goodman & Silverstein, 2002), and other ethnicities have been overlooked entirely. It is also often the case that studies which investigated varying ethnic groups were undertaken to identify the needs of such persons (e.g., Strom, Buki, & Strom, 1997; Strom, Strom, Fournet, Wang, Behrens, et al., 1997), and not to determine the effect that cultural specificity has upon their attitudes toward raising their grandchildren. In this respect, understanding cultural differences is not only important in itself, but such knowledge allows us to better understand persons in each cultural context, underscoring the relativistic nature of the experience of raising one's grandchildren. Moreover, an appreciation of the cultural influences on custodial grandparenting helps us understand this role in terms of not only its personal, social, and familial antecedents, but also those cultural traditions that codefine one's role expectations and limitations, opportunities for formal and informal support from others, and predispositions to seeking help from others when necessary.

On a broader level of understanding, Fry (1995) points out (see Ekels, 1998) that extending our knowledge about culture and grandparenting is valuable in many respects: it broadens the empirical base upon which theory rests, it promotes a more realistic view of human experience, and it gives us greater insight into our own social institutions. In these respects, custodial grandparenting research has to this point been largely atheoretical (see Hayslip & Hicks Patrick, 2003), and our knowledge of what adjustments grandparents make when they volunteer to raise their grandchildren is largely, and unfortunately, colored by a literature which has emphasized the negative antecedents and consequences of raising a grandchild (see Hayslip & Kaminiski, 2005).

As noted above, our attention to not only variation across cultures in custodial grandparenting, but also to that within cultures deepens our knowledge about variations in grandparental caregiving within our own culture. While cross cultural research is scarce, our understanding of the commonalities and differences between the experiences of Caucasian grandparent caregivers and other grandparents raising their grandchildren has been enhanced by comparisons with African Americans (e.g., Caputo, 2000; Pruchno, 1999), with Hispanic grandparents (see e.g., Burnette, 1997; Cox, Brooks, & Valcarcel, 2000) as well as with both Latino and African American grandparent caregivers (Goodman & Silverstein,

2002). This of course, is equally true regarding our understanding of African American, Hispanic, and Latino grandparent caregivers. While not specifically targeting grandparent caregivers, in-depth portrayals of grandparents of a variety of ethnicities can be found in Falk and Falk (2002) (re: Jews, Amish, Mormons, Chinese, African Americans, Hispanics), Hunter and Taylor (1998) (re: African Americans), Williams and Torrez (1998) (re: Hispanics), and Ikamo (1998) (re: Asians).

Ekels (1998) has pointed out that grandparenthood can be understood in terms of its primacy as a kinship relationship (i.e., one becomes a grandparent through the birth of one's grandchildren). However, in the context of the distinction between bilateral (one's descent is defined by joints in terms of the paternal and fraternal line) and unilineal descent (where descent is defined by either paternal or maternal lines, but not both) (Ekels, 1998), we might characterize cross cultural (or ethnic) variation in custodial grandparenting in terms of whether one's cultural or ethnic background uniquely defines one's role as a middle aged or older grandparent who is raising a grandchild, that is, whether this role is a valued one, whether it is distinct from the role of grandparent per se, and what aspects of the role influence the allocation of resources allocated to meeting the needs of such persons. Thus, studying the cultural context in which custodial grandparenting occurs can enhance our understanding of what is likely a non-normative life transition (Baltes, 1987) for most adults. An appreciation for the role of such influences are brought into sharper focus when traditional grandparents are studied.

Cultural (and subcultural) variations (see Thomas, 1999) may also impact the functions that accompany the grandparent role, that is, viewing grandparents as mentors for younger parents, as transmitters of cultural values and heritage (see Kopera-Frye & Wiscott, 2000), as persons who are agents of socialization for and influence over their grandchildren, or as persons who can enjoy their grandchildren but not be responsible for their raising, all of which may or may not conflict with the demands of grandparent caregiving. Especially relevant to custodial grandparenting is the issue of how such persons are influenced by cultural norms and expectations governing the extent to which one is expected to fulfill a parental role after one's own children are grown. For example, in American culture, the "empty nest" (i.e., that one's usefulness to and influence over one's children end when the latter leave home) constitutes a crisis for many middle-aged persons, for whom grandparenthood may alleviate feelings of parental worthlessness. Thomas (1990) has highlighted this conflict in role demands in discussing the "double bind" in which many grandparents find themselves (i.e., they are expected to be available to help when necessary in the care of grandchildren, but are nevertheless expected to keep their opinions about how the children should be raised to themselves). Such feelings may be brought into sharp contrast from grandparents who are now raising their grandchildren. On the other hand, for traditional grandparents or for those custodial grandparents who coreside with their grandchildren, conflicts over child-rearing may emerge in light of the latter's desire to be involved in the everyday decisions about child care and discipline (Chase-Lansdale, Gordon, Coley, Wakschlag, & Brooks-Gunn, 1999).

In Hispanic and African American cultures, familism is a primary influence on (a) how persons in the family define their relationships to one another, (b) the independence of roles within the family system, as well as (c) impacting both household composition and living arrangements (see Ekels, 1998) and role boundaries associated with parenthood and grandparenthood. Each of these constructs (i.e., the empty nest and familism) consequently may represent manifestations of cultural norms that impact persons' expectations of their roles as not only traditional grandparents, but also as grandparent caregivers.

Despite the in-depth attention given the grandparenting role in adulthood (see Szinovacz, 1998), and in spite of the seminal research by scholars such as Cox, Burnette, Goodman, Minkler, and Burton dealing with subcultural ethnic or racial variations in the experience of grandparents raising their grandchildren, little if any cross-cultural work has been conducted with such grandparents. As noted above (see Frye, 1995; Ekels, 1998), such work, at the minimum, can better inform us regarding our own culture's influence on grandparent caregivers and provide a broader basis for theory construction and intervention. In this respect, there are indications of recent interest in the experiences of grandparent caregivers in other cultures (i.e., Poindexter's (2003) qualitative study of the stresses faced by grandmothers in Uganda caring for AIDS orphaned children). This project stresses such persons' resilience, social support, and sense of spirituality in the face of the stigma attached to AIDS, poverty, death, and the physical demands of raising a grandchild whose parent has died from HIV disease. Likewise, Musil and her colleagues (2003) compared U.S. born and Uganda grandmothers raising their grandchildren, finding the latter to be in poorer health, to report more depression, but yet reporting that the caregiving demands and concerns over the well-being of grandchildren were similar across cultures.

In this light, several years ago, we reported on a cross-cultural study of both traditional and custodial U.S. and native-born Mexican grandparents, utilizing objective self-report measures of role satisfaction, personal well-being, role meaning, social support, and quality of relationships with their grandchildren (Toledo, Hayslip, Emick, Toledo, & Henderson,

2000). We found both cultural (United States vs. Mexico) differences and grandparent group (traditional versus custodial) differences to exist, suggesting that Mexican grandparents, versus those in the United States, invested more meaning into their roles, yet were more depressed, experienced less satisfying relationships with their grandchildren, and reported more financial/parental stress and less role satisfaction.

For purposes of the present study, our working hypothesis is that the salience of the family as an entity with which one identifies and is defined by others with whom one may not even coreside (i.e., familism) permits persons to persist in raising their grandchildren and/or value the role of grandparent despite poorer relative health, poverty, or unemployment, wherein such individuals' needs are redefined in terms of those of the family. These dynamics may allow them to derive more personal meaning from being a grandparent caregiver. In this light, in Mexico, grandparents assume a more dominant role in the family hierarchy, leading to greater expectation of social support and a more even distribution of caregiving responsibilities among men and women, all of which would be in contrast to grandparents in the United States (for a discussion of such literature, see Toledo et al., 2000).

This chapter explores this hypothesis of the centrality of the family in the United States and Mexico by utilizing open-ended qualitative data from the Toledo et al. (2000) sample to further elucidate cross-cultural differences in traditional and custodial grandparenting. Such qualitative data may further elucidate the influence of factors permitting Mexican grandparents who are raising their grandchildren to persist in deriving meaning from their roles as grandparents despite living in poverty, having less social support, and experiencing less self-esteem and more depression relative to their counterparts in the United States.

METHOD

Sample and Procedure

The samples in this study were 75 U.S.-born grandparents (23 traditional, 52 custodial), M age = 58, and 54 native-born Mexican grandparents (16 traditional, 38 custodial), M age = 57. All custodial grandparents reported raising their grandchildren on a full-time basis, and coresided with them. All interviews were conducted in persons' homes or in a place that was convenient to each grandparent. Prior to completing the self-report questionnaire (see Toledo et al., 2000), each person was asked the following open ended questions: "What are your experiences as a grandparent?" "What is good about being a grandparent?" "Is there anything bad about being a grandparent?" "Has your role as a grandparent changed, and if so, how, and why?" "Is your role as a grandparent better or worse than it was previously?" and "What advice to other grandparents do you have?" All open-ended questions were framed in general terms (i.e., regarding grandparenting in general) to permit comparisons between traditional and custodial grandparents. Mexican-born grandparents were interviewed by 2 native-born, Spanish speaking, undergraduate students who were under the supervision of the second and last authors. The responses to the above questions were written down verbatim by each interviewer, and in the case of Mexican grandparents, translated and retranslated back to English by the second author and the last two authors to assure their veracity. Responses were then transcribed by the third author for each of the above questions without his or her knowledge of whether the respondent was Mexican or American in origin, or whether one was a traditional or custodial grandparent.

RESULTS AND DISCUSSION

Views of the Grandparent Role Across Cultures

American Grandparent Sample

American grandparents, whether custodial or not, clearly saw distinct boundaries to exist between parental and grandparental family units and viewed themselves as tangential to the lives of the lives of their children and grandchildren. This theme of separateness and boundary-bound roles principally differentiated the American and Mexican samples.

Indeed, separation from parental duties was cherished and often listed by traditional American grandparents when responding to what they considered "best" about being a grandparent. Examples of such responses were: "The ability to give and receive love without feeling responsible for the ultimate outcome of their upbringing," and "Having the fun of the child and very little responsibility." In addition, many of the traditional American grandparents relished their limited involvement in the lives of their grandchildren: "I can play with him, watch him as he sleeps, and enjoy! Then he goes home." "We play and have a great time, then he goes home. I enjoy the fact that I am not the primary caregiver." Such grandparents looked upon parental responsibilities as undesirable: "You can have warm, loving relationships with them (grandchildren) without all the negatives," "Knowing that the child is not your full responsibility, you can just enjoy her and not have to deal with all the negative things about raising a child."

Traditional American grandparents saw themselves most often as playmates, and a "lightness" in their relationships with the grandchildren was conveyed in their responses to questions about being a grandparent. Indeed, the word "joy" appeared 44 times in the responses of the traditional sample, and the word "enjoy" was used nearly 80 times. "It's great—I can enjoy them and send them home," "It's positive since I don't have total responsibility," "I love babysitting for short vacations," "Grandkids are more fun than kids," "They are special—I can make up for mistakes with my children," "I'm glad I'm not the primary caregiver." Clearly, the sense of these answers among traditional American grandparents emphasized the importance of autonomy to them and yet, being able to contribute to their grandchildren's lives. There were little or no negative comments about being a grandparent, except that some traditional grandparents wished that they had more grandchild contact. American traditional grandparents stressed the enjoyment of the grandparent role, valued their grandchildren, and enjoyed the maturation of the relationship with the adult child and grandchildren over time. Indeed, they felt that their role as a grandparent was tangential to that of the child's parent's, and stressed that they could come and go in their grandchildren's lives at will. They valued the fact that they did not have primary responsibility for their grandchildren.

Custodial American grandparents, whether they characterized the grandchild(ren) they were raising as problematic or not (based upon ratings of the behavioral and emotional difficulties their grandchildren were experiencing, see Toledo et al., 2000), also valued separate parental and grandparental units, expressing this attitude when asked what they liked *least* about being grandparents. Indeed, custodial grandparents grieved over the loss of the traditional grandparental role, for example: "From only offering love and caring in the past, now we are required to give guidance and discipline," "I am a primary caregiver. The child is now my responsibility," "Instead of spoiling them and sending them home I have to be the disciplinarian, caregiver, instiller of dreams and goals," "You can't send them home with Mom and Dad," "Being a grandparent meant that I could keep them when I want to and take them home when I got tired of them." Such persons often went as far as to assert they were denied the opportunity to be grandparents at all: "They are our first grandchildren, and since we have raised them for 99% of the time, we are parents. We do not know what grandparenting is like." Indeed, in the American sample, custodial grandparents validated the importance of the grandparental role of companion by lamenting its loss:

"We have not experienced the joy of just being a grandparent." In fact, it is only in listening to custodial American grandparents do the *expectations* of grandparenthood become apparent. The loss of time to oneself, with one's spouse, for travel, or for social engagements was lamented, and the necessity of changing lifestyles was frequently mentioned, a theme echoed in much of the contemporary research on custodial grandparenting (see e.g., Jendrek, 1994). Not surprising, American custodial grandparents rarely said that their lives had not changed: "I have no privacy and nothing in common with friends," "I provide care, but I'm not appreciated," "Disciplining them takes out all of the enjoyment," "I am too busy being a parent," "I wish I could just enjoy that special bond," "Missing out on life," "Times with spouse are limited," "Sacrifice in time and lifestyle," "Guilt over relationships with other grandchildren."

Among U.S. custodial grandparents, despite the personal costs of doing so, providing a safe environment was most salient for many, as was knowing that the grandchildren are being cared for in the best way possible, for example, "A challenge but I'm doing the right thing," "Responsibility and discipline are most important," "I have less energy and patience." Indeed, some American grandparents said they felt "forced" into raising their grandchild, and often felt that in light of the demands on their time, the impact on their energy, health, and vitality, and the need to return to work or to relearn parenting skills, that they were "doing someone else's job."

A further indication of the desire for the autonomy of American family units is found in the respect, if not fear, expressed by the grandparents toward the parents. Traditional grandparents were mindful of a need to maintain a positive relationship with their children in order to have access to the grandchildren: "Support your children with encouragement, not too much advice," "Don't forget to compliment the (grand)child's parents on their parenting skills." In contrast, some custodial grandparents went so far as to advise others to "hire a lawyer" and "get custody to keep the parents away from the grandchildren."

Mexican Grandparent Sample

Traditional grandparents in the Mexican sample presented grandparenthood as a stage in life that was expected and cherished. Although some grandparents expressed concerns about their ability to raise a grandchild: "I despair when I see my grandchildren and don't have the means to help them," mention of personal difficulties was notably absent. Their sense of family continuity was clear and involvement in the lives of the grandchildren was considered a privilege. Indeed, a sense of family obligation prevailed, and many spoke of particular responsibilities they felt toward their grandchildren: "It is a privilege to arrive at this stage of life." "God gave (me) the gift to be a grandmother and to be the mother of a mother." This theme was echoed in what custodial Mexican grandparents said was most negative about being a grandparent: to be overwhelmed with total responsibility—to feel alone in this. For example: "To take seriously the role of mother instead of grandmother because I feel a great sense of responsibility for my grandchild. . . . Because it's not the same to be a grandmother and to see the grandchildren from time to time other than to just visit, than to be totally in charge of them, because it represents big responsibility to take full care of one of them."

Interestingly, a loss of purpose existed among the traditional Mexican grandmothers that appeared to be alleviated by the presence of a grandchild. For example, "Sometimes I feel alone because our grandchildren do not live near us, but there are some days of happiness," "If I didn't have my grandchildren, I would feel alone and sad." The experience of motherhood was relived and often extended to the grandchildren, relieving loneliness and restoring meaning to their lives. Mexican traditional grandparents stressed relationship between their earlier parenting and the quality of grandchildren's life. For example: "I feel that I've reached my goals in being able to see my grandchildren," "My grandchildren are a reflection of my own children," "I get to relive my experiences as a mother," "My grandchildren treat me better than my own kids!" "Life makes more sense now." Indeed, Mexican custodial Grandparents stressed the positive aspects of their roles: "It's good to feel like a mom again," "It's like starting over again to raise them," "I love them as much as my own kids." Among such grandparents, there were few negative aspects of raising their grandchildren: "Getting angry/upset," "My own kids are jealous of how I treat my grandchildren." These understandably negative aspects of raising children were countered by the many personal and familial advantages Mexican custodial grandparents associated with the parental roles: "I wish everyone were as happy as me," "I get to share the best moments with my family," "I love them like my own kids."

Additional Themes Differentiating the American and Mexican Samples

A theme that differentiated the American and Mexican samples of grandparents was the role of grandchildren in enabling them to relive past experiences as a parent. A traditional Mexican grandparent stated: "It brings back memories of your children when they were small," "To me to be grandmother is beautiful, because you relive the moments when your children were small. To me it's the most beautiful gift from God." Indeed, for custodial Mexican grandparents, the experience of parenting was in fact being played out again in their lives, for example: "It is to start a new life, because I have new experiences with my grandchildren. It's like to start another life again. Because you have to start to raise another human being." Thus, raising a grandchild alleviated loneliness and added meaning to their lives, in contrast to American custodial grandparents, who stressed the loss of the traditional grandparent role and the disruptions in their lives that raising a grandchild brought about.

Another theme that clearly differentiated the American and Mexican (regardless of custodial status) samples was the sense that they expected that their grandchildren would "give back" to them. For example: "To receive the love of a new being in this world," "It is a wonderful experience to know there is more than one person who loves you," "That they give the same love that my children gave me," "It's nice to know there is another person in the family who loves you," "That they give me their attention," "And tomorrow when I turn old they are the ones who are going to offer me a glass of water." This sense of giving back transcended the custodial roles that some Mexican grandparents played, and may indeed explain the objective findings reflecting enhanced grandparental role meaning in the face of many personal and economic obstacles in their lives the custodial grandparents in Mexico reported (Toledo et al., 2000). While American custodial grandparents often expressed fear about what the future may hold (Emick & Hayslip, 1999), the future was defined in terms of joys yet to be experienced with one's grandchildren—that one might enjoy the fruits of one's labor, so to speak, for Mexican grandparents.

CONCLUSIONS

In order to compare the attitudes of the two populations toward raising their grandchildren, it is necessary to examine the overall context in which they view grandparenthood, for it is there that the greatest differences are found. Traditional grandparents, both American and Mexican, had the most clearly defined perspective on the meanings and roles assigned to being grandparents, while the American custodial samples reflected on their actual or perceived losses associated with this role. This disconnect between the roles of grandparent and custodial grandparent is reflected in the words of an American grandmother raising two grandchildren: "Raising grandchildren is just not the same as being a grandparent." Sadly, such losses may go unrecognized or they may be minimized by others (Miltenberger, Hayslip, Harris, & Kaminiski, 2003–2004), contributing to custodial grandparents' isolation from other age peers, and contributing to feelings of depression or hopelessness that their situation will improve. This orientation was clearly absent in the Mexican custodial sample.

In sum, our qualitative data suggested that traditional U.S.-born grandparents emphasized the enjoyment and value of grandparental role autonomy, desired more contact with grandchildren, and yet valued the maturation of such relationships over time. In contrast, Mexican-born traditional grandparents saw their roles as extensions of earlier parenting, and viewed their grandchildren in such terms. While custodial U.S.-born grandparents emphasized the negative impact of caregiving on them, regretted having to assume an authoritative parental role, and were otherwise burdened by caregiving, Mexican-born custodial grandparents not only stressed that their lives had not changed, and that they not only welcomed the opportunity to parent again, but also saw their new roles as extensions of their relationships with their own adult children.

These findings highlight cross-cultural differences in perceptions of the family as central to the lives of both traditional and custodial grandparents. U.S.-born grandparents emphasized familial structure in their roles, and regretted the loss of such structure when they raised their grandchildren. In contrast, for Mexican-born grandparents, the salience of family provided continuity in their lives. Consequently, they valued and benefited from the structure that their families had provided them regardless of their custodial status.

In this light, this study's qualitative approach highlights the cultural and role-specific differences in the perception of the centrality of the family (i.e., familism, in the context of the traditional and custodial grandparenting role), and is consistent with the impact of sociodemographic and cultural change on the experience of grandparents, particularly custodial grandparents in the United States, leading to a greater need to structure the grandparent role among such persons. The dissolution of this role seems to be a dominant theme in the lives of U.S. custodial grandparents in this sample. In contrast, no such boundaries have been erected among Mexican grandparents and consequently their lives do not change to the degree that their U.S. counterparts do when they assume care of the grandchildren.

REFERENCES

Baltes, P. (1987). Theoretical propositions of life span developmental psychology: On the dynamics of growth and decline. *Developmental Psychology, 23,* 611–626.

Burnette, D. (1997a, Sept–Oct). Grandparents raising grandchildren in the inner city. *Families in Society: The Journal of Contemporary Human Services, 6,* 489–499.

Burnette, D. (1997b). Grandmother caregivers in inner city Latino families: A descriptive profile and informal supports. *Journal of Multicultural Social Work, 5,* 121–138.

Burton, L. (1992). Black grandparents raising children of drug-addicted parents: Stressors, outcomes, and social service needs. *The Gerontologist, 32*(6), 744–751.

Burton, L. M. (1992, Summer). Challenges and rewards: African American grandparents as surrogate parents. *Generations,* pp. 51–54.

Burton, L. M. (1996). Age norms, the timing of family role transitions, and intergenerational caregiving among aging African American women. *The Gerontologist, 38*(2), 199–208.

Burton, L. M., & Bengtson, V. L. (1985). Black grandmothers: Issues of timing and continuity of roles. In V. L. Bengston & J. F. Robertson (Eds.), *Grandparenthood* (pp. 61–77). Beverly Hills, CA: Sage.

Caputo, R. (2000). Trends and correlates of coresidency among Black and White grandmothers and their grandchildren: A panel study 1967–1992. In B. Hayslip & R. Goldberg-Glen (Eds.), *Grandparents raising grandchildren: Theoretical, empirical, and clinical perspectives* (pp. 351–368). New York: Springer.

Chalfie, D. (1994). *Going it alone: A closer look at grandparents parenting grandchildren.* Washington, DC: American Association of Retired Persons, Women's Initiative.

Chase-Lansdale, P. L., Gordon, R. A., Coley, R. L., Wakschlag, L. S., & Brooks-Gunn, J. (1999). Young African American multigenerational families in poverty: The contexts, exchanges, and processes of their lives. In E. M. Hetherington (Ed.), *Coping with divorce, single parenting, and remarriage: A risk and resiliency perspective* (pp. 165–191). Mahwah, NJ: Lawrence Erlbaum.

Cox, C., Brooks, L., & Valcarcel, C. (2000). Culture and caregiving: A study of Latino grandparents. In C. Cox (Ed.), *To grandmothers house we go and stay: Perspectives on custodial grandparents* (pp. 218–232). New York: Springer.

Ekels, C. (1998). Grandparenthood in cross cultural perspective. In M. E. Szinovacz (Ed.), *Handbook on grandparenthood* (pp. 40–52). Westport, CT: Greenwood.

Emick, M., & Hayslip, B. (1999). Custodial grandparenting: Stresses, coping skills, and relationships with grandchildren. *International Journal of Aging and Human Development, 48,* 35–61.

Falk, U. A., & Falk, G. (2002). *Grandparents: A new look at the supporting generation.* Amherst, NY: Prometheus Books.

Frye, C. (1995). Kinship and individuation: Cross cultural perspectives on intergenerational relations. In V. L. Bengston & L. Burton (Eds.), *Adult intergenerational relations: Effects of social change* (pp. 126–156). New York: Springer.

Fuller-Thomson, E., Minkler, M., & Driver, D. (1997). A profile of grandparents raising grandchildren in the United States. *The Gerontologist, 37*(3), 406–411.

Goodman, C., & Silverstein, M. (2002). Grandparents raising grandchildren: Family structure and well-being in culturally diverse families. *The Gerontologist, 42,* 676–689.

Hayslip, B., & Hicks-Patrick, J. (2003). Custodial grandparenting viewed from within a life span perspective. In B. Hayslip & J. Hicks Patrick (Ed.), *Working with custodial grandparents* (pp. 3–11). New York: Springer.

Hayslip, B., & Kaminski, P. (2005). Grandparents raising their grandchildren: A review of the literature and suggestions for practice. *The Gerontologist, 45,* 262–269.

Hunter, A. G., & Taylor, R. J. (1998). Grandparenthood in African American Families. In M. E. Szinovacz (Ed.), *Handbook on grandparenthood* (pp. 70–86). Westport, CT: Greenwood.

Ikamo, Y. (1998). Asian grandparents. In M. E. Szinovacz (Ed.), *Handbook on grandparenthood* (pp. 97–112). Westport, CT: Greenwood.

Jendrek, M. (1994). Grandparents who parent their grandchildren: Circumstances and decisions. *The Gerontologist, 34*(2), 206–216.

Joslin, D. (2002). *Invisible caregivers: Older adults raising children in the wake of HIV/AIDS.* New York: Columbia University Press.

Kopera-Frye, K., & Wiscott, R. (2000). Intergenerational continuity: Transmission of beliefs and culture. In B. Hayslip & R. Goldberg-Glen (Eds.), *Grandparents raising grandchildren: Theoretical, empirical, and clinical perspectives* (pp. 65–84). New York: Springer.

Kornhaber, R. (1996). *Contemporary grandparenting.* Thousand Oaks, CA: Sage Publications.

Miltenberger, P., Hayslip, B., Harris, B., & Kaminski, P. (2003–2004). Perceptions of the losses experienced by custodial grandmothers. *Omega: Journal of Death and Dying, 48,* 245–262.

Minkler, M. (1994). Grandparents as parents: The American experience. *Aging International, 21,* 24–28.

Minkler, M. (1997, October). *Intergenerational households headed by grandparents: Demographic and social contexts.* Generations United Expert Symposium. Washington, DC.

Minkler, M., & Roe, K. (1993). *Grandmothers as caregivers: Raising children of the crack cocaine epidemic.* Newbury Park, CA: Sage Publications.

Minkler, M., Roe, K. M., & Price, M. (1992). The physical and emotional health of grandmothers raising grandchildren in the crack cocaine epidemic. *The Gerontologist, 32,* 5752–5761.

Morrow-Kondos, D., Weber, J., Cooper, K., & Hesser, J. (1997). Becoming parents again: Grandparents raising grandchildren. *Journal of Gerontological Social Work, 28*(1/2), 35–46.

Musil, C., Fitzpatrick, J., Eagan, S., Okonsky, J., Walusimbi, M., Mutabaazi, J., et al. (2003, November). *Grandmothers raising grandchildren in Uganda.* Paper presented at the Annual Scientific Meeting of the Gerontological Society of America. San Diego, CA.

Pinson-Milburn, M., Fabian, E., Schlossberg, N., & Pyle, M. (1996). Grandparents raising grandchildren. *Journal of Counseling and Development, 74,* 548–554.

Poindexter, C. C. (2003, November). "Mama Jaja" (Mother-Granny): *The stress and strength of Ugandan grandmothers caring for AIDS orphans.* Paper presented at the Annual Scientific Meeting of the Gerontological Society of America. San Diego, CA.

Pruchno, R. (1999). Raising grandchildren: The experiences of Black and White grandmothers. *The Gerontologist, 39*, 209–221.

Simmons, T., & Dye, J. L. (2003). *Grandparents living with grandchildren: 2000. Census 2000 Brief*, 1–10. Washington, DC: U.S. Department of Commerce.

Strom, R., Buki, L., & Strom, S. (1997). Intergenerational perceptions of English speaking and Spanish speaking Mexican American grandparents. *International Journal of Aging and Human Development, 46*, 41–50.

Strom, R., Fournet, L., Wang, C.-M., Behrens, J., & Griswold, D. (1997). Learning needs of African-American, Caucasian, and Hispanic grandparents. *Journal of Instructional Psychology, 28*(2), 119–134.

Szivovacz, M. (1998). *Handbook on grandparenthood*. Westport, CT: Greenwood.

Thomas, J. (1990). The grandparent role: A double bind. *International Journal of Aging and Human Development, 31*, 169–177.

Thomas, R. M. (1999). *Human development theories: Windows on culture*. Thousand Oaks, CA: Sage.

Toledo, R., Hayslip, B., Emick, M., Toledo, C., & Henderson, C. (2000). Cross cultural differences in custodial grandparenting. In B. Hayslip & R. Goldberg-Glen (Eds.), *Grandparents raising grandchildren: Theoretical, empirical, and clinical perspectives* (pp. 107–124). New York: Springer.

Williams, N., & Torrez, D. (1998). Grandparenthood among Hispanics. In M. E. Szinovacz (Ed.), *Handbook on grandparenthood* (pp. 87–96). Westport, CT: Greenwood.

Wilson, M. N. (1984). Mothers' and grandmothers' perceptions of parental behavior in three-generational Black families. *Child Development, 55*, 1333–1339.

Wilson, M. N. (1986). The Black extended family: An analytical consideration. *Developmental Psychology, 22*(2), 246–258.

CHAPTER 12

Grandparent Caregiving Among First Nations Canadians[*]

Esme Fuller-Thomson

Over the past decade, there has been a growing body of research on grandparents raising grandchildren in the United States. Only in the last three years has the issue of grandparent caregiving in Canada begun to receive the attention of the media (e.g., Growe, 2003; Waytiuk, 2001), some elected officials (e.g., Kormos, 2002; Kwan, 2002) and a few scholars (e.g., Fuller-Thomson, 2003; Inwood, 2002). The growing awareness of the issue mirrored a substantial increase in Canada in the number of grandchildren being raised by grandparents. Between 1991 and 2001 there was a 20% increase in the number of children under 18 years old

[*]The author would like to thank Real Lortie, senior consulting analyst, Statistics Canada, for conducting the custom tabulations; Leanne McCormack, M.S.W., for assistance with manuscript preparation; and Rose Mandamin, Ph.D. (candidate), for her helpful comments and suggestions on an earlier draft. The author also gratefully acknowledges the Program for Research on Social and Economic Dimensions of an Aging Population (SEDAP) for its support of this research.

who were living with their grandparents without a parent present in the household (Statistics Canada, 2003a).

The most compelling finding of recent Canadian research on skipped generation families was that First Nations[1] Canadians were vastly overrepresented among grandparent caregivers (Fuller-Thomson, 2004). Skipped generation households are defined as households that contain only members of the grandparent and the grandchild generation, no parents or aunts or uncles of the grandchildren are coresident. More than 17% of caregiving grandparents in such households were of First Nations descent although First Nations persons comprise only 2.8% of the total population and 1.4% of the Canadian population aged 45 and over (Statistics Canada, 1998, January 13).

Using custom tabulations of the 1996 Census of Canada, this article provides the first nationally representative data profiling the characteristics of Aboriginal grandparent caregivers in skipped generation families in Canada. Differences in demographic characteristics, household composition and tasks, and disability status between First Nations and other grandparent caregivers are examined.

REVIEW OF THE LITERATURE

First Nations Grandparent Caregivers

Elders have traditionally played key roles as wise advisers and keepers of the cultural legacy in First Nations communities (Castellano, 2002). Historically, grandparents in Aboriginal communities in Canada and the United States have helped to socialize and instruct their grandchildren and often played an important role in their physical care as well (Bahr, 1994; Castellano, 2002; Human Resources and Development Canada, 2002; Shomaker, 1989). When grandparents helped raise the grandchildren, mothers were able to secure food and provide for their families (Bahr, 1994) and grandchildren in turn provided needed assistance to grandparents (Shomaker, 1989). The vibrant tradition of grandparent caregiving has continued until the present day. Some grandparents relish

---

[1]The author is aware of the debate over which is the most appropriate term for Canada's First Peoples. In keeping with the majority of the literature by First Nations scholars (e.g., Assembly of First Nations, 2002; Castellano, 2002), this article will use the terms "Aboriginal Peoples" and "First Nations Canadians" interchangeably to define a group which includes North American Indian, Métis or Inuit and/or those who reported being a Treaty Indian or a Registered Indian as defined by the Indian Act of Canada (Status Indians) and/or those who were members of an Indian Band or First Nation (Non-status Indians).

the role of "cultural conservator" and actively seek out the opportunity to parent or coparent grandchildren in order to enhance children's understanding of traditional ways and values (Weibel-Orlando, 1997). In at least one Canadian tribe—the Ojibwe—paternal grandparents may coparent their first grandchild with the child's parents (Mandamin, 2003). This practice is to honor the grandparents and to allow the child full access to the elders' teachings. In effect, this custom assists to mitigate the pressures of young parenthood. However, in contrast to these positive reasons for caregiving, many First Nations grandparents, similar to non-Aboriginal grandparents, provide care in response to crisis, such as alcohol and drug addiction or imprisonment of the grandchildren's parents. These crises often carry a social stigma for the grandchildren's parents, and may extend to the whole family. Furthermore, these grandparents are additionally burdened with their concerns about the well-being of their adult children.

The Canadian Royal Commission on Aboriginal Peoples (1996), echoing many American studies (e.g., AARP, 1995), reported on the serious social and economic conditions among First Nations peoples including high levels of morbidity, short life spans, inadequate schooling, extremely high teenage pregnancy rates, high levels of drug and alcohol abuse, overcrowded housing, poverty, and family breakdown. These social conditions, in turn, fuel the number of grandchildren coming into their grandparent's care and provide the context within which grandparents have to provide care.

Grandparent caregiving in First Nations communities cannot be understood without understanding the historical context of Aboriginal peoples (Castellano, 2002; Royal Commission on Aboriginal Peoples, 1996). Throughout North America, Aboriginal communities have been dispossessed of their traditional territory and relocated. A large proportion of First Nations children were taken from their families' home and sent to residential schools far from their communities, while others were removed by child welfare agencies and placed in non-Aboriginal foster and adoptive homes. Residential schools followed a policy of forced acculturation, prohibiting native language use and cultural practices, and minimizing contact with families of origin. Furthermore, many First Nations children were physically and sexually abused in the schools. As the Royal Commission on Aboriginal Peoples (1996) points out, the effect of child welfare and residential school policies . . . "was to tear more holes in the family web and detach more Aboriginal people from their roots."

Castellano (2002) discussed the generational impact of removing children from the home and community. Upon return to their home community, these children had often lost their sense of identity and their ability to communicate in their mother tongue. Furthermore, many of these children had been deprived of adequate parental role modeling and consequently had difficulties coping when they became parents. Furthermore, residential school placements have been associated with higher levels of drug disorders among First Nations men (Robin, Rasmussen, & Gonzales-Santin, 1999). Foster care placement during childhood has been found to be associated with adult drug, alcohol, and anxiety disorders in a study of Native Americans (Robin, Rasmussen, & Gonzales-Santin, 1999). Although residential schools have been closed and transracial adoptions and foster care placements have declined, the healing will take a long time. An executive director of an urban First Nations Child and Family Service agency reported that 90% of the agency's single parent clients were foster care wards themselves and the majority of the children's grandparents had been in residential schools (Royal Commission on Aboriginal Peoples, 1996).

The First Nations Child and Family Services Program has recently been developed to redress some of the injustices of the previous child welfare policies and practices. This program substantially expanded child and family services agencies that are designed, managed, and controlled by First Nations. Approximately 90% of on-reserve children of First Nations descent are currently receiving services from these agencies (Indian and Northern Affairs Canada, 2001). These agencies are mandated to provide culturally appropriate care and rely heavily upon grandparents and other relatives for foster care placements. Unfortunately, First Nations Canadian children are four to six times more likely than other Canadian children to come into the care of child welfare agencies. In addition, Aboriginal children are the fastest growing segment of the Canadian population (Indian and Northern Affairs Canada, 2001).

Outcomes Associated With Grandparent Caregiving

Some of the outcomes of grandparents raising grandchildren are positive. In a large, representative study, Solomon and Marx (1995) concluded that the health and the behavior of children raised by grandparents were similar to children who lived with both biological parents despite the considerably lower financial resources typically available to grandparent households. Grandparents consistently emphasized the love that the grandchildren in their care provide. They also reported feeling relieved knowing that the grandchildren were now in a safe environment and that the family had been kept together (Minkler & Roe, 1993). Grandparent caregivers also felt closer to their grandchildren than did non-caregiving grandparents (Fuller-Thomson & Minkler, 2001). Weibel-Orlando

(1997) noted that adult grandchildren often were key supports to the Native American grandparents who had raised them decades earlier.

Grandparent caregivers, however, are also vulnerable to many negative outcomes. In comparison to non-caregiving grandparents, grandparents who were raising their grandchildren had lower levels of life satisfaction (Shore & Hayslip, 1994), higher levels of poverty (Strawbridge, Wallhagen, Shema, & Kaplan, 1997), and experienced more depressive symptoms (Burton, 1992; Fuller-Thomson, Minkler, & Driver, 1997; Kelley, Whitley, Sipe, & Yorker, 2000) and limitations in their daily activities (Kelley et al., 2000; Minkler & Fuller-Thomson, 1999). Although we do not have, to date, any studies documenting the outcomes for First Nations Canadian grandparent caregivers, in a recent U.S. study Native American grandparents raising grandchildren were more likely than their non-caregiving Native American peers to be living in poverty and in overcrowded conditions and to have a disability (Fuller-Thomson & Minkler, 2003). Despite the often substantial financial, emotional, and physical costs involved, First Nations grandparents are willing to raise their grandchildren who are in need. Bahr (1994, p. 234) described Native American grandparent caregivers as "caretaker of last resort, . . . [devoting] extraordinary effort and personal sacrifice to performing the grandmother role" and emphasized that grandparents raising grandchildren are a sign of the strength and resilience of First Nations communities despite "almost insurmountable odds."

In sum, research on First Nations grandparent caregiving is essential due to the paucity of studies in the area, the over-representation of Aboriginals among Canadian grandparent caregivers, and the unique historical and current context of care provision in First Nations communities.

METHODS

Sample

Data presented in this article were primarily based on custom tabulations of the 1996 Census of Canada. These tabulations were prepared by Statistics Canada for the author. The long form of the 1996 Census was given to a 20% sample of all Canadian households (Hull, 2001). The Census long form included questions on a wide range of demographic, economic, and social characteristics of household members. Weighting the long-form sample to the national population generated national prevalence numbers. Please see Statistics Canada (1997) for a complete discussion of sample size and weighting.

Skipped generation households were defined as households that contain only members of the grandparent and the grandchild generation, where no parents or aunts or uncles of the grandchildren are co-resident. Only households in which all the grandchildren were under 18 were included in the analysis. Although many grandparents may have been the primary caregivers to grandchildren in three-generational households, the census data was not sufficiently detailed to clarify the respective caregiving roles in the household when the grandchildren's parents and/ or aunts and uncles were present. One can assume with more certainty that grandparents are the care providers when they are the only adults in the household. Thus, the study was restricted to the smaller sample of skipped generation households.

The demographic characteristics of grandparents in skipped generation households and of the households themselves were presented for both First Nations and non-First Nations respondents. To determine whether differences between the two groups were statistically significant, chi-square tests were conducted for categorical variables and independent *t*-tests were calculated for ratio-level variables.

Measures

First Nations status, as defined by Statistics Canada, referred to those persons who reported identifying with at least one Aboriginal group, [i.e., North American Indian, Métis, or Inuit (Eskimo) and/or those who reported being a Treaty Indian or a Registered Indian as defined by the Indian Act of Canada or who were members of an Indian Band or First Nation] (Statistics Canada, 1997). In addition, disability status was defined as a limitation in the kind or amount of a person's activity because of a long-term physical condition, mental condition, or health problem (Statistics Canada, 1997).

The hours spent doing household activities were obtained through the following three-part question. Last week how many hours did this person spend doing the following activities? (a) Doing unpaid housework, yardwork, or home maintenance for members of this household, or others. (Examples include preparing meals, doing laundry, household planning, shopping, and cutting the grass.) (b) Looking after one or more of this person's own children, or the children of others, without pay. (Examples include bathing or playing with young children, driving children to sports activities or helping them with homework, and talking with teens about their problems.) (c) Providing unpaid care or assistance to one or more seniors. (Examples include providing personal care to a senior family member, visiting seniors, talking with them on the telephone and helping them with shopping, banking, or with taking medication.) Where activities overlapped, respondents were instructed to report the same hours in more than one part. Therefore, the reader should view these data with caution due to potential overcounting.

RESULTS

Grandparent caregivers of First Nations origin differed markedly from caregivers who were not of First Nations descent. Aboriginal grandparent caregivers were more likely to be female (64% vs. 58%), and were less likely to be married (57% vs. 72%). First Nations grandparent caregivers were less likely to be employed (29% vs. 40%) and more likely to define themselves as being outside of the labor force (65% vs. 55%) than were non-Aboriginal caregivers. Almost three quarters (73%) of First Nations caregivers had not completed high school in comparison to 59% of grandparent caregivers who were not of First Nations descent. More than three in five First Nations Canadian grandparent caregivers (62%) had a language other than English or French as a mother tongue although only 8% could not communicate in either of Canada's official languages. In comparison, only 15% of non-Aboriginal Canadian grandparents raising grandchildren had a mother tongue that was not English or French and only 3% could not communicate in either official language.

This study's findings revealed that some grandparents devoted minimal time to care provision, while others designated a good portion of their waking hours. The findings indicated that First Nations grandparents were disproportionately in the latter group. First Nations caregivers were more likely than their non-Aboriginal Canadian peers to spend 30 or more hours per week on unpaid child care (46% vs. 30%) or on unpaid housework (41% vs. 34%). However, not all grandparent caregivers spent a large part of their week on caregiving tasks. For example, among First Nations grandparent caregivers, 32% provided less than 5 hours per week of unpaid child care and 21% spent a comparable time on unpaid housework. Among other grandparent caregivers, these figures were 41% and 22%, respectively.

More than three quarters of all grandparent caregivers did not provide any unpaid care to seniors. However, 15% of Aboriginal grandparents spent 5 or more hours per week providing such assistance in comparison to 8% of caregivers who were not of First Nations descent.

Although tribal group data was not available, the grandparent caregivers identified their mother tongue. Forty-five percent of grandparent caregivers of First Nations descent reported one of the major Aboriginal languages as their mother tongue. The three largest language groups were Cree ($n = 1150$), Ojibwe ($n = 495$) and Inuktitut/Eskimo ($n = 125$).

When household-level information was considered, grandparent caregivers of First Nations descent were twice as likely as those in non-Aboriginal caregiving households to have two or more grandchildren in the home (34% vs. 17%). Despite having more dependents in the household, First Nations grandparent caregiving households had median incomes less than 70% than that of their non-Aboriginal caregiving peers. Forty-two percent of First Nations families had household incomes less than $15,000 in comparison to 28% of non-Aboriginal families. More than two in five Aboriginal skipped generation households (44%) were on First Nations Reservations. Forty-four percent of First Nations skipped generation households had at least one grandparent living with a disability, in comparison to 31% of non-Aboriginal households. Seven percent of both First Nations and non-Aboriginal skipped generation households had a child with a disability.

DISCUSSION

This study's findings indicate that First Nations Canadian grandparents who are raising grandchildren are considerably disadvantaged when compared with other grandparents in skipped generation households. More than likely, First Nations grandparent caregivers have a disability, are poor and not unmarried, provide more hours of child care and housework, are raising two or more children, and have not completed high school—in comparison with other grandparents in skipped generation households. These findings are partially a function of the disproportionate burden of ill health, unemployment, and poverty that afflict First Nations communities (Indian and Northern Affairs Canada, 2000; Royal Commission on Aboriginal Peoples, 1996).

The median income for First Nations skipped generation households is well below the poverty line for three-person families. Skipped generation families are disproportionately poor (Chalfie, 1994; Fuller-Thomson, 2004), but the extreme poverty apparent among First Nations Canadian skipped generation families reflects in part, the far higher poverty rates evident among First Nations Canadians in general. However, skipped generation households appear to be further disadvantaged with an average household income $2,000 lower than that of all First Nation households in Canada (Indian and Northern Affairs Canada, 2000). Similarly, a recent nationally representative American study found that Native American caregiving grandparents also had higher rates of poverty and of disability than their non-caregiving Native American peers (Fuller-Thomson & Minkler, 2003). Easier access to kinship care payments and reimbursement levels for grandparents at non-familial foster care rates could alleviate some of the economic hardship.

In order to determine additional policy and programmatic responses to alleviate poverty among First Nations Canadian grandparent caregivers, further understanding of the reasons for the problem are necessary. For instance, it is important to investigate potential barriers to labor force participation including inadequate employment opportunities on reservations, the competing time demands of care provision, and high levels of disability.

Undoubtedly, some of the financial difficulties are related to the fact that two thirds of First Nations Canadian grandparent caregivers are not in the labor force. This is a surprisingly high proportion in light of the fact that three quarters of grandparent caregivers are under 65 years of age. This reflects limited employment opportunities on reservations, where 44% of the First Nations caregivers reside. Almost two thirds of First Nations caregiving grandparents are women who, especially in the older age groups, are less likely than men to have worked outside the home and are more likely to be poor.

It is possible that the lower level of employment among First Nations Canadians is due to grandparents' inability to reconcile multiple role demands with their concomitant time demands. A qualitative study in the United States found one third of the study participants had relinquished their jobs in order to care for a grandchild (Burnette, 1999). Although most grandparent caregivers in this study had substantial demands on their time with respect to care provision and housework, First Nations Canadians were more likely than other caregivers to spend 30 or more hours per week on each of these tasks. Almost half (46%) of First Nations Canadian grandparent caregivers provided 30 or more hours per week of child care, in comparison to 30% of non-First Nations grandparents. Similarly, First Nations Canadians were more likely than other Canadian grandparent caregivers to be spending 30 or more hours per week on housework. This greater time commitment may be due to the fact that First Nations Canadians are twice as likely as other grandparent caregivers to be raising two or more grandchildren, with concomitant increases in child care and housekeeping responsibilities. Furthermore, the emotional, physical, and economic toll of raising multiple grandchildren appears to be particularly acute (Minkler & Roe, 1993). The availability of financial assistance and supportive services may be particularly beneficial for these resource-stretched families.

Another explanation for the higher time demands experienced by First Nations households relates to the age of the grandchildren. In comparison to 16% of First Nations Canadian skipped generation households, one quarter of non-Aboriginal households contained only older teenage grandchildren, who obviously require less child care and may assist with some of the housework. First Nations grandparent caregivers are also less likely to have a spouse and thus are less likely to have someone with whom to share the caregiving and homemaking duties. Lastly, the more limited economic resources available to many First Nations Canadian families makes it less likely that they can afford to purchase labor saving devices such as dishwashers or to hire babysitters or cleaners to assist them.

For those grandparents who do leave the labor force in midlife to raise their grandchildren, there are serious long-term repercussions on public and private pensions and on the accumulation of retirement savings. Furthermore, grandparents who wish to reenter the workforce once their grandchildren are in school full time may find it difficult to obtain employment. Work opportunities are more limited for older workers in general and this is particularly true for those with less education. More than half of First Nations grandparent caregivers had no high school education and only a quarter had completed high school, thereby minimizing their opportunity to reenter the workforce. For grandparents to remain in the workforce, adequate, affordable, and accessible child care must be available to those grandparents raising young children. Long waiting lists, few subsidized spots and difficulties registering grandchildren without legal custody papers present significant barriers to obtaining day care for all grandparent caregivers.

Castellano (2002) has encouraged the expansion of Headstart programs for First Nations Canadians both on and off reserve. In addition to allowing grandparents to remain in the workforce, preschool and intensive, scholastically oriented, and culturally appropriate after-school programs would be an invaluable resource for grandchildren who have disabilities. These programs could provide grandparents with helpful assistance and information on creative ways to cope with learning difficulties and other issues. Grandparent caregivers raising grandchildren with psychological and physical problems often have extensive demands on their time and energy and experience high levels of stress (Sands & Goldberg-Glen, 2000) and less satisfaction with the grandparental role (Hayslip, Shore, Henderson, & Lambert, 1998).

High rates of disability among First Nations Canadian grandparents may provide another explanation for the low labor force participation rates. More than 40% of First Nations skipped generation households contained a grandparent with a disability and 10% of grandparent caregivers were providing unpaid care to a senior for 10 or more hours per week. The higher rates of disability in Aboriginal families are not surprising considering the much higher level of morbidity among First Nations populations (Royal Commission on Aboriginal Peoples, 1996). Despite such high levels of need, Aboriginal Canadians receive less governmental health funding per person than do other Canadians (Assembly of First Nations, 2002). Health care services are very limited on reservations, particularly in remote areas, and there is often little access to specialist care. A 1999 survey indicated that 60% of First Nations Canadians believe they do not receive the same health services as other Canadians (Assembly of First Nations, 2002). Recent program proposals to increase access to in-home supportive care for on-reserve populations are promising. Respite care could be creatively designed to provide assistance to grandparent caregivers with disabilities who have the physical tasks of caregiving such as bathing children. Further development for employment retraining opportunities would also improve the possibility for grandparent caregivers with disabilities to reenter the labor force.

There is a strong potential for all grandparent caregivers to experience interrole conflict and role overload (Burnette, 1999; Cox, 2000; Davis, 1996). Adaptation to this major role transition is hindered by the unanticipated, ambiguous, and off-time nature of grandparental caregiving (Burnette, 1999). Grandparent caregivers speak of their lack of preparation for undertaking care of grandchildren (Minkler & Roe, 1993). Many grandparents face uncertainty about when, or if, parents will resume their primary caregiving role. As discussed earlier, the data reveal that grandparent caregivers in general and First Nations grandparents, in particular, have a high level of involvement in many distinct and potentially conflictual roles. Many grandparents in skipped generation families are attempting to fulfill their obligations as homemakers, spouses, parents to adult children (many of whom have serious problems), or employees, in addition to their custodial grandparenting role. Almost a quarter of First Nations grandparent caregivers are also providing some care to seniors. As noted previously, many grandparent caregivers have insufficient financial resources as well as health problems that undoubtedly make it difficult to fulfill the expectations that come with the caregiving role. Burnette's (1999) study found many grandparents were overloaded with too many role demands and inadequate resources to meet those demands, which in turn undermined their self-esteem. Bahr's (1994) qualitative study of Native American grandparent caregivers described the elder's struggle to provide food and other basic necessities in the context of extreme poverty and documented the substantial financial, emotional, and physical burden this placed on grandmothers.

In Bahr's (1994) study, many Native American grandparent caregivers were proud of their traditional upbringing and knowledge and saw themselves as continuing the caregiving traditions of their foremothers. Although we do not know the role of traditional values in the lives of these grandparents, we do have information on their mother tongue. These data highlight the fact that 60% of First Nations Canadian grandparent caregivers did not have English or French as a mother tongue. This rate is more than twice that of the total Aboriginal community (Statistics Canada, 2003b). It is likely that most individuals who spoke an Aboriginal language in their youth had substantial exposure to traditional First Nations culture. Further research is needed to investigate the relative contribution of cultural tradition, financial necessity, and social inequality in the formation of First Nations grandparent caregiving households (Rosenthal & Gladstone, 2000).

The vast majority of grandparents who reported having an Aboriginal mother tongue had also mastered either English or French. However, one in twelve First Nations Canadian grandparent caregivers reported that they could not communicate in either English or French. Without language skills in one of the official languages, it is much more difficult for these grandparent caregivers to access employment, health, social, and financial services. Furthermore, there may be communication problems if the grandchildren do not speak the Aboriginal language of their grandparents. Burnette (1999) noted a similar problem among Latino grandparent caregivers, where the grandchildren tended to be culturally and linguistically assimilated into the dominant society.

There are several limitations to this study. Grandparents in skipped generation households represent only a portion of grandparent caregivers. One American study found that more than half of grandparents who were raising their grandchildren had a coresident child (Fuller-Thomson & Minkler, 2001). Findings should not be generalized to grandparent caregivers in three-generation households who may differ from grandparents in skipped generation households. Due to the wording of the Census question on hours spent in household tasks, it is possible that some double counting occurred and thus, the hours may be inflated. In all likelihood, however, this error affected First Nations and other grandparent caregivers in the same manner. The Census did not provide information on whether grandparents had legal custody of the child, whether they were receiving kinship care payments and the duration of care provision. All these factors have been shown to impact grandparent caregivers (Minkler & Roe, 1993).

Further focused research on role-related processes, strains, and social supports should improve our theoretical understanding of social roles among grandparent caregivers (Burnette, 1999). Qualitative studies among First Nations grandparent caregivers are definitely warranted due to their large numbers and significantly higher rates of disability and poverty.

The findings from our study reveal a portrait of Native Canadian grandparents in skipped generation households as resilient caregivers who often are raising their grandchildren in the context of extreme poverty and ill health. As Bahr (1994) suggests, grandparent caregivers "rather than signaling family failure . . . (are) a testimony to one of the great strengths of . . . (First Nations) families, a traditional pattern of responsibility and care that continues to serve families and protect children" (p. 233).

REFERENCES

American Association of Retired Persons (AARP) Minority Affairs. (1995). A portrait of older minorities. Washington, DC: AARP. Retrieved October 18, 2002, from http://research.aarp.org/general/portmino.html#NATIVE

Assembly of First Nations (2002, April 4). Presentation notes to the commission on the future of healthcare in Canada. Ottawa, Canada. Retrieved February 8, 2002, from http://www.afn.ca/Programs/Health%20Secretariat/assembly_of_first _nations_presen.htm

Bahr, K. S. (1994). The strengths of Apache grandmothers: Observations on commitment, culture & caretaking. *Journal of Comparative Family Studies, 25*, 233–248.

Burnette, D. (1999). Social relationships of Latino grandparent caregivers: A role theory perspective. *The Gerontologist, 39*(1), 49–58.

Burton, L. M. (1992). Black grandparents rearing children of drug-addicted parents: Stressors, outcomes, and social service needs. *The Gerontologist, 32*(6), 744–751.

Castellano, M. B. (2002). Aboriginal family trends: Extended families, nuclear families, families of the heart. Vanier Institute of the Family. Retrieved November 15, 2002, from http://www.vifamily.ca/cft/aboriginal/aborignl.htm

Chalfie, D. (1994). *Going it alone: A closer look at grandparents parenting grandchildren.* Washington, DC: American Association of Retired Persons.

Cox, C. B. (2000). Why grandchildren are going to and staying at grandmother's house and what happens when they get there. In C. B. Cox (Ed.), *To grandmother's house we go and stay: Perspectives on custodial grandparents* (pp. 3–19). New York: Springer.

Davis, L. V. (1996). Role theory and social work treatment. In I. J. Turner (Ed.), *Social work treatment: Interlocking theoretical approaches* (4th ed., pp. 581–600). New York: Free Press.

Fuller-Thomson, E. (2003). Grandparents raising grandchildren in Canada: A grounded theory study of Caribbean-Canadian, First Nations and White custodial grandmothers. Unpublished manuscript.

Fuller-Thomson, E. (2004). Grandparents raising grandchildren in Canada: A profile of skipped generation families. Manuscript submitted for publication.

Fuller-Thomson, E., & Minkler, M. (2001). American grandparents providing extensive child care to their grandchildren: Prevalence and profile. *The Gerontologist, 41*(2), 201–209.

Fuller-Thomson, E., & Minkler, M. (2003). Native American grandparents raising grandchildren: Findings from the Census 2000 Supplementary Survey and implications for social work practice. Manuscript submitted for publication.

Fuller-Thomson, E., Minkler, M., & Driver, D. (1997). A profile of grandparents raising grandchildren in the United States. *The Gerontologist, 37*(3), 406–411.

Growe, S. J. (2003, January 11). Grandparents with custody are "punished." *Toronto Star*, pp. L11.

Hayslip, B., Shore, J., Henderson, C. E., & Lambert, P. L. (1998). Custodial grandparenting and the impact of grandchildren with problems on role satisfaction and role meaning. *Journals of Gerontology: Social Sciences, 53B*(3), S164–S173.

Hull, J. (2001). Aboriginal single mothers in Canada, 1996: A statistical profile. Indian Affairs and Northern Development, Ottawa, Canada. Retrieved January 9, 2003, from http://www.ainc-inac.gc.ca/pr/ra/smt_e.pdf

Human Resources and Development Canada. (2002). Child welfare in Canada 2000. Retrieved December 3, 2002, from http://www.hrdc-drhc.gc.ca/sp-ps/socialp-psociale/cfs/rpt2000/rpt 2000e_2.shtml

Indian and Northern Affairs Canada. (2000). Comparison of social conditions, 1991 and 1996: Registered Indians, registered Indians living on reserves and the total population of Canada. Indian Affairs and Northern Development, Ottawa, Canada. Retrieved January 4, 2002, from http://www.ainc-inac.gc.ca/pr/sts/hac/socl_e.pdf

Indian and Northern Affairs Canada. (2001). First Nations child and family service program. Indian Affairs and Northern Development, Ottawa, Canada. Retrieved December 12, 2002, from: http://www.ainc-inac.gc.ca/ps/fnc_e.html

Inwood, S. (2002). Grandparents raising grandchildren. *Canadian Nurse, 98*(4), 21–25.

Kelley, S. J., Whitley, D., Sipe, T. A., & Yorker, B. C. (2000). Psychological distress in grandmother kinship care providers: The role of resources, social support, and physical health. *Child Abuse and Neglect, 24*(3), 311–321.

Kormos, P. (2002, December 12). Speech by N.D.P. House Leader on grandparents raising grandchildren. Paper presented at the Ontario House of Parliament, Queen's Park, Toronto, ON.

Kwan, J. (2002). Debates of the Legislative Assembly: B.C., 2002 Legislative session: 3rd session, 37th Parliament, MAY 28 Afternoon sitting, Vol. 8(7). Hansard. Retrieved January 14, 2003, from: http://www.legis.gov.bc.ca/hansard/37th3rd/h20528p.htm#3657

Mandamin, R. (2003, January 19). Personal communication: Ph.D. Candidate, Faculty of Social Work, University of Toronto, ON.

Minkler, M., & Fuller-Thomson, E. (1999). The health of grandparents raising grandchildren: Results of a national study. *American Journal of Public Health, 89*(9), 1384–1389.

Minkler, M., & Roe, M. (1993). *Grandmothers as caregivers: Raising children of the crack cocaine epidemic.* Newbury Park, CA: Sage.

Robin, R. W., Rasmussen, J. K., & Gonzales-Santin, R. (1999). "Impact of childhood out-of-home placement on a Southwestern American Indian tribe." *Journal of Human Behavior in the Social Environment* 2(1/2), 69–89.

Rosenthal, C. J., & Gladstone, J. (2000). Contemporary family trends: Grandparenthood in Canada. Vanier Institute for the Family, Ottawa. Retrieved December 19, 2002, from: http://www.vifamily.ca/cft/grandpt/intro.htm

Royal Commission on Aboriginal Peoples. (1996). People to people, nation to nation: Highlights from the report of the Royal Commission on Aboriginal Peoples. Minister of Supply and Services, Canada. Retrieved December 15, 2002, from: http://www.ainc-inac.gc.ca/ch/rcap/rpt/index_e.html

Sands, R. G., & Goldberg-Glen, R. S. (2000). Factors associated with stress among grandparents raising their grandchildren. *Family Relations, 49,* 97–105.

Shomaker, D. J. (1989). Transfer of children and the importance of grandmothers among Navajo Indians. *Journal of Cross-Cultural Gerontology, 4,* 1–18.

Shore, R. J., & Hayslip, B. (1994). Custodial grandparenting: Implications for children's development. In A. Godfried & A. Godfried (Eds.), *Redefining families: Implications for children's development* (pp. 171–218). New York: Plenum.

Solomon, J. C., & Marx, J. (1995). "To grandmother's house we go": Health and school adjustment of children raised solely by grandparents. *The Gerontologist, 35,* 386–394.

Statistics Canada (1997). 1996 Census Dictionary, First Edition: (Catalogue No. 92-351-XPE). Ottawa, ON: Minister of Industry.

Statistics Canada (1998, January 13). The Daily: Aboriginal data, 1996 census. Statistics Canada. Retrieved January 7, 2003, from: http://www.statcan.ca/Daily/English/980113/d980113.htm#ART1

Statistics Canada (2003a). Age groups, number of grandparents and sex for grandchildren living with grandparents with no parent present, for Canada, Provinces and Territories, 1991 to 2001 censuses—20% sample data. Statistics Canada. Retrieved January 16, 2003, from: http://www12.statcan.ca/english/census01/products/standard/themes/

Statistics Canada (2003b). Aboriginal population by mother tongue, 1996 Census. Statistics Canada. Retrieved February 7, 2003, from: http://www.statcan.ca/english/Pgdb/demo36a.htm

Strawbridge, W. J., Wallhagen, M. I., Shema, S. J., & Kaplan, G. A. (1997). New burdens or more of the same? Comparing grandparent, spouse, and adult-child caregivers. *Gerontologist, 37*(4), 505–510.

Waytiuk, J. (2001). A lifeline of love. *Today's Grandparent,* Winter. Retrieved December 14, 2002, from: http://www.todaysparent.com/grandparent/article.jsp?cId=5014

Weibel-Orlando, J. (1997). Grandparenting styles: The contemporary American Indian experience. In J. Sokolovsky (Ed.), *The cultural context of aging: Worldwide perspectives* (2nd ed., pp. 139–155). Westport, CT: Bergin & Garvey.

CHAPTER 13

Social Support Among Custodial Grandparents Within a Diversity of Contexts*

Steven J. Kohn and Gregory C. Smith

This chapter investigates whether or not key aspects of diversity within a large and nationally representative sample of custodial grandmothers are related to their encounters with social support systems. Although national profiles of custodial or "skipped generation" grandparents show this type of family caregiving to transcend race, social class, and geography (Fuller-Thomson & Minkler, 2000; Pebley & Rudkin, 1999), past research on diversity within this population has focused narrowly upon race and ethnicity. Furthermore, investigators have paid scarce attention to the social support systems of these caregivers. Yet, as described in this

*At the time that this chapter was written, the first author was project director of the NIMH grant that funded the research. Steven J. Kohn is now a member of the Department of Psychology and Counseling faculty at Valdosta State University. The research reported here was supported by grant 5RO1MH66851-01 from the National Institute of Mental Health (NIMH) to the second author.

chapter, it is likely that important aspects of diversity in addition to race are quite relevant to how custodial grandparents use and perceive various kinds of social support systems. Thus, in addition to race, we will also examine social support among custodial grandparents in terms of geographic region (i.e., southern vs. non-southern states) and residential locale (i.e., urban, suburban, rural).

THE SIGNIFICANCE OF SOCIAL SUPPORT

Traditional definitions of social support generally encompass informal support provided by family, friends, and neighbors, as well as formal support from professionals and social systems (Sarason, Pierce, & Sarason, 1990). A focus on custodial grandparents' use and appraisal of both formal and informal supports is important because as they assume the caregiver role in increasing numbers they will need greater support from family, friends, community services, and professionals from many disciplines to help them cope with the physical and emotional challenges of providing care to their grandchildren (Roberto & Qualls, 2003). Unfortunately, despite the recognized importance social support provides in mediating stress and coping among custodial grandparents (see, for discussion, Musil, Schrader, & Mutikani, 2000), many see themselves as having to manage their caregiving situation alone and report feeling judged, criticized, and abandoned by their families, communities, and society (Baird, John, & Hayslip, 2000; Hirshorn, Van Meter, & Brown, 2000; Roberto & Qualls, 2003). Indeed formal support systems often display contempt and indifference toward custodial grandparents (Hayslip, Silverthorn, Shore, & Henderson, 2000; Pebley & Rudkin, 1999), and accessing informal and formal support is made difficult by the shame and stigma associated with the reasons (e.g., parental irresponsibility) for becoming a caregiving grandparent (Fuller-Thomson & Minkler, 2000; Porterfield, Dressel, & Barnhill, 2000). The net result of these dilemmas in obtaining support from others is a heightened sense of rejection, loneliness, social isolation, and frustration (Baird et al., 2000; Morrow-Kondos, Weber, Cooper, & Hesser, 1997; Musil, 1998).

It is important to note, however, that we broaden our definition of social support to include appraisals of neighborhood quality and a perceived sense of isolation (i.e., loneliness and rejection). Although these are not measures of social support in the traditional sense, they are conceptually relevant to social support and represent salient issues in the lives of many custodial grandparents. For example, problems linked to the overall quality and safety of the neighborhood are said to be factors that can heighten the chronic stress and strain associated with custodial grandparenting (Cox, 2000; Musil et al., 2000). Likewise, Fuller-Thomson and Minkler (2000) point out that social isolation, rejection, and alienation are quite common among custodial grandparents, and often linked to the social stigma associated with the reasons for caregiving such as poor parenting, incarceration, and drug abuse by the parent generation.

THE CONTEXT OF DIVERSITY WITHIN A DIVERSITY OF CONTEXTS

Our decision to explore diversity with respect to race, residential locale, and regional differences is rooted in an ecological perspective which holds that diversity occurs within a framework of multiple and often interactive contexts (Trickett, Watts, & Birman, 1994). A central tenet of this view is that various types of human diversity of interest to social scientists must be examined within a range of environmental contexts. In other words, the diversity associated with such traits as race or gender cannot be adequately investigated from a global perspective because they are shaped by specific or localized sociocultural conditions that are present within the unique context of one's environment. This caveat is particularly important with respect to the study of custodial grandparents because these caregivers come from all walks of life and live in a wide variety of settings (Butts, 2000; Pebley & Rudkin, 1999). Thus, it is insufficient to examine race or other forms of diversity among custodial grandparents without further considering how any differences that are observed may be mitigated by such contextual factors as residing in an urban versus rural area or being from a particular geographic region of the United States.

RACE AND SOCIAL SUPPORT

Although race is the most frequently investigated type of diversity regarding custodial grandparents (Goodman & Silverstein, 2002; Pruchno, 1999), past studies have typically failed to (a) compare racial groups explicitly (see, for exceptions, Pruchno, 1999; Pruchno & McKenney, 2002), (b) involve large representative samples to warrant generalizability across the entire nation, and (c) explore potential linkages between race and social supports. These specific failures of past studies are addressed in the present investigation.

The question of whether or not meaningful racial differences exist among custodial grandparents is somewhat controversial. On one hand, key differences in family life, cultural traditions, and sociohistorical contexts commonly noted between the two races may be expected to yield differences in how custodial grandparenting is experienced by Blacks and Whites, particularly with respect to formal and informal social supports. Blacks, for instance, are more likely to live in extended families which respond to the needs of their members, less likely to embrace the grandparental "norm of non-interference," and have historically played much different roles in family maintenance than Whites (Brown & Mars, 2000; Watson & Koblinsky, 1997).These combined influences suggest that Black custodial grandparents may be more advantaged than their White counterparts in terms of informal support from family and friends (Musil et al., 2000). In contrast, historic patterns of racial discrimination, coupled with the fact that Blacks are also likely to be poorer, less educated, and in poorer health than Whites suggest that they may be disadvantaged with respect to their involvement with formal supports (Butts, 2000).

However, there are equally compelling reasons to expect few, if any, differences in social supports between Black and White custodial grandparents once sociodemographic differences are taken into account (Caldwell, Antonucci, & Jackson, 1998; Pearson, Andrea, Cook, Ialongo, & Kellam, 1997). Bengtson, Rosenthal, and Burton (1995), for example, concluded that the view of pervasive strength in the extended kin networks of minority elders is not supported empirically and that the strength of ties in minority families is more heterogeneous than reported in the historical literature. Furthermore, the experience of many of today's Black grandparents who assume care for grandchildren as a result of drug addiction, incarceration, teen pregnancy, or parental incapacity due to AIDS, differs from that of their ancestors who assumed caregiving under much different sociohistorical circumstances (Burton, 1992; Burton & Dilworth-Anderson, 1991; Minkler & Roe, 1993). Thus, custodial grandparents from diverse ethnic backgrounds may now be more alike than before because they are raising their grandchildren due to social necessities rather than to personal choice or historical customs (Cox, 2000; Jendrek, 1994).

PLACE OF RESIDENCE AND SOCIAL SUPPORT

Even though U.S. Census data show that custodial grandparents reside in a variety of urban, suburban, and rural locations, research to date has primarily focused on those living in large metropolitan urban areas. Likely reasons for this emphasis on urban grandparents are that (a) approximately 75% of this population is estimated to reside in urban areas

(Pebley & Rudkin, 1999), (b) the chronic strain related to neighborhood and community problems of urban life are believed to impact the lives of these grandparents (Cox, 2000), and (c) the causes of custodial grand-parenting (e.g., drug abuse, crime) are highly prevalent in urban settings (Burton, 1992; Robinson, Kropf, & Myers, 2000).

The social forces described in the preceding paragraph are not unique to urban areas, however, and custodial grandparents from urban and rural areas share many common stressors (Robinson et al., 2000). Nevertheless, within rural areas, access to and availability of various basic health and social services for families often are seriously lacking. Grandparents in rural areas may encounter a variety of unmet needs due to few available resources, poor economic infrastructures, ill-equipped or poorly staffed social service agencies, transportation concerns, and geographic isolation (Cohen & Pyle, 2000; Cuellar & Butts, 1999). Rural custodial grandparents may also experience more social isolation than their urban dwelling counterparts due to a remote geography and the vast physical distance between neighboring families (Roberto, Richter, Bottenberg, & MacCormack, 1992). To date, however, direct comparisons between rural and urban custodial grandparents have been entirely speculative and devoid of explicit empirical investigations (e.g., Robinson et al., 2000).

Another deficiency in the literature on custodial grandparents has been a failure to explore the potentially unique circumstances of those families who reside in suburban locales. In fact, the tendency among most investigators has been to classify suburban dwelling custodial grandparents into either the urban or non-urban categories (see, for example, Fuller-Thomson, Minkler, & Driver (1997). This general neglect of suburban custodial grandparents may be attributed to the post–World War II idealization of the suburbs as pockets of affluence devoid of stress and hardship (Jackson, 1985). In the present study, we explore the possibility of explicit differences in the use and appraisal of social supports by custodial grandparents who reside either in urban, suburban, or rural areas.

POTENTIAL GEOGRAPHIC REGIONAL
DIFFERENCES IN SOCIAL SUPPORT

The particular region of the country where a family resides is another important environmental context that may be related to use and appraisal of social supports. Although attention to regional differences among custodial grandparents has been scarce and limited to basic demographic profiles, the few prior attempts to examine this variable have made a key distinction between grandparents from the southern and non-southern regions of the United States (Caputo, 2001; Fuller-Thomson & Minkler, 2000). One obvious reason for distinguishing between the South and non-South is because approximately 43% of all custodial grandparents reside in the South, making it by far the most prevalent region of the country for this form of caregiving to occur (U.S. Bureau of the Census, 2002). In turn, this heightened prevalence in the South may be associated with various factors related to how custodial grandparents encounter social supports such as greater community acceptance, less social stigma, or more abundant services than exist in those regions of the United States with fewer caregiving grandparents.

The southern region of the United States also possesses a unique historical legacy, which is partly due to the Civil War and slavery (Kulikoff, 1993). This has helped perpetuate a common and sometimes accurate image of the South as an underdeveloped, depressed, and neglected social, economic, and educational region (Kasarda, Irwin, & Hughes, 1986; Rowley & Freshwater, 1999). Although the South has experienced a renaissance in terms of social growth and economic prosperity (Goldfield, 1987), policy experts maintain that this region still lags behind the rest of the United States with respect to social, economic, and instrumental support services for children and their caregivers (Adams, Schulman, & Ebb, 1998; Shuptrine & Grant, 1996). Thus, it seems quite possible that such deficiencies have an impact on families headed by custodial grandparents.

Specific Goals of the Present Study

As stated earlier, the purpose of the study reported here is to explore whether or not the following three types of diversity within a large and nationally representative sample of custodial grandparents are related to their interactions with social support systems: *Race* (White and Black), *Residential Locale* (urban, suburban, and rural), and *Geographic Region* (South vs. non-South). Although the literature described in the previous sections illustrates how each of these three types of diversity may influence custodial grandparents' use and appraisals of social support, no specific hypotheses are tested due to the dearth of previous research in this area. Thus, two broad research questions are addressed in this study: (a) Do statistically significant differences exist among custodial grandparents in the use and appraisal of formal and informal social support with respect to the independent variables of *race*, *residential locale*, and *region*?; and

(b) Do any significant interactions exist between these three independent variables?

METHOD

Participants

The participants were a national sample of 733 grandmothers (M age = 56.9 years, SD = 7.92, Range = 34–83 years) providing full-time care to a grandchild between ages 4 and 16 years for at least 3 months in the absence of the child's parents. Recruitment involved a combination of probability (i.e., letters mailed to randomly selected households with children ages 0 to 17 years) and convenience (e.g., social service agencies; Internet, radio, TV, and newspaper ads) sampling methods. Potential participants were promised a $60 incentive for completing the study. By study design, the sample was approximately one half Black and one half White.

The resulting sample is from a total of 48 states and, as can be seen in Table 13.1, was diverse in terms of place of residence (urban: 47.7%; suburban: 19.8%; rural: 32.5%). More than half were married (55.3%), most worked full or part time (41%) and were either high school graduates (27.7%) or attended some college (35.5%). A target grandchild was used as a reference point during the entire interview, and the most recent birthday method (Kish, 1965) was used to select a target grandchild if a respondent was providing care to more than one grandchild within the specified age range. The target grandchildren were 391 girls and 342 boys (M age = 9.8 years, SD = 3.70, range = 4 to 16 years). The length of care provided by their grandmothers ranged from 3 months to 16 years (M = 8.14 years, SD = 4.50). A diagnosis of at least one physical condition was reported for 18.3% of the target grandchildren, whereas 27% were diagnosed with at least one psychiatric disorder.

Interview Procedure

Each grandmother was interviewed over the telephone by professionally trained and supervised interviewers at Kent State University. The interview was completed over a span of two to three separate telephone calls, and it encompassed questions on family issues, coping processes, interactions with the target grandchild, caregiving appraisals, well-being

TABLE 13.1   Descriptive Demographic Statistics of Participants

Variable	n	%
Race		
White	367	50.1
Black	366	49.9
Marital status		
Married	405	55.3
Widowed	102	13.9
Divorced	159	21.7
Single, never married	67	9.1
Education		
Less than 5 years	5	0.7
5 to 8 years	19	2.6
Some high school	99	13.5
High school graduate	203	27.7
Some college	260	35.5
College graduate	95	13.0
Graduate/professional training	52	17.1
Locale		
Urban	350	47.7
Rural	238	32.5
Suburban	145	19.8
Region		
Non-southern states	491	67.0
Southern states	242	33.0
Work status		
Not working	219	29.9
Working full or part time	329	44.9
Retired	144	19.6
Full-time homemaker	41	5.6
Income		
Under $10,000	123	16.8
$10,000–$15,000	109	14.9
$16,000–$20,000	85	11.6
$21,000 –$25,000	90	12.3
$26,000–$35,000	140	17.3
$36,000–$50,000	99	13.5
$51,000–$75,000	59	8.0
$76,000–$100,000	19	2.6
$101,000–$125,000	4	0.5
More than $125,000	5	0.7

of both grandparents and grandchild, as well as formal and informal social supports.

MEASURES

Independent Variables

Race was obtained through grandmothers' self-report of being either Black or White. *Locale* was determined by asking respondents if they considered the area in which they lived to be either urban, rural, or suburban. *Geographic Region* was operationalized according to the U.S. Bureau of the Census' (2000) designation of regional divisions (i.e., Northeast, South, Midwest, West), with grandmothers residing in southern states classified as "Southerners" and those living in either the Northeast, Midwest, or West considered "non-Southerners."

As part of the comprehensive telephone interview, grandmothers completed the measure described below regarding informal and formal social support. Each measure was preceded by the following statement to elicit the respondent's view of how things had changed since the inception of providing care to the target grandchild: "Since you began caring for your grandchild. . . . "

Dependent Variables

Informal Social Support

Family Support was measured with the Satisfaction with Family Life Scale from the Medical Outcomes Study Family Functioning Battery (Sherbourne, Kamberg, & Wells, 1992). Respondents rated from 1 (excellent) to 5 (poor) their satisfaction with three items regarding emotional support provided by family members (e.g., "The support and understanding you give each other"). Items were summed and the arithmetic average was then computed to yield a possible score ranging from 1 to 5 with lower scores indicating more positive support among family members (Cronbach's alpha = .88).

Expressive Social Support was measured with the eight-item Expressive Support scale (Pearlin, Mullan, Semple, & Skaff, 1990). Respondents rated each item (e.g., "You have at least one friend or relative you want to be with when you are feeling down or discouraged") from 1 (strongly disagree) to 5 (strongly agree). A mean score was calculated with a possible range of 1 to 4, with higher scores indicating greater perceived support from family members (Cronbach's alpha = .89).

Satisfaction with Friends and Neighbors was measured by one item developed for this study: "Overall, how satisfied are you with the emotional support and understanding that you receive from your friends and neighbors?" (rated from 0, not at all satisfied to 5, extremely satisfied).

Loneliness was measured by one item developed for this study: "You find your circle of friends and acquaintances too limited" (rated from 1, strongly disagree to 5, strongly agree).

Feeling Rejected was measured by one item developed for this study: "You feel rejected" (rated from 1, strongly disagree to 5, strongly agree).

Formal Social Support

Support from Formal Systems in the Community was measured with respect to each of the following six service systems: legal, social service, school, medical, mental health, and clergy/religious community. For each service system, respondents were asked the following question, "The _____ has been supportive of my needs as a caregiving grandparent." Response alternatives for each item ranged from 1 (strongly disagree) to 4 (strongly agree).

Use of Mental Health Services was measured by asking respondents whether or not they had used each of five different mental health-related services (i.e., family counseling, support groups, psychiatric treatment, substance abuse treatment/prevention, telephone crises/help lines) for either themselves or the target grandchild in the past year. Respondents received a 1 for each service that was used, and a total score was calculated with a possible range of 0 to 5.

Use of Instrumental Supportive Services was measured by asking respondents whether or not they had used each of five different instrumental supportive services (i.e., food banks, financial assistance, transportation, respite, day care) for either themselves or the target grandchild in the past year. Respondents received a 1 for each service that was used, and a total score was calculated having a possible range of 0 to 5.

The Quality of the Neighborhood/Community Environment was measured by the following four separate items: "My community is a safe, clean, and comfortable environment"; "My community provides the resources and services necessary for raising a child"; "My community is a good place to raise a child"; and "My community is a good place to live." Response alternatives for each item ranged from 1 (strongly disagree) to 4 (strongly agree).

RESULTS

An initial 2 (race) × 2 (region) × 3 (locale) multivariate analysis of variance (MANOVA) was performed to test for statistically significant group differences in terms of the key demographic variables of income, education, grandmother's age, and target grandchild's age. Statistically significant multivariate differences were found only with respect to income and education. In turn, univariate differences were observed such that income was significantly greater for those grandmothers who were White, lived in suburbs, and were non-Southerners ($p \leq .01$). The only significant univariate difference regarding education was that suburban grandmothers had higher educational levels ($p \leq .01$). Chi-square analyses were performed to look for possible differences in marital and work status among the three categories of independent variables. The only statistically significant difference found involved race and marital status such that more White grandmothers were married than Blacks (chi-square = 89.39, $p \leq .001$).

Because income was the only demographic variable found to show statistically significant differences across the independent variables, it was entered as a covariate in all subsequent analyses. Income is also regarded as a key variable in the receipt of various forms of social support and service usage (Streeter & Franklin, 1992; Turner, Pearlin, & Mullan, 1998).

Multivariate Effects

A series of 2 (race) × 2 (region) × 3 (locale) multivariate analyses of covariance (MANCOVA) with income entered as a covariate were performed using the SPSS General Linear Model (GLM) procedure to examine potential group differences in the dependent variable domains of informal support, formal support, and neighborhood quality. We used MANCOVA because this method (a) creates a linear combination of related dependent variables and then tests for differences in this new variable using methods similar to analysis of variance (ANOVA), (b) diminishes the likelihood of Type I errors, and (c) makes necessary adjustments if any of the dependent variables are intercorrelated. The GLM procedure is also quite robust with respect to departures from the principle multivariate assumptions of (a) independence among observations, (b) equality of variance-covariance matrices, and (c) normality of dependent variables (Hair, Anderson, Tatham, & Black, 1998). Nevertheless, inspection of the data revealed that they acceptably met these assumptions, and as recommended by Olson (1976), Pillai's trace criterion was used in order to maximize robustness due to sample size inequalities.

Overall Multivariate Effects

Statistically significant multivariate effects were found (a) within the informal support variable cluster for both race (multivariate $F = 5.11$; $df = 5/688$; $p \leq .001$) and locale (multivariate $F = 1.92$; $df = 10/1376$; $p \leq .05$). In spite of the multivariate effects, no univariate differences were observed by locale. In the formal support variable cluster multivariate effects were observed for both race (multivariate $F = 2.08$; $df = 8/669$; $p \leq .05$) and geographic region (multivariate $F = 5.33$; $df = 8/669$; $p \leq .001$). In the neighborhood quality variable cluster multivariate effects were found for race (multivariate $F = 4.76$; $df = 4/689$; $p \leq .001$), and a statistically significant race locale (multivariate $F = 2.73$; $df = 8/1378$; $p \leq .01$) interaction was also present.

Univariate Between Group Main Effects

Main effects associated with each of three separate MANCOVAs described in the preceding paragraph are presented in Table 13.2, and the corresponding adjusted means and standard deviations are shown in Table 13.3.

Informal Social Support

Within the informal support cluster statistically significant differences were found only by race, with White grandmothers reporting feeling significantly lonelier and more rejected than Black grandmothers.

Formal Social Support

Statistically significant univariate group differences were found for (a) race, with Black grandmothers reporting significantly lower satisfaction with support received from both the school system and the medical community than their White counterparts; and (b) region, with Southern grandparents reporting less satisfaction with the legal system and mental health community, in meeting their needs as caregivers. Southern grandmothers were also found to utilize significantly fewer instrumental services than grandmothers residing in other parts of the country.

TABLE 13.2 Results of Multivariate Analysis of Covariance (MANCOVA) for Social Support Variables

| | Univariate Statistics | | | | | |
| | Race | | Region | | Locale | |
Source	f	df	f	df	f	df
Informal social supports						
Family support	10.14***	1	0.03	1	1.83	2
Friends and neighbors	0.03	1	0.002	1	2.18	2
Expressive support	0.37	1	1.46	1	0.37	2
Loneliness	18.09***	1	0.73	1	0.04	2
Rejection	7.29***	1	0.16	1	1.39	2
Formal social supports						
Legal system	0.004	1	6.75**	1	0.41	2
Social service system	0.10	1	3.26	1	0.19	2
School system	4.47*	1	0.89	1	0.27	2
Medical community	8.96**	1	4.36*	1	0.49	2
Mental health community	0.96	1	13.23***	1	1.11	2
Religious community	0.33	1	1.97	1	1.81	2
Mental health service use	2.15	1	3.82	1	1.27	2
Instrumental service use	0.47	1	21.25***	1	0.69	2
Neighborhood quality						
Safe and clean place	13.61***	1	1.03	1	2.75	2
Necessary resources/ services	12.70***	1	2.78	1	0.89	2
Good place to raise children	12.82***	1	0.04	1	1.16	2
Good place to live	1.33	1	2.33	1	3.24*	2

Note: Income served as a covariate in each analysis.
*$p \leq .05$. **$p \leq .01$. ***$p \leq .001$.

TABLE 13.3 Adjusted Means and Standard Deviations for Social Support Variables

| | Race | | | | Region | | | | Locale | | | | | |
| | White | | Black | | Non-Southern | | Southern | | Urban | | Suburban | | Rural | |
	M	SD	M	SD	M	SD	M	SD	M	SD	M	SD	M	SD
Informal social supports														
Family support	2.28	0.92	2.31	0.94	2.29	0.92	2.30	0.95	2.32	0.93	2.36	0.96	2.22	0.90
Friends and neighbors	3.30	1.11	3.28	1.11	3.28	1.10	3.32	1.12	3.32	1.15	3.18	1.09	3.31	1.05
Expressive support	3.31	0.51	3.23	0.45	3.29	0.50	3.23	0.42	3.25	0.47	3.33	0.46	3.25	0.49
Loneliness	**2.72**	**1.05**	**2.35**	**0.89**	**2.59**	**1.01**	**2.44**	**0.9 3**	2.46	0.95	2.53	0.93	2.65	1.07
Rejection	**2.18**	**1.00**	**2.03**	**0.88**	2.11	0.95	2.21	1.00	2.19	1.02	1.97	0.84	2.11	0.93
Formal social supports														
Legal system	2.62	1.01	2.56	0.94	**2.65**	**0.99**	**2.46**	**0.94**	2.59	1.01	2.53	0.94	2.61	0.95
Social service system	2.66	0.98	2.57	0.88	**2.65**	**0.95**	**2.53**	**0.89**	2.60	0.97	2.59	0.91	2.64	0.89
School system	**3.31**	**0.73**	**3.12**	**0.74**	**3.23**	**0.75**	**3.18**	**0.72**	3.19	0.79	3.26	0.73	3.22	0.68
Medical community	**3.35**	**0.65**	**3.17**	**0.70**	**3.31**	**0.66**	**3.16**	**0.71**	3.26	0.72	3.26	0.66	3.25	0.64
Mental health community	3.08	0.79	2.94	0.77	**3.10**	**0.76**	**2.84**	**0.81**	2.98	0.82	3.13	0.75	2.99	0.76

TABLE 13.3 (continued)

| | Race | | | | Region | | | | Locale | | | | | |
| | White | | Black | | Non-Southern | | Southern | | Urban | | Suburban | | Rural | |
	M	SD	M	SD	M	SD	M	SD	M	SD	M	SD	M	SD
Religious community	3.39	0.65	3.38	0.66	3.40	0.63	3.36	0.71	3.40	0.67	3.39	0.58	3.36	0.68
Mental health service use	1.63	1.50	1.39	1.42	1.48	1.43	1.58	1.54	1.54	1.46	1.39	1.44	1.54	1.50
Instrumental service use	1.28	1.23	1.08	1.15	**1.36**	**1.22**	**0.82**	**1.05**	1.21	1.19	1.18	1.21	1.14	1.19
Neighborhood quality														
Safe and clean place	**3.31**	**0.66**	**3.02**	**0.72**	3.17	0.71	3.16	0.69	3.07	0.75	3.29	0.62	3.24	0.66
Necessary resources/services	**3.12**	**0.69**	**2.93**	**0.69**	3.04	0.69	3.00	0.71	3.00	0.72	3.10	6.40	3.02	0.70
Good place to raise children	**3.24**	**0.63**	**3.04.**	**0.68**	3.12	0.68	3.18	0.62	3.15	0.74	3.14	0.69	3.15	0.69
Good place to live	3.22	0.68	3.07.	0.74	3.18	0.68	3.07	0.78	**3.07**	**0.67**	**3.29**	**0.61**	**3.15**	**0.66**

Note: Bold and underscored values represent statistically significant differences.

213

Appraisals of Neighborhood Quality

Statistically significant differences, however, were found by both race and locale. Black grandmothers rated their neighborhood less favorably than Whites in terms of it being a safe and clean environment for children ($p \leq .001$), providing resources and services needed to raise a child ($p \leq .001$), and being a good place to raise children ($p \leq .001$). The only significant difference involving locale was that urban grandmothers were less favorable of the neighborhood being an overall good place to live ($p \leq .05$). It should be noted, however, that despite the univariate difference, no multivariate effects were found for neighborhood quality and locale.

Univariate Interaction Effects

A significant race by locale interaction was found for grandmothers' ratings of the neighborhood providing resources and services needed to raise a child (F $(2/692) = 3.63$, $p \leq .05$), and their general view of the neighborhood being a good place to live (F $(2/692) = 4.65$, $p \leq .01$), with urban-dwelling Black grandmothers providing significantly lower ratings for these two neighborhood appraisals.

DISCUSSION

The purpose of the present study was to explore whether or not diversity regarding race (White and Black), residential locale (urban, suburban, and rural), and geographic region (South versus non-South) was related to custodial grandmothers' experience with various aspects of social support as conceptualized into three distinct variable clusters: informal support, formal support, and neighborhood quality.

Central to the meaningfulness of this study is that few studies have explicitly examined social support among custodial grandparents (see for exception, Musil, 1998). Although social support from both formal and informal sources is widely recognized as a key component of one's ability to cope with stressful situations (Aneshensel, Pearlin, Mullan, Zarit, & Whitlatch, 1995), the main findings are discussed below according to the respective independent variables of race, residential locale, and geographic region. This section concludes with a description of study limitations and directions for future research.

The Salience of Race

The most striking finding of the present study concerns the extent to which race, in contrast to residential locale and region, was associated with custodial grandmothers' use and appraisal of social support. In fact, race was the only independent variable for which statistically significant differences were found across all three dependent variable clusters. Moreover, because the differences between White and Black grandmothers emerged after income (a proxy measure of socioeconomic status) was treated as a covariate, it is likely that the racial differences found in this study are largely due to long standing cultural and historical forces rather than to differences in social status. Our findings regarding race are also consistent with those reported by Pruchno (1999) in the only other large-scale national study of Black and White caregiving grandparents.

That Black grandmothers in our study reported feeling less lonely and rejected since taking on the role of custodial grandparent than their White counterparts is congruent with Pruchno's (1999) findings that Black grandmothers were more likely than Whites to (a) have friends who also live with their grandchildren, (b) report that it was not unusual for multiple generations to live together in their family, (c) have been raised by a grandparent themselves, and (d) feel that caregiving responsibilities had less of a negative impact on their social life. Thus, the results of both studies reinforce the widespread assertion that Blacks feel less stigmatized and more in tune with their social peers within the custodial grandparenting role than Whites due to traditions of kinship caregiving within the Black multigenerational family structure (Burton & Dilworth-Anderson, 1991; Cox, 2000; Scannapieco & Jackson, 1996). It should be noted, however, that the mean values observed in the present study (see Table 13.3) suggest that both Black and White custodial grandmothers are at risk with respect to feeling isolated and rejected as a result of becoming a custodial grandparent. Moreover, the overall magnitude of the observed race differences on these particular variables was small.

In terms of the formal social support variable cluster, use of both mental health and instrumental services appears to be low regardless of race, region, or locale. Within the formal support cluster, all grandmothers reported overall higher levels of satisfaction regarding the legal and social service systems than with the other four service systems. Use of both mental health and instrumental services appears to be low regardless of race, region, or locale. Significant racial differences, however, were found where Blacks were less likely than Whites to report that their needs as custodial grandparents were being met by either the school system or the medical community. However, there are two key reasons why these particular differences should be regarded as being modest in scope: (a) The overall mean levels of satisfaction with formal services were consistently high for both Blacks and Whites (see Table 3); and (b) No statistically significant differences by race were found for any of the other formal services examined (i.e., legal, social service, mental health, and religious) or for the two indices of service use examined in the present study. Thus, both the White and Black custodial grandmothers in this sample seemed to be generally pleased with how a wide variety of formal support systems were meeting their needs as caregivers.

The particular finding that Black custodial grandmothers within our national sample were less satisfied with the medical community than White grandmothers is consistent with a long-standing pattern of distrust of medical health professionals held by Black patients, which is said to be due to indifference and unethical treatment by both physicians (Byrd, Clayton, & Blendon, 2000; Savitt, 1985) and medical researchers (Corbie-Smith, Thomas, Williams, & Moody-Ayers, 1999). Similarly, the finding that Blacks were less satisfied than Whites in terms of how well the school system was meeting their needs as custodial grandparents may reflect a heritage of distrust associated with school segregation and racial bias in the classroom (Ogbu & Davis, 2003). The modest differences found between White and Black grandmothers in this study, however, should not minimize the fact that custodial grandparents of both races are known to experience problematic interactions with the educational system due to a belief among school staff and administrators that these caregivers are not legitimate parental figures (Grant, Gordon, & Cohen, 1997; Jendrek, 1994).

Although neighborhood appraisals were generally quite favorable regardless of grandmothers' race, region, or locale (Table 13.3), statistically significant differences were found by both race and locale. Even after controlling for income, Black grandmothers were less likely than Whites to view their neighborhood or community as providing resources and services necessary for raising a child; being a safe and clean place to live; and being a good place to raise children. We also found a statistically significant race × locale interaction such that Black grandmothers from urban settings held the least favorable evaluations of their neighborhood as being an overall good place to live. This latter finding is in line with the belief that neighborhood problems are most prevalent among Black custodial grandparents residing in the inner city (Burton, 1992; Minkler, Roe, & Price, 1992). Nevertheless, since the mean ratings (see Table 13.3) across the various neighborhood quality measures indicate overall favorable perceptions among both Black and White grandmothers, it appears that custodial grandparents from both races generally view their neighborhoods and communities as good settings in which to raise their grandchildren. Nevertheless, the finding that Black custodial grandmothers reported less favorable evaluations than White grandmothers is consistent with the assertion that Black individuals often see their communities as devalued relative to predominantly White neighborhoods (due to a long history of racism and inequality), which prompts them to believe that they are receiving public services and amenities of reduced quality (Feagin & Sikes, 1994; Feagin, Early, & McKinney, 2001). In turn, these perceptions may foster feelings of distrust of formal public service providers among Black custodial grandparents (Baird et al., 2000).

Residential Locale

As stated in the introduction, many reasons exist for suspecting that custodial grandparents from rural environments encounter less accessibility to formal and informal social supports than their counterparts who reside in urban or suburban settings (Cohen & Pyle, 2000; Cuellar & Butts, 1999; Roberto et al., 1992). It has also been stated that concerns regarding neighborhood crime, safety, and overall quality are highest among grandparents living within urban areas (Burton, 1992; Cox, 2000; Minkler et al., 1992). Yet, despite the many reasons for suspecting differences regarding social supports between urban, rural, and suburban custodial grandparents to emerge, only two modest differences emerged in the present study within the neighborhood quality variable cluster. First, urban custodial grandmothers were less likely than rural and suburban grandparents to rate their neighborhood as a "good place to live." Second, as noted above, a significant race by locale interaction where Black urban grandmothers reported the least favorable evaluations of their neighborhood as being an overall good place to live was also found.

One possible explanation for the surprising dearth of differences found among rural, urban, and suburban custodial grandparents is that we statistically controlled for income, on account of our preliminary finding that suburban custodial grandmothers reported significantly higher income than their rural and urban counterparts. As noted earlier, income is seen as an important variable in the receipt of social support and the use of services (Streeter & Franklin, 1992; Turner et al., 1998). Yet, upon reanalyzing the data without controlling for income, the results remained virtually the same.

Another potential reason for the scarcity of differences found between urban, suburban, and rural custodial grandparents concerns the way in which we operationalized locale. More specifically, a major disadvantage of our reliance on grandmothers' self-report is that respondents may have been unfamiliar with key distinctions between the various types of residential locales that are held by experts. For instance, some respondents from suburbs of large metropolitan regions may have incorrectly reported themselves as residing in urban locales. Thus, it is conceivable that the use of a more objective and quantitative method for differentiating between urban, suburban, and rural locales, such as the geographic designations of the U.S. Bureau of the Census (2002), which are based on Metropolitan Statistical Areas (MSAs) and involve calculations of both population size and the density of a residential population, may have yielded different findings. Yet, it has been argued that this statistical approach fails to capture important qualitative aspects of those who actually reside in these areas (Rios, 1988).

Another possible explanation for the scarcity of differences between urban, suburban, and rural custodial grandparents in the present study is that as much heterogeneity may exist within urban, suburban, and rural areas as it does between them. For example, due to the phenomenon referred to as "urban sprawl" (Duany, Plater-Zyberk, & Speck, 2000), certain rural areas now border on and share similar services and amenities with nearby urban and suburban communities. Yet other rural areas continue to exist within remote and isolated areas of the United States. Social scientists have also maintained that suburban and rural areas are becoming as diverse as urban areas in terms of income, education, occupation, race, ethnicity, culture, and the type of neighborhood or community in which one lives (Bull, 1993; Choldin, 1985; Duany et al., 2000).

Thus, future research is needed to determine the extent to which variability within urban, suburban, and rural locales may be related to important social support outcomes for custodial grandparents and their families.

South Versus Non-South

Although we found a substantial number of statistically significant differences between custodial grandparents from southern versus non-southern states, these differences were solely within the formal support variable cluster with no regional differences found within either the neighborhood quality or informal support clusters. Compared to non-southern custodial grandmothers, those in the South used fewer instrumental services within the past year and reported less satisfaction with the legal system, the medical community, and the mental health community in meeting their needs as caregivers. This pattern of findings is remarkably consistent with the observation by policy experts that a gap exists regarding the quality and delivery of resources and services related to child care between the

South and the rest of the country (Adams, Schulman, & Ebb, 1998; Shuptrine & Grant, 1996; Southern Institute on Children and Families, 2002). These results are particularly disturbing in view of the fact that custodial grandparenting is most prevalent in the South and that the South's overall population of children has increased to a point where their numbers are larger than other regions of the country (U.S. Bureau of the Census, 2002). It is anticipated that this population increase will raise the consumption of important services related to child care (e.g., education, medical), place a financial strain on the formal service system, and thus reduce the ability of southern states and municipalities to adequately deliver these services in a high quality manner (Guillory, Beyle, & Quinterno, 2004). Indeed, these growing deficiencies in child care-related services in the South represent a serious widespread issue for all parental caregivers and not just a problem unique to custodial grandparents.

Study Limitations and Directions for Future Research

Several important limitations of this study limit the generalizability of the findings reported in this chapter. Although the sample is large, diverse, and contains respondents from across the United States, participation in this study was entirely voluntary. Thus, it is unknown to what extent the views of those custodial grandmothers who chose not to participate were either alike or different from those of study participants. Also, by restricting our sample to Whites and Blacks, we are unable to generalize our findings to custodial grandparents from other racial or ethnic groups (e.g., Latinos, Asians, Native Americans). Another limitation is that our data came entirely from grandmothers' self-reports which may not have accurately captured the true objective circumstances of these caregivers. It should also be acknowledged that social support is an extremely complex and multidimensional construct (Sarason et al., 1990) and that many important aspects of formal and informal support were overlooked in this study. Finally, the cross-sectional nature of the data prohibits us from concluding that any of the differences found in this study are truly associated with taking on the role of custodial grandparent.

Despite these limitations, the present study is the first to provide important new information on how diversity associated with race, residential locale, and geographic region is related to custodial grandparents' perceptions and use of formal and informal social supports. The findings should be useful to policy makers and provide an impetus for future research. However, further studies are needed that (a) expand diversity to encompass multiple racial and ethic groups; (b) examine differentiation within categories of urban, suburban, and rural; (c) include more in-depth and objective measures of social support; and (d) explore potential linkages between social support and the overall well-being of custodial grandparents and the grandchildren to whom they provide care.

REFERENCES

Adams, G., Schulman, K., and Ebb, N. (1998). Locked doors: States struggling to meet the child care needs of low-income working families. Washington, DC: Children's Defense Fund.

Aneshensel, C. S., Pearlin, L. I., Mullan, J. T., Zarit, S. H., & Whitlatch, C. J., (1995). *Profiles in caregiving: The unexpected career*. New York: Academic Press.

Baird, A., John, R., & Hayslip, B., Jr. (2000). Custodial grandparenting among African Americans: A focus group perspective. In B. Hayslip Jr. & R. Goldberg-Glenn (Eds.), *Grandparents raising grandchildren: Theoretical, empirical, and clinical perspectives* (pp. 125–144). New York: Springer.

Bengtson, V. L., Rosenthal, C. J., & Burton, L. M. (1995). Paradoxes of families and aging. In R. H. Binstock & L. K. George (Eds.), *Handbook of aging and the social sciences* (4th ed., pp. 253–282). San Diego, CA: Academic Press.

Brown, D. R., & Mars, J. (2000). Profile of Contemporary Grandparenting in African-American families. In C. B. Cox (Ed.), *To grandmother's house we go and stay: Perspectives on custodial grandparents* (pp. 203–217). New York: Springer.

Bull, C. N. (Ed.). (1993). *Aging in rural America*. Newbury Park, CA: Sage.

Burton, L. M. (1992). Black grandparents rearing children of drug-addicted parents: Stressors, outcomes, and social service needs. *The Gerontologist, 32*(6), 744–751.

Burton, L. M., & Dilworth-Anderson, P. (1991). The intergenerational family roles of aged Black Americans. *Marriage and Family Review, 16*(3/4), 311–330.

Butts, D. (2000). Organizational advocacy as a factor in public policy regarding grandparents raising grandchildren. In B. Hayslip & R. Goldberg-Glen (Eds.), *Grandparents raising grandchildren: Theoretical, empirical, and clinical perspective* (pp. 341–350). New York: Springer.

Byrd, M. W., Clayton, L. A., & Blendon, R. (2000). *An American health dilemma: A medical history of African Americans and the problem of race*. New York: Routledge.

Caldwell, C. H., Antonucci, T. C., & Jackson, J. S. (1998). Supportive/conflictual family relations and depressive symptomatology: Teenage mother and grandmother perspectives. *Family Relations, 47*, 395–402.

Caputo, R. K. (2001).The intergenerational transfer of grandmother-grandchild coresidency. *Journal of Sociology & Social Welfare, 28*(1), 79–86.

Choldin, H. (1985). *Cities and suburbs: An introduction to urban sociology*. New York: McGraw-Hill.

Cohen, C. S., & Pyle, R. (2000). Support groups in the lives of grandmothers raising grandchildren. In C. B. Cox (Ed.), *To grandmother's house we go and stay: Perspectives on custodial grandparents* (pp. 235–252). New York: Springer.

Corbie-Smith, G., Thomas, S. B., Williams, M. V., & Moody-Ayers, S. (1999). Attitudes and beliefs of African Americans toward participation in medical research. *Journal of General and Internal Medicine, 14,* 537–546.

Cox, C. B. (Ed.). (2000). *To grandmother's house we go and stay: Perspectives on custodial grandparents.* New York: Springer.

Cox, C. B., Brooks, L. R., & Valcarcel, C. (2000). Culture and caregiving: A study of Latino grandparents. In C.B. Cox (Ed.), *To grandmother's house we go and stay: Perspectives on custodial grandparents* (pp. 218–232). New York: Springer.

Cuellar, N., & Butts, J. (1999). Caregiver distress: What nurses in rural settings can do to help. *Nursing Forum, 34*(3), 24–30.

Duany, A., Plater-Zyberk, E., & Speck, J. (2000). *Suburban nation: The rise of sprawl and the decline of the American dream.* New York: North Point Press.

Feagin, J. R., Early, K. E., & McKinney, K. D. (2001). The many costs of discrimination: The case of middle-class African Americans. *Indiana Law Review, 34,* 1313–1360.

Feagin, J. R., & Sikes, M. (1994). *Living with racism: The Black middle class experience.* Boston: Beacon Press.

Frey, W. H. (2001). Melting pot suburbs: A Census 2000 study of suburban diversity. *The Brookings Institution Center on Metropolitan and Urban Policy, Census 2000 Series,* 1–17.

Fuller-Thomson, E., & Minkler, M. (2000). African American grandparents raising grandchildren: A national profile of demographic and health characteristics. *Health & Social Work, 25,* 109–118.

Fuller-Thomson, E., Minkler, M., & Driver, D. (1997). A profile of grandparents raising grandchildren in the United States. *The Gerontologist, 37,* 406–411.

Goldfield, D. R. (1987). *Promised land the South since 1945.* Wheeling, IL: Harlan Davidson.

Goodman, C. C., & Silverstein, M. (2002). Grandmothers who parent their grandchildren: An exploratory study of close relations across three generations. *Journal of Family Issues, 22*(5), 557–578.

Grant, R., Gordon, S. G., & Cohen, S. T. (1997). An innovative school-based intergenerational model to serve grandparent caregivers. *Journal of Gerontological Social Work, 281*(1–2), 47–61.

Guillory, F., Beyle, T., & Quinterno, J. (2004). *SouthNow update* (March 12, Issue no. 55). Program on Southern Politics, Media, and Public Life. Chapel Hill, NC: University of North Carolina.

Hair, J., Anderson, R., Tathem, R., & Black, W. (1998). *Multivariate data analysis* (5th ed.). Upper Saddle River, NJ: Prentice Hall.

Hayslip, B., Silverthorn, P., Shore, R. J., & Henderson, C. (2000). Determinants of custodial grandparents' perceptions of problem behaviors in their grandchildren. In B. Hayslip & R. Goldberg-Glen (Eds.), *Grandparents raising grandchildren: Theoretical, empirical, and clinical perspectives* (pp. 255–268). New York: Springer.

Hirshorn, B. A., Van Meter, M. J., & Brown, D. R. (2000). Intervening when grandparents raise grandchildren due to substance abuse: Responding to a uniquely destabilizing factor. In B. Hayslip, Jr. & R. Goldberg-Glenn (Eds.), *Grandparents raising grandchildren: Theoretical, empirical, and clinical perspectives* (pp. 269–288). New York: Springer.

Jackson, K. (1985). *Crabgrass frontier.* New York: Oxford University Press.

Jendrek, M. P. (1994). Grandparents who parent their grandchildren: Circumstances and decisions. *The Gerontologist, 34*(2), 206–216.

Kasarda, J. D., Irwin, M. D., & Hughes, H. L. (1986). The South is still rising. *American Demographics, 6,* 32–39.

Kish, L. (1965). *Survey sampling.* New York: John Wiley.

Kulikoff, A. (1993). The southern tidewater and piedmont. In M. K. Cayton, E. J. Gorn, & P. W. Williams (Eds.), *Encyclopedia of American social history* (Vol. 2, pp. 1017–1029). New York: Scribner.

Minkler, M., & Roe, K. (1993). *Grandmothers as caregivers.* Newbury Park, CA: Sage.

Minkler, M., Roe, K., & Price, M. (1992). The physical and emotional health of grandmothers raising grandchildren in the crack cocaine epidemic. *The Gerontologist, 32,* 752–760.

Morrow-Kondos, D., Weber, J., Cooper, K., & Hesser, J. (1997). Becoming parents again: Grandparents raising grandchildren. *Journal of Gerontological Social Work, 28*(1–2), 35–46.

Musil, C. M. (1998). Health, stress, coping and social support in grandmother caregivers. *Health Care for Women International, 19,* 441–455.

Musil, C. M., Schrader, S., & Mutikani, J. (2000). Social support, stress, and special coping tasks of grandmother caregivers. In C. B. Cox (Ed.), *To grandmother's house we go and stay: Perspectives on custodial grandparents* (pp. 56–70). New York: Springer.

Ogbu, J. U., & Davis, A. (2003) *Black American students in an affluent suburb: A study of academic disengagement.* Mahwah, NJ: Erlbaum.

Olson, C. L. (1976). On choosing a test statistic in multivariate analyses of variance. *Psychological Bulletin, 83,* 579–586.

Pearlin, L. I., Mullan, J. T., Semple, S. J., & Skaff, M. M., (1990). Caregiving and the stress process: An overview of concepts and their measures. *The Gerontologist, 30,* 583–594.

Pearson, J. L., Andrea, G., Cook, J. M., Ialongo, N. S., & Kellam, S. G. (1997). Grandmother involvement in child caregiving in an urban community. *The Gerontologist, 37*(5), 650–657.

Pebley, A. R., & Rudkin, L. L. (1999). Grandparents caring for grandchildren: What do we know? *Journal of Family Issues, 20*(2), 218–242.

Porterfield, J., Dressel, P., & Barnhill, S. (2000). Special situation of incarcerated parents. In C. B.Cox (Ed.), *To grandmother's house we go and stay: Perspectives on custodial grandparents* (pp. 184–202). New York: Springer.

Pruchno, R. (1999). Raising grandchildren: The experiences of Black and White grandmothers. *The Gerontologist, 39*(2), 209–221.

Pruchno, R. A., & McKenney, D. (2002). Psychological well-being of Black and White grandmothers raising grandchildren: Examination of a two-factor model. *Journal of Gerontology: Psychological Sciences, 57B,* P444–P452.

Rios, B. R. D. (1988). "Rural"—A concept beyond definition? *ERIC*(5), 47–51.

Roberto, K., & Qualls, S. (2003). Intervention strategies for grandparents raising grandchildren: Lessons learned from the late life caregiving literature. In B. Hayslip & J. Hicks Patrick (Eds.), *Working with custodial grandparents*. New York: Springer.

Roberto, K., Richter, J., Bottenberg, D., & MacCormack, R. (1992). Provider/client views: Health care needs of the rural elderly. *Journal of Gerontological Nursing, 18*, 31–37.

Robinson, M., Kropf, N., & Myers, L. (2000). Grandparents raising grandchildren in rural communities. *Journal of Mental Health and Aging, 6*(4), 353–365.

Rowley, T. D., & Freshwater, D. (1999). Are workers in the rural South ready for the future? *U.S. Department of Agriculture, Economic Research Service, Rural Development Perspectives, 14*(3), October.

Sarason, B. R., Pierce, G. R., & Sarason, I. G. (1990). Social support: The sense of acceptance and the role of relationships. In B. R. Sarason, I. G. Sarason, & G. R. Pierce (Eds.), *Social support: An interactional view* (pp. 97–128). New York: Wiley.

Savitt, T. (1985). Black health on the plantation: Masters, slaves and physicians. In J. Walzer Leavitt & R. Numbers (Eds.), *Sickness and health in America* (pp. 313–330). Madison: University of Wisconsin Press.

Scannapieco, M., & Jackson, S. (1996). Kinship care: The African American response to family preservation. *Social Work, 41*(2), 190–195.

Sherbourne, C. D., Kamberg, A. H., & Wells, K. B. (1992). Physical/psychophysiologic symptoms measure. In A. L. Stewart & J. E. Ware (Eds.), *Measuring functioning and well-being: The medical outcomes study approach* (pp. 260–276). Durham, NC: Duke University Press.

Shuptrine, S. C., & Grant, V. C. (1996). *Uninsured children in the South: Second report*. The Henry J. Kaiser Family Foundation (November).

Southern Institute on Children and Families (2002). *Chartbook of major indicators: conditions placing children in the South at risk (August)*.

Streeter, C. L., & Franklin, C. (1992). Defining and measuring social support: Guidelines for social work practitioners. *Research on Social Work Practice, 2*(1), 81–98.

Turner, H. A., Pearlin, L. I., & Mullan, J. T. (1998). Sources and determinants of social support for caregivers of persons with AIDS. *Journal of Health and Social Behavior, 39*(2), 137–151.

U.S. Bureau of the Census. (2002). *Profile of general demographic characteristics: 2000*. Washington, DC: U.S. Bureau of the Census.

Watson, J., & Koblinsky, S. (1997). Strengths and needs of working-class African-American and Anglo-American grandparents. *International Journal of Aging and Human Development, 44*(2), 149–165.

Whitley, D. M., Kelley, S. J., & Sipe, T. A. (2001). Grandmothers raising grandchildren: Are they at increased risk of health problems? *Health and Social Work, 26*(2), 105–114.

CHAPTER 14

Stress-Related Factors Among Primary and Part-Time Caregiving Grandmothers of Kenyan Grandchildren

Paul Odhiambo Oburu and Kerstin Palmérus

Research on kinship care, especially during the past three decades, has consistently reported an upward trend in the number of sub-Saharan African orphans (children below 15 who have lost one or both parents) due to HIV/AIDS-related deaths. In 2001, it was estimated that about 14.3 million of these orphans (12% compared to 6.5% for Asia and 5% for Latin America) were raised on a full-time basis by elderly and impoverished grandparents. Their numbers were expected to exceed 16% (over 44 million sub-Saharan African and 2 million Kenyan children) by 2010 (UNICEF/UNAIDS, 2002).

Full-time care is potentially very stressful to caregiving grandmothers. Limited state involvement in welfare systems and lack of social institutions that potentially could take in the large number of orphans has meant that Kenyan adoptive grandmothers have to sacrifice their own self-interests and limited financial resources when they assume full-time caregiving responsibilities for their orphaned grandchildren (UNICEF, 1999, 2000). Pressure exerted on grandmother caregivers to fend for their grandchildren at a time when they are grieving over the deaths of their adult children (these children's parents) generates in them feelings of loss, being used, and abused (Adepoju & Mbugua, 1997; UNICEF/UNAIDS, 2002).

This chapter compares the levels of stress experienced by Kenyan caregiving grandmothers who assumed full-time (FTC) and partial (PTC) caregiving responsibilities for their grandchildren. This chapter specifically examines whether the total stresses experienced was moderated by these grandmothers' perception of child manageability, and perceived availability of emotional and instrumental support. It is evident from the literature reviewed that studies comparing stress experienced by non-U.S. grandmothers with full-time and partial caregiving responsibilities for their grandchildren are still lacking (Musil, 1998; Rodgers, 1999). Existing analyses have mainly focused on U.S. grandmothers with primary responsibility for their grandchildren or used predominantly White, middle- to upper-class grandmothers of children with at least one of the parents still living (e.g., Kelley, 1993; Rodgers, 1999).

The McCubbin and Patterson (1982) "double ABCX" stress-coping model was used to examine the possibility that the total stress experienced was mediated by availability of family resources (i.e., social and instrumental support) and caregivers' perception of child manageability or behavioral difficulty. In this model "A" refers to the initial stressful event (i.e., caregiving load). The model suggests that apart from the initial stressors, there are always competing or "double" stressors (i.e., changes in life roles, competing family, work, friendship, and financial demands) that further predispose caregivers to experience elevated levels of stress. In the mentioned model, "B" is the mediator or family resources (e.g., emotional and instrumental support, "C" is caregivers' subjective appraisal of the crisis (e.g., appraisal of caregiving as manageable, upsetting, or a breach in their life courses), and "X" is the outcome, experienced stress, or sense of strain (Gatz, Bengtson, & Blum, 1990).

The FTC was expected to experience significantly higher levels of stress than did the PTC (who only supplemented caregiving responsibilities to transient biological parents). This was anticipated due to the combination of socioemotional problems related to deaths of their own children (Minkler, Fuller-Thomson, Miller, & Driver, 1997) and the numerous responsibilities associated with full-time caregiving roles (Bowers & Myers, 1999).

It was also anticipated that caregivers high on stress would perceive their children to be behaviorally difficult due to the "reciprocal determinism" that has been reported between caregiving stress and child difficulty (Edwards, 1998). Elevated levels of experienced stress have also been associated to primarily responsible caregivers" perception of children's conduct problems to be difficult (e.g., Bowers & Myers, 1999; Eyberg, Boggs, & Rodriguez, 1992). In addition, the potential sources of instrumental and emotional support available to FTC could be reduced by the magnitude of the orphan crisis where many families have been affected, and modern Kenyans" gravitation toward individualistic lifestyles and limited state involvement in family support systems (Adepoju & Mbugua, 1997).

However, previous investigations that assessed the links between assumption of extensive caregiving duties, perceived role satisfaction, and experienced stress (e.g., Pruchno & McKenney, 2002) has shown that resumption of duty in old age is an activity that can either have positive or negative valence among caregiving grandmothers. This suggests that in the traditional and contemporary Luo societies (the ethnic group used in the present study), where partial responsibility has different connotations to the Euro-American "part-time" or "half-time" work schedules, assumption of extensive parenting responsibilities did not necessarily connote that full-time adoptive grandmothers were more inclined to experience elevated levels of stress than did those with limited responsibilities. In the traditional Luo family contexts, children born out of wedlock, children of ailing sons and daughters, those neglected by their own parents, and orphaned breastfeeding babies were brought up either on partial or full-time basis by grandmothers who had reached menopause stage (Nyambedha, Wandibba, & Aagaard-Hansen, 2003; Ocholla-Ayayo, 1976). This connotes that Luo grandmothers with partial caregiving responsibilities for their non-orphaned grandchildren could sometimes have direct parenting roles resulting into elevated levels of caregiving stress (Nyambedha et al., 2003).

The implication is that the PTC operating within the traditional norms but with limited duties or lacking clear-cut caregiving roles could sometimes experience greater or different stresses than did the FTC, especially when their instrumental and emotional support needs were unmet (e.g., Gatz et al., 1990; Jendrek, 1994). The research questions addressed in this study were: Do full-time caregiving grandmothers experience higher levels of stress than did the partially responsible grandmothers? Were the expected higher levels of experienced stress among the primarily responsible grandmothers linked to extensive caregiving roles, perceived lack of emotional and instrumental support, and child behavioral difficulty?

METHOD

Sample and Procedures

Information provided by social workers, government officers, and local leaders was used to select 128 full-time (FTC) and 113 part-time (PTC) caregiving grandmothers residing in the rural areas of Rachuonyo district of Nyanza Province, Kenya. They all belonged to the Luo ethnic group (see Ocholla-Ayayo, 1976 for ethnographic description of the Luo). The participants were individually interviewed within their own homes but away from others. They were first asked to choose one child below 10 years of age currently living within their household for whom they had provided full-time or supplementary care for the longest period. A target was randomly chosen in cases where more than one child met the criteria. They were assured of the confidentiality of information obtained.

The mean age of the FTC grandmothers was 62.2 years (SD = 9.3, range 42–82 compared to mean = 60.4; SD = 8.9, range 41–96 for PTC; p > .05). The FTC had lived with their grandchildren for a period ranging between 1 and 9 years (M = 3.2; SD = 2.1 compared to M = 2.9; SD = 1.4; range = 1 to 6 years for PTC; p > .05). Almost all participants from both groups (97%) had less than 7 years of basic education. Most of the FTC grandmothers (59%) were currently widowed (compared to 37% for the PTC; X^2 = 9.1; df = 1; p < .001). The main sources of income for both groups of participants included peasant farming (81% for FTC and 65% PTC), small-scale businesses (16% FTC and 22% PTC), and remittances from friends and relatives (3% FTC and 13% PTC; X^2 = 9.0; df = 2; p < .05). The FTC grandmothers had on average three children under their custody (compared to two for the PTC; F (1, 239) = 47.6; p < .001). Most of them (98%) were orphans (compared to 64% of PTC children who had two biological parents, 25% born out of wedlock, 6% were neglected, and 5% had one sick parent). The mean age was 73.1 months (SD = 26.7, range = 12 to 120 months for the FTC grandchildren and 52 months (SD = 24.49, range = 12 to 96) for the PTC grandchildren; F (1,239) = 41.9; p < .01).

Instruments

The Parenting Stress Index–short form (PSI–SF) with a total stress index and subscales addressing parent distress, child difficulty, and parent-child dysfunctional interaction was used to assess experienced stress (see Abidin, 1990). The alpha reliability coefficient was .72 for the items of the parent distress subscale, .75 for the child difficulty and parent-child dysfunctional interaction subscales, and .68 for the total parenting stress index. Perceived emotional support from spouses, friends, and relatives was investigated using the emotional support scale (Marshall & Barnett, 1993). Availability of instrumental assistance in carrying out child care tasks and household chores was assessed using the instrumental support scale (Cowan & Cowan, 1987). These two scales have high internal consistency (alpha = .94; Deater-Deckard & Scarr, 1996). Child behavioral difficulty was measured using Scarr and Ricciuti's (1987) manageability scale (alpha = .75).

RESULTS

Parenting Stress

The total stress experienced by the FTC ranged from 63 to 153 (M = 130.3, SD = 19.6 compared to M = 114, SD = 23.2, range = 75 to 151 for PTC; p < .001). Twenty-seven percent of the FTC's obtained scores fell at or above the 85th percentile score of 145 (compared to 15% for the PTC). Child difficulty subscale scores for FTC ranged from 14 to 65 (M = 55.4, SD = 12.5 compared to M = 49.5, SD = 13.9, range = 23 to 65 for the PTC; 38% of the scores for FTC and 26% for PTC were above the 85th percentile score of 65). The mean scores obtained by the FTC in the parent-child dysfunctional interaction (M = 51, SD = 7.6, range = 20 to 60 in contrast to M = 47.5, SD = 7.8, range = 32 to 60 for PTC; 16% of FTC had scores above 55 compared to 13% for the PTC) and parental distress (M = 45.3, SD = 6.5, range = 16 to 56 compared to M = 36.2, SD = 8.6, range = 20 to 52) were above that of the PTC. Parental distress scores for the PTC that fell at or above the 85th percentile slightly exceeded that of the FTC (15% had scores above 45 while 13% of the FTC had scores above 52).

Perceived Child Behavioral Difficulty, Instrumental and Emotional Support

The PTC reported significantly lower levels of emotional support (M = 44, SD = 5.1, range = 28 to 50 for PTC and M = 46, SD = 5.8, range = 16 to 50 for FTC; F (1,239) = 5.5, p <. 05) and child behavioral difficulty (M = 61, SD = 25, range = 38 to 158 for PTC and M = 87, SD = 44, range = 38 to 182 for FTC; F (1,236) = 33.2; p < .001) than did the FTC. The differences between the PTC (M = 28.6, SD = 5.7, range = 18 to 46) and FTC (M = 27.3, SD = 7.6, range = 18 to 53) in their perceived availability of instrumental support were not statistically significant $(F (1,239) = 2.1; p = .15)$.

Demographic and Contextual Variables Related to Parenting Stress

The total stress experienced by the FTC was significantly linked to their perception of their grandchildren's behavioral difficulty $(r = .52; p < .001)$. Approximately 20% of the variance of total stress experienced by FTC $[F(3,124) = 11.3; p <. 001]$ was explained by their perception of child managerial difficulty. For the PTC, experienced stress was related to instrumental $(r = -.39, p < .001)$, and emotional support $(r = .31, p < .001)$. These significant variables accounted for 47% of experienced stress $(F(3,106) = 33; p < .001)$. Univariate Analysis of Covariance (ANCOVA) was used to test for the possible interaction effects of perceived child difficulty, and availability of emotional and instrumental support on the total stress experienced by FTC and PTC.

In these analyses, child age and number of children cared for were controlled. Scores above the median splits were also expected to correspond to perceived availability of instrumental assistance, emotional support, and child behavioral difficulty. The total PSI-SF was the dependent variable while predictors included child behavioral difficulty (0 = not difficult, 1 = difficult), instrumental assistance (0 = available, 1 = not available) and emotional support (0 = available, 1 = not available).

Significant main effects of perceived child behavioral difficulty $(F(1,100) = 30.3$ for PTC and $F(1,106) = 28.5$ for FTC; $p < .001)$, lack of emotional support $(F(1,100) = 38.9; p < .001$ for PTC), instrumental assistance $(F(1,100) = 11.5; p < .01$ for PTC) and two-way interaction effects of lack of instrumental support and perceived child difficulty $(F(1,100) = 5.4; p < .05$ for PTC) on the total stress experienced were obtained. These results suggested that perceived child behavioral difficulty for both groups, and availability of emotional support (especially among the PTC) and lack of instrumental assistance corresponded to elevated levels of experienced stress. The PTC caregivers who lacked instrumental support were also likely to perceive their grandchildren's behaviors as managerially difficult.

DISCUSSION

Data from the present study suggested that the full-time caregivers (FTC) occupying multiple caregiving roles experienced elevated levels of stress than did the part time caregivers (PTC). The total stress experienced was linked to grandchildren's perceived behavioral difficulty for the two groups and limited instrumental support and availability of emotional support among the PTC. These results partly confirmed earlier investigations (e.g., Bowers & Myers, 1999; Kelley, 1993; Minkler & Fuller-Thomson, 2001; Pruchno & McKenney, 2002; Rodgers, 1998) that linked increased levels of experienced stress among grandmothers adopting their grandchildren to higher levels of caregiving load and children's difficult behaviors. Evidence obtained from previous studies suggest that children with managerially difficult behaviors require more resources (i.e., caregiver time and patience) that may not be available to grandmothers rearing grandchildren, particularly at a time when they are least expecting extensive or restrictive child-rearing duties (e.g., Bowers & Myers, 1999; Kelley, 1993).

On the part of the PTC, limited care-taking responsibilities meant that they were not likely to have similar levels of experienced stress and perceived child behavioral difficulty as did the FTC (e.g., Bowers & Myers, 1999). However, the nonsignificant differences in levels of available instrumental support suggested that either they had similarly assumed burdensome nontraditional grandmother roles or were dissatisfied with instrumental and emotional support provided to them by their grandchildren's parents (e.g., Musil, 1998). Shared residency also implied that apart from caregiving load, limited instrumental support and pressures caused by the transitions or changed timings of their child minding duties from non-restrictive, nocturnal education sessions characteristic of the traditional three-generation Luo families, to restrictive child minding duties during the day (Geissler, 1998), could have led to the obtained non-significant differences between FTC and PTC in their perceived availability of instrumental support (e.g., Musil, 1998).

The finding that availability of emotional support was linked to higher levels of total stress experienced by the PTC grandmothers was in contrast to earlier investigations (e.g., Crnic & Greenberg, 1990) that reported that at times of psychological distress, emotional support from friends and relatives enhances self-esteem and consequently increases an individual's positive appraisal of stressful situations. The positive relationship obtained between experienced stress and availability of emotional support among the PTC should however be treated with caution due to the complex nature of stress-support relationships (e.g., Rodgers, 1998). Experienced stress and availability of emotional support are also two opposite constructs of the same continuum such that not having beneficial or expected emotional support could be associated with an escalation in the total stress experienced (e.g., Dunn, Burbine, Bowers, & Tantleff-Dunn, 2001; Rodgers, 1998).

Highly distressed grandmothers who perceived their grandchildren's behaviors as managerially difficult were also likely to seek out more social support from friends and relatives leading to the obtained positive correlations. In the Kenyan context, where grandmothers traditionally are the "glue" that holds the extended family units together (Ocholla-Ayayo, 1997), it is likely that the challenges to traditional grandmothers" roles could further have distressed the PTC leading to the observed positive correlations obtained between emotional support and total stress experienced (e.g., Abidin, 1990).

Results from this particular study suggested that the total stress experienced was linked to levels of caregiving, perceived child managerial difficulty, lack of beneficial emotional support (Rodgers, 1998, 1999), and inadequacy of instrumental assistance. We recommend that efforts be made in reducing the clinically significant stress levels experienced by grandmother caregivers through the provision of required emotional and instrumental support to these Kenyan grandmother caregivers. We also recomment that support be made available in the form of financial assistance, respite care, and capacity-building programs that make those grandmother caregivers perceive themselves as competent managers of grandchildren's difficult behaviors. Increasing their self-reliance in their daily provisions to their grandchildren and bolstering their self-confidence in parenting responsibilities could also be beneficial in reducing the total stress experienced.

There are, however, several limitations of the present study that must be considered. The key limitation was on the reliance on self-report instruments. There is a possibility that without other confirmatory independent measurement scales, social desirability could have inflated some of the observed results. The other limitation is in the psychological model of the stress tested. Although previous research (e.g., Bowers & Myers, 1999; Pruchno & McKenney, 2002) demonstrated that a two-model factor consisting of both negative (e.g., experienced stress, perception of caregiving as burdensome) and positive affect (caregiving satisfaction) are necessary for a comprehensive understanding of psychological well-being of full-time caregiving grandmothers, the theoretical model tested in the present study did not concern itself with positive affect. Potential determinants of parental distress including overall attitudes toward child rearing, appraisal of stressful situations, and emotional and behavioral adjustment of children were also not part of the model tested in the present study.

Future studies using two-factor stress models would thus assess the predictive roles of social support, and emotional and behavioral adjustment of (totally) orphaned grandchildren, in determining the total stress experienced by caregiving grandmothers. Preferably, the participants should be samples drawn from other Kenyan ethnic groups. The linkages between psychological well-being, parental positive affect, and competence in handling children's inappropriate behaviors should also be assessed.

REFERENCES

Abidin, R. R. (1990). *The Parenting Stress Index—Short form.* Charlottesville, VA: Paediatric Psychology Press.

Adepoju, A., & Mbugua, W. (1997). The African family: An overview of changing forms. In A. Adepoju (Ed.), *Family population and development in Africa* (pp. 41–59). London & New York: Zed Books.

Bowers, B., & Myers, B. J. (1999). Grandmothers providing care for their grandchildren: Consequences of various levels of care giving. *Family Relations, 48,* 303–311.

Cowan, C. P., & Cowan, P. A. (1987). A preventive intervention for couples becoming parents. In C. F. Z. Boukydis (Ed.), *Research on support for parents and infants in postnatal period* (pp. 225–251). Ablex.

Crnic, K. A., & Greenberg, M. T. (1990). Minor parenting stress with young children. *Child Development, 61,* 1628–1637.

Deater-Deckard, K., & Scarr, S. (1996). Parenting stress among dual-earner mothers and fathers: Are there gender differences? *Journal of Family Psychology, 10*(1), 45–59.

Dunn, M. E., Burbine, T., Bowers, C. A., & Tantleff-Dunn, S. (2001). Moderators of stress in parents of children with autism. *Community Mental Health Journal, 37*(1), 39–52.

Edwards, O. W. (1998). Helping grandkin-grandchildren raised by grandparents: Expanding psychology in schools. *Psychology in the Schools, 35,* 173–181.

Eyberg, S. M., Boggs, S. R., & Rodriguez, C. M. (1992). Relationships between maternal parenting stress and child disruptive behaviour. *Child & Family Behaviour Therapy, 14,* 91–92.

Gatz, M., Bengtson, V. L., & Blum, M. J. (1990). Care giving families. In J. E. Birren & K. W. Schaie (Eds.), *Handbook of the psychology of aging* (3rd ed., pp. 304–338). San Diego, CA: Academic Press.

Geissler, P. W. (1998). "Worms are our life." Part two: Luo children's thoughts about worms and illness. *Anthropology and Medicine, 5,* 133–144.

Jendrek, M. (1994). Grandparents who parent their grandchildren: Circumstances and decisions. *The Gerontologist, 34*(2), 206–216.

Kelley, S. J. (1993). Caregiver stress in grandparents raising grandchildren. *Image: Journal of Nursing Scholarship, 25,* 331–337.

Marshall, N. L., & Barnett, R. C. (1993). Work-family strains and gains among two-earner couples. *Journal of Community Psychology, 21*(81), 64–78.

McCubbin, H. I., & Patterson, J. M. (1982). Family adaptation to crises. In H. I. McCubbin, A. E. Cauble, & J. M. Patterson (Eds.), *Family stress, coping and social support* (pp. 5–25). Springfield, IL: Thomas.

Minkler, M., & Fuller-Thomson, E. (2001). Physical and mental health status of American grandparents providing extensive childcare to their grandchildren. *Journal of American Women's Medical Association, 56*(4), 199–205.

Minkler, M., Fuller-Thomson, E., Miller, D., & Driver, D. (1997). Depression in grandparents raising their grandchildren: Results of a national longitudinal study. *Archives of Family Medicine, 6,* 445–452.

Musil, C. M. (1998). Health, stress, coping and social support in grandmother caregivers. *Health Care for Women International, 19,* 441–455.

Nyambedha, E. O., Wandibba, S., & Aagaard-Hansen, J. (2003). "Retirement lost": The new role of the elderly as caretakers for orphans in Kenya. *Journal of Cross-Cultural Gerontology, 18,* 33–52.

Ocholla-Ayayo, A. B. C. (1976). *Traditional ideology and ethics among Southern Luo.* Uppsala, Sweden: Scandinavian Institute of African Studies.

Ocholla-Ayayo, A. B. C. (1997). The African family between tradition and modernity. In A. Adepoju (Ed.), *Family, population & development* (pp. 60–77). London & New York: Zed Books Ltd.

Pruchno, R. A., & McKenney, D. (2002). Psychological well-being of Black and White grandmothers raising grandchildren: Examination of a two factor model. *Journal of Gerontology: Psychological Sciences, 57B*(5), 444–452.

Rodgers, A. Y. (1998). Multiple sources of stress and parenting behavior. *Children and Youth Services Review, 20,* 525–546.

Rodgers, A. Y. (1999). Parenting stress, depression, and parenting in grandmothers raising their grandchildren. *Children and Youth Services Review, 21*(5), 377–388.

Scarr, S., & Ricciuti, A. (1987). *The manageability scale.* University of Virginia, unpublished manuscript.

UNICEF: United Nations Children's Fund. (1999). The AIDS emergency league table: Children orphaned by AIDS. *The Progress of Nations 1999.* New York: Author.

UNICEF: United Nations Children's Fund. (2000). *The state of the world's children 2000.* New York: Author.

UNICEF/UNAIDS (2002). Children on the brink: A joint report on orphan estimates and program strategies. Author: Washington, DC.

SECTION 4

Variation Across Race and Ethnicity

CHAPTER 15

Latina Grandmothers Raising Grandchildren: Acculturation and Psychological Well-Being[*]

Catherine Chase Goodman and Merril Silverstein

INTRODUCTION

The number of grandparents raising grandchildren in the United States has been increasing over the past 30 years (Casper & Bryson, 1998). Similar to grandparents of other ethnicities, Latino grandparents provide for grandchildren when their adult children are unable to parent due to drugs, incarceration, mental illness, teen pregnancy and single parenthood, and death. In addition, they may assist their adult children by providing child care and economic support, including housing. Thus, grandparents may provide a home for adult children and grandchildren (coparenting), or assume full care when the parent is unable to care

*This study was supported by grant RO1AG14977 from the National Institute on Aging and in part by a Scholarly and Creative Activity Award, California State University, Long Beach.

for the grandchild and does not live with the family (custodial). Latino grandparent caregivers represent an under studied, but rapidly emerging subgroup of caregivers to their grandchildren. This is particularly true in Los Angeles County, which is home to 4.2 million Latinos in 2000—more than any other county in the nation (Guzman, 2001). In this study, we focus on the level of language acculturation in relation to psychological well-being in a sample of caregiving Latina grandmothers.

DOMAINS OF ACCULTURATION

Acculturation and Well-Being

Acculturation is defined as the capacity of immigrants and their descendants to participate in mainstream institutions of the host society (Caetano & Clark, 2003). However, the process of acculturation has been viewed both in a negative light—as an erosion of traditional values, customs, and language—and in a positive light—as a process by which mainstream culture is adopted while traditional culture is maintained (Cuéllar, 2000). Supporting the more negative view, researchers have found that acculturation is associated with increases in deviant behavior, such as substance abuse, alcohol use, and family disruption (Caetano & Clark, 2003; Organista, Organista, & Kurasaki, 2003; Rogler, Cortés, & Malgady, 1991; Silverstein & Chen, 1999).

Recent reviews of epidemiological literature (Cuéllar, 2000; Organista et al., 2003) have found that immigrant Mexican Americans had a lower incidence of mental disorders than U.S.-born Mexican Americans, but were no different than residents in Mexico City, ruling out the explanation that those with good mental health are more apt to immigrate (Vega, Kolody, Aguilar-Gaxiola, Alderete, Catalano, & Caraveo-Anduaga, 1998). Therefore, explanations focus on cultural protective factors, such as family values.

Family resources may be of help in facing the stresses involved in immigration, but new immigrants have also been shown to be depressed and struggle with language and cultural adaptation, poverty, and discrimination (Baca Zinn & Wells, 2000; González, Haan, & Hinton, 2001; Organista et al., 2003; Rogler et al., 1991). Some scholars have proposed that acculturation is not linear (Aranda & Miranda, 1997; Cuéllar, 2000). Bicultural persons—those who have access to aspects of both cultures—may adapt best to their host societies because they are able to choose desired aspects from each culture. For example, bicultural Latinos have been shown to have less internal conflict and greater family support than low- and high-acculturated groups (Miranda, Estrada, & Firpo-Jimenez, 2000).

Acculturation and Familism

An important value of Latino groups of many nationalities has been familism, an emphasis on the centrality of family identity and support. However, an aspect of reliance on family may be an exclusion from majority culture and an unresponsive social service system (Williams & Torrez, 1998). Thus, any consideration of familism in the Latino population requires that socioeconomic resources be taken into account. Aranda and Miranda (1997) reviewed literature on familism among Latinos and concluded that familism persisted in spite of acculturation, including such dimensions as perceived support from family, preference for interacting with relatives, ethnic identity, and the strength of extended family relationships. Thus, family support—such as that found in grandparent caregiving—persists in spite of acculturation (Aranda & Miranda, 1997; Baca Zinn & Wells, 2000; Sabogal, Marín, Otero-Sabogal, VanOss Marín, & Pérez-Stable, 1987). Sabogal and colleagues (1987) found that family support was consistent among Latinos regardless of acculturation, and was higher than for non-Latino Whites, whereas family obligation and family as an attitudinal referent decreased with acculturation.

Latino Caregiving Grandparents

Grandparent caregivers nationally are apt to experience depression (Minkler, Fuller-Thomson, Miller, & Driver, 1997). Similarly, Burnette (2000) found that nearly half of the grandparent caregivers in her Puerto Rican sample scored above the clinical range on the Geriatric Depression Scale. Stress is particularly extreme for grandmothers caring for children with behavior problems, as demonstrated in a rare cross national study of Latino grandparent caregivers from the United States and Mexico (Toledo, Hayslip, Emick, Toledo, & Henderson, 2000).

While the incidence of coparenting grandparent-headed families in 2002 was higher for Latino than White families (4.6% versus 2.6% respectively), custodial rates were similar (1.5% versus 1.2% respectively; Fields, 2003). Thus, coparenting appears more normative for Latino families: Coparenting, in comparison to custodial caregiving, has been related to higher well-being among Latina grandmothers (Goodman & Silverstein, 2002). Generally, caregiving in Latino groups takes place more in the context of the three-generation household, where other family members may assist grandparent caregivers. Almost half of the grand-mothers in Burnette's Latino sample had an adult child other than the parent who was available as a helper (Burnette, 1999). Another study (Cox, 2000) comparing African American and Latino grandparents found that grandchildren of Latino caregivers were more apt than African American grandchildren to have frequent contact with their parents and that grandparents were less likely to be custodial. More often Latino grandchildren lived with the parent while the grandparent provided care during the day, which suggests collaborative parenting.

Latino custodial grandparents represent a certain paradox with regard to the values of familism. While caregiving itself is a form of familism, being a surrogate parent may induce feelings that the normative ideals of familism have not been fulfilled by the adult child, thereby negatively affecting the grandmother's well-being.

Hypotheses

This chapter examines the relationship between acculturation and psychological well-being and predictors of well-being among Latina caregiving grandparents. Specifically, we hypothesize that (1) bicultural grandmothers would have greater well-being than those whose orientations were toward only one culture; (2) aspects of family functioning and cohesion would be related to well-being, especially (a) the parent's presence in the household (coparenting versus custodial families), and (b) a lower level of the grandchild's behavior problems.

METHODS

Sample and Data Collection

The sample consists of 357 Latina grandmothers living in Los Angeles County who were caring for their dependent grandchildren. National ancestry was known for 84%, and of those 78% were from Mexico. Overall, 64% were foreign born and had immigrated to the United States. This sample was a subsample from a larger multi-ethnic study (Goodman, 1998). Sample recruitment was primarily through the Los Angeles Unified School District (77%) and media announcements (23%) during 1998 through 2001. At the time of recruitment, 68.5% of students in LAUSD were Latino. Notices in Spanish and English were sent home with children from 223 schools. Potential respondents were screened to assure they were caregiving grandmothers and a grandparent was head of household.

Face-to-face interviews, lasting about one hour, were conducted by University of California at Los Angeles Survey Research Center in Spanish or English by linguistically and ethnically matched interviewers. Most of the interviews with Latina grandmothers were conducted in Spanish (59.2%). The sample consisted primarily of middle-aged grandmothers (mean 55 years), with an average of 9 years of education. Over half were married (53%) and 40% were working. Poverty rate for the family was 35%. The parent lived in the household in over half of the families (55.7%).

Measures

Grandmothers were the sole respondents and they described one grandchild, selected to avoid bias as either the one from the targeted school or a randomly selected grandchild. Measures that were not already available in Spanish were translated by a bilingual mental health professional and reviewed by three bilingual persons of different nationalities (Mexican, Spanish, and Salvadoran).

Acculturation

Acculturation was measured using four items from a language-use measure (Marín, Sabogal, Marín, Otero-Sabogal, & Pérez-Stable, 1987), focused on preference in general, at home, in thinking, and with friends. Response scales ranged from 1 (only Spanish) to 5 (only English) and coefficient alpha for the four items was .95. Respondents whose average score reflected prefer or only use Spanish or English were classified as Spanish preferred or English preferred, respectively, and those in the middle range were classified as bicultural. Almost half preferred Spanish (47%), 25.5% were bilingual, and 27.5% preferred English. Generation of immigration was defined as first generation (foreign born), second generation (one or both parents foreign born), and third generation (neither grandmother nor her parents foreign born).

Demographic Factors and Parental Presence

Grandmother's demographic factors were marital status, age, education, working status, per capita family income, poverty, recruitment method, and health. The SF-36 health survey (Ware, 1993) was used to describe health. Subscale internal consistency ranged from .70 to .92 in this sample. Parental presence refers to current presence (coparenting) or absence (custodial) in the household of whichever parent was the grandmother's adult child. Presence of adult children includes the parent and other adult children living in the household.

Family Functioning and Cohesion Factors

The grandchild's behavior problems were measured using by a 10-item Behavior Rating Index for Children (BRIC), with problems rated on a 5-point scale from 1 (rarely or never) to 5 (most or all of the time) (Stiffman, Orme, Evans, Feldman, & Keeney, 1984). Coefficient alpha in this sample was .77. Emotional closeness between grandmother and both grandchild and parent were measured using five items from the affective solidarity measure developed by Bengtson (affection, understanding, emotionally close, communication, and getting along together) (Gronvold, 1988). Items were rated from 1 (not at all or none) to 6 (extremely or a great deal) and coefficient alpha for this sample was .80 (grandmother and grandchild) and .92 (grandmother and her adult son or daughter). Grandmother-parent conflict over decisions about the grandchild was a single item, rated from 1 (none at all) to 6 (a great deal). Reasons the grandmother assumed care were described and reasons suggesting dysfunction were summed for a parental dysfunction index (drug use, alcohol use, child neglect, emotional/mental problem, and legal trouble; coefficient alpha = .74).

Grandmother Well-Being

Subjective well-being is considered to be the cognitive evaluation of life with related emotional states, both positive and negative. The Positive and Negative Affect Scale (PANAS) was used to measure mood (Watson, Clark, Tellegen, 1988). This is a 20-item measure of mood using descriptive positive adjectives, such as "interested," "strong," or negative adjectives, such as "distressed," or "hostile." Respondents answer on a 5-point scale describing how they felt during the past few weeks, from 1 (very slightly or not at all) to 5 (extremely). A Spanish version was available, the SPANAS, developed through forward and back translations and the two-factor structure was validated in a Spanish sample (Joiner, Sandín, Chorot, Lostao, & Marquina, 1997). Coefficient alpha for this sample was .85 for positive affect and .87 for negative affect. Life satisfaction, a cognitive judgement of well-being, was measured using the Satisfaction With Life Scale (Diener, Emmons, Larsen, & Griffin, 1985). The measure consists of five items scored on a 7-point scale, from 1 (strongly agree) to 7 (strongly disagree). The coefficient alpha for this sample was .80.

RESULTS

Acculturation and Socioeconomic and Family Factors

Table 15.1 shows that grandmothers who preferred the use of Spanish tended to be younger, have less education, fewer working, and lower income compared to those who preferred English. More Spanish-preferred grandmothers were recruited through the schools, which was shown previously to be associated with higher well-being. Furthermore, more grandmothers in the Spanish-preferred group were married and had the parent present in their households. The Spanish-preferred group also had more adult children (parent and others) living in their households.

No acculturation differences were evident for grandmother's health, grandchild's behavior, closeness with the parent, and conflict with the parent over decisions. However, fewer Spanish-preferred grandmothers assumed care because of parental substance abuse or related issues. On the other hand, Spanish-preferred grandmothers were less close to their grandchildren. Thus, bivariate results show the Spanish-preferred group having the greatest socioeconomic disadvantages (low income and education), and the English-preferred group having the least socioeconomic disadvantages. The reverse was the case for the availability of social resources, with more married grandmothers, more coresident parents, and lower incidence of parental substance use or related issues among Spanish-preferred families.

Predictors of Grandmother Well-Being

Table 15.2 shows hierarchical regression equations that predicted positive affect, negative affect, and life satisfaction. Each outcome variable is represented by three regression models. Model 1 examined the effect of acculturation with no controls. Model 2 added covariates representing socioeconomic resources (per capita family income; grandmother's education, marital status, age, and physical health; parent's presence; and recruitment method). Model 3 added covariates representing family functioning and cohesion (grandchild's behavior problems, closeness grandmother-grandchild, closeness grandmother-parent, conflict grandmother-parent over decisions, and parental dysfunction index). Predictor variables were selected to minimize multicollinearity and include variables that differentiated acculturation groups or were related to well-being at the bivariate level. Presence of outliers lead to deletions beyond ±3 standardized residuals (1 outlier for positive affect and life satisfaction and 6 for negative affect; Tabachnick & Fidell, 2001).

TABLE 15.1 Family Characteristics by Language Acculturation

Characteristics		Prefer Spanish (n = 168)	Bilingual (n = 91)	Prefer English (n = 98)	Total (n = 357)	F or χ^2	df
		Grandmother's Characteristics and Socioeconomic Resources					
Age	M	54.04$_a$	56.68$_b$	56.30	55.33	3.70*	2,354
	SD	(8.38)	(8.83)	(8.51)	(8.60)		
Years of education	M	5.68$_a$	9.96$_{bc}$	11.76$_{bd}$	8.44	106.90***	2,354
	SD	(3.72)	(3.96)	(2.34)	(4.38)		
Per capita income ($)[a]	M	4,764.50$_a$	6,571.39$_b$	7,434.91$_b$	5,958.13	13.72***	2,354
	SD	(2,929.71)	(4,848.08)	(5,311.36)	(4,361.63)		
Family poverty[a]	%	39.90	35.20	25.50	34.70	5.65	2,357
School recruitment	%	88.70	71.40	60.20	76.50	29.64***	2,357
Working	%	29.80	25.50	46.90	39.50	12.71**	2,357
Married	%	60.70	50.50	40.80	52.70	10.05**	2,357
Health[b]	M	49.87	47.19	47.32	48.48	2.80	2,351
	SD	(8.69)	(11.62)	(11.71)	(10.43)		
Immigrant status						217.60***	4,356
1st generation	%	98.20	61.50	8.20	64.30		
2nd generation	%	1.80	18.70	46.40	18.30		
3rd or higher	%	—	19.80	45.40	17.40		
Parent present currently	%	69.0	40.7	46.9	55.7	23.985***	2,357

244

TABLE 15.1 *(continued)*

Characteristics		Prefer Spanish (n = 168)	Bilingual (n = 91)	Prefer English (n = 98)	Total (n = 357)	F or χ^2	df
All adult children in HH						31.54***	6, 357
None	%	18.50	42.90	34.70	29.10		
One	%	39.90	27.50	44.90	38.10		
Two	%	24.40	22.00	17.30	21.80		
Three or more	%	17.30	7.70	3.10	10.90		
Family Factors							
GC behavior	M	20.95	24.66	22.22	22.24	1.76	2,354
problems	SD	(14.25)	(16.81)	(15.29)	(15.25)		
Close GC to GM	M	24.70$_a$	25.01$_a$	26.34$_b$	25.23	8.11***	2,354
	SD	(3.21)	(3.32)	(3.34)	(3.34)		
Close GM to	M	22.42	20.80	21.69	21.81	1.85	2,354
parent	SD	(6.33)	(5.91)	(7.25)	(6.51)		
Conflict GM and	M	1.48	1.57	1.65	1.55	.78	2,354
parent	SD	(1.14)	(1.03)	(1.19)	(1.13)		
Parental	M	.44$_a$	1.04$_b$	1.26$_b$	.82	15.29***	2,354
substance issues	SD	(.94)	(1.32)	(1.58)	(1.29)		

Note: HH = Household, GM = Grandmother, GC = Grandchild.
[a]Data on yearly income were collected in categories with intervals of $5000, and midpoint used for dollar amount. Mean substitution was used for missing income data. Poverty is based on U.S. Health and Human Services Guidelines issued in 2000, reflecting the year 1999.
[b]Contains some missing data.
* $p \leq .05$. ** $p \leq .01$. *** $p \leq .001$. Tukey Post Hoc tests, $p \leq .05$, $_a < _b$; $_c < _d$.

TABLE 15.2 Predictors of Well-Being: Standardized Beta Coefficients

Characteristics	Positive Affect			Negative Affect			Life Satisfaction		
	1	2	3	1	2	3	1	2	3
Acculturation									
Bilingual vs. prefer English	-.08	-.04	.02	-.08	-.06	-.07	.03	.01	.03
Prefer Spanish vs. prefer English	-.28***	-.21**	-.12	-.17**	-.05	-.05	.15*	.05	.07
Socioeconomic resources									
Per capita income		.14**	.10*		-.04	-.03		.09	.07
Years of school		.10	.11		-.01	-.02		-.02	-.02
Parent present currently		.12*	.05		-.15**	.01		.20***	.04
Married		.01	.01		-.09	-.05		.21***	.18***
Age		-.02	.01		-.04	-.01		.11*	.11*
Physical health		.26***	.23***		-.20***	-.15**		.15**	.12*
School recruitment		-.07	-.11*		-.20***	-.13*		.08	.01

TABLE 15.2 *(continued)*

Characteristics	Positive Affect			Negative Affect			Life Satisfaction		
	1	2	3	1	2	3	1	2	3
Family factors									
Grandmother-grandchild closeness			.25***			.03			.08
Grandmother-parent closeness			.11			−.17**			.16*
Conflict over decisions—parent[a]			−.04			.12*			−.05
Behavior rating for children			−.05			.21***			−.11
Substance factor—parent			.01			.12			−.13*
R^2	.06	.18	.26	.02	.13	.26	.02	.14	.22
F	11.04***	8.19***	8.57***	3.45*	5.78***	8.34***	3.53*	6.23***	6.72***
df	2, 350	9, 343	14, 338	2, 345	9, 338	14, 333	2, 350	9, 343	14, 338

Note: Dichotomous variables coded 1 = yes.
[a]A log linear transformation used to correct for positive skew.
*$p \leq .05$. **$p \leq .01$. ***$p \leq .001$

Positive Affect

Spanish-preferred grandmothers had lower positive affect than the English-preferred group in Model 1, showing that this aspect of well-being was higher among the more acculturated. In Model 2, with the addition of socioeconomic resources, this acculturation effect was sustained. Parental presence (coparenting), higher income, and better health were related to greater positive affect. However, if only education and income were added by themselves, the acculturation effect (Spanish preferred versus English preferred) was no longer significant ($\beta = -.15$, $t_{(1, 348)} = -1.91$, $p = .06$), suggesting these two benefits of acculturation explained most of the acculturation effect. In Model 3, acculturation was no longer significant and emotional closeness between the grandmother and grandchild was a significant predictor. Notably, parental presence was no longer a significant predictor, suggesting family factors, particularly closer relations with grandchildren, were more salient than having the parent currently at home.

Negative Affect

In marked contrast to results for positive affect, Spanish-preferred grandmothers had lower negative affect than English-preferred grandmothers in Model 1, showing higher well-being among the less acculturated. In Model 2, acculturation was no longer significant with the addition of socioeconomic resources. Parental absence (custodial), poor health, and recruitment through the media were related to negative affect. To clarify the impact of these socioeconomic resource factors, the addition of only marital status and parental presence eliminated the significant acculturation effect for Spanish preferred versus English preferred ($\beta = -.11$, $t_{(1, 343)} = -1.65$, $p = .10$), suggesting these two factors alone explained much of the initial relationship. In Model 3, family factors predicting negative affect were the grandchild's behavioral problems and greater conflict and less closeness with the parent. Parental absence ceased to be significant as a predictor after family factors were entered into the model. Apparently, it is the problematic aspects of family relationships that were apt to make the parent's absence negative.

Life Satisfaction

Similar to results for negative affect, Spanish-preferred grandmothers had higher life satisfaction than English-preferred grandmothers in Model 1. In Model 2, acculturation was no longer significant. Parental presence (coparenting), good health, being married, and older were related to life satisfaction. Even with the addition of only marital status and parent present, acculturation (Spanish preferred versus English preferred) was no longer related to life satisfaction ($\beta = .07$, $t_{(1, 348)} = 1.12$, $p = .27$), suggesting these two factors explained the initial acculturation and life satisfaction relationship. In Model 3, family factors predicting life satisfaction were greater closeness between grandmother and parent and a lower level of parental dysfunction. As with both other indices of well-being, parental presence ceased to be significant as a predictor of improved life satisfaction after family factors are entered into the model. Apparently, close relations with the parent and the parent's freedom from substance abuse and related issues were the underlying reasons why grandmothers living with the grandchild's parent were advantaged in their life satisfaction.

DISCUSSION

Acculturation and Well-Being

In this investigation we tested a model of acculturation to identify sources of psychological well-being and distress among Latina grandmothers who were caring for their grandchildren. The study supports a multidimensional view of well-being in which different indices relate to acculturation in distinct ways. Contrary to our main hypothesis, we found no apparent mental health advantage for bilingual grandmothers. Spanish-preferred grandmothers were distinct in their lower levels of positive affect compared to bilingual and English-preferred groups. Apparently, isolation from mainstream institutions that is implied by using only Spanish— particularly income and education—are responsible for the lower positive affect in this group, supporting results of previous studies demonstrating immigration stress (González et al., 2001; Organista et al., 2003; Rogler et al., 1991). Lesser acculturated grandmothers in the Spanish-preferred group suffered monetary disadvantages: They were less educated, less likely to be employed, and had lower household income.

In marked contrast, there was some evidence that the Spanish-preferred group enjoyed higher well-being (better life satisfaction and lower negative affect) compared to the English-preferred group. This result is consistent with research that has established higher mental health among new immigrants (Vega et al., 1998; Organista et al., 2003; Cuéllar, 2000). However, this advantage was explained by the greater resources related to being married and having the parent of their grandchild currently in the household. Thus, traditionally oriented Latina grandmothers may have had greater life satisfaction and lower negative mood because they had their child care efforts supported or complemented by their spouse and the coresident parent. Clearly, among grandmothers with greater English language use, there were more seriously disruptive circumstances surrounding the adoption of their caregiving role. The grandmother's English preference was related to the parent's involvement in social problems prevalent in mainstream society, specifically substance abuse and related legal, child neglect, and emotional problems. This is consistent with other studies of substance use and acculturation (Caetano & Clark, 2003). Overall, being married and having parental involvement appear to be protective factors for new immigrant grandmothers that reduce the negative impact of exposure to mainstream societal problems.

Parental Presence and Grandchild's Behavior

Coparenting with a parent who lived in the household was related to higher well-being for Latina grandmothers with consistency across well-being measures, until more sensitive family relationship factors were controlled. Thus, the more influential family factors were family cohesion between grandmother, grandchild, and parent; and higher functioning family members, such as less frequent parental substance related reasons for care and fewer disturbed grandchildren. Thus, the cooperative and mutually reinforcing intergenerational relationships are at the heart of the positive association between parental presence and psychological outcomes for Latina caregiving grandmothers—a situation that likely emerges from values of familism inherent in traditional Latino culture. As another aspect of familism, over 70% of the families had one or more adult children living in the household, and the grandchild's parents lived in the household for 56%. Therefore, the custodial grandmother's other adult children were sometimes available to assist and support her, consistent with previous research (Burnette, 1999).

The grandmother's relationship with her grandchild was another dominant theme explaining her well-being. The child's behavior problems increased negative affect among these grandmothers, suggesting that the challenges of managing a difficult child have emotional consequences. Previous research has also demonstrated that raising children with behavior problems is distressing for grandmother caregivers (Hayslip, Shore, Henderson, & Lambert, 1998), including a cross national study with Mexico (Toledo et al., 2000). Furthermore, emotionally close grandmother-grandchild relationships were related to the grandmother's positive affect. Closer relationships with grandchildren were evident among the English-preferred grandmothers: Previous research has identified some relationship inhibition across three generations when traditional grandparents relate to highly acculturated grandchildren (Silverstein & Chen, 1999).

Other factors were related to well-being that suggest certain grandmothers are particularly at risk. Poorer health elevated distress levels across all three well-being indicators, reflecting the disabling impact of poor health in coping with the demands of providing for young children. Additionally, more mature and married grandmothers found life more satisfying: Consequently younger and unmarried grandmothers were at greater psychological risk.

Limitations

It should be noted that the sample volunteered based on recruitment through the schools and media, although broad recruitment made it possible to identify families with diverse characteristics across a wide geographic area. The sample is predominantly of Mexican descent, and therefore results may not apply to Latinos of other national origin. Additionally, our requirement for subject recruitment that households be *grandparent-headed* may be an ambiguous criterion for many Latino families who flexibly share housing with members of other generations in order to adapt to difficult economic circumstances. Finally, we rely only on language as an indicator of acculturation, a measure that may have somewhat limited utility for comparison to other studies that rely more on value and lifestyle measures.

Implications for Practice

Family income was related to positive mood, and a lack of vitality and happiness may result from the stress of caregiving with few resources. Poverty was markedly high overall (35%) demonstrating that many Mexican Americans are economically marginalized, with poor access to higher status employment and upward mobility (Baca Zinn & Wells, 2000). Professionals working with Latina grandmothers must be attentive to financial stress and assist with access to resources. Economic and cultural barriers to service utilization have been identified for health and mental health services, particularly for undocumented Latino immigrants (Berk & Schur, 2001). Therefore, culturally relevant and accessible interventions that assist the family to cope with children's difficult behaviors, conflicted relationships with the parent, and parental substance abuse would have an impact on the grandmother's well-being. Cuéllar (2000) recommends the use of an ecological framework to promote health and well-being, which includes evaluation of the context, attention to acculturation stresses, and consideration of social problems that impact individual functioning. Particularly younger, low income, unmarried, or ill grandmothers are at risk for psychological distress. They should be targeted for assistance with basic needs and help managing difficult family relationships in order to optimize their caregiving capacity to nurture and protect their grandchildren.

REFERENCES

Aranda, M. P., & Miranda, M. R. (1997). Hispanic aging, social support, and mental health: Does acculturation make a difference? In K. S. Markides & M. R. Miranda (Eds.), *Minorities, aging, and health* (pp. 271–294). Thousand Oaks, CA: Sage.

Baca Zinn, M., & Wells, B. (2000). Diversity within Latino families: New lessons for family social science. In D. H. Demo, K. R. Allen, & M. A. Fine (Eds.), *Handbook of family diversity* (pp. 252–273). New York: Oxford University Press.

Berk, M. L., & Schur, C. L. (2001). The effect of fear on access to care among undocumented Latino immigrants. *Journal of Immigrant Health, 3*(3), 151–156.

Burnette, D. (1999). Social relationships of Latino grandparent caregivers: A role theory perspective. *The Gerontologist, 39*, 49–58.

Burnette, D. (2000). Latino grandparents rearing grandchildren with special needs: Effects of depressive symptomatology. In P. McCallion & M. Janicki (Eds.), *Grandparents as carers of children with disabilities: Facing the challenges* (pp. 1–16). New York: Haworth Press.

Caetano, R., & Clark, C. L. (2003). Acculturation, alcohol consumption, smoking, and drug use among Hispanics. In K. M. Chun, P. B. Organista, & G. Marín (Eds.), *Acculturation: Advances in theory, measurement, and applied research* (pp. 223–239). Washington, DC: American Psychological Association.

Casper, L. M., & Bryson, K. R. (1998). *Co-resident grandparents and their grandchildren: Grandparent maintained families* (Population Division Working Paper No. 26). Washington, DC: U.S. Census Bureau.

Cox, C. (2000). Empowerment practice: Implications for interventions with African American and Latina custodial grandmothers. *Mental Health and Aging, 6*(4), 385–397.

Cuéllar, I. (2000). Acculturation and mental health: Ecological transactional relations of adjustment. In I. Cuéllar & F. A. Paniagua (Eds.), *Handbook of multicultural mental health* (pp. 45–62). San Diego, CA: Academic Press.

Diener, E., Emmons, R. A., Larsen, R. J., & Griffin, S. (1985). The Satisfaction With Life Scale. *Journal of Personality Assessment, 49*, 71–75.

Fields, J. (2003). *Children's living arrangements and characteristics: March 2002* (Current Population Reports P20-547). Washington, DC: Bureau of the Census. Retrieved July 18, 2003, from: http://www.census.gov/prod/2003pubs/p20-547.pdf

González, H. M., Haan, M. N., & Hinton, L. (2001). Acculturation and the prevalence of depression in older Mexican Americans: Baseline results of the Sacramento Area Latino Study on Aging. *Journal of the American Geriatrics Society, 49,* 948–953.

Goodman, C. C. (1998). *Grandmothers who parent: Family relations and well-being* (Funded Grant RO1AG14977). Bethesda, MD: National Institute on Aging, U.S. Health and Human Service.

Goodman, C., & Silverstein, M. (2002). Grandmothers raising grandchildren: Family structure and well-being in culturally diverse families. *The Gerontologist, 42,* 676–689.

Gronvold, R. L. (1988). Measuring affectual solidarity. In D. J. Mangen, V. L. Bengtson, & P. H. Landry, Jr. (Eds.), *Measurement of intergenerational relations* (pp. 74–97). Newbury Park, CA: Sage.

Guzman, B. (2001). *The Hispanic population: Census 2000 brief.* Washington, DC: U.S. Census Bureau. Retrieved December 11, 2002, from: http://www.census.gov/prod/2001pubs/c2kbr01-3.pdf

Hayslip, B., Jr., Shore, R. J., Henderson, C. E., & Lambert, P. L. (1998). Custodial grandparenting and the impact of grandchildren with problems on role satisfaction and role meaning. *Journal of Gerontology: Social Sciences, 53B,* S164–S173.

Joiner, T. E., Sandín, B., Chorot, P., Lostao, L., & Marquina, G. (1997). Development and factor analytic validation of the SPANAS among women in Spain: (More) cross-cultural convergence in the structure of mood. *Journal of Personality Assessment, 68,* 600–615.

Marín, G., Sabogal, F., Marín, B. V., Otero-Sabogal, R., & Pérez-Stable, E. J. (1987). Development of a short acculturation scale for Latinos. *Journal of Behavioral Sciences, 9,* 183–205.

Minkler, M., Fuller-Thomson, E., Miller, D., & Driver, D. (1997). Depression in grandparents raising grandchildren: Results of a national longitudinal study. *Archives of Family Medicine, 6,* 445–452.

Miranda, A. O., Estrada, D., & Firpo-Jimenez, M. (2000). Differences in family cohesion, adaptability, and environment among Latino families in dissimilar stages of acculturation. *The Family Journal: Counseling and Therapy for Couples and Families, 8,* 341–350.

Organista, P. B., Organista, K. C., & Kurasaki, K. (2003). The relationship between acculturation and ethnic minority mental health. In K. M. Chun, P. B. Organista, & G. Marín (Eds.), *Acculturation: Advances in theory, measurement, and applied research* (pp. 139–161). Washington, DC: American Psychological Association.

Rogler, L. H., Cortés, D. E., & Malgady, R. G. (1991). Acculturation and mental health status among Hispanics: Convergence and new directions for research. *American Psychologist, 46,* 585–597.

Sabogal, F., Marín, G., Otero-Sabogal, R., VanOss Marín, B., & Pérez-Stable, E. J. (1987). Hispanic familism and acculturation: What changes and what doesn't? *Hispanic Journal of Behavioral Sciences, 9,* 397–412.

Silverstein, M., & Chen, X. (1999). The impact of acculturation in Mexican-American families on the quality of adult grandchild-grandparent relationships. *Journal of Marriage and the Family, 61,* 188–198.

Stiffman, A. R., Orme, J. G., Evans, D. A., Feldman, R. A., & Keeney, P. A. (1984). A brief measure of children's behavior problems: The Behavior Rating Index for Children. *Measurement and Evaluation in Counseling and Development, 17*(2), 83–90.

Tabachnick, B. G., & Fidell, L. S. (2001). *Using multivariate statistics* (4th ed.). Boston: Allyn & Bacon.

Toledo, J. R., Hayslip, B., Jr., Emick, M. A., Toledo, C., & Henderson, C. E. (2000). Cross-cultural differences in custodial grandparenting. In B. Hayslip, Jr., & R. Goldberg-Glen (Eds.), *Grandparents raising grandchildren: Theoretical, empirical, and clinical perspectives* (pp. 107–124). New York: Springer.

U.S. Department of Health and Human Services. (2000). *The 2000 HHS poverty guidelines: Office of the Assistant Secretary for Planning and Evaluation, 65 Fed.Reg. 7555-7557.* Retrieved October 1, 2002, from: http://www.aspe.hhs.gov/poverty/00poverty.htm

Vega, W. A., Kolody, B., Aguilar-Gaxiola, S., Alderete, E., Catalano, R., & Caraveo-Anduaga, J. (1998). Lifetime prevalence of DSM-III-R psychiatric disorders among urban and rural Mexican Americans in California. *Archives of General Psychiatry, 55,* 771–782.

Ware, J. E., Jr. (1993). *SF-36 health survey: Manual and interpretation guide.* Boston: The Health Institute, New England Medical Center.

Watson, D., Clark, L. A., & Tellegen, A. (1988). Development and validation of brief measures of positive and negative affect: The PANAS Scales. *Journal of Personality and Social Psychology, 54,* 1063–1070.

Williams, N., & Torrez, D. J. (1998). Grandparenthood among Hispanics. In M. E. Szinovacz (Ed.), *Handbook on grandparenthood* (pp. 87–96). Westport, CT: Greenwood Press.

CHAPTER 16

African American Grandmothers as Health Educators in the Family*

Jeffrey A. Watson, Suzanne M. Randolph, and James L. Lyons

Between 1995 and 1997 more than 18,000 10- to 19-year-olds died in the United States each year from accidents with bicycles, motorcycles, cars, and trucks (Department of Transportation, 1998). However, experts argue that the mortality rate from such accidents can and should be reduced (Centers for Disease Control and Prevention, 1999; Department of Health and Human Services, 1990), in part through family-based prevention efforts (Resnick, Bearman, Blum, Bauman, Harris, et al., 1997); in particular, families who talk to, monitor, and model safety for young people may help protect them from known risk factors (Beck, Ko, & Scaffa, 1997; Beck, Scaffa, Swift, & Ko, 1995).

Since African American grandmothers do a significant amount of teaching with their grandchildren (Watson & Koblinsky, 1997), this investigation sought to measure the relationship between the frequency

*Funding for this research was provided by the Minority Health Research Laboratory, Department of Health Education, University of Maryland, College Park, MD.

of African American grandmothers talking to, monitoring, and modeling safety for their 10- to 19-year-old grandchildren about the risk behaviors with bicycle, motorcycle, car, and truck accidents and the variables which may predict those frequencies. This study sought to answer the question: "How much of the variance in the grandmother's teaching frequencies can be explained by key variables in grandparenting research and from the Theory of Planned Behavior (Ajzen, 1991)?" The answer may contribute to innovations within the grandparent education movement (Jordan, 1994; Strom & Strom, 1993; Watson, 1997b), reducing injuries among grandchildren and improving cognitive mastery among grandparents (Wallen, 1993).

Since 1900, African Americans in the United States have gained more than thirty years in life expectancy (Kain, 1993). Thus, African American grandparents in the United States now number over 8 million, with more than 900,000 maintaining a household with at least one minor grandchild (age < 18; Casper & Bryson, 1998; U.S. Bureau of the Census, 1993). Although the majority of householding grandparents in the United States are of European descent (56%), the most common denominator in surrogate grandparenting is substance abuse in the middle generation (Burnette, 1997; Pinson-Millburn, Fabian, Schlossberg, & Pyle, 1996). Even in homes not challenged by addiction, the average child in the United States has lost an average of 10 to 12 hours of direct time with parents per week since 1960 due largely to work force pressures (Resnick et al., 1997); this loss of parental time has created a greater opportunity for risk behavior and for the emergence of the grandparents' role.

THE THEORY OF PLANNED BEHAVIOR

The National Institutes of Health summarize the state of grandparenting research as incomplete, atheoretical, and often neglecting the roles of gender, age, social class, and ethnicity (Pruchno, 1995). Thus, the current examination uses the Theory of Planned Behavior (Ajzen, 1988, 1991) to guide its research on African American grandmothers of minor grandchildren.

The Theory of Planned Behavior (Ajzen, 1988, 1991) originated in the field of social psychology and evolved from the Theory of Reasoned Action (Fishbein & Ajzen, 1975). The earlier theory had suggested that health outcomes (e.g., lung cancer) had been conditioned, in part, by health behaviors (e.g., smoking or not smoking cigarettes). Health behaviors, in turn, had been influenced by behavioral intention (e.g., purposing to abstain or not abstain from smoking). Intention, according to this theory, had been largely determined by attitudes (e.g., wanting or not wanting to stop smoking) and beliefs (e.g., subjective norms: believing that others did or did not want the smoker to quit smoking).

The Theory of Planned Behavior (Ajzen, 1988, 1991) added another precursor to intention: perceived behavioral control. Accordingly, intention had three precursors: attitudes, beliefs, and control (e.g., gaining confidence to overcome barriers—like "the nicotine jitters"—through the help of a smoking cessation workshop). Since two of the precursors (i.e., attitudes, norms) in the theory are mediated through intention, the current study focused on intention and control as predictors of the health behavior of grandmothers (e.g., grandmothers talking to, monitoring, and modeling safety for their grandchildren regarding known risk behaviors).

AFRICAN AMERICAN GRANDMOTHERS: A REVIEW OF LITERATURE

When the U.S. government published its health care agenda for the decade 1990 through 2000 (Department of Health and Human Services, 1990), it recognized the family as a primary context for studying, promoting, and changing health behavior (Bloomberg, Myers, & Braverman, 1994; Dougherty & Campbell, 1988; U.S. Administration for Children, Youth, and Families, 1993).

The Intentions of African American Grandmothers

Based on 510 telephone surveys with middle class grandparents, Cherlin and Furstenberg (1986) described three basic styles of grandparenting (i.e., involved, companionate, and remote) based on the frequency of contact, the type of contact, and the parent-like nature of contact between grandparents and grandchildren. The interviews suggested that African American grandparents in the sample ($n = 51$) were nearly twice as likely (27%) to model the involved style than grandparents of European descent (15%); as such, African American grandparents were more likely than Anglo grandparents to pursue daily or nearly daily contact; to enact serious, parent-like relationships; and to correct the misbehavior of grandchildren.

In a 12-week experiment, the Stroms demonstrated that grandparents ($N = 395$) can grow through grandparent education (Strom & Strom, 1989; 1991; 1993); indeed, the experimental group significantly improved in 19 out of 60 areas. The investigators further reported (Strom, Collinsworth, Strom, & Griswold, 1993) that grandmothers ($n = 292$) and

African Americans ($n = 204$) were more successful and stronger in teaching than grandfathers ($n = 103$) and European Americans ($n = 204$), respectively; however, the grandparents of color also encountered more difficulty with grandchildren and sought more information about their grandchildren than their counterparts. In follow-up studies with working-class ($N = 192$) and middle-class ($N = 117$) grandparents (Watson & Koblinsky, 1997, 2000), evidence confirmed that grandmothers and African Americans of both classes made more frequent attempts to teach and felt more successful in doing so than grandfathers and European Americans, respectively; yet grandparents of color also expressed more frustration and sought more information concerning their grandchildren than their Caucasian counterparts.

At a university, 52 college students were asked to compare the role of their grandparents to that of their great-grandparents (Roberto & Skoglund, 1996). The results suggested that grandparents interact more frequently with college-age grandchildren than do great-grandparents.

Through telephone interviews with coresiding grandmothers ($N = 123$; 80% African American, 20% Caucasian), family researchers (Pearson, Hunter, Cook, Ialongo, & Kellam, 1997) concluded that the grandmother's role was not associated with her age or her employment; it was, however, correlated to household structure and race. Among the six household structures identified, two were most likely to have the grandmothers engaged in the full range of parenting activities: grandmother-alone and grandmother-and-grandfather. In the households where at least one parent was present, the grandmother did less of the parenting; when both parents were present, the grandmother did the least. After controlling for household economics and coresidency, the African American grandmother was still more likely than the Caucasian grandmother to get the grandchild up in the morning, to feed the grandchild, and to make sure the grandchild made it to school and bed on time; yet the grandmother of color was not more likely to set rules nor to provide emotional support, compared to the Caucasian grandmothers.

The previous body of research suggests that the typical African American grandmother exhibits a high degree of intention in her grandparenting role (e.g., greater involvement, more frequent teaching, more interaction, and more child-rearing activities) compared to Anglo-American grandparents, grandfathers, and great-grandparents.

The Control of African American Grandmothers

Based upon years as a family therapist, Boyd-Franklin (1989) describes the African American grandmother as occupying a highly constructive role in the family. At times challenged by poverty and early childbearing, Black grandmothers have headed more three- and four-generation households, initiated more fictive kin relationships, and experienced more role salience than grandmothers of European descent. Thus, African American grandmothers have often provided leadership during times of family stress (McAdoo, 1978), supporting grandchildren with advice, problem solving, and encouragement. Indeed, grandchildren have been more likely to graduate from high school and to maintain steady employment after high school, if their mothers and grandmothers had developed a strong relationship; similarly, children raised by their grandparents did better in school behaviorally than children raised in single-parent and blended-family homes.

Burton cautions, however, against idealizing the African American grandmother (Burton & Dilworth-Anderson, 1991; Burton & Hagestad, 1986), pointing out that younger grandmothers (age < 38) often refuse to accept the role of surrogate mother. Similarly, Wilson reports less role flexibility in household and child care responsibilities than is frequently suggested (Wilson, Tolson, Hinton, & Kiernan, 1990), especially with the growing number of grandmothers in the workforce. In keeping with this caution, three studies of African American grandmothers as surrogate parents (Burton, 1992; Jendrek, 1994) reported that grandmothers sometimes assume custody because of alcohol or drug addiction in the middle generation; although these grandmothers expressed universal concern for the welfare of the grandchildren, they also described themselves as living with chronic stress, negligible support, and external pressure to provide the care (38%).

In one study on family transitions (Burton, 1996), 61 triads of African American women described their role as first-time mothers, grandmothers, and great-grandmothers. Based on interviews, Burton grouped the triads into clusters: normative/on-time, normative/early, and non-normative/early; the most recent births were considered early (versus on-time) if the mother was an adolescent, yet the births were considered normative (versus non-normative) if the women considered the timing to be normal. Normative/on-time births introduced women to their roles at the ages of 21, 45, and 67, respectively. Normative/early births triggered the roles at 18, 37, and 56, whereas non-normative/early roles began at 16, 32, and 56. Burton (1996) further summarized that most of the women (87%) welcomed their role transitions; that normative transitions distributed caregiving duties equitably; that many (83%) of the youngest grandmothers (median age 32) refused to assume an active surrogate parent role because of their need for work, education, friendship, romance, or childbearing; and that the child-rearing responsibility was pushed up the generational ladder to the great-grandmother, when both the mother and the grandmother did not assume this responsibility. Similarly, Watson (1997a) found that women who became grandmothers later in life felt they had more information about their grandchildren and were able to make stronger efforts in teaching their grandchildren.

The previous body of research suggests that the average African American grandmother exhibits a high degree of control (i.e., confidence to overcome barriers) in her grandparenting role. Thus, at times, she has successfully met challenges posed by poverty, early childbearing, child custody, alcohol and drug addiction in the middle generation, and extended family stress.

METHOD

This study sought cross-sectional, correlational data from a convenience sample of African American women in Christian churches in the Washington, D.C., area because research had suggested that African American grandmothers were strong family teachers (Billingsley, 1992; Watson & Koblinsky, 1997) and that church-affiliated grandmothers were more likely to confront the problem behaviors of grandchildren than those not affiliated (Walters, 1996). The investigation sought to answer the question: "How much of the variance in the grandmother's teaching frequencies can be explained by key variables from grandparenting research"? (See Table 16.1, block 1) and from the Theory of Planned Behavior (Ajzen, 1991; see Table 16.1, block 2.) Full Model Fitted Multiple Regression Analysis was chosen because the study sought to include all ten predictor variables in the explanatory model. As a one-tailed test, this study utilized the following statistical levels: significance ($\alpha = .05$), effect size ($\delta = .50$), power ($1 - \beta = .80$), and sample ($N \geq 95$).

The dependent variables were based upon seven risk behaviors for unintentional injury in the *Youth Risk Behavior Survey* (Centers for Disease Control and Prevention, 1995): riding a bicycle, not wearing a bicycle helmet, riding a motorcycle, not wearing a motorcycle helmet, not wearing a seat belt, riding with a driver who has been drinking alcohol, and driving a motor vehicle after drinking alcohol. These behaviors were combined with three health education behaviors of grandmothers (Beck et al., 1995, 1997): talking to, monitoring, and modeling safety for grandchildren.

Churches were randomly selected from the only published list of African American churches in the Washington, D.C., area (Thomas & Shields, 1985) and an African American minister was recruited as the

TABLE 16.1   Regression Analyses: Frequency With Which African American Grandmothers Talk to, Monitor, and Model Safety for Their Grandchildren

Predictor Variables	Outcome: *Talking*	Outcome: *Monitoring*	Outcome: *Modeling*
Block 1 (variables 1 to 7)	$R^2 = .26^*$	$R^2 = .17$	$R^2 = .10$
1. Grandmother's information	$r^2 = .01$	$r^2 = .00$	$r^2 = .01$
2. Grandmother's social support	$r^2 = .01$	$r^2 = .01$	$r^2 = .01$
3. Grandmother's age	$r^2 = .02$	$r^2 = .04$	$r^2 = .00$
4. Grandmother's frequency of contact	$r^2 = .10^*$	$r^2 = .12^{**}$	$r^2 = .09^*$
5. Grandchild's age	$r^2 = .01$	$r^2 = .03$	$r^2 = .01$
6. Grandchild's sex	$r^2 = .00$	$r^2 = .00$	$r^2 = .00$
7. Grandchild's coresidency	$r^2 = .13^{**}$	$r^2 = .04$	$r^2 = .03$
Block 2 (variables 8 to 9)	$R^2 = .51^{****}$	$R^2 = .35^{****}$	$R^2 = .24^{***}$
8. Grandmother's intention	$r^2 = .45^{****}$	$r^2 = .28^{****}$	$r^2 = .18^{**}$
9. Grandmother's control	$r^2 = .08^*$	$r^2 = .07^*$	$r^2 = .12^{**}$
Blocks 1+2 combined (variables 1 to 9)	$R^2 = .56^{****}$	$R^2 = .38^*$	$R^2 = .44^{**}$

$^*p < .05.$ $^{**}p < .01.$ $^{***}p < .001.$ $^{****}p < .0001.$

gatekeeper (i.e., telephoning church leaders, reading Informed Consent statements, distributing surveys following the service to grandmothers who volunteered to participate). The gatekeeper and congregations received a small stipend. Grandmothers were asked to complete the survey within 1 week and to mail it to a research address in a prepared envelope. Questionnaires were precoded to seek approximately equal numbers of grandmothers writing about granddaughters and grandsons, as well as 10- to 14-year-old and 15- to 19-year-old grandchildren.

A series of 2 (sex of grandchild) × 2 (age group of grandchild) analyses of variance was conducted on interval variables, while a series of chi square procedures were conducted on nominal variables. These series tested whether the subgroups differed on any of the variables of interest as a function of the sex or age group of the grandchild, or the interaction of the two.

Each of the dependent variables—frequency of grandmothers talking to, monitoring, and modeling safety for their 10- to 19-year-old grandchildren about risk factors for accidental transportation injury—were individually regressed on nine predictor variables and on two blocks of variables (see Table 16.1). The regressions produced parameter estimates and correlation coefficients for each predictor variable (or block) and the dependent variable of interest. Using Full Model Fitted Multiple Regression Analysis, this study sought to evaluate whether block 1 or the addition of block 2 would explain more of the variance in the grandmother's health education role with her 10- to 19-year-old grandchildren concerning risk factors. This study conceptualized the grandmother's role as growing out of her commitment (i.e., intentions), confidence (i.e., control), and, in view of custodial grandparenting, context (i.e., coresidency, frequency of contact).

A total of 105 African American grandmothers with an eligible index grandchild completed the survey (52.5% response rate). A series of reliability analyses using Cronbach's alpha revealed a reasonable level of internal consistency for the subscales used in the study: .89 (talking), .84 (monitoring), .85 (modeling), and .99 (control); frequency distributions for these subscales were normally distributed, suggesting that the composite scores had scalar properties.

The average African American grandmother in the study was 62.07 years of age; had educational and occupational characteristics typical of the working class; and had 7.31 grandchildren. About half (51.9%) of the study participants were not currently married or partnered. Almost all (98.1%) were living in a house or apartment and had typically spent their lives in an urban (52.9%) or suburban setting (43.3%). Most were interested in attending a grandparent education workshop (60.3%), were not the main caretaker for the index grandchild (81.8%), and had chosen the index grandchild because that grandchild was the only one who fit the profile of the study (49.2%) or was the one with whom the grandmother had the most contact (40.0%). A series of post-hoc t-tests compared coresidential grandmothers with non-coresidential grandmothers; utilizing the Bonferroni correction, results suggest that grandmothers who lived with any grandchild (29.5%) and grandmothers who lived with the index grandchild (17.6%) were both significantly more likely to report frequent contact.

RESULTS

The outcome variables were individually regressed on nine of the ten predictor variables and on three blocks of predictor variables. One of the original independent variables, grandmother's willingness to correct, was not analyzed because it was a constant (i.e., 100% of the grandmothers said they would correct their grandchildren if they saw them misbehaving).

As shown in Table 16.1, five of the predictor variables did not significantly contribute to the variance in the frequency of grandmothers talking to their 10- to 19-year-old grandchildren about the risk of injury with bicycles, motorcycles, cars, and trucks. However, four of the predictor variables did significantly contribute to such variance: grandmother's frequency of contact ($r^2 = .10$; $p < .02$), grandchild's co-residency ($r^2 = .13$; $p < .01$), grandmother's intention ($r^2 = .45$; $p < .0001$), and grandmother's control ($r^2 = .08$; $p < .03$). As also shown in Table 16.1, the frequency of talking was predicted by block 1 ($R^2 = .26$; $p < .04$), by block 2 ($R^2 = .51$; $p < .0001$), and by blocks 1 and 2 combined ($R^2 = .56$; $p < .0001$).

As shown in Table 16.1, six of the predictor variables did not significantly contribute to the variance in the frequency of grandmothers monitoring their 10- to 19-year-old grandchildren about the risk of injury. However, three of the predictor variables did significantly contribute to such variance: frequency of contact ($r^2 = .12$; $p < .01$), intention ($r^2 = .28$; $p < .0001$), and control ($r^2 = .07$; $p < .05$). As also shown in Table 16.1, the frequency of monitoring was not predicted by block 1 ($R^2 = .17$; ns), but was predicted by block 2 ($R^2 = .35$; $p < .0001$), and by blocks 1 and 2 combined ($R^2 = .38$; $p < .02$).

As shown in Table 16.1, six of the predictor variables did not significantly contribute to the variance in the frequency of grandmothers modeling safety for their 10- to 19-year-old grandchildren. However, three of the predictor variables did significantly contribute to such variance: frequency of contact ($r^2 = .09$; $p < .02$), intention ($r^2 = .18$; $p < .002$) and control ($r^2 = .12$; $p < .008$). As also shown in Table 16.1, the frequency of modeling was not predicted by block 1 ($R^2 = .10$; ns), but was predicted by block 2 ($R^2 = .24$; $p < .001$), and by blocks 1 and 2 combined ($R^2 = .44$; $p < .004$).

DISCUSSION

If there are more than 70 million grandparents in the United States—including more than 8 million of African descent (Casper & Bryson, 1998; U.S. Bureau of the Census, 1993)—why do they all not adopt an optimal, health education role with their grandchildren? Because grandparenting is a diverse experience. Some grandmothers resolve to play a safety-oriented role with their grandchildren. Others confidently overcome barriers and find resources to help their grandchildren. But how much information does the typical grandmother have about risk behaviors? How much social support does she have to teach in the family? How old is she? How often does she see her grandchildren? Is she willing to correct them? How old are they? Are they boys or girls? Does the grandchild live under the same roof with the grandmother?

Typical grandmothers in this study were 62 years old, had seven grandchildren, came from the working class, lived in a house or apartment, and were not the main caretaker for the index grandchild. Most were interested in a free, 12-session, grandparent education workshop.

The frequency of grandmothers talking to their grandchildren about the risk of accidental transportation injury was predicted by frequency of contact, coresidency, intention, and control. These findings are consistent with previous research that suggested that grandparents with more frequent contact tend to have a relationship which is more parent-like in nature; grandparents who coreside make more frequent efforts to teach their grandchildren; grandparents who engage in health behavior do so because they want to, because they believe others want them to, and because they feel they can overcome barriers that might stand in their way. These findings are also consistent with previous research which suggests that the average African American grandmother exhibits a high degree of intention (i.e., commitment) in her grandparenting role (e.g., greater involvement, stronger teaching, more influence, and more child-rearing activities) compared to White grandparents, grandfathers, and great-grandparents. These findings are also consistent with previous research which reports that many Black grandmothers exhibit a high degree of perceived behavioral control (i.e., confidence to overcome barriers) in their grandparenting role, successfully meeting the challenges posed by poverty, early childbearing, child custody, alcohol and drug addiction in the middle generation, and extended family stress. Thus, grandparent educators should adapt their programming to reflect potential differences among grandmothers: differences in family structure (i.e., coresiding grandchild versus not), differences in family interaction (i.e., frequent grandchild contact versus not), differences in family attitudes (i.e., those who want grandmothers to teach grandchildren versus not), and differences in family resources (i.e., confidence to overcome barriers in the teaching of grandchildren versus not).

Regression analyses indicated that the frequency of grandmothers talking was predicted by block 1 (26% explained), by block 2 (51% explained), and by blocks 1 and 2 combined (56% explained). Thus, grandparent educators might need to consider that a grandmother's health education role could be related to her context (e.g., frequency of contact and coresidency), her commitment (e.g., intention to teach grandchildren), and her confidence (e.g., perceived control to overcome barriers in teaching grandchildren). Specifically, grandmothers may gain a greater sense of control for teaching 10- to 19-year-old grandchildren, if grandparent educators could address barriers (time, opportunity, permission, confidence) and resources (materials, media, community leaders, church leaders, or life stories). Indeed, a post hoc stepwise regression suggested that the best way to elevate a grandmother's intention to teach is to elevate her sense of control over teaching (i.e., empowerment, self-efficacy, mastery).

The frequency of grandmothers monitoring was predicted by three variables: frequency of contact, intention, and control. These variables had also predicted talking. While monitoring was not predicted by block 1 (17% explained), it was predicted by block 2 (35% explained) and by the combination of blocks 1 and 2 (38% explained). Thus, the grandmother who checks to see if her grandchildren are engaging in accident-prone behavior with bicycles and motorcycles is also more likely to have frequent interaction with those grandchildren. Similarly, the grandmother who pays attention to whether her grandchildren are wearing seat belts and helmets is also more likely to believe that this type of watching is part of her role. Furthermore, if this grandmother wants to help her grandchild to avoid mixing alcohol and motor vehicles, whether as a passenger or a driver, she needs a certain degree of confidence to engage in this type of supervision. Thus, when grandparent education workshops are conducted or new curriculum materials are developed, it would be important to recognize the strategic nature of a grandmother's context (i.e., how often does she have contact?), a grandmother's commitment (i.e., how thoroughly does she intend to monitor her behavior?), and a grandmother's confidence (i.e., how much control does she feel she has to overcome the barriers in "watching out" for her grandchild's safety?).

The frequency of grandmothers modeling was predicted by three variables: frequency of contact, intention, and control. These findings support the same research discussed earlier for talking and monitoring. While frequency of modeling was not predicted by block 1 (10% explained), it was predicted by block 2 (24% explained) and by the combination of blocks 1 and 2 (44% explained). When a grandmother believes that "actions speak louder than words," she seizes the opportunity to teach her grandchildren by example (e.g., buckling her seat belt, avoiding bicycles and motorcycles or wearing helmets when she does, and not drinking and driving or riding with intoxicated drivers); such role modeling could save lives on prom night, for instance. However, this kind of role modeling would not even exist as a family resource, if the grandmother had not made up her mind to live a safer lifestyle and to overcome the hurdles involved in doing so; furthermore, her powerful health education lessons would have little intergenerational benefit, unless there were some regular opportunity for her grandchildren to observe her behavior. Therefore, when grandparent educators write curricula or run workshops, they should consider that all of their target audience is not the same. Some grandmothers intend to live safer lifestyles than others; some are more effective at overcoming barriers than others; and some actually have more contact with their grandchildren than others. So based on evidence in this current study, innovative grandparent educators might conduct needs assessments or ask questions such as: "Is this grandmother committed to modeling safety for her grandchildren? Is she confident that she can overcome barriers that might stand in her way? Is she in a geographic and interactional context which allows her to cast her example in front of the grandchildren?"

In conclusion, grandparent specialists should continue to practice educational diversity (e.g., targeting older and younger grandmothers, grandmothers with differing levels of information and social support, grandmothers of boys and girls, and grandmothers with grandchildren of different ages). Yet, these same grandparenting programs might be even stronger if they specifically acknowledged the role of the grandmother's context (e.g., frequent contact, coresidency), commitment (e.g., intention), and confidence (e.g., control). Additional research might focus on other risk behaviors; other ethnicities; other kinship positions; or children of other ages. New studies could also utilize qualitative methods; could explore causal relationships; could apply the subscales to new inquiries; or could explore the differing estimates on the grandmother's willingness to correct.

REFERENCES

Ajzen, I. (1988). *Attitudes, personality, and behavior*. Chicago: Dorsey Press.

Ajzen, I. (1991). The theory of planned behavior. *Organizational Behavior and Human Decision Processes, 50*, 179–211.

Beck, K., Ko, M., & Scaffa, M. (1997). Parental monitoring, acceptance, and perceptions of teen alcohol misuse. *American Journal of Health Behavior, 21*, 26–32.

Beck, K., Scaffa, M., Swift, R., & Ko, M. (1995). A survey of parent attitudes and practices regarding underage drinking. *Journal of Youth and Adolescence, 24*, 315–334.

Billingsley, A. (1992). *Climbing Jacob's ladder*. New York: Simon & Schuster.

Bloomberg, L., Myers, J., & Braverman, M. T. (1994). The importance of social interaction: A new perspective on social epidemiology, social risk factors and health. *Health Education Quarterly, 21*, 447–463.

Boyd-Franklin, N. (1989). *Black families in therapy: A multisystems approach*. New York: Guildford Press.

Burnette, D. (1997). Grandparents raising grandchildren in the inner city. *Families in Society, 72,* 489–499.

Burton, L. (1992). Black grandparents rearing children of drug-addicted parents: Stressors, outcomes, and social service needs. *The Gerontologist, 32,* 744–751.

Burton, L. (1996). Age norms, the timing of family role transitions, and intergenerational caregiving among aging African American women. *The Gerontologist, 36,* 199–208.

Burton, L. M., & Dilworth-Anderson, P. (1991). The intergenerational family roles of aged Black Americans. *Marriage & Family Review, 16,* 311–330.

Burton, L. M., & Hagestad, G. O. (1986). Grandparenthood, life context, and family development. *The American Behavioral Scientist, 29,* 471–484.

Casper, L. M., & Bryson, K. R. (1998). *Co-resident grandparents and their grandchildren: Grandparent maintained families.* Washington, DC: U.S. Bureau of the Census.

Centers for Disease Control and Prevention (1993). *Mortality trends, causes of death, and related risk behaviors among U.S. adolescents* (CDC Publication No. 099-4112). Atlanta, GA: Centers for Disease Control and Prevention.

Centers for Disease Control and Prevention (1995). *Youth Risk Behavior Survey.* Atlanta, GA: Centers for Disease Control and Prevention.

Centers for Disease Control and Prevention (1999). *Youth Risk Behavior Survey 1997.* [CD-ROM]. Atlanta, GA: Centers for Disease Control and Prevention.

Cherlin, A. J., & Furstenberg, F. F., Jr. (1986). *The new American grandparent: A place in the family, a life apart.* New York: Basic Books.

Department of Health and Human Services. (1990). *Healthy people 2000: National health promotion and disease prevention objectives* (DHHS Publication No. PHS 91-50212). Washington, DC: U.S. Government Printing Office.

Department of Transportation. (1998). *Annual report file—Fatal accident reporting system: 1997—National Highway Traffic Safety Administration* (1998). Washington, DC: Department of Transportation.

Dougherty, W. J., & Campbell, T. L. (1988). *Families and health.* Newberry Park, CA: Sage Publications.

Fishbein, M., & Ajzen, I. (1975). *Belief, attitude, intention and behavior: An introduction to theory and research.* Reading, MA: Addison-Wesley.

Jendrek, M. P. (1994). Grandparents who parent their grandchildren: Circumstances and decisions. *The Gerontologist, 34,* 206–216.

Jordan, C. F. (1994). *Grandparenting by grace: Leader's guide.* Nashville, TN: Lifeway Press.

Kain, E. L. (1993). Race, mortality, and families. In H. P. McAdoo (Ed.), *Family ethnicity: Strength in diversity* (pp. 60–78). Newberry Park, CA: Sage.

McAdoo, H. P. (1978). Factors related to stability in upwardly mobile Black families. *Journal of Marriage and Family, 40,* 761–776.

Pearson, J. L., Hunter, A. G., Cook, J., Ialongo, N., & Kellam, S. (1997). Grandmother involvement in child caregiving in an urban community. *The Gerontologist, 37,* 650–657.

Pinson-Millburn, N. M., Fabian, E. S., Schlossberg, N. K., & Pyle, M. (1996). Grandparents raising grandchildren. *Journal of Counseling and Development, 74,* 548–554.

Pruchno, R. (1995). *Grandparents in American society: Review of recent literature*. Beachwood, OH: Myers Research Institute.

Resnick, M. D., Bearman, P. S., Blum, R. W., Bauman, K. E., Harris, K. M., Jones, J., et al. (1997). Protecting adolescents from harm: Findings from the National Longitudinal Study on Adolescent Health. *Journal of the American Medical Association, 278*, 823–832.

Roberto, K., & Skoglund, R. (1996). Interactions with grandparents and great-grandparents: A comparison of activities, influences, and relationships. *International Journal of Aging and Human Development, 43*, 107–117.

Strom, R., Collinsworth, P., Strom, S., & Griswold, D. (1993). Strengths and needs of Black grandparents. *International Journal of Aging and Human Development, 36*, 255–268.

Strom, R., & Strom, S. (1989). *Grandparent development: Final report submitted to the American Association of Retired Persons*. Washington, DC: Andrus Foundation.

Strom, R., & Strom, S. (1991). *Grandparent education: A guide for leaders*. Newbury Park, CA: Sage.

Strom, R., & Strom, S. (1993). *Grandparent strengths and needs inventory manual*. Bensenville, IL: Scholastic Testing Service.

Strom, R., Strom, S., Collinsworth, P., Strom, P., & Griswold, D. (1996). Black grandparents: Curriculum development. *International Journal of Aging and Human Development, 43*, 119–134.

Thomas, V., & Shields, L. (1985). *Directory of Black churches and other religious-related organizations in the Washington, D.C. metropolitan area*. Washington, DC: Mental Health Research and Development Center in The Institute for Urban Affairs and Research at Howard University.

United States Administration for Children, Youth, and Families. (1993). Designing health promotion approaches to high-risk adolescents through formative research with youth and parents. *Public Health Reports, 108*, 68–77.

United States Bureau of the Census. (1993). *Current population reports, estimates, and projections* (Series P-25 No. 1127). Washington, DC: U.S. Government Printing Office.

Wallen, J. (1993). Protecting the mental health of children in dangerous neighborhoods. *Children Today, 22*, 24–27.

Walters, L. M. (1996). *A descriptive study of problems faced by African American grandmothers raising grandchildren*. Unpublished doctoral dissertation, California State University, Long Beach.

Watson, J. (1997a). Grandmothering across the lifespan. *The Journal of Gerontological Social Work, 28*, 45–62.

Watson, J. (1997b). Factors associated with African American grandparents' interest in grandparent education. *The Journal of Negro Education, 66*, 73–82.

Watson, J. (1999). Lois, Eunice, and Timothy: A New Testament example of family ministry in the three-generation household. *Marriage & Family: A Christian Journal, 2*, 89–100.

Watson, J., & Koblinsky, S. (1997). Strengths and needs of African-American and Anglo-American grandparents. *International Journal of Aging and Human Development, 44*, 149–165.

Watson, J., & Koblinsky, S. (2000). The strengths and needs of African-American and Anglo-American grandmothers in the working class and middle classes. *Journal of Negro Education, 69,* 198–213.

Wilson, M. N., Tolson, T. F., Hinton, I. D., & Kiernan, M. (1990). Flexibility and sharing of childcare duties in Black families. *Sex Roles, 22,* 409–425.

CHAPTER 17

Religious Beliefs and Practices Among African American Custodial Grandparents

Martha R. Crowther, Leslie M. Swanson, Rachel L. Rodriguez, Melissa Snarski, and Hyoun-Kyoung Higgerson

There has been a steady increase in the number of grandparents who are raising their grandchildren. Many grandparent caregivers experience stress, decreased social and economic well-being, and reduced physical health as a result of caregiving (Burton, 1992; Joslin & Brouard, 1995; Joslin & Harrison, 1998; Minkler & Fuller-Thomson, 1999; Minkler & Roe, 1993; Minkler, Roe, & Price, 1992; Sands & Goldberg-Glen, 2000). As interest in this area of research grows, questions as to the methods grandparents use to cope with the stress of caregiving increase. Although many grandparents experience stress, not all do. Crowther and Rodriguez (2003) examined African American custodial grandparents and found that overall, the grandparent caregivers in their study reported high levels of health and well-being, and their psychological distress fell within normal limits. There are several possible explanations for this phenomenon. First, grandparents in poor health would be less likely to become custodial grandparents. Second, grandparents who want to become custodial grandparents would deemphasize their health concerns for fear that their grandchildren would be taken away from them. Third, their prior exposure to and mastery of life stress, or experience of caregiving may serve to better prepare African American custodial grandparents for the demands of caregiving. In this chapter, we explore religious beliefs and practices as an additional explanation for the decrease in stress among African American custodial grandparents.

The literature on African Americans has consistently indicated that African Americans report a religious or spiritual component to their lives (e.g., Armstrong & Crowther, 2002; Chatters, 2002). Religious/spiritual coping is especially common among elderly African Americans. This may be due to the role that the Black Church plays in African American culture. The Black Church in the African American experience has undoubtedly contributed to the spiritual formation of African American individuals (Lincoln & Mamiya, 1990).

Conceptualization of Religiousness and Spirituality

Religion and spirituality are the most important factors that structure human experience, beliefs, values, behavior, and illness patterns. Some regard the constructs as indistinguishable, while others argue that religion and spirituality are uniquely different with religion referring to a group activity that involves specific behavioral, social, doctrinal, and denominational characteristics (Abeles, Ellison, Goerge, Idler, Krause, et al., 1999). Religious practices encourage spiritual growth, while spiritual practices are often a salient aspect of religious participation. Many scholars argue that it is possible to adopt the outward form of religious behavior without developing a relationship with God, sometimes referred to as an extrinsic orientation to religion (e.g., Allport & Ross, 1967).

The Role of Religion and Spirituality in the Lives of African Americans

Religion and spirituality shape individual, family, and communal relations across the life course. Sanders (2002) suggests that a primary source of support for many African Americans is spirituality. This spirituality is often tied into some form of organized religion.

There is some evidence to suggest that there are ethnic differences in spiritual beliefs and practices (e.g., Armstrong, 1999; Cavendish, Welch, & Leege, 1998); thus, we might expect some differences in the content and transmission of spirituality between ethnic groups. Characteristic of African American families is the significant interplay between spirituality and religiosity. The impact of the Black Church as an institution on African American families is difficult to overestimate. The Black Church has long served as a type of extended family (Boyd-Franklin, 1989; Lincoln & Mamiya, 1990) and even today continues to provide initial training in leadership for many African American youth that is not systematically offered in most mainstream educational settings. Moreover, the Church helps to address systemic problems in the culture (Richardson, 1991). A spiritual approach must encompass history, racism, discrimination, economic loss, and the like, if it is to be relevant to most African American families (Smith, 1997). Unfortunately, as Smith (1997) noted, spirituality is often marginalized in the service of economic values.

In addition to the Black Church, Black families exert significant influence on the spiritual development of children. In a qualitative study of African American parents, Hurd, Moore, and Rogers (1995) reported that the cultivation of spirituality through belief in and respect for God was a common theme across the interviews. Because of the oral tradition that has been highly developed in African cultures, the role and impact of storytelling is a primary means of such cultivation (Boyd-Franklin, 1989). More research is needed to understand the specific mechanisms by which African American families transmit distinctly spiritual values to their children.

In turn, the transmission of spiritual values in Black families is best fostered in the context of a supportive community. Haight (1998) conducted a four-year ethnographic study of an African American community, which revealed that spirituality played an active part in how children were socialized and resulted in a sense of support. Haight suggested that this support contributed to coping with racism, discrimination, and inadequate educational and occupational opportunities. Morevoer, Brody, Stoneman, and Flor (1996) demonstrated in a sample of African American youth ages 9 to 12 that formal religiosity was positively associated with family cohesion and negatively associated with family conflict, internalizing, and externalizing problems.

Religious Coping

Religious coping is a broad term used to describe many different actions. Recently, Koenig and his colleagues examined the association between 21 types of religious coping and mental health characteristics. Offering religious help to others was one of the most powerful predictors of low depressive symptoms, greater level of cooperativeness, and greater stress-related growth (Koenig, Larson, & Larson, 2001). It is noted that coping behaviors focused primarily on the self without depending on God were related to greater depression and significantly lower stress-related growth.

Empirical studies have shown a clear connection between stressful life events and various forms of religious/spiritual involvement (e.g., Bearon & Koenig, 1990).

Some studies report that though religious coping may reduce the affective symptoms of depression, it is less effective for biological symptoms. In a study done by Koenig et al. (1992), they examined the relationship between nonreligious and religious coping. Participants were given the RCI (Religious Coping Index) to measure the level of religious coping used. They found that religious coping was significantly and inversely related to depressive symptoms. However, religious coping was only associated with the cognitive symptoms of depression and not its somatic symptoms.

METHOD

Participants

The data used in this chapter was collected as part of a larger study on custodial grandparenting (Crowther, 1998, 2001). A subset of the participants were given the Brief Measure of Religion and Spirituality (BMRS) developed by the Fetzer Institute (Fetzer Institute, 1999) in an attempt to understand the relation between religion and spirituality among the grandparent caregivers. Eighty-two African American grandparent caregivers aged 38 to 75 years (M = 53) were recruited for this study. Sixty percent of the women were single, 57.3% of the grandparents had completed some college education or more, and 46.3% of the grandparents were providing care for one to two grandchildren.

Eligibility

Grandparent caregivers were considered eligible for inclusion in the study if they met all of the following criteria:

1. The subject had to be at least 25 years of age at the time of entry into the study.
2. The subject was not institutionalized.
3. The subject must be the primary caretaker for at least one child under the age of 18 who is not their own son or daughter.

Participant Recruitment

Participants were recruited with the help of community persons, organizations, and fliers. The individuals and organizations were given an information sheet describing the project and stating the eligibility criteria. Persons and organizations that assisted in subject recruitment were: community health centers, directors of child advocacy programs, Head Start programs, school counselors and teachers, and psychologists who work with the sample population. A contact number was provided for persons interested in participating. Those who expressed interest in participating were prescreened to insure that they met eligibility criteria. If eligibility criteria were met, an appointment was made for participation in the project. At the time of interview, a "snowball technique" was employed; that is, subjects were asked if they knew of anyone else who fit the study criteria.

Procedure

After meeting eligibility criteria, each participant was interviewed in a neutral location chosen by the interviewer and the participant. One 2-hour assessment was conducted. The purpose and requirements of the study were explained to the participant and any questions were answered. Participants were ensured of the anonymity of their responses. Participants were then interviewed and asked to complete standardized questionnaires. Grandparents received monetary compensation for their participation in the project. They were also provided with information regarding a support group in their area.

Measures

Sociodemographics

Sociodemographic characteristics of the sample provided a basis for understanding the personal context of grandparent caregivers. The format included both closed and open-ended questions and covered the following topic areas: demographics, religious affiliation and practices, household composition, number of children, grandchildren, and great-grandchildren, number of persons respondent is primary caregiver for in addition to grandchildren, the amount of time the respondent has been in the grandparent caregiver role, presence or absence of a substance abusing parent in the home, and physical and psychological status of the grandchildren.

Subjective Well-Being

Subjective well-being was assessed using three single-item measures relating to evaluations of life satisfaction, happiness, and goal attainment. The items combined represent the affective and cognitive dimensions of subjective well-being (Tran, Wright, & Chatters, 1991). Additionally, these items arrive at a global versus domain-specific evaluation of life quality. When the items were combined, the scores ranged from 3 to 9, with higher scores indicating greater subjective well-being (alpha coefficient = 0.63). The three items in this study have been used with African American participants in the past and were found to be predictive in determining health, stress, and psychological resources (Tran et al., 1991)

Coping

Pearlin, Mullan, Semple, and Skaff (1990) used the coping scale (alpha coefficient = 0.44), which comprised three components that address coping in response to life problems: management of the situation causing stress (alpha coefficient = 0.48), management of the meaning of the situation such that its threat is reduced, and management of the stress symptoms that result from the situation (alpha coefficient = 0.54). The items that measure management of the meaning of the situation have three factors: reduction of expectations (alpha coefficient = 0.52), use of positive comparisons (alpha coefficient = 0.52), and a search for a larger sense of meaning (alpha coefficient = 0.48). The response categories for the subscale items range from 1 to 4 and the higher the score, the higher the coping.

Appraisal of Caregiving

Appraisal was measured by economic and intrapsychic strain questionnaires (Pearlin et al., 1990). Economic strain is comprised of three items measuring the following dimensions: reduction in household income, increase in expenditures related to the care and treatment of the care recipient and whether there is enough money to subsist month to month. Intrapsychic strain is measured by the following scales: role captivity, loss of self, caregiving competence, and personal gain. Role captivity is a four-item scale that measures the reluctance of the caregiver to perform the role (alpha coefficient = 0.49). Loss of self is assessed by a two-item scale that assesses the sense of personal identity the caregiver may have lost because of the caregiving role (alpha coefficient = 0.56). Caregiving competence is measured by a four-item scale and asks caregivers to rate their level of competence in the caregiving role (alpha coefficient = 0.60).

Personal gain is a four-item scale that assesses whether the caregiver has grown from the caregiving experience (alpha coefficient = 0.52). The response categories are continuous for each item and range from 1 to 4; the higher the score, the higher the appraisal of caregiving.

Brief Multidimensional Measure of Religiousness and Spirituality

The BMRS is a measure developed by the Fetzer Institute (Fetzer Institute, 1999) to assess religiousness and spirituality, as well as links between health outcomes and religiousness and spirituality. The BMRS consists of several measurement domains. This study specifically examined the following domains: daily spiritual experiences, values, beliefs, forgiveness, private religious practices, religious/spiritual coping, religious support, organizational religiousness, and meaning.

RESULTS

As presented in Table 17.1, the majority of participants reported that they considered themselves either very (52%) or moderately religious (45%). In terms of religious affiliation, 75% of the participants indicated that they were protestant and 24% indicated that they were other.

Predictors of Coping and Well-Being

The majority of participants' scores indicated that they had a high level of coping (see Table 17.2). Utilizing multiple regression analysis, findings suggested that while not statistically significant ($p < .0597$), as participants' religiousness increased, "reduction of expectations" also tended to increase. Utilizing the inclusion of an interaction term, findings suggested that there was a significant interaction between the number of grandchildren under a grandparent's care and subjective well-being (SWB) and degree of religiosity ($B = .07$, $t = 2.04$ $p = < .05$). For grandparents who have custody of four or fewer grandchildren, increased religiousness is associated with decreased SWB. However, for those grandparents who have custody of five or more grandchildren, SWB *increases* with increased religiousness. It appears that when faced with the increased stress of caring for a substantial number of grandchildren, religiosity may serve as a potential moderator to facilitate SWB for custodial grandparents faced with such responsibility. Thus, religiosity moderates the relationship between the number of children under a grandparent's care and well-being in this sample of African American grandparent caregivers.

TABLE 17.1 Demographic Characteristics (N = 82)

Characteristics		N (%)
Age (years)	30–39	5 (6.1)
	40–49	26 (31.7)
	50–59	35 (42.7)
	60–69	12 (14.6)
	70–79	4 (4.9)
Marital status	Married	33 (40.2)
	Separated	6 (7.3)
	Divorced	20 (24.4)
	Widowed	14 (17.1)
	Single/never married	8 (9.8)
	Other	1 (1.2)
Education	Grade school	6 (7.3)
	Some high school	14 (17.1)
	High school graduate	15 (18.3)
	Some college or technical school	35 (42.7)
	College graduate or higher	12 (14.6)
Religious preference[a]	Baptist	55 (69.6)
	Methodist	4 (5.1)
	Presbyterian	1 (1.3)
	Other	19 (24.1)
How religious	1 Not at all religious	1 (1.2)
	2	1 (1.2)
	3 Somewhat religious	20 (24.4)
	4	17 (20.7)
	5 Very religious	43 (52.4)
Number of children	1–2	28 (34.1)
	3–4	31 (37.8)
	5–6	14 (17.1)
	7–9	8 (9.8)
Number of grandchildren[a]	0	1 (1.2)
	1–2	25 (30.5)
	3–4	21 (25.6)
	5–9	20 (25.2)
	10–21	13 (16.5)
Number of grandchildren for care now	1–2	38 (46.3)
	3–4	27 (32.9)
	5–9	14 (17.0)
	10–15	3 (3.6)

[a]Missing value was not included to the percentage.

TABLE 17.2 Coping

	N	Mean	Std. Dev	Max	Min
Management of the situation causing stress	81	3.4290	.42616	4.00	2.00
Management of meaning					
Reduction of expectations	81	3.4033	.55457	4.00	2.00
Use of positive comparisons	81	3.2407	.83707	4.00	1.00
A search for a larger sense of meaning	80	3.5188	.58701	4.00	2.50
Management of the stress symptoms	80	2.8875	.45770	3.75	1.88
Total	78	12.1000	1.2557	14.40	8.2

Reduction of expectations (DV)	b	p-value
Religiousness (IV)	0.37003	0.0597
Number of grandchildren (IV)	−0.07586	0.0803

Organizational Religiousness and Meaning

Participants reported that they spend an average of 6 hours per week in activities on behalf of their church or activities that they do for religious or spiritual reasons. On average, participants reported that they have spiritual and religious experiences every day or more often. The grandparents reported that they engage in private religious practices (i.e., prayer outside of church, meditation, watching religious programs on the television, reading religious literature) on average, at least once a day.

Eighty-seven percent of the participants also reported that because of their religious or spiritual beliefs, they have almost always forgiven others for hurting them and themselves for things that they have done wrong. When asked how involved their chosen religion is in understanding or dealing with stressful situations, the majority of the participants ($n = 16$) reported that their chosen religion is "very involved," and six participants reported that their chosen religion is "somewhat involved" (see Figure 17.1). Many of the participants ($n = 12$) reported that, if they were ill, the people in their congregation would help them out "a great

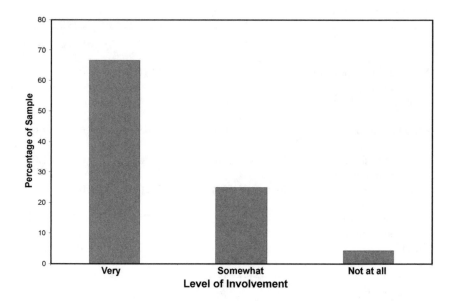

FIGURE 17.1 Level of involvement of participant's religion in dealing with stressful situations

deal," and if they were faced with a difficult situation, the people in their congregation would be willing to give them "a great deal" of comfort ($n = 13$).

When faced with major problems in their lives, the majority of the participants used religiosity and spirituality to cope. Half of the participants reported that they work together with God as partners "a great deal" when they are faced with major problems (see Figure 17.2). Over 80% of the participants reported that they look to God for strength, support, and guidance "a great deal." When coping with a major problem, 50% of the grandparents reported that they think about how their life is a part of a larger spiritual force "a great deal" (see Figure 17.3). All of the participants reported that they pray for strength to keep going "very often" or "fairly often" (see Figure 17.4). Ninety-five percent of the participants reported that they pray for strength to keep going "very often."

DISCUSSION

The data suggest that custodial grandparents are quite religious. Almost all of the grandparents surveyed indicated that they are moderately to very religious and spiritual. The results of this study indicate that spiritual-

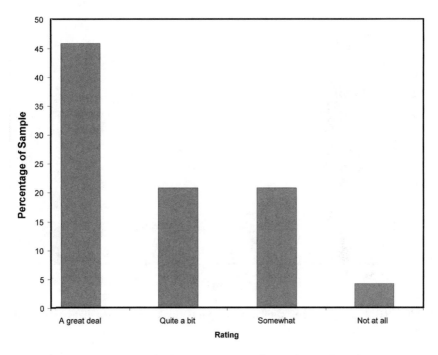

FIGURE 17.2 Extent to which participants work together with God as partners.

ity and religiousness may serve as coping mechanisms that grandparents employ in dealing with the demands they encounter as primary caregivers for their grandchildren.

Clinical Applications

While designed primarily to assess the degree of religiousness and spirituality found among African American custodial grandparents, this study has clinical implications. Clinically, the results could help identify topics to be addressed in grandparent caregiver support groups, such as coping skills utilizing religion and spirituality. Psychotherapists who have clients that are raising their grandchildren may want to take into account the roles that spirituality and religiosity play in therapy and their clients' well-being.

Limitations

Given the location, size, and demographics of this sample, it would be very difficult to apply these conclusions to grandparents raising their

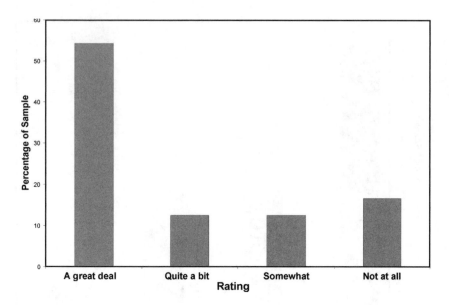

FIGURE 17.3 Extent to which participants think about their lives as part of a larger spiritual force.

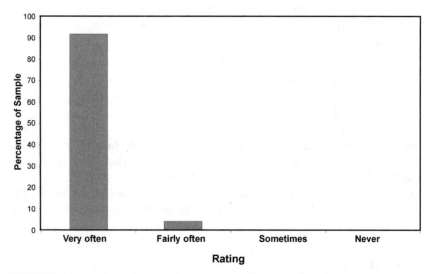

FIGURE 17.4 How often participants pray for strength to keep going?

grandchildren outside of the South. Future research should examine the role of religiosity and spirituality in grandparent caregivers across the country to aid in generalizability.

The sample size of the study is quite small, and all of the participants are female. Although the majority of grandparents raising their grandchildren are grandmothers, there are grandfathers who are responsible for the primary care of their grandchildren. Future studies should address the issue of grandfathers who raise their grandchildren, as their use of religiosity and spirituality as a coping mechanism may differ from that of females. Measurement concerns (alphas) for several scales also emerge as limitations here.

This study sheds some light on the use of religious and spiritual practices by grandmothers that are raising their grandchildren. The results of this study suggest that future research into the mechanisms by which religion and spirituality help grandparents cope with the demands placed upon them would help further our understanding of this growing phenomenon.

REFERENCES

Abeles, R., Ellison, C., George, L., Idler, E., Krause, N., Levin, J., Ory, M., Pargament, K., Powell, L., Underwood, L., & Williams, D. (1999). *Multidimensional measurement of religiousness/spirituality for use in health research.* A John E. Fetzer Publication.

Allport, G. W., & Ross, J. M. (1967). Personal religious orientation and prejudice. *Journal of Personality and Social Psychology, 5,* 432–443.

Armstrong, T. D. (1999). The impact of spirituality on the coping process of families dealing with pediatric HIV or pediatric nephrotic syndrome (Doctoral dissertation, University of North Carolina at Chapel Hill, 1998). *Dissertation Abstracts International, 59*(12-B), 64–82.

Armstrong, T., & Crowther, M. (2002). Spirituality among older African Americans. *Journal of Adult Development, 9*(1), 3–12.

Bearon, L. B., & Koenig, H. G. (1990). Religious cognition and use of prayer in health and illness. *Gerontologist, 30,* 249–253.

Boyd-Franklin, N. (1989). *Black families in therapy: A multisystems approach* (pp. 78–91). New York: The Guilford Press.

Brody, G. H., Stoneman, Z., & Flor, D. (1996). Family wages, family processes, and youth competence in rural married African American families. In E. M. Hetherington & E. A. Blechman (Eds.), *Stress, coping, and resiliency in children and families* (pp. 173–188). Mahwah, NJ: Lawrence Erlbaum Associates.

Burton, L. (1992). Black grandmothers rearing children of drug-addicted parents: Stressors, outcomes, and social service needs. *The Gerontologist, 32*(6), 744–751.

Cavendish, J. C., Welch, M. R., & Leege, D. C. (1998). Social network theory and predictors of religiosity for Black and White Catholics: Evidence of a "Black sacred cosmos"? *Journal for the Scientific Study of Religion, 37*, 397–410.

Chatters, L. (2002). Religion and health: Public health research and practice. *Annual Review of Public Health, 21*, 335–367.

Crowther, M. R. (1998). *Compensatory grandparenting.* Dissertation. Duke University.

Crowther, M. R. (2001). *Kincare: Grandparents raising grandchildren.* Funded by the American Studies Program, University of Alabama, Tuscaloosa.

Crowther, M., & Rodriguez, R. (2003). A stress and coping model of custodial grandparenting among African Americans. In B. Hayslip, Jr. & J. H. Patrick (Eds.), *Working with custodial grandparents* (pp. 311–330). New York: Springer Publishing.

Fetzer Institute (1999). *Multidimensional measurement or religiousness/spirituality for use in health research.* Kalamazoo, MI: John E. Fetzer Institute.

Haight, W. L. (1998). Gathering the spirit at First Baptist Church: Spirituality as a protective factor in the lives of African American children. *Social Work, 43*(3), 213–221.

Hurd, E. P., Moore, C., & Rogers, R. (1995). Quiet success: Parenting strengths among African Americans. *Families in Society: The Journal of Contemporary Human Services, 76*, 434–443.

Joslin, D., & Brouard, A. (1995). The prevalence of grandmothers as primary caregivers in a poor pediatric population. *Journal of Community Health, 20*(5), 383–401.

Joslin, D., & Harrison, R. (1998). The hidden patient: Older relatives raising children orphaned by AIDS. *Journal of the American Medical Women's Association, 5*, 65–71.

Kanner, A. D., Coyne, J. C., Schaefer, C., & Lazarus, R. S. (1981). Comparison of two modes of stress measurement: Daily hassles and uplifts versus major life events. *Journal of Behavioral Medicine, 4*, 1–39.

Koenig, H. G., Cohen, H., Blazer, B., Pieper, C., Meadov, K., Shelp, F., et al. (1992). Religious coping and depression among elderly hospitalized medically ill men. *American Journal of Psychiatry, 14*, 1693–1700.

Koenig, H. G., Larson, D. B., & Larson, S. S. (2001). Religion and coping with serious medical illness. *The Annals of Pharmacotherapy, 35*(3), 352–359.

Lincoln, C. E., & Mamiya, L. H. (1990). *The Black church in the African American experience.* Durham, NC: Duke University Press.

Minkler, M., & Fuller-Thomson, E. (1999). The health of grandparents raising grandchildren: Results of a national study. *American Journal of Public Health, 89*(8), 1–6.

Minkler, M., & Roe, K. M. (1993). *Grandmothers as caregivers: Raising grandchildren of the crack cocaine epidemic.* Newbury Park, CA: Sage.

Minkler, M., Roe, K. M., & Price, M. (1992). The physical and emotional health of grandmothers raising grandchildren in the crack cocaine epidemic. *The Gerontologist, 32*, 752–761.

Pearlin, L. I., Mullan, J. T., Semple, J. S., & Skaff, M. M. (1990). Caregiving and the stress process: An overview of concepts and their measures. *The Gerontologist, 30*, 583–594.

Pearson, J. P., Hunter, A. G., Ensminger, M. E., & Kellam, S. G. (1990). Black grandmothers in multi-generational households: Diversity in family structure and parenting involvement in the Woodlawn community. *Child Development, 61,* 434–442.

Richardson, B. L. (1991). Utilizing the resources of the African American church: Strategies for counseling professionals. In C. C. Lee & B. L. Richardson (Eds.), *Multicultural issues in counseling: New approaches to diversity* (pp. 368–394). American Counseling Association.

Sanders, R. G. W. (2002). The Black church: Bridge over troubled water. In J. L. Sanders & C. Bradley (Eds.), *Counseling African American families* (pp. 73–84). The Family Psychology and Counseling Series. Alexandria, VA: American Counseling Association.

Sands, R. G., & Goldberg-Glen, R. S. (2000). Factors associated with stress among grandparents raising their grandchildren. *Family Relations, 49*(1), 97–105.

Smith, A. (1997). *Navigating the deep river: Spirituality in African American families.* Cleveland, OH: United Church Press.

Taylor, R. J., Mattis, J., & Chatters, L. M. (1999). Subjective religiosity among African Americans: A synthesis of findings from five national samples. *Journal of Black Psychology, 25,* 524–543.

Tran, T. V., Wright, R., & Chatters, L. (1991). Health, stress, psychological resources, and subjective well-being among older Blacks. *Psychology & Aging, 6,* 100–108.

U.S. Bureau of the Census. (1996). *Current population reports: Marital status and living arrangements.* Washington, DC: U.S. Government Printing Office.

CHAPTER 18

A Stress Process Model of Grandparent Caregiving: The Impact of Role Strain and Intrapsychic Strain on Subjective Well-Being

Rachel L. Rodriguez and Martha R. Crowther

The past 30 years have seen a dramatic increase in the number of grandparents serving as primary caregivers to their grandchildren and great-grandchildren. The United States Census Bureau reported that between 1970 and 1997, the percentage of children living with their grandparents or other relatives rose from 3.2% to 5.5%. In one third of these homes, neither parent was present, typically making the grandparent or other relative the primary caregiver (Saluter, 1992). The 2000 Census data show that these numbers are continuing to rise. This data estimates that 4.5 million children, or 6.3% of all children under the age of 18, were living in a grandparent-maintained household with no biological parent present in 2000 (Bryson, 2001).

Attempts to profile grandparent caregivers suggest that approximately 30% of African American grandmothers and 14% of African

American grandfathers reported being the primary caregiver for a grand-child for at least 6 months (Szinovacz, 1998), compared to 10.9% of all grandparents (Fuller-Thomson, Minkler, & Driver, 1997). Grandparent caregivers have also been found to be more likely to live in the South and have income levels below the poverty line (Fuller-Thomson et al., 1997). In sum, the research implies that grandparents who raise their grandchildren are more likely to be African American, female, poor, and live in the South.

Previous research also suggests that the stresses of the caregiving role make grandparent caregivers vulnerable to a host of physical, psycho-logical, and psychosocial problems, including depression, social isolation, and poverty (Burton, 1992; Dressell & Barnhill, 1994; Fuller-Thomson et al., 1997; Jendrek, 1994; Joslin & Harrison, 1998; Minkler & Roe, 1993; Minkler, Roe, & Price, 1992). Many grandparent caregivers report decreased socialization with friends and family as a consequence of their caregiving responsibilities (Burton, 1992; Jendrek, 1994; Minkler & Roe, 1993; Pruchno, 1999; Shore & Hayslip, 1994). Research examining the physical health of grandparent caregivers has also demonstrated poorer self-assessed health status, considerable comorbidity, delayed help seek-ing, and a frequent tendency to minimize the severity of health problems among grandparents in the study samples (Joslin & Harrison, 1998; Minkler & Fuller-Thomson, 1999; Minkler & Roe, 1993, 1996; Minkler et al., 1992; Shore & Hayslip, 1994). Depression is a frequently docu-mented psychological effect for grandparents raising their grandchildren (Burton, 1992; Fuller-Thomson & Minkler, 2000; Minkler, Fuller-Thom-son, Miller, & Driver, 1997; Minkler & Roe, 1993). On a national scale, a study by Minkler et al. (1997) found that grandparents raising their grandchildren were almost twice as likely to be clinically depressed when compared to grandparents who do not raise their grandchildren. Financial burdens stem from the fact that many grandparent caregivers are forced to quit their jobs or take a leave of absence from their place of employment to care for their grandchildren (Roe & Minkler, 1998; Pruchno, 1999). Moreover, Pruchno (1999) reported that of those who were able to continue to work after taking on the caregiving role, 40% of grandparent caregivers had missed work, come to work late, left work suddenly be-cause of their grandchild, or left work for a grandchild's medical appoint-ment. The implication of these findings is that no employment or less time at employment means less money for the grandparent caregiver to use to support the grandchild.

A STRESS PROCESS MODEL
OF GRANDPARENT CAREGIVING

While the literature has elucidated the problems and stressors that these caregivers face, there has been no offer of a comprehensive theoretical model of grandparent caregiving. The present will present a modified stress and coping model of caregiving similar to those proposed by Haley, Levine, Brown, and Bartolucci (1987) and Pearlin, Mullan, Semple, and Skaff (1990). Within this model of caregiving, stress is the result of the relationship between an individual and his or her environment. There are a number of factors that can be potential stressors for the caregiver, including the needs of the care recipient and include the cognitive status and problematic behaviors of the care recipient, as well as the number of activities for which the care recipient is dependent on the caregiver. Of particular interest are a group of stressors collectively referred to as role strains and intrapsychic strains (Pearlin et al., 1990). Role strains for the caregiver include family conflict, job-caregiving conflict, economic problems, and constriction of social life. Intrapsychic strains have a global component that includes self-esteem and mastery over the forces affecting their lives, as well as a situational component which includes loss of self and role captivity.

Mediators of stress are used to explain why caregivers exposed to similar stressors are affected by them in dissimilar ways. In this model, coping responses, social support, and appraisals are possible explanations of this phenomenon. Coping represents behaviors and practices of individuals as they act on their own behalf, and has three possible functions: management of the situation causing stress, management of the meaning of the situation such that its threat is reduced, and management of the stress symptoms that result from the situation (Pearlin & Aneshensel, 1986). Social support can be used to buffer effects of stress, as well as prevent or inhibit the development of secondary stressors. Appraisals of caregiving include both feelings of competence in the caregiving role and feelings of personal gain from the caregiving role.

As applied to grandparent caregivers, the proposed stress and coping model would predict that grandparent caregivers are vulnerable to a host of stressors. The background and context of the stress would include factors such as the grandparent caregivers' age, their socioeconomic status, caregiving history, and their family and social support systems. Stressors would include the problematic behaviors of their grandchildren and the number of activities for which the grandchildren are dependent upon the grandparent. Role strains for grandparent caregivers would include conflicts with their children or children's spouses, increased absences from work due to caregiving responsibilities, loss of social support, and financial burden. Intrapsychic strains may be exhibited in grandparent caregivers feeling trapped in the caregiving situation, and experiencing a loss in their identity.

While grandparent caregivers may be beset with a myriad of stressors, they may not experience them as such. In these instances, factors such as the grandparent caregiver's coping skills and social support network may be diffusing the stress. For example, when stressed, the grandparent caregiver may exercise or watch television to relax, or he or she may call a friend to discuss the situation or get advice. The custodial grandparent's own feelings of competence may also mediate the stressful experience.

In accordance with the Stress-Process Model, the outcome domain for grandparent caregivers may be manifested in anxiety, depression, irascibility, cognitive disturbance, physical health, and yielding of role. For the model put forth in the current study, the outcome domain is the grandparent's subjective well-being. Simply stated, subjective well-being refers to how people evaluate their lives, and includes variables such as life satisfaction, happiness, and goal attainment (Tran, Wright, & Chatters, 1991).

Previous work indicates that stress has a negative impact on evaluations of life quality (Kessler, Price, & Wortman, 1985; Tessler & Mechanic, 1978). Conceptually, it has been suggested that the effects of stress operate though psychological components that are important to the maintenance of positive self-concept (Tran et al., 1991). In other words, stress negatively impacts one's sense of self, which in turn affects one's subjective well-being. Thus, in the case of grandparent caregivers, a logical assumption would be that the numerous stressors experienced would negatively impact the grandparent's quality of life, resulting in a lowered report of subjective well-being.

In summary, the proposed model suggests that there exists a relation between grandparent caregiver's role strain, psychological stress, and subjective well-being, and that this relation is mediated by the grandparent's coping skills, social support systems, and caregiver appraisals. It is hypothesized that grandparent caregivers will experience numerous role strains and intrapsychic strains as a result of their situation. It is further hypothesized that these strains will cause grandparent caregivers to report that they are less satisfied with their lives, experience more unhappiness, and state less goal attainment. In other words, a negative relation is expected between measures of role strain and subjective well-being as well as between measures of intrapsychic strain and subjective well-being. It is also hypothesized that coping skills, social support, and caregiver appraisals will have positive effects on grandparent caregivers' subjective well-being, thereby reducing the impact of stress on subjective well-being.

A TEST OF THE CONCEPTUAL MODEL: METHODS AND RESULTS

Participants

Grandparent caregivers aged 25 and over were recruited from two sites for this study. The studies conducted at both sites were designed to assess the nature, impact, and consequences of custodial caregiving among African Americans (Crowther, 1998, 2001). Grandparents were considered eligible for inclusion if they were over 25 at the time of entry into the study, had been caring for a grandchild for 6 months or more, and were non-institutionalized. The resulting sample consisted of 76 grandmothers.

Procedure

After meeting eligibility criteria, each participant was interviewed in a neutral location agreed upon by the interviewer and the participant. One 2-hour assessment was conducted. The purpose and requirements of the study were explained to the participant and any questions were answered. Participants were ensured of the anonymity of their responses. Compensation for participation at both sites included monetary compensation as well as information regarding a support group in their area. The support group included professionals from the community who provided useful information to the participants. The support group was not offered as a coercive measure but as assistance in a tangible manner.

Measures

Sociodemographics

Sociodemographic characteristics of the sample provided a basis for understanding the personal context of grandparent caregivers. The format included both closed and open-ended questions and covered a variety of topic areas including: demographics, religious affiliation and practices, household composition, number of care recipients in addition to grandchildren, the amount of time the respondent has been in the grandparent caregiver role, location of grandchildren's parents, and physical and psychological status of the grandchildren.

Coping

The coping scale comprises three components that address coping in response to life problems: management of the situation causing stress, management of the meaning of the situation such that its threat is reduced, and management of the stress symptoms that result from the situation (Pearlin et al., 1990). The components measure different aspects of coping and are specific to the study of caregivers. The items used to measure management of the situation are not factored; they are intended to be single items. The items that measure management of the meaning of the situation have three factors: reduction of expectations (alpha coefficient = 0.48), use of positive comparisons (alpha coefficient = 0.63), and a search for a larger sense of meaning (alpha coefficient = 0.49). Pearlin et al. (1990) acknowledge, "the reliability coefficients are not robust." Given this, results for these subscales should be interpreted with caution. The items that measure management of distress were analyzed separately. The response categories for the subscale items range from 1 to 4, and the higher the score, the higher the coping. The coping scale was originally designed for use with Alzheimer's caregivers. As such, the subscales were slightly modified to make the wording relevant to custodial grandparents. The coping scale was used to assess one of the mediators of stress described in the stress process model.

Social Support

The Duke Social Support Index (Hughes, Blazer, & Hybels, 1991) was used as a multidimensional measure of social support. The index consists of 35 items that measure 4 dimensions of social support: subjective social support, frequency of social interaction, size of social network, and instrumental support (Landerman, George, Campbell, & Blazer, 1989). The total score is the sum of the individual items. The higher the score, the greater the social support for each scale. In a biracial community sample of approximately 3,000 adults aged 18 and over the subjective social support scale was found to be the best predictor of health outcomes among the four subscales (Landerman et al., 1989) and produced an alpha coefficient of 0.79. The social support scale was used to assess one of the mediators of stress described in the stress process model.

Appraisal of Caregiving

The appraisal of caregiving scale (Pearlin et al., 1990) was used to assess role strain, intrapsychic strain, and possible mediators as proposed in the caregiving model. Role strain was measured by questions concerning economic strain. Economic strain is comprised of three items measuring reduction in household income, increase in expenditures related to the care and treatment of the care recipient, and whether there is enough money to subsist month to month. Intrapsychic strain is measured by the following scales: role captivity (alpha coefficient = 0.83) and loss of self (alpha coefficient = 0.76). The intrapsychic scales may appear dependent because they are closely linked construct; however the intercorrelations between them are not very high ($r = 0.35$). Appraisal of caregiving was measured by a caregiving competence subscale (alpha coefficient = 0.74) and personal gain subscale (alpha coefficient = 0.76). Like intrapsychic strain, these two constructs may appear to be linked, however, the correlation between them is also not very strong ($r = 0.32$). The response categories are continuous for each item and range from 1 to 4. The higher the score, the higher the construct being measured.

Hassles

The original scale consisted of two subscales: the Hassles Scale and the Uplifts Scale (Kanner, Coyne, Schaefer, & Lazarus, 1981). However, for the purposes of this study, only the Hassles Scale, which measures secondary role strains, is relevant. This version of the Hassles scale has been used in previous studies and has been found to accurately represent the hassles experienced by grandparent caregivers (Crowther, 1998). Participants responded if the hassle had occurred in the past month and a 3-point severity rating was used to determine the severity of the item. The scale is scored by the frequency and intensity of the ratings. Test-retest correlation coefficients for the Hassles Scale were .79 for frequency and .48 for intensity. The Hassles Scale was used to assess secondary role strain as described in the stress process model.

Subjective Well-Being

Subjective well-being (Tran et al., 1991) was assessed using three single-item measures relating to evaluations of life satisfaction, happiness, and goal attainment. The single-item subjective well-being questions chosen are examples of subjective social indicators. When the items have been combined, the scores ranged from 3 to 9 ($M = 7.44$, $SD = 1.40$), with higher scores indicating greater subjective well-being (Tran et al., 1991). The life satisfaction item is focused on the immediate past with a relative emphasis on cognitive versus affective elements. The happiness item is focused on events occurring in the present with an emphasis on affective over cognitive elements. The goal attainment item is focused on past events and emphasizes a comparison between the respondent's goals and attainments and incorporates a high degree of cognitive components. The Subjective Well-Being Scale was used to assess one of the outcome variables described in the stress process model.

RESULTS

Characteristics of Study Sample

Table 18.1 shows the sociodemographic characteristics of the 76 participants included in the study. Participants ranged in age from 35 to 75

TABLE 18.1   Demographic Characteristics of Study Sample ($N = 76$)

Variable	M	SD	Range
Age (in years)	53.03	9.07	35–75
Number of grandchildren raising	1.83	1.39	1–7
Time in caregiving role (in months)	82.83	58.64	3–216
Number of people dependent upon caregiver	3.07	2.38	1–15

Category	N	%	
Sex			
Female	74	97.4	
Male	2	2.6	
Education			
Less than high school	20	26.3	
High school graduate/GED	14	18.4	
Some college/technical school	30	39.5	
College graduate and beyond	12	15.8	
Marital Status			
Married	27	35.5	
Divorced	20	26.3	
Separated	6	7.9	
Widowed	14	18.4	
Single/never married	8	10.5	
Other	1	1.3	
Employment Status			
Employed	44	57.9	
Not employed	32	42.1	

years, with a mean age of 53.08 years. The number of grandchildren that the participants reported raising ranged from 1 to 7, although the majority (59.2%) reported that they were the primary caregiver for 1 grandchild ($M = 1.83$, $SD = 1.39$). Furthermore, participants reported being in the caregiving role an average of 82 months ($M = 82.83$, $SD = 58.64$).

The sample was 97.4% female. All of the participants were African American. In terms of education, 73.7% of the sample reported having graduated high school or obtaining a general equivalency diploma (GED). More than one third of the sample, 35.5% reported being married at the time of the interview. Additionally, 7.9% were separated, 26.3% were divorced, 18.4% were widowed, 10.5% were never married, and 1.3% listed other as their marital status. Over half of the participants, 57.9%, were employed.

Bivariate Analyses

Table 18.2 shows the results of bivariate correlations between subjective well-being and measures of role strain and intrapsychic strain. These analyses revealed significant correlations in the hypothesized direction for role captivity ($r = -.529$, $p < .001$) and self-loss ($r = -.486$, $p < .001$). No variables measuring role strain were found to be significantly correlated with the dependent variable.

Social support, coping responses, and caregiver appraisals were hypothesized to mediate the effects of role strain and intrapsychic strain on subjective well-being. Of the 19 social support and coping variables, only one, taking medication to calm oneself, was found to be significantly correlated with the dependent variable ($r = -.263$, $p < .05$). A significant positive correlation was also found between caregiver competence, a variable measuring appraisal of caregiving, and subjective well-being ($r = .450$, $p < .001$). Results of these bivariate correlations are also reflected in Table 18.2.

Hierarchical Multiple Regression Analyses and Tests of Mediation

To test for possible mediation effects, two hierarchical regressions were performed. Only those variables that were found to be significantly related to the dependent variable were included in the regression equation. One set of predictors, those variables measuring intrapsychic strain that were found to be significantly correlated in the hypothesized direction were used in the hierarchical regressions. Next, the main effects of (a) the sole coping variable that showed a significant correlation with the dependent variable and (b) caregiver competence were tested in separate equations.

The variables of role captivity and self loss explained 30.6% of the variability in subjective well-being for grandparent caregivers. As seen in Table 18.3, Model 3a, those grandparent caregivers who experienced less role captivity and felt that they had lost less of their personal identity as a result of the caregiver role had higher subjective well-being.

The significant coping variable, taking medication to calm oneself, was then added to the model to test for possible mediation (Model 3b). Though it increased the R^2 to .316, the change in R^2 from Model 3a to Model 3b was not significant. Furthermore, adding this coping variable to the equation did not significantly reduce the effects of role captivity and self-loss on subjective well-being (Models 3a and 3b). Therefore it was concluded that this variable was not a mediator of the effects of intrapsychic strain on subjective well-being.

TABLE 18.2   Means, Standard Deviations, and Bivariate Correlations between Subjective Well-Being and Intrapsychic Strain, Role Strain, Social Support, and Coping

Variable	M	SD	Measure Subjective Well-Being
Intrapsychic strain			
Role captivity	5.91	3.00	−.529**
Self-loss	2.89	2.00	−.486**
Role strain			
Economic strain	7.11	1.97	−.047
Frequency of hassles	18.69	13.61	.033
Severity of hassles	0.45	0.66	−.132
Social support			
Size of social support group	10.29	8.32	.049
Frequency of interactions	9.21	3.56	−.113
Subjective social support	18.77	2.47	−.014
Instrumental support	11.16	2.85	−.070
Coping			
Reduce expectation	10.14	1.79	.037
Positive comparisons	6.49	1.66	−.196
Larger construction of illness	6.97	1.37	−.144
Be firm with grandchild	3.78	.506	.036
Let things slide	2.87	1.02	−.149
Keep grandchild busy	3.66	.684	.119
Learn about the situation	3.49	.902	−.168
Spent time alone	2.31	.972	.067
Eat differently than usual	2.11	1.19	−.162
Smoke	1.59	1.11	. 003
Exercise	2.30	1.10	.123
Watch television	2.89	1.01	−.117
Read	2.73	1.16	−.177
Drink	1.12	.399	.139
Medicate	1.53	.945	−.263*
Appraisal of caregiving			
Caregiver competence	15.34	16.00	.450**
Personal gain	10.86	1.36	−.040

*$p < .05$. **$p < .001$.

TABLE 18.3   Hierarchical Regressions of Subjective Well-Being on Intrapsychic Strain, With Mediation Effects of Coping and Caregiver Competence ($n = 76$)

Variable	Model 3a	Coping Model 3b	Caregiver Competence Model 3c
Role captivity	−.199*	−.203*	−.190*
Self loss	−.268	−.215	−.175
Medicate		−.165	
Caregiver competence			.358**
R^2	.306	. 316	.409
δ R^2	.306***	.01	.103**

*$p < . 05.$ **$p = .001.$ ***$p < .001$

A separate set of regressions then tested the effects of caregiver competence on subjective well-being (Model 3c). Adding caregiver competence to the model increased the R^2 to .409, and resulted in a significant change in R^2 from Model 3a to Model 3c. As shown in regression Models 3a, higher subjective well-being was associated with less role captivity (β = −.199) and less self-loss (β = −.268). As required for mediation, impact of role captivity (Model 3c) on subjective well-being was significantly reduced (β = −.190, $p < .01$) when the effect of caregiver competence was considered. Though the impact of self-loss was also reduced when caregiver competence was added to the model, it was not a significant reduction (β = −.175, $p = .252$). Therefore, it was concluded that caregiver competence mediated the impact of role captivity, but not self-loss on subjective well-being.

DISCUSSION

In accord with previous research, the results of this study indicate that grandparent caregivers' subjective well-being is negatively impacted by some measures of intrapsychic strain. More specifically, feeling trapped in the caregiving role and feeling as though they have lost a sense of personal identity because of their role as custodial grandparent is detrimental to grandparent caregivers' subjective well-being. Caregiver competence was found to have a moderately strong positive relation with subjective well-being. This implies that as grandparent caregivers' feelings of caregiver competence increase, so will their subjective well-being. Only one coping variable proved to have a relationship with subjective well-being. It was found that taking medication to calm oneself had a negative effect on grandparent caregivers' subjective well-being.

More important, it was found that the amount of competence the caregiver feels was a mediator of the stress. In other words, caregiver competence significantly reduced the negative impact of stress on subjective well-being. This latter finding has also been documented with regard to African American caregiving populations by other researchers (Dilworth-Anderson, Williams, & Cooper, 1999; Haley, Roth, Coleton, Ford, & West, 1996). In particular and paralleling the results of the current study, these studies have found that high levels of caregiver competence and feelings of mastery in the caregiving role buffer the effects of stress for African American caregivers.

Though the findings of high levels of caregiver competence in the current study correspond with the literature, there were several other interesting findings in this study that do not. For example, the current study's sample did not report experiencing role strains, nor were social support or coping variables found to be mediators of the stressors that were reported. This contradicts what has been found in the literature regarding caregivers. The literature consistently cites numerous role strains experienced in the caregiving situation and have found social support and coping to be mediators of this stress, most often regardless of the race of the sample (Dilworth-Anderson et al., 1999; Haley et al., 1996; Musil & Ahmad, 2002).

Overall, the results of this study find somewhat weak support for the proposed model of grandparent caregiving. However, there are a number of limitations to the study in question that could explain these results. The number of respondents is small ($n = 76$) and the sample itself is homogeneous. The respondents consisted mainly of southern, single, middle-aged employed African American grandmothers. While the literature would indicate that the sample is representative of the population most likely to be raising their grandchildren, the simple lack of variance among the respondents combined with poor power could have skewed the results. The lack of demographic differences also makes it difficult to generalize beyond African American grandparent caregivers who live in the South. The fact that the majority of the respondents were working may have impacted study results also. This finding is different than that reported in the literature. Furthermore, the current population had been the primary caregiver for their grandchildren for an average of approximately 7 years ($M = 82.83$ months, $SD = 58.54$ months). In other words, the respondents were well established in the caregiver role. Thus, the demands of the caregiving role may no longer be perceived as a strain or stress, but as a fact of everyday life.

Along with this finding, it should be noted that the grandparent caregivers in this study reported a mean rating for subjective well-being of 7 on a scale of 3 to 9 ($M = 6.88$, $SD = 1.46$). This indicates that the grandparent caregivers in the current study had a relatively high level of subjective well-being, and may not have been a "stressed" population. It should also be noted that grandparent caregivers have been found to minimize the severity of health problems (Joslin & Harrison, 1998; Minkler & Fuller-Thomson, 1999; Minkler & Roe, 1993, 1996; Minkler et al., 1992; Shore & Hayslip, 1994). It may be that this tendency to downplay one's problems may extend to other domains as well and explain the lack of stressors reported in the current study. In other words, the grandparent caregivers in the current study could be underreporting their experience of role strains.

It is also a possibility that the measures used did not accurately tap into the experience of the grandparent caregiver population. For example, the Coping Scale and the Appraisal of Caregiving Scale were designed to be used with Alzheimer's caregivers. While the questions were reworded to be relevant to the caregiving population used in this study, they may have been altered such that they are no longer accurately measuring the intended constructs.

While there are several methodological explanations for the findings of the current study, a sociocultural explanation may also be appropriate. The literature notes that the experience of African American caregivers is significantly different from that of White caregivers (Dilworth-Anderson & Rhoden, 1999; Haley et al., 1996; Pruchno, 1999). Part of this difference is that African Americans are socialized to expect to be placed in the caregiving role during their lifetime. Therefore, when placed in the caregiving role, it may not be perceived as a disruption in their life, but as a cultural norm (Haley et al., 1996). More specifically, Dilworth-Anderson and Rhoden (1999) note that African American women are socialized to view their caregiving duties to include older family members as well as grandchildren and thus adjust expectations and support systems to meet their needs. In other words, the respondents in the current study may have been primed to step into the caregiving role and therefore do not view it as stressful, unusual, or unfair, and thus have a high level of psychological resiliency.

CONCLUSION

Future Research

Despite not fully supporting the proposed model, the results of the current study suggest that grandparent caregivers do experience negative psychological effects as a result of their role. Since the number of grandparent caregivers is continuing to rise, there is a need for further research in this area. Future studies may want to evaluate the experience of grandparent caregivers across race, genders, and age. More specifically, future studies may need to include more definitive measures of caregiver competence and even include a measure of self-efficacy across roles. There is also a need to more thoroughly examine the differences in time as the primary caregiver for one's grandchildren. It would also be fruitful to look at the varying levels of caregiving in which grandparents engage (i.e., primary caregiver, intermittent caregiver, and the traditional grandparent role). Additionally, the current study highlights the resiliency of many grandparent caregivers. Future studies may want to examine the strengths of this caregiving population.

REFERENCES

Bryson, K. (2001). New Census Bureau data on grandparents raising grandchildren. Paper presented at The Gerontological Society of America Annual Scientific Meeting, Chicago, November 2001.

Burton, L. (1992). Black grandmothers rearing children of drug-addicted parents: Stressors, outcomes, and social service needs. *The Gerontologist, 32*(6), 744–751.

Crowther, M. R. (1998). *Compensatory grandparenting*. Dissertation. Duke University.

Crowther, M. R. (2001). Kincare: Grandparents raising grandchildren. Funded by the American Studies Program, University of Alabama, Tuscaloosa.

Dilworth-Anderson, P., & Rhoden, L. (1999). A sociocultural view of African American women and their caregiving roles. In N. Burgess & E. Brown (Eds.), *African American women: An ecological perspective*. New York: Garland Press.

Dilworth-Anderson, P., Williams, S. W., & Cooper, T. (1999). The contexts of experiencing emotional distress among family caregivers to elderly African Americans. *Family Relations, 48*, 391–396.

Dressell, P., & Barnhill, S. (1994). Reframing gerontological thought and practice: The case of grandmothers with daughters in prison. *The Gerontologist, 34*, 685–690.

Fuller-Thomson, E., & Minkler, M. (2000). African American grandparents raising grandchildren: A national profile of demographic and health characteristics. *Health and Social Work, 25*, 109–118.

Fuller-Thomson, E., Minkler, M., & Driver, D. (1997). A profile of grandparents raising grandchildren in the United States. *The Gerontologist, 37*, 406–411.

Haley, W. E., Levine, E. G., Brown, S. L., & Bartolucci, A. A. (1987). Stress, appraisal, coping and social support as predictors of adaptational outcome among dementia caregivers. *Psychology and Aging, 2*, 323–330.

Haley, W. E., Roth, D. L., Coleton, M. I., Ford, G. R., West, C. A. C., Collins, R. P., et al. (1996). Appraisal, coping and social support as mediators of well-being in Black and White family caregivers of patients with Alzheimer's Disease. *Journal of Counseling and Clinical Psychology, 64,* 121–129.

Hughes, D., Blazer, D., & Hybels, C. (1991). *Duke Social Support Index (DSSI): A working paper (revised).* Center for the study of Aging and Human Development, Duke University Medical Center.

Jendrek, M. P. (1994). Grandparents who parent their grandchildren: Circumstances and decisions. *The Gerontologist, 34,* 206–216.

Joslin, D., & Harrison, R. (1998). The hidden patient: Older relatives raising children orphaned by AIDS. *Journal of the American Medical Women's Association, 5,* 65–71.

Kanner, A. D., Coyne, J. C., Schaefer, C., & Lazarus, R. S. (1981). Comparison of two modes of stress measurement: Daily hassles and uplifts versus major life events. *Journal of Behavioral Medicine, 4,* 1–39.

Kessler, R. C., Price, R. H., & Wortman, C. B. (1985). Social factors in psychopathology: Stress, social support, and coping processes. *Annual Review of Psychology, 35,* 463–478.

Landerman, R., George, L. K., Campbell, R. T., & Blazer, D. G. (1989). Alternative models of the stress buffering hypothesis. *American Journal of Community Psychology, 17,* 625–643.

Minkler, M., & Fuller-Thomson, E. (1999). The health of grandparents raising grandchildren: Results of a national study. *American Journal of Public Health, 89,* 1–6.

Minkler, M., Fuller-Thomson, E., Miller, D., & Driver, D. (1997). Depression in grandparents raising grandchildren. *Archives of Family Medicine, 6,* 445–452.

Minkler, M., & Roe, K. M. (1993). *Grandmothers as caregivers: Raising grandchildren of the crack cocaine epidemic.* Newbury Park, CA: Sage.

Minkler, M., & Roe, K. M. (1996). Grandparents as surrogate parents. *Generations, 20,* 34–38.

Minkler, M., Roe, K. M., & Price, M. (1992). The physical and emotional health of grandmothers raising grandchildren in the crack cocaine epidemic. *The Gerontologist, 32,* 752–761.

Musil, C. M., & Ahmad, M. (2002). Health of grandmothers: A comparison by caregiver status. *Journal of Aging and Health, 14,* 96–121.

Pearlin, L. I., & Aneshensel, C. (1986). Coping and social supports: Their functions and applications. In L. H. Aiken & D. Mechanic (Eds.), *Applications of social science to clinical medicine and health* (pp. 417–439). New Brunswick, NJ: Rutgers University Press.

Pearlin, L. I., Mullan, J. T., Semple, J. S., & Skaff, M. M. (1990). Caregiving and the stress process: An overview of concepts and their measures. *The Gerontologist, 30,* 583–594.

Pruchno, R. (1999). Raising grandchildren: The experiences of Black and White grandmothers. *The Gerontologist, 39,* 209–221.

Roe, K. M., & Minkler, M. (1998). Grandparents raising grandchildren: Challenges and responses. *Generations, 22,* 25–32.

Saluter, A. F. (1992). Marital status and living arrangements: March 1991. *U.S. Bureau of the Census Current population reports*. (Series P-20 No. 461). Washington, DC: U.S. Government Printing Office.

Shore, R. J., & Hayslip, B. (1994). Custodial grandparenting: Implications for children's development. In A. Godfried & A. Godfried (Eds.), *Redefining families: Implications for children's development*. New York: Plenum.

Szinovacz, M. E. (1998). Grandparents today: A demographic profile. *The Gerontologist, 38*, 37–52.

Tessler, R., & Mechanic, D. (1978). Psychological distress and perceived health status. *Journal of Health and Social Behavior, 19*, 254–262.

Tran, T. V., Wright, R., & Chatters, L. (1991). Health, stress, psychological resources, and subjective well-being among older Blacks. *Psychology & Aging, 6*, 100–108.

CHAPTER 19

The Voices of Black Grandmothers Parenting Grandchildren With TANF Assistance

Tammy L. Henderson and Jennifer L. Cook

CUSTODIAL GRANDPARENTING: THE EXPERIENCES OF BLACK GRANDMOTHERS

According to Generations United (2002), in 1997, 34.5% of grandparent-led households were Black compared to 43.8% of White and 17.6% of Hispanic families. Thomson, Minkler, and Driver (2000) found that Black grandparents had an 83% higher odds ratio of being the primary caregiver of their grandchildren than other racial group, although the increase in grandparent-led families has occurred among families of all racial, ethnic, socioeconomic, and geographic locations (Lugalia, 1998). The increased probability of Black grandparents parenting their grandchildren is not surprising in light of the fact that kinship care and quasi-kinship networks were part of the West African familial traditions and an adaptive behavior of Black families in the United States (Sudarkasa, 1988). Kinship networks have been used as an adaptive response to parental death and illness, unmarried parenthood, and family migration (Stack & Burton, 1993; Sudarkasa, 1988) and demonstrate role flexibility (i.e., Burton, 1992; Hunter & Taylor, 1998). Grandparents, in particular, have played a pivotal kinship role in the support and maintenance of Black families, especially in situations in which parents are not capable of rearing their children due to illness, incarceration, financial stress, and parental death due to AIDS and other illnesses (i.e., Burton, 1992; Hunter & Taylor, 1998; Jendrek, 1994). Research on the pivotal role of Black grandparents provides insights into the lives of Black family life; yet, research on the experiences and views of Black grandmothers whose grandchildren are receiving Temporary Assistance for Needy Families (TANF), welfare, remains a road less traveled.

The Economic Challenges of Poor Grandparent-Led Families

What Is TANF?

The Personal Responsibility and Work Opportunity Reconciliation Act of 1996 [PRWORA/96] (H.R. 3734) replaced Aid to Families with Dependent Children (AFDC) with TANF (Karger & Stoesz, 2002; Mullen & Einhorn, 2000). The social objectives behind PRWORA/96 were to reduce welfare dependency, promote economic self-efficiency, help poor families acquire a work ethnic, discourage out-of-wedlock births, and to provide work skills training. To give states more flexibility in administering public assistance programs, TANF (a) provides a lump-sum federal block grants to states to operate their own welfare and work programs, (b) requires states to spend no less than 80% of their nonfederal funds to receive the full block grant or 75% for states that meet their workforce requirements, (c) limits assistance to adults to 60 months, and (d) maintains rigorous work requirements (for a summary see Administration for Children and Families at http://www.acf.dhhs.gov/programs/ofa/ or Karger & Stoesz, 2002).

TANF (42 USCS § 601, 2000; U.S. Congress, House of Representative's, Committee on Ways and Means, 1998) is one of a few social programs that assist grandparents caring for a grandchild. To qualify for TANF, grandparents' household income must not exceed the state's eligibility requirements, their grandchild must not have access to parental support, and the grandparent must be the primary caregiver (Mullen, 2000a). Some eligibility determinations do not include the income of grandparents, making it a child-only case, although generally, all household members' resources are included in eligibility requirements. The federal government does not require grandparents to obtain legal custody of their grandchildren, yet, the Commonwealth of Virginia and several other states (a) require grandparents to have legal custody of the grandchild, (b) include the grandchild's income and resources in eligibility requirements, and (c) maintain that parents must not reside in the home. Unlike parents, grandparents face delays in the TANF eligibility processing, have problems meeting eligibility requirements, and experience other difficulties accessing services including Medicaid and food stamps (i.e., Minkler & Roe, 1996; Mullen, 2000a).

Besides challenges with eligibility, generally, families headed by grandparents are more likely to live in poverty (Generations United, 2002). If 9.1 million Black families are impoverished (U.S. Census Bureau, 2000, September) and 19% of grandparent-led families lived in poverty (U.S. Census Bureau, 2003, October), then it is reasonable to assert that Black families headed by grandparents are economically at risk. Current welfare and foster care policies compound the economic vulnerabilities of grandparent-led families. Because they are related to the child, using the TANF program instead of foster care, grandparents may get only a third of the cash assistance given to licensed group homes or licensed foster care parents who are not related to the child (Scarcella, Ehrle, & Green, 2003). Many grandparents do not know how to access foster care resources (Cox, 2000), therefore, they rely on Temporary Assistance for Needy Children, the current welfare policy.

THE SOCIAL CONSTRUCTION OF POVERTY AND RACE

The Social Meanings of Poverty

The experiences of grandparent-led families are influenced by PRWORA/ 96 and two social constructs: poverty and race. Historically, to obtain assistance, poor families must abide by rigid rules and policies enacted to establish moral and gendered norms and prevent fraudulent behavior (Abramovitz, 1996). For example, in colonial times and pre-Revolutionary times, local governments intruded upon the privacy rights of parents under three circumstances: (a) when children lived in single-mother or fatherless homes, (b) when families were poor, and (c) when parents were not capable of educating their children (Davidson, 1994). Communities during this period had little tolerance for single-mother homes and poor families. Consequently, children from single-mother homes were placed in boarding homes, fatherless children were placed in indentured apprenticeships, and children from poor families were placed in collective living arrangements.

Currently, society has created a way to address child welfare and to make parents responsible for their economic situations by enacting PRWORA/96 (Bogenschneider, 2001) and the Adoption and Safe Families Act (ASFA, PL 105-89) of 1997. ASFA was enacted to reduce barriers to terminating parental rights and creating stable, adoptive families for children whose parents were deemed unfit, a deep-seated departure from the theme of family preservation in prior child welfare laws. These shifts demonstrate the fluidity of values toward poor families. Likewise, these shifts reveal the legal limits placed on poor families, including the privilege of exercising their right to family and parental autonomy.

First, welfare is associated with laziness and fraudulent behavior. Welfare serves as a symbol of shame and immorality branded on the faces and experiences of welfare recipients in the same way that the "A" signified shame and immorality in the *Scarlet Letter*. Second, using individualism as an explanation, welfare-reliant or poor people are assumed to lack a work ethic and to be lazy, slothful people. Third, to remove these negative meanings, several researchers have asked welfare-reliant participants for their views on welfare. For example, Rank (1994) provided insights from a random sample of welfare-reliant families in Wisconsin; Seccombe's (1999) 47 participants resided in Florida; Monroe and Tiller (2001) interviewed 84 women in rural Louisiana.

Despite the negative stigmas attached to poverty and welfare, some researchers found that welfare-reliant women desire economic independence (Monroe & Tiller, 2001; Rank, 1994; Seccombe, 1999). Welfare-reliant women worked, yet they experienced seasonal employment or underemployment, low wages, and few or no benefits. To cope with the social and economic stressors, welfare-reliant women conceal their identity, distinguish and distance themselves from poor people, deny any differential treatment of poor and nonpoor persons, identify external for their impoverished state, and focus on the importance of caregiving (i.e., Monroe & Tiller, 2001; Rank, 1994; Seccombe, 1999). Yet, few researchers have asked Black grandparents their views toward welfare and poverty, which is the goal of the current study.

The Social Meanings of Race

Despite the socially constructed views that most Blacks are dependent upon welfare, access to social insurance (Social Security) and welfare programs (Gordon, 1994) were not available to Black mothers until the early 1900s. In 1931, 3% of recipients of Mother's Pension, the first federal welfare policy, were Black. The enactment of the War on Poverty programs in the 1960s resulted in Blacks gaining access to public assistance programs, yet they remain ineligible for social insurance programs. By 1969, 45% of welfare recipients were Black (Malveaux, 1995; Roberts, 2002), facilitating the social construction of racial stigmas attached to welfare. These occurrences gave Patrick Moynihan's some evidence, though taken out of context, to substantiate his report (1965), *The Negro Family: The Case for National Action*, which portrayed the Black family as deviant and pathological and attaching welfare dependency to Black families. Although the percentage of Black welfare recipients has dropped from 45% in 1969 to 38% in 1999, proportions that are larger than the population of Blacks in the United States (Karger & Stoesz, 2002). Based on the social meanings attached to welfare and race, most people believe that most welfare recipients are Black and Hispanic. In actuality, race is among many factors (i.e., education, marital status, work experience, and disability) that influence the length of time on and the returned use of welfare (Bane & Ellwood, 1994).

THEORETICAL FRAMEWORK

This research draws on the symbolic interaction perspectives to examine the views, experiences, and recommendations of Black grandmothers. Symbolic interaction theorists seek to explain how individuals generate symbolic worlds through human interactions and how these socially created worlds mold human behavior. This perspective allows researchers (a) to interpret the events and symbols in the environment of participants, (b) to understand the meanings and socialized interpretations held by participants, and (c) to know how individuals identify themselves (Klein & White, 1996; LaRossa & Reitzes, 1993). Although capturing the influence of race is beyond the scope of this study, this theoretical perspective allowed us to explore Black grandmothers of southwest Virginia's views, experiences, and analyses of welfare, making a marginalized group the expert of their lives, experiences, and the research on poverty.

METHOD

Conducting secondary analysis, our sample was drawn from 20 grandparent-led families on the TANF case rolls of two Virginia counties. Departments of Social Services provided our research team with a list of child-only cases (grandparents were not part of the assistance unit) in which grandparents had legal custody of their grandchildren. Because study participants were drawn from child-only cases, time limits for receipt of assistance were not applicable to most grandparents in our study (Mullen, 2000a). The interview encompassed open-ended questions to explore demographic characteristics, personal views of and recommendations about TANF, food security, social support resources, adult and child health, and housing information. We conducted personal interviews within the home and recorded, transcribed, and verified each interview. One grandmother did not allow us to record the interview.

We used Grounded Theory Methods (GTM), an approach that allows the research to reveal the nature of individuals' experiences and to understand what lies behind a phenomenon about which little is known (Strauss & Corbin, 1990). In teams of two and during the initial stage or opening coding stage, we reviewed Black grandmothers' responses to questions about their experiences with and views toward TANF and poverty, what others needed to understand about TANF, and suggestions for changes in the TANF program. Then, using a constant-comparative method, we went back and forth from the raw data to the open coded data to create categories and linkages. We asked these questions to guide the axial coding: (a) What were grandmothers' views about poor people, themselves, and TANF? (b) What did grandmothers want others to understand? (c) What problems existed in the current social welfare program?

The relationship of themes to categories required an additional review of the data. During the selective coding or the process of determining core categories, related themes, and validation of linkages between categories and themes, we continued to reexamine the data to verify our explanatory theory about their experiences, views, and suggestions. We then posed these questions: (a) What were the meanings assigned to welfare, TANF, and others? (b) What were grandmothers recommended changes?

RESULTS

Profiling Black Grandmothers in Southwest Virginia

As shown in Table 19.1, the average age of grandmothers was 57.6 years and their mean educational level was 11.7 years. Four of the 20 grandmothers had associate's or bachelor's degrees; nine completed high school or obtained a GED. Seven grandmothers completed 7 to 11 years of education. Of the grandmothers without spouses, only 3 of 20 had never married. Contrary to the myth related to unmarried mothers making up the largest group of welfare recipients (Karger & Stoesz, 2002), they were underrepresented among the current and larger sample of participants. Five grandmothers were divorced or separated; six were married;

TABLE 19.1   Description of Black Grandmothers

Category	Percentage (*n*)
Age	
39–49	20% (*n* = 4)
50–59	40% (*n* = 8)
60–69	30% (*n* = 6)
70+	10% (*n* = 2)
Education	
7 to 11 grade	35% (*n* = 7)
12 grade	45% (*n* = 9)
Associate's +	20% (*n* = 4)
Marital status	
Single, never married	15% (*n* = 3)
Married	30% (*n* = 6)
Divorced/separated	25% (*n* = 5)
Widow	30% (*n* = 6)
Number of grandchildren	
One grandchild	35% (*n* = 7)
Two grandchildren	50% (*n* = 10)
Three or more grandchildren	15% (*n* = 3)
Reasons for parenting grandchildren	
Parental drug problems	25% (*n* = 5)
Parental death	5% (*n* = 1)
Parental incarceration	20% (*n* = 4)
Parental migration	10% (*n* = 2)
Child abuse	15% (*n* = 3)
Other parental issues	25% (*n* = 5)

and six were widows. Seven grandmothers were caring for one grandchild; 10 were parenting two grandchildren; three had three grandchildren in the home.

Consistent with other research findings of others (Burton, 1992; Mullen, 2000a), grandparents were parenting their grandchildren due to parental drug problems (*n* = 5), death (*n* = 1), incarceration (*n* = 4), and migration to secure better jobs (*n* = 2). Some grandparents were parenting their grandchildren because of child abuse (*n* = 3). Parents' inability to care for their child due to parental immaturity, depression, or recognition of their poor parenting skills (*n* = 5) required grandparents to intervene in the lives of their grandchildren.

Experiences with TANF

Nine Black grandmothers had positive experiences when interacting with the Department of Social Services. Two grandmothers, one 76 years old with a 10th-grade education and the other 43 years old with an associate's degree, noted that the caseworkers failed to show respect toward them and others. A 46-year-old, married grandmother noted: "I don't know. I've always paid taxes and done what I had to do to take care of my own. So, I just figured that if you go there, they should at least treat people with respect I just believe in treating people with respect." Two grandmothers believed that caseworkers lacked sufficient training, thereby, making interactions with the Department of Social Services some-what difficult.

One of the predominant issues conveyed by Black grandmothers related to insufficient formal social support resources. Grandmothers noted that TANF was "little bit of money, it does not pay for child care, it does not purchase basic toiletries, it does not pay my car note, it does not raise a child for a month," nor does it "feed a family of four" [sic]. TANF was "supplemental money for my grandchildren," firmly declared the 62-year-old, divorced grandmother. In fact the average cash assistance for families in our study was $247. The low mean cash assistance seems minuscule in light of the fact that 13 of 20 (65%) were parenting two to three grandchildren. To be more specific, 9 of 20 Black grandmothers received $157 to $243 in cash assistance; 8 obtained $248 to $291; 3 received $320 to $455.

Consistent with the research (Mullen, 2000b), grandparents also told of challenges accessing child care, food stamps, Medicaid or health care, and local social support programs. Four of 20 (20%) grandmothers received food stamps to help care for their grandchildren; the mean amount was $259. The four grandmothers who received food stamps had two grandchildren in the home. A 53-year-old widow received $355 in food stamps; a 55-year-old separated grandmother obtained $70; a 43-year-old never married grandmother received $306; as a 51-year-old divorced grandmother received $328.

The social goal of personal responsibility and subsequent punitive consequences of noncompliance also emerged in the experiences of Black grandmothers. The biannual recertification of benefits was of concern to six grandmothers; they articulated that when the letter arrives for the next appointment, you must report to social services with the correct documents or face the loss of assistance. Compliance also translated into little respect for grandparents' time. A 62-year-old widow noted: "I have to and sit there and wait. I know I'm not more important than anybody else. I guess that's just the rule." Another Black grandmother declared: "You can't be a half hour late; you can't go down there with half of your stuff," meaning your information.

Grandmothers, like other welfare-reliant participants, faced time demands and constraints that sometimes undermined their ability to balance work-family responsibilities with TANF policies. Time is one concern; however, missing work was another. Ten of 20 grandmothers who worked outside the home had to leave or miss work to make the TANF recertification and other related appointments. Employers of grandparent-led families and of older adults in general may not be cognizant of the need for work-life policies such as flexible time, sick leave, and family leave that are typically associated with families with young children or welfare-reliant families (Thomas, Sperry, & Yarbrough, 2000).

Views Toward TANF and Poverty

We asked why people were on TANF to determine the views toward TANF and poverty. In general, five grandmothers believed that people were on welfare because they needed help. A widow noted that people were doing the best that they knew how to do. According to two of five grandmothers, others were on TANF for the same reasons that they were on TANF; they needed help. Grandmothers displayed compassion and understanding for people who did not have a choice but to accept public assistance—a view at the less condemning end of the continuum, meaning participants did not place complete fault on the individual, but were willing to explore the complexities of poverty. Yet, seven grandmothers, whose ages ranged from 43 to 76, had mixed beliefs about why people were receiving TANF. They mentioned larger structural constraints. According to our grandparents, individuals who were mentally ill or who lacked sufficient education, skills, and training had to use TANF to support their families (Monroe & Tiller, 2001; Rank, 1994; Seccombe, 1999). Yet, at the same time, they said that some people are lazy. As expected, fatalism emerged at the far end of the continuum; two grandparents believed that people had no choice but to accept welfare.

Black grandmothers were not immune to the myths and stereotypes associated with welfare or poverty (Abramovitz, 1996; Edin & Lien, 1997; Karger & Stoesz, 2002) with six grandmothers holding strong views of individualism. They held the belief that people were too lazy to work, thereby allowing themselves to become dependent on welfare. Three grandmothers—a 66-year-old married one, a 58-year-old widow, and a 59-year-old separated woman—held firm beliefs about people being lazy and fraudulent. A 59-year-old widow repeated the belief that people do not want to work.

To determine the negative stigmas attached to welfare, we asked grandmothers how does your situation differ from other welfare recipients (Monroe & Tiller, 2001; Rank, 1994; Seccombe, 1999)? As expected, Black grandmothers coped by disassociating themselves from other TANF recipients by proclaiming that they did not know anything about TANF before becoming the primary caregiver of their grandchild ($n = 3$) and they did not know about the circumstances of others on TANF ($n = 1$). Identifying social norms related to work, 8 of the 20 grandmothers were disabled or unable to work, but they clearly desired to work. An additional four grandparents proudly explained that they work and use TANF to assist them with their grandchildren; it did not directly help grandparents. A 53-year-old grandmother stated that she needed the additional assistance because her husband—the grandfather—was disabled. Yet, three grandmothers used compliance with family norms to disassociate themselves from other TANF recipients. One grandmother proudly stated that her husband provided for her, another participant clarified that she was raising someone else's children, and a 53-year-old married grandmother explained that she voluntarily took care of their grandchildren.

Not all Black grandmothers, however, disassociated themselves from other welfare recipients. One Black grandmother did not view their situation as different from others; she admitted that her family needed help. Among this small group, they mentioned other factors that influenced people's use of welfare. Black grandmothers noted other problems that contributed to people's impoverished state or use of welfare: "some people cannot function," so they need some additional help.

Personal Responsibility and Fault

We then explored the meanings Black grandmothers had toward personal responsibility when asking whose fault is it that people are poor. The responses created a continuum of beliefs that extend from no one's, theirs, and the government's fault. Ten grandmothers believed that it was no one's fault. They noted that neither the individual nor society were at fault; many factors contributed to people being poor. Participants went on to explain that people are not getting the help that they need and they lacked knowledge or understanding, family financial management skills, and money. Some participants in our study also demonstrated the fatalist view of participants in Seccombe's (1999) study. They believed that people "don't have a choice; they must get help where ever they can get it."

Five grandmothers believed that people's own laziness and behaviors caused their poverty, whereas one grandmother believed it was the individual's fault combined with other factors. Yet, others did not hold this fatalist view. Five of twenty Black grandmothers blamed the government for people's impoverished existence. As she identified structural issues such as education, employment availability, and job skills, one divorcee had these words to share about government's responsibility to citizens:

> I think that the fault lies in the government. I don't think anybody is poor by choice unless they have a mental illness or are disabled. . . . People are poor who work every day. Minimum wage jobs do not allow a person to live, so they have 2 or 3 minimum wage jobs. I have a 2-year degree, but I don't make enough money. . . . Before this job, actually, I worked a job 24 years and the company went out of business. So my choice was to go to school and make some decisions that I needed to make for myself. I stumbled onto this job. My salary is under the poverty level, but I work every day. I have schooling and experience. So people that don't have any type of schooling or experience have jobs paying minimum wage, and most of them want to live decent. Some people work two or three minimum wage jobs a day. (A 62-year-old divorcee with a high school education)

Interestingly so, a 48-year-old married grandmother commented on how the government manages to help individuals in other countries, but fails to help its own citizens.

Understanding of TANF

We also asked participants what they wanted others to understand about TANF. They wanted to be viewed as any other citizen. The importance of education and financial freedom were viewed as an essential credential and buffer to poverty. Two of the seven grandmothers who did not have a high school education discussed the desire to *better* themselves or to provide an opportunity for others to improve their circumstances. Obtaining additional education, learning to operate a computer, and improving their ability to parent their grandchildren were among the meanings attached to bettering themselves or improving the circumstances of others. Three grandmothers, a 53-year-old widow, a 53-year-old never married, and a 65-year-old married, noted that "you must know how to budget and how to use money wisely." A very forthcoming 62-year-old divorcee acknowledged "I never depend on TANF." The money that my granddaughter "receives goes for her hair, church tithes, and clothes. She has a savings account, and that money goes into that. It helps; it's not a lot of money [*sic*]. Eight grandmothers considered adopting their grandchild; nonetheless, none were the adoptive parent of the child. The hope of parents returning to care for their children was consistent among the grandmothers, at least the ones whose children were still living. A 43-year-old never married grandmother, whose own child died from AIDS, wanted to formally adopt her grandchildren to ensure that they were taken care of after her death. The funeral program rested on the table as the interviewer walked into the home; the loss occurred seven years prior. But, what cannot be gathered in the transcriptions were the interviewers', undergraduate, and graduate student's conviction about the children being loved. Because of the low adoption rate and a tradition of informal kinship care in Black families, grandparents may need assistance with child custody, adoption, and visitation rights (Henderson & Stevens, 2003; Mullen & Einhorn, 2000).

They spoke of sacrificing or "giving up a lot" to parent their grandchildren. They faced the challenge of starting over, and raising another child. "Sometimes it's hard. I'm thinking. What am I doing? But, somebody has to do it," stated a 53-year-old married grandmother. As a 51-year-old divorced grandmother said: "You know it's not easy. Even though I'm going to get my blessings, at this age it's hard and stressful. If I were a little bit younger, maybe it would not be so hard." The voice of a married 53-year-old grandmother sheds additional light on the issue, stating that "having to start over and raise another child is not easy. Especially in the time we live in now. It is very hard. Sometimes it's difficult. I pray and ask God to help me through this and He does give me the strength to do it."

Suggestions for Changes in TANF Policies

One goal of this study was to examine the recommendations of a disenfranchised group to examine family strengths and challenges. Over half of grandmothers ($n = 11$) noted that the amount of the cash assistance was insufficient to really make a difference in their grandchildren's lives. All of the participants believed that the government should assist the poor, but this response was seasoned with personal responsibility. One predominant theme was the need for additional social services, including mental health services, housing assistance, assistance to develop financial management skills, parenting skills, and child care. Some grandmothers believed that Social Security was insufficient to meet their family's financial needs—a 66-year-old widow and 48-year-old married grandmother.

Black grandmothers spoke with conviction and gave concrete recommendations about TANF. Grandmothers believed that TANF should have different policies for grandparents and other relatives, a suggestion argued by Thomas and associates (2000). Eligibility requirements posed a problem—a 76-year-old married grandmother whose income was too high for her to qualify for TANF. Similarly, a 58-year-old homeowner was ineligible for Medicaid and food stamps. Harvard Law Review (1999) articulated the current TANF and foster care policies penalize relative caregivers. In short, children in the care of relatives may qualify for TANF, but this program offers fewer social support services and has the lowest amount of cash assistance available to needy families. Otherwise, relatives must surrender children to the foster care system, a program that has additional support services, such as food allowance, housing subsidy, food stamps, Medicaid, and larger cash assistance award. A 65-year-old married grandmother further illuminates this concern:

> It's hard. I was a foster care parent two years ago. I had foster kids. If these kids go into a foster home, they would give that person $700 to $800 a month to be a foster care parent. But because I listed as the grandmother, I am penalized for being a grandparent. I get around $250 each month. That is supposed to provide everything that my grandchild needs? Yet, and still, if they take them out of my home and place them in foster care, that person would get much more.

As demonstrated in the words of grandmothers, differential supports of the foster care and welfare systems were viewed as inappropriate, *unfair*, and inconsistent with helping poor children. Their wisdom resembled the recommendations of Mullen & Einhorn (2000), who stated that the implementation of TANF policies need to be clear, fair, and consistent. Grandmothers believed that they should receive the same resources that foster care parents obtained. Using the voice of a 62-year-old divorcee describes the problem:

> Grandparents, these days, have two and three children that they are raising. TANF does not provide enough for these kids. I think that there should be a clause for grandparents to be able to have enough support to be comfortable to raise their grandchildren. You take grandparents who are over 65 who are not able to work and depend on their Social Security or retirement to raise their grandchildren; the help of TANF does not allow them properly to raise their grandchildren. I know a woman in my church whose 66 but still working because she can't afford to retire. She has three grandchildren and she gets TANF. Because Food Stamps are based on her income, she can't get Food Stamps. It is not fair. And I think that Food Stamps, Medicaid, and TANF should be available for grandparents and it should not be based on grandparents' income. So I have a big problem with that. Just like,

I don't qualify for Food Stamps because of my income. That's not fair to me. I had to take my grandchild; foster care was not an option for her. If she was in foster care, foster care parents would be getting food stamps, Medicaid, and everything. But because I am the grandparent, I don't qualify for the Food Stamps because they say I am over the income limit. But my income provides for two people, not one. I don't understand how they can say that my income is sufficient to rear my grandchild.

In short, the implementation of TANF and foster care policies need to reflect the realities of contemporary familial concerns and structures, such as kinship care by grandparents.

DISCUSSION

This study changes our image of welfare-reliant families from being poor single mothers and poor Black single women to include grandparents' assuming responsibility for their grandchildren. The experiences, views, and recommendations of Black grandmothers demonstrate the meanings attached to poverty, TANF, poor people, and themselves. We were committed to giving Black grandparents an opportunity to express their views and educate others about their experiences (Seccombe, 1999). The historical and cultural roots of kinship care and intergenerational ties permeated their experiences as they voluntarily assumed responsibility for rearing their grandchildren and keeping them out of the foster care system. Although they faced the challenges and stigmas that accompany poverty, they are parenting grandchildren because of parental challenges that range from substance abuse to poor parenting skills. They, like most citizens, value education and personal responsibility, but they made sacrifices for their families. Their family roles, while flexible, included husbands who serve as economic providers and they wanted their own children to be responsible parents.

Experiences With TANF

The meanings attached to TANF and poverty were complex, varied, and mixed. A few grandparents conveyed negative experiences with TANF, mentioning rigid regulations and demonstrating the stagnate and historical nature of U.S. social policies for poor families (Abramovitz, 1996; Gordon, 1994). Black grandmothers had to adhere to biannual and other meetings, wait until their inspection time arrived, and release personal pride to receive on average $247 per month for all 20 households.

The differential treatment of poor families (e.g., Seccombe, 1999), even the elders of the community, also was depicted in the lack of respect for a few Black grandmothers by caseworkers and the implementation of welfare and foster care policies that undermine the contributions of adults engaged in kinship care or grandparents rearing grandchildren. Black grandmothers understood the realities of differential treatment in the child welfare systems, but they did not accept them. They welcomed an opportunity to express their views and wisdom about life and the social welfare system.

Views Toward TANF, Poverty, and Personal Responsibility

Based on symbolic interaction theory, Black grandmothers' views created a continuum of beliefs toward TANF, poverty, and personal responsibility, but they were not exempt from holding negative images toward welfare-reliant families. Demonstrating that individualism continues to be associated with poverty and welfare, at one end of the continuum, grandparents associated poverty and TANF to laziness, welfare-reliant women having children to collect checks, and people defrauding the system (Karger & Stoesz, 2002). Demonstrating moderate views inside this continuum were a few Black grandmothers who believed that individualism and structural constraints (i.e., poor education and skills) resulted in the people being poor or reliant on welfare. Fatalistic views also arose as they declared that people have no choice but to accept welfare.

Despite the continuum of beliefs, grandparents could not fully escape the negative stigmas attached to poverty and welfare, which they addressed by disassociating themselves from other TANF recipients. Participants denied any knowledge of TANF, acknowledged being disabled or employed, and held up social and family norms. Yet the complexities of real life emerged as Black grandmothers appeared to be empathetic toward the poor families. When assigning fault, only five grandmothers blamed the victim or the individual. Others stated that no one was at fault and a combination of issues, such as education and training force some families into poverty. Some of them held the government responsible for the impoverished state of U.S. citizens.

Recommendations

Recognizing the differential treatment of relatives and nonrelatives, Black grandmothers recommended changes in or the creation of social support services that resemble the supports given to foster care parents. The law, as implemented, penalizes families involved in kinship care and demonstrates that kinship care is less valued by society than care by nonrelatives (Harvard Law Review, 1999; Mullen & Einhorn, 2000). They recommended (a) increasing cash assistance for grandparents parenting grandchildren to some intermediate level between TANF and foster care assistance; (b) changing the qualification guidelines for TANF, food stamps, and Medicaid; and (c) giving grandparents the same resources offered to foster care parents.

Finally, grandparent-led families—much like single-parent and dual-career families—need work-life family policies. Grandparents are required to comply with TANF policies during biannual recertification and to attend any required meetings. Employed grandparents need work-life family policies that focus on sick or family leave, information and referral service, and health care (Thomas et al., 2000). Black grandmothers identified a need for mental health services, child care, parent education, housing assistance, and financial management skills.

REFERENCES

Abramovitz, M. (1996). *Regulating the lives of women: Social welfare policy from colonial times to the present.* (Revised Edition). Boston: South End Press.

Bane, M. J., & Ellwood, D. T. (1994). *Welfare realities: From rhetoric to reform.* Cambridge, MA: Harvard University Press.

Burton, L. (1992). Black grandparents rearing children of drug-addicted parents: Stressors, outcomes, and social service needs. *The Gerontologist, 32,* 744–751.

Cox, C. B. (Ed.). (2000). *To grandmother's house we go and stay: Perspectives on custodial grandparents.* New York: Springer.

Davidson, C. E. (1994). Dependent children and their families: A historical survey of United States policies. In F. H. Jacobs & M. W. Davies (Eds.), *More than kissing babies: Current child and family policy in the United States* (pp. 65–89). Westport, CT: Auburn House.

Edin, K., & Lien, L. (1997). *Making ends meet.* New York: Russell Sage Foundation.

Ehrle, J., Geen, R., & Clark, R. L. (2001). *Children cared for by relatives: Who are they and how are they fairing.* Retrieved October 8, 2003, from http://www.urban.org/urlprint.cfm?ID=7256

Generations United. (2002). Fact Sheet—Grandparents and other relatives raising children: Challenges of caring for the second family. Washington, DC: Author.

Gordon, L. (1994). *Pitied but not entitled: Single mothers and the history of welfare 1890–1935.* New York: The Free Press.

Harden, A. W., Clark, R. L., & Maguire, K. (1997). *Informal and kinship care.* Washington, DC: U.S. Department of Health and Human Services.

Harvard Law Review. (1999). The policy of penalty in kinship care. Retrieved on December 11, 2002, from: http://www.lexis-nexis.com

Henderson, T. L., & Stevens, M. (2003). *Grandparents raising grandchildren: Rights and responsibilities.* (Publication No. 350–255). Virginia Cooperative Extension, Virginia Tech, Blacksburg.

Hunter, A. G., & Taylor, R. J. (1998). Grandparenthood in African American families. In M. E. Szinovacz (Ed.), *Handbook of Grandparenthood* (pp. 70–86) Westport, CT: Greenwood Press.

Jendrek, M. P. (1994). Grandparents who parent their grandchildren: Circumstances and decisions. *The Gerontologist, 34,* 206–216.

Karger, H. J., & Stoesz, D. (2002). *American social welfare policy: A pluralist approach.* Boston: Allyn & Bacon.

Klein, D., & White, J. (1996). The symbolic interaction framework. In D. Klein & J. White (Eds.), *Family theories* (pp. 87–117). Thousand Oaks, CA: Sage.

LaRossa, R., & Reitzes, D. (1993). Symbolic interactionism and family studies. In. P. Boss, W. Doherty, R. LaRossa, W. Schumm, & S. Steinmetz (Eds.), *Sourcebook of family theories and methods: A contextual approach* (pp. 135–163). New York: Plenum Press.

Lugalia, T. (1998). Marital status and living arrangements: March 1997. In *Current Population Reports.* Washington, DC: U.S. Bureau of Census.

Malveaux, J. (1995, February). The GOP's war against poor women. *Black Enterprise, 25,* 32.

Menaghan, E. G., & Parcel, T. L. (1990). Parental employment and family life: Research in the 1980's. In A. Booth (Ed.), *Contemporary families: Looking forward, looking back* (pp. 361–380). Minneapolis, MN: National Council of Family Relations.

Minkler, M., & Roe, K. M. (1996). Grandparents as surrogate parents. *Generations, 20,* 34–38.

Monroe, P. A., & Tiller, V. V. (2001). Commitment to work among welfare-reliant women. *Journal of Marriage and Family, 63,* 816–828.

Moynihan, P. (1965). *The negro family: The case for national action.* Washington, DC: Office of Policy Planning and Research, U.S. Department of Labor.

Mullen, F. (2000a). Grandparents and welfare reform. In C. B. Cox (Ed.), *To grandmother's house we go and stay: Perspectives on custodial grandparents* (pp. 113–131). New York: Springer.

Mullen, F. (2000b). Why grandchildren are going to and staying at grandmother's house and what happens when they get there. In C. B. Cox (Ed.), *To grandmother's house we go and stay: Perspectives on custodial grandparents* (pp. 3–19). New York: Springer.

Mullen, F., & Einhorn, M. (2000). The effects of state TANF choices on grandparent-headed households. Washington, DC: American Association of Retired Persons (AARP).

Perry-Jenkins, M., Repetti, R. L., & Crouter, A. C. (2001). Work and family in the 1990s. In R. Milardo (Ed.), *Understanding families into the new millennium: A decade in review* (pp. 200–217). Minneapolis, MN: National Council of Family Relations.

Rank, M. R. (1994). A view from the inside out: Recipients' perceptions of welfare. *Journal of Sociology and Social Welfare, 21,* 27–47.

Roberts, D. (2002). *Shattered bonds: The color of child welfare.* New York: Basic Civitas Books.

Scarcella, C. A., Ehrle, J. & Green, R. (2003). *Identifying and addressing the needs of children in grandparent care* (Document No. B-55 in Series, New Federalism: National Survey of American Families). Washington, DC: Urban Institute.

Seccombe, K. (1999). *So you think I drive a Cadillac? Welfare recipients' perspective on the system and its reform.* Boston, MA: Allyn and Bacon.

Stack, C. B., & Burton, L. M. (1993). Kinscripts. *Journal of Comparative Family Studies, 24,* 157–170.

Strauss, A., & Corbin, J. (1990). *Basic of qualitative research: Grounded theory procedures and techniques.* Newbury Park, CA: Sage.

Sudarkasa, N. (1988). Interpreting the African heritage in Afro-American family organization. In H. P. McAddo (Ed.), *Black families* (2nd ed., pp. 27–43). Newburg, CA: Sage.

Thomas, J. L., Sperry, L., & Yarbrough, M. S. (2000). Grandparents as parents: Research findings and policy recommendations. *Child Psychiatry and Human Development, 31,* 3–22.

Thomson, E. F., Minkler, M., & Driver, D. (2000). A profile of grandparents raising grandchildren in the United States. In C. B. Cox (Ed.), *To grandmother's house we go and stay: Perspective on custodial grandparents* (pp. 20–33). New York: Springer.

U.S. Congress, House Committee on Ways and Means. (1998, May). Overview of Entitlement program: 1998 green book (p. 419). Washington, DC: 105th Congress. 2nd session.

U.S. Census Bureau. (2000, September). *The Black population in the United States* (Document No. P20-530). Washington, DC: Author.

U.S. Census Bureau. (2003, October). *Grandparents living with grandchildren: 2000* (Report Number C2KBR-31) Washington, DC: Author.

Toward an Understanding of Diversity Among Grandparents Raising Their Grandchildren

Julie Hicks Patrick and Bert Hayslip Jr.

> There are years that ask questions and years that answer.
> —Zora Neale Hurston (as cited By Power Dynamics, 1997)

In the past few decades, much has been learned about custodial grandparents and the demands they face as a consequence of living with and helping to raise young grandchildren. This knowledge has had profound effects for custodial grandparents and the children with whom they live. Based on this knowledge, we have educated the general public, developed supportive programs and interventions, and informed policies.

Being able to respond to and understand diversity among custodial grandparents presents us as researchers and practitioners with powerful tools for changing attitudes toward grandparents raising their grandchildren. It allows persons from different disciplines to communicate more effectively about the needs of grandparent caregivers. It helps us more effectively educate the public about such persons' needs, and avoids the tendency to see grandparent caregivers as a homogenous group. Indeed, in light of the attention to the phenomenon of custodial grandparents in recent years, one's tendency is to view them from the "outside" (i.e., the public, other grandparents, service providers, teachers, other grandchildren see such persons in terms of their commonalities), creating what social psychologists have termed an "in group-out group" mentality. This often leads to stereotypical assumptions about such grandparents as a group—what their needs are, the issues they face, and how they cope with such issues.

Although attending to variability across grandparent caregivers sharpens our awareness of how they are different, we must be careful in not overemphasizing these differences to the exclusion of what custodial grandparents have in common. In this context, the truth probably lies somewhere in the middle. As custodial grandparents will have first been parents and then grandparents, and the grandchildren they are raising will have most likely (at least for a time) grown up in a two-parent family and seen their grandparents in a much different light, it would indeed not be surprising to find that grandparents raising their grandchildren do share some commonalities, and that despite their uniqueness, they do overlap in many respects.

In the next few paragraphs, we briefly evaluate where we currently stand and outline a path for the next decade in order for the research base to bring us closer to a richer and fuller understanding of diversity and custodial grandparenting.

THE CURRENT GENERATION
OF GRANDPARENTING RESEARCH

Empirically, we began by simply describing different subgroups of grandparents who raise their grandchildren (i.e., African American or Latina grandparent caregivers, women) to a more in-depth understanding of the inherent differences in the effects of such different family constellations on grandparents themselves. These empirical findings have been translated to the greater public, increasing their awareness and understanding of the important contributions made by custodial grandparents. This awareness is key in advocating for services tailored to meet the diverse and changing needs of grandparents and their grandchildren. In many cases, this knowledge has already been translated into therapeutic programs and policies to support grandparents who are raising grandchildren (see Hayslip & Kaminski, 2005).

As in any new area of inquiry, it is important for persons from a variety of disciplines to first conduct a variety of descriptive studies, and it is in this context that we have learned that the experience of raising one's grandchildren affects millions of adults. As these experiences cut across racial, ethnic, and socioeconomic lines, it would not be surprising to learn that the demands of grandparenting, as well as the resources available to cope with these demands varies greatly across groups. We have also learned that certain aspects of custodial grandparenting are particularly difficult for some middle-aged and older adults, and that these caregiving challenges often pose risks to one's physical and psychological well-being. Indeed, attention to diversity heightens our sensitivity to grandparents who may be especially at risk in these respects. In addition, we have discovered that for many custodial grandparents, support groups and specific interventions are helpful for alleviating some of the stresses associated with raising one's grandchildren. Yet, such support may be more or less beneficial for some grandparents and not others. Indeed, much has been learned from this first generation of studies.

As our knowledge of custodial grandparenting and its many variations deepens, we see the growth of research studies are increasingly multidisciplinary and rigorous in terms of their empirical and clinical methods. For example, during the past decade, researchers and clinicians from a variety of disciplines and perspectives have adopted more precise definitions of custodial grandparenting, examined univariate associations with important outcome measures, and contrasted the experiences of various groups of custodial grandparents. We have focused explicitly on differences in the experiences of custodial grandparents as a function of race, ethnicity, and the reasons prompting coresidence. Our work has been strengthened through the use of appropriately sized samples and an emerging set of common measures that allow us to compare across grandparent samples and to link their experiences to the broader family caregiving literature.

Much progress has occurred in understanding the ways in which diversity influences grandparents who are raising grandchildren. However, as we continue to move the field forward, it will be important to acknowledge additional sources of diversity among custodial grandparents. The chapters presented in this volume mark a strong step toward that goal.

The four chapters in Section 1 expand the typical caregiving model to include custodial grandparents. Pruchno and McKenney advance our understanding of diversity among custodial grandparenting in multiple ways. First, by focusing on employment interruptions, they address an important, yet understudied effect of custodial grandparenting. Second, they demonstrate unanticipated effects of advanced education, with grandmothers with more years of education, and presumably more flexible and higher status jobs, missing more hours of work due to caregiving. Finally, they use rigorous multivariate analyses with a cross-validation group, increasing the validity of their findings. Hayslip, Temple, Shore, and Henderson advance our knowledge of custodial grandparenting by contrasting positive outcomes between different subgroups of grandparents. Although the research focus in the past has highlighted the negative effects on grandparents, Hayslip et al. expand the focus to include the factors unique to custodial grandparenting which dampen the positive experiences that one anticipates having in grandparenthood. This is an important approach in that it enables us to place the experiences of custodial grandparents within the larger framework of families in middle to late adulthood. We therefore learn more about both subgroups of grandparents. Qualls and Roberto emphasize the benefits of learning from the broader caregiving field, discussing the ways in which services and interventions for custodial grandparents can be strengthened by lessons learned in other areas. Finally, King, Hayslip, and Kaminiski discuss self-reported barriers to both formal and informal social support services. Interestingly, in this sample, about half of the grandparents reported having difficulties receiving the formal services they needed.

The six chapters in Section 2 address the ways in which age and gender influence grandparents who are raising their grandchildren. Hayslip, Shore, and Emick explore the relations among age, gender, and subjective health assessments across different samples of custodial grandparents. Such informal meta-analyses are an important precursor to more rigorous statistical analyses that will inform theory and service provision. Musil and Standing employ qualitative analyses to examine day-to-day hassles expressed by grandmothers using diary methods. Including such qualitative methods is a useful way to gain insight into the subjective experiences of grandmothers, and their results highlight both common and unique themes across different grandmother-grandchild relationships. McCallion and Kolomer extend the investigation of the effects of raising grandchildren to the often under-studied group of grandfathers. The finding that grandfathers with primary care responsibilities expressed more concerns about time disruption in retirement than did grandmothers is an important addition to our knowledge, demonstrating that we need to focus more attention on this select group of caregivers. Lee, Ensminger, and LaVeist also examine differences and similarities across differing grandmother-grandchild relationships, with a focus on African American families. Lee and colleagues highlight the need for separate examinations of varying household constellations. Chase Goodman, using a large sample and multivariate analyses, examines a host of factors, including age, that influence grandmothers' well-being. Notably, her findings highlight the importance of race and the importance of child factors in the explanation of grandmothers' well-being. Hayslip, Kaminiski, and Earnheart echo this idea, asserting that the experiences of grandfathers have yet to be examined systematically. Looking across several studies, their analyses suggest that, like grandmothers, grandfathers who raise grandchildren may be at greater risk for negative physical and psychological effects. Future research will need to further explore the role of gender in custodial grandparenting as increasing numbers of the current cohort of adults, whose gender role definitions will likely differ from those of the current generation, are asked to raise their grandchildren.

The four chapters in Section 3 highlight the importance of cultural differences in the experience of custodial grandparenting. Utilizing qualitative methods, Hayslip, Baird, Toledo, Toledo, and Emick provide rich statements from U.S.-born and Mexican-born grandparents. These data represent an important step in understanding the ways in which the grandparent role differs across subgroups of custodial and traditional grandparents. Such information is crucial to developing appropriate services and interventions. Such knowledge, however, can also strengthen the research endeavor, as we develop culturally sensitive constructs and measures. Fuller-Thomson presents data on a different cultural group in the Americas: First Nations grandparents in Canada. Using Census data to identify her sample, Fuller-Thomson contrasts the experiences of Aboriginal and non-Aboriginal grandparents, with results showing that First Nations grandparents raise their grandchildren with significantly fewer resources than other Canadians. Kohn and Smith focus on geographic diversity among custodial grandparents, reminding us that caregivers from rural, suburban, and urban America often face different challenges and bring different resources to bear on these challenges. Equally important, however, is their finding that even when geography and income are considered, differences remain between African American and Caucasian grandmothers. Finally, Oburu and Palmerus expand our investigation of diversity to a non-American group of grandmothers. That the relations among perceived stress, grandchild behavior problems, and social support are different among Kenyan grandmothers than American grandmothers has important implications for both service delivery and for theory. These results speak to the importance of testing the generalizability of our models predicting grandparent well-being in other cultures.

The five chapters in Section 4 continue to focus on the effects of race and ethnicity among grandparents in the United States. Chase Goodman and Silverstein examine a host of culturally sensitive measures, including degree of acculturation. They also are among the handful of researchers who explicitly include measures of intrafamily functioning. Their careful analyses demonstrate that closeness with the grandchild is associated with higher positive affect, whereas conflict with the middle generation is associated with increased negative affect for grandparent caregivers. Watson, Randolph, and Lyons extend investigations of African American grandmothers by focusing on the ways in which grandparents might influence young grandchildren. Important findings demonstrate that grandmothers who had more frequent contact with the grandchild, who were confident in their ability to guide the child, and who were committed to their role within the family were more likely to engage in all measured forms of health education, from talking to monitoring to modeling. Such instrumental roles, however, may result in distress for the grandmothers, as discussed by Rodriguez and Crowther. In a separate chapter, Crowther, Swanson, Rodriguez, Snarski, and Higgerson examine religiousness as a resource for custodial grandmothers. Significantly, a large percentage of African American grandmothers reported that their religion helped them deal with the stresses of raising their grandchildren. Finally, Henderson and Cook examine custodial grandmothers' experiences with the formal service system as related to raising grandchildren. The statements of these grandmothers, who are struggling economically, demonstrate the deep commitment many custodial grandparents feel toward their own independence, their connection to their families, and ultimately, to the desire to be a positive force in the lives of their grandchildren.

The Next Generation of Grandparenting Studies

Despite these advances to our understanding of diversity among custodial grandparents represented in these chapters, the focus on diversity must continue to grow over the next ten years. We must move our research and clinical foci to asking, "for which grandparents will this intervention be effective?" In order to accomplish this new goal, it will be necessary to include a diversity of predictive models and theories, data collection methods, and analytic strategies. We began this epilogue with a quote that suggested the promise of progress and growth over time. As researchers and clinicians, we hold the tools to move the field beyond "years that ask questions" into the "years that answer." As we close this text, we briefly outline several directions for future research.

When research on custodial grandparenting has been guided by a theoretical model, it most often has been a stress and coping approach (Crowther et al.; Rodriguez & Crowther) or a role-strain model (e.g.,

Pruchno & McKenney). These approaches are a useful way to examine group differences in the effects of specific demographic characteristics, resources, and outcomes. However, we need to extend our examinations to include models that link custodial grandparenting to the broader literature on family caregiving (Qualls & Roberto), and life span development (Hayslip & Hicks Patrick, 2003). For example, the stress and coping model implicitly assumes that custodial grandparenting is a non-normative and stressful event. Studies of Latina grandmothers, however (Chase Goodman & Silverstein; Hayslip, Baird, Toledo, Toledo, & Emick) demonstrate that some grandparents view custodial grandparenting as a normative extension of their roles within the family. Similar perspectives have been identified among African American grandmothers, although the experiences of part-time caregiving grandmothers in Kenya (Oburu & Palmerus) tell a different story. Thus, if our empirical models assume a non-normative approach, it is possible, and even likely, that our interventions to support custodial grandparents will not be viewed as relevant by some grandparents. In addition, although early studies focused on a variety of outcomes, the stress and coping model has pushed the field away from examinations of some of the positive aspects of custodial grandparenting—there are moments of joy in the task of raising one's grandchild. Just as the literature examining caregiving to older adults is refocusing on positive outcomes (Kramer, 1997), we need to expand the range of outcomes that we examine among custodial grandparents.

One way to accomplish these goals is to move beyond multidisciplinary research toward transdisciplinary studies. Although multidisciplinary studies often acknowledge and incorporate useful models and measures from other areas of investigation (such as a link between sociology and psychology), few studies have used such collaborations to strengthen and shape the respective disciplines. A transdisciplinary approach to diversity among custodial grandparents would certainly benefit the science, but it also has the potential to advance the usefulness of that knowledge and to enrich the services available to families in mid to late life. For example, although King, Hayslip, and Kaminiski have identified several barriers to the use of support groups, a family ecology or business administration emphasis might suggest novel ways to help grandparents deal with those barriers.

The next generation of grandparenting studies should also be enriched through a diversity of research methods. To date, most studies have relied on convenience samples of custodial grandparents who express their views through telephone interviews or self-administered surveys. We know that research participants' responses are influenced by the mode of interview (Dillman, 2000) as well as by the study's title and hypotheses

(Cook & Campbell, 1979). Several advances in recruitment are represented in the current chapters, most notably Fuller-Thomson's and Kohn and Smith's use of known sampling frames. In addition, insightful qualitative methods are being employed, as evidenced by Musil and Standing's use of daily diaries, Henderson and Cook's use of open-ended interviewing, McCallion and Kolomer's focus groups, and Hayslip, Baird, Toledo, Toledo, and Emick's coding of grandmothers' own words. Such investigations must be continued because they highlight the value of such sensitive measures and interpretations.

Finally, it is time to move our analytic strategies to include a fuller range of statistical tools. With few exceptions, multivariate analyses are not often conducted within custodial grandparenting studies. In addition, few researchers have focused on statistical interaction terms. For example, we know that there are consistent group differences in negative well-being between genders and between European and African Americans. Examining the ways in which race and gender interact would provide important information to researchers and service providers. Kohn and Smith's use of well-controlled multivariate analyses reminds us that even when we allow resource variables such as education and income to account for shared variance in outcomes, race often continues to contribute uniquely to the variance explained in well-being. Similarly, Pruchno and McKenney's use of a validation group adds an additional level of confidence to their results. Work by Hayslip and his colleagues represents another important step for the field: We may soon have enough large scale studies to permit a statistical meta-analysis examining the effects of age, race, and gender on well being among custodial grandparents. It will be necessary to include sufficient information in our published research (e.g., means, standard deviations, standard errors, effect sizes) to support the use of this important statistical tool. As we continue to explore the full range of diversity among custodial grandparents, other constructs can be included in such analyses.

Finally, in order to move our research to the next level of sophistication, we need to acknowledge the dynamic nature of custodial grandparenting. Most of our research relies on cross-sectional studies, and has focused on grandparents to the exclusion of their grandchildren. These snapshots in time provide important information, but we must begin to conduct and report true longitudinal examinations of grandparents raising grandchildren, and emphasize more the dynamic nature of grandparent-grandchild relationships over time. For example, in light of the disparity across subgroups of custodial grandparents in access to health care and in health itself, how will such grandparents fare in the long run? What might be the consequences for their grandchildren? How will age-related changes in health impact the grandparent-grandchild dyad? These questions remain to be answered.

REFERENCES

Cook, T., & Campbell, D. (1979). *Quasi-experimentation: Design and analysis issues for field settings*. Boston: Houghton Mifflin.

Dillman, D. (2000). *Mail and internet surveys: The Tailored Design Method* (2nd ed.). New York: John Wiley & Sons.

Hayslip, B., & Kaminski, P. (2005). Grandparents raising their grandchildren: A review of the literature and suggestions for practice. *The Gerontologist, 45,* 262–269.

Hayslip, B., & Hicks Patrick, J. (2003). Custodial grandparenting viewed from within a lifespan perspective. In B. Hayslip & J. Hicks Patrick (Eds.), *Working with custodial grandparents* (pp. 3–12). New York: Springer.

Kramer, B. J. (1997). Gain in the caregiving experience: Where are we? What next? *The Gerontologist, 37,* 218–232.

Power Dynamics Publishing. (1997). Words of Women Quotations for Success. New York: http://www.creativequotations.com, retrieved May 22, 2005.

Index

Note: 't' indicates a table